The Violent Peace

Carl Mydans & Shelley Mydans

THE VIOLENT PEACE

Atheneum New York 1968

All photographs not otherwise attributed were taken for Life

Maps drawn by Guy Fleming

Authors' Note

WE HAVE been living for more than twenty years in what we often call "the postwar period." We speak of things that happened "before the war" and "after the war," and in so doing we seem to be saying that we live in a time of peace. Nevertheless, we are all uneasily aware that this peace has been broken almost continuously and in all parts of the world ever since World War II. We read of violence in Africa, rebellion in South America, something that looks like all-out war in the Middle East or Asia.

The purpose of this book is to look closely at this period of peace, at the kinds of warfare that have threatened and still threaten it, so that we may gain a clearer understanding of the times in which we live.

The best way to look at these wars, we found, was through the eyes of correspondents who covered them and photographers who, by the necessity of their profession, had penetrated into the midst of them. And since the eyewitness accounts of these reporters—written in the immediacy of the violence they observed—give dramatic dimension to the story, we have constructed the book around them, adding the background necessary to make each episode clear in its historical setting. We have grouped the pictures in separate folios because they are not illustrations but the visual means by which we can feel the impact of war itself.

Since the very gathering together of these episodes and pictures may give the impression that our most recent two decades have been more violent than any other two decades that might be wrenched out of history, it is important to remember that this is not a report on our times, but a report on the wars of our times.

It has been a sobering experience for us to keep our attention fixed on violence for many months. No one likes to absorb himself in the record of men in pain or to look long at the dead. But as John Shaw Billings, editor of *Life*, wrote thirty years ago, when he decided to publish Robert Capa's photographs of corpses on the battlefield of the Spanish Civil War, "The love of peace has no meaning or no stamina unless it is based on a knowledge of war's terrors. . . . Dead men have indeed died in vain if live men refuse to look at them."

There is no avoiding the fact that men have been dying on a dismaying number of battlefields all over the world in the past two decades, and it is up to the living to try to understand the reasons for the violence in which they died. We cannot hope to control what we do not understand, nor to confront our adversary, war, with our eyes averted.

When we first took on this project, the problem arose of what wars to include, and we consulted many experts in order to draw up a comprehensive list. But we found them at some variance with each other and in the end chose to include not only those conflicts which were of obvious world importance but also some less important but no less violent episodes because they contributed to a general revelation of how men act and what happens in warfare, or simply because they were best covered by vivid accounts.

For these accounts we went to the files of *Time* and *Life*, not because they necessarily contain the best dispatches to have come out of the wars of this era, but because these publications have encouraged detailed eyewitness reporting and their reference libraries provide a rich source for such material.

There have been so many opportunities for war reportage in the past two decades that some reporters and photographers have virtually traveled the world from war to war, but the present-day correspondent is not an adventurer and we have never known one who has become calloused to suffering and death. Most of their dispatches are based on thoughtful and informed analysis of the background of the events they cover. From this solid material provided by a great number of gifted correspondents, we have extracted only the highlights of action to which a reporter was an actual eyewitness. In doing this we have sometimes had to cut and edit the cables that came fresh from the field, and we have usually deleted the writers' references to fellow correspondents. Very often a reporter will choose other members of the press corps to travel and work with when he has respect for their experience or even their reputation for survival, and frequently they are named in his dispatches. In most cases we have omitted these names and changed the pronoun "we" to the first person singular. We did this in order to erase as much as possible anything that might get between the reader and the event itself.

Some people will be curious as to the division of labor in a joint effort such as this book. In our case, each of us searched for eyewitness accounts and pictures, each wrote first drafts of various chapters as they fell to our lot in a rather hit-or-miss fashion, and each edited and rewrote the other's preliminary drafts. Both of us have seen something of war and we were both correspondents in World War II. Since that time only Carl Mydans has continued as a correspondent, and when the pronoun "I" is used in the text it refers to him.

We had the invaluable assistance of Betsy Peirce Prince to help us with the research and check our copy for accuracy. And of course the project could never have been attempted without the editors of *Life*, who suggested it to us and made available the tremendous resources and files of the Time organization. Their generosity has been unfailing, but they have not influenced our opinions in any way. Only we are responsible for what is said here.

A final note seems necessary. Some of the conflicts included in the book are still in battle, others are quiescent or smoldering and may erupt again. It is therefore important to know that we have closed this book on January 1, 1968.

Contents

Photographs

The Violent Peace

I

The Rites of Peace

THERE WAS a time when men knew how to bring wars to a close. Throwing the total weight of all their resources against the enemy, they rained destruction on him until his will to fight collapsed. The war was won and finished—until the next war was declared. The last time that this happened was in the second great world war, when the allies emerged victorious and the rites of peace were solemnly gone through.

I was witness to such a ceremony, set on the wide veranda deck of the U.S.S. *Missouri*, when the victors and the vanquished acted out their formal parts, accepting the rewards of triumph and acknowledging defeat. The great ship strained on its heavy anchor chain, blown by the winds of an early Japanese autumn, and inscribed wide arcs upon the choppy waters of Tokyo Bay. Around it a host of smaller naval craft pulled at their moorings in parallel sweeps, and beyond them, on that Sunday morning, the ships of the line of the U.S. and allied navies extended over the horizon, across the Pacific Ocean, and into every other ocean on the globe. Some five hundred miles southwest of us lay the molten ruins of Hiroshima and Nagasaki. The date was September 2, 1945. That night I wrote the following report:

▶ The planked veranda deck of the *Missouri* had been sanded and bleached to a stark whiteness, and in the dismal gray of the ocean overcast it caught an unexpected light and cast it back into the faces of the allied officers who stood pressed into tight formations along the deck. It highlighted their stern expressions as they waited stiffly for the Japa-

3

nese to come. From my position in the 40-mm. gun tub just above them, I could see the green baize-covered table with the surrender papers all laid out. And behind me every railing and deck and yardarm was festooned with sailors, marines, and soldiers straining to get a look at their fallen enemy.

There were eleven men in the Japanese surrender party, and as they came up the ladder and across the deck they seemed to move with difficulty, their steps uncertain. The two principals were Yoshijiro Umezu, chief of the Imperial General Staff, and Foreign Minister Mamoru Shigemitsu. Umezu looked as I expected him to: dour, chunky, very military in his polished boots and khaki uniform with gold braid and three rows of ribbons on his chest. Shigemitsu was in morning clothes—top hat and cutaway—and it was he who set the mood of uncertainty and hesitation, even anguish, as he came toward the surrender table. He limped badly and used a cane; long ago he had lost a leg when a Korean terrorist threw a bomb to protest the subjugation of that country. And now, at the end of a long succession of other bombings and subjugations, this broken man had been chosen to represent surrender. As he advanced along the deck, leaning heavily on his cane, his face pursed with effort, the breeze whipped his striped trousers so that they blew tight against his wooden leg that tapped out each step grotesquely in the hush of waiting men.

It was he who signed for the Emperor. At the surrender table he paused and looked around. Then, in an ungainly struggle before the thousands of eyes that watched him, he balanced his cane against the table and lowered himself onto a chair. Once more that fleeting look around. Then he peeled off a yellow glove and, bending forward, signed the unconditional surrender. ▶

Ever since that September day the world has been at peace. Not a single war has been declared in more than twenty years; there has been no repetition, even on the smallest scale, of that glorious victory or that total defeat. Yet violence and warlike episodes have not diminished in these two decades. From the very minute that the peace treaties were signed, marking the end of the war, the stresses which that war had left were leading to new military confrontations: the bitter contest for supremacy between the power nations, the struggle for independence in the colonies, the clashes over territory, and the civil wars and insurrections against established governments.

There have been some fifty military conflicts that could be graced by the name of war since 1945, sixteen of them fought between sovereign nations, the others anti-colonial or anti-governmental uprisings, twenty of these with foreign troops involved. Eleven of these conflicts were of such a nature that they threatened global peace, but far outnumbering the major crises have been the outbreaks of local violence, some of them almost unnoticed by the world at large but where, in some, the dead were counted in the hundreds of thousands.

What is new since the last war is the external pressure that compels men to seek peace, even to stop mid-conflict, rather than fight for victory at all costs. It is the force of fear—fear of Armageddon, of world destruction, should total war be waged by nuclear powers—that has compelled these powers to draw back from risking yet another worldwide war. They have had to learn to put a limit on themselves, in a way that men have never done before, both as to their objectives and their means of seeking dominance.

Less than a month after the first atomic bomb was dropped, this threat to world survival was officially recognized. In his solemn speech from aboard the U.S.S. *Missouri*, General Douglas MacArthur said, "A new era is upon us. Even the lesson of victory itself brings with it a profound concern, both for our future security and the survival of civilization. The destructiveness of the war potential, through the progressive advances in scientific discovery, has in fact now reached a point which revises the traditional concept of war."

This revision has not meant that men have ceased to fight. It has meant only that in nuclear war they can no longer fight for total victory. Their perfection of the means of war, developed slowly through the centuries, precludes it. The peace that came in 1945 did not mean, as we had hoped, the end of war. Men have fought since then in almost every corner of the globe—from Greece to South Vietnam, from Kashmir to the Congo—and insurrections sprout like mushrooms in the poor nations of the world. But none of these conflicts has been carried to a conclusion in the old traditional sense with the victor poised triumphant, his foot upon his foe.

The scene on the *Missouri* is probably the last such tableau that the world will ever see. Far more typical of our era is the ending of another war, a war that never was declared and went under the name of a police action. Eight years after the final victory in World War II, the guns were silenced in Korea, the fighting stopped—not with a formal surrender but with an inconclusive armistice that has not yet been ratified. Twenty-four nations were involved in the Korean War; some 1,900,000 soldiers were killed or wounded, millions of noncombatants killed, wounded or made homeless; three years of gigantic effort had been spent. It ended with the drawn-out conferences at Panmunjom, the two sides haggling, exchanging insults and recriminations. We may say that the United Nations "won" the Korean War in that the Communists did not win their immediate objective. But there is no aura of victory at Panmunjom, where now, more than a decade later, patrols still clash and heated meetings of an Armistice Commission still take place. Nor was there when the cease-fire papers first were signed, on July 27, 1953. A correspondent on the scene, Dwight Martin, cabled at the time:

▶ An air of disquieting unreality hung over the ceremony in the sprawling T-shaped "peace pagoda" that the Communists had built. It was hot and the atmosphere smelled strongly of sweat and the odor of raw pine exuded by the bleak, unpainted interior. On one wall was the outline of a huge "peace dove" which the Communists had nailed in place a day or so before and then removed at the United Nations' insistence.

As the United Nations' chief delegate, Lieutenant General William K. Harrison, and the North Koreans' Nam Il strode in, promptly at ten a.m., neither gave any indication that he was aware of the other's presence. Nam Il was sweating in his heavy uniform, a row of gold medals, each approximately the size of a small orange, glittering on his breast. Harrison wore no decorations except for the three stars of his rank. Both men sat down immediately and began signing the documents. Batteries of cameramen popped off a twinkling barrage of flashbulbs and set up a steady whir and click from movie and television cameras. From time to time during the ten minutes required for signing, heavy bursts of outgoing and incoming artillery in the ridges a mile or so away rocked the heavy air inside the building. . . .

An armistice for the Korean War had finally been signed, but there was no rejoicing, no exultation. On the contrary there was an almost palpable feeling of discomfort, perhaps even embarrassment. A correspondent asked a top-ranking British officer if the Commonwealth Division would observe the occasion with the traditional *feu de joie.* "No," the commander said. "There is nothing to celebrate. Both sides have lost." ▶

In such scenes do wars and the ends of wars, like any other acts in human history, present themselves. And the excuse for journalism is that for those who could not be there to hear the tapping cane upon the deck or smell the smell of sweat in a raw pine room, the journalist supplies the vehicle to take them there. Through him we learn that war is not a distant happening, either in time or place, but is a part of our daily lives, and we a part of it.

Few men ever wanted war, but many want the things that seem obtainable only through war. It is said that when Bismarck was asked if he wanted war he replied, "Certainly not. What I want is victory." But this statement was made before the advent of nuclear explosives. It is this latest weapon that has curtailed the means of obtaining victory and brought a new dimension to international warfare in our day. To wage general, unlimited war would be to assure defeat not only for your enemy but for yourself. And defeat in this nuclear age is to lose not only everything that one might fight for, but very nearly everything that man has achieved since he first ascended from the primordial slime.

In 1954 President Eisenhower said, "We have arrived at that point ... when war does not present the possibility of victory or defeat." And in his notable address in the House of Commons in 1955, Winston Churchill gave his judgment on the present and the future. "It may well be," he said, "that we shall, by a process of sublime irony, have reached a stage in this story where safety will be the sturdy child of terror, and survival the twin brother of annihilation." The balance of terror, he said, had replaced the possibility of victory.

Yet, more than twenty years after the development of nuclear explosives, it is still difficult for men to discard the notion that military might is the ultimate source of power in world affairs. We have been conditioned by European history to think in terms of alternate, clear-cut times of peace and times of war. War was an instrument of foreign policy, "the mere continuation of policy by other means," in Clausewitz' famous phrase. And there was no set limit to the amount of military force that might be brought against a rival nation.

Now, in this age of "over-kill," power must be sought in other fields than that of military force, and responsible governments—no matter what their foreign policy may be—must recognize the perils of international warfare and exercise self-limitation both as to means and to goals.

All of the confrontations between the nuclear powers in this new age have been either wars fought by proxy, as in the Greek civil war of 1946–49, where aid was given by each to his chosen side, or else they have been bloodless tests of wills, as in the Berlin airlift of 1948 and the Cuban missile crisis of 1962. When the United States sent troops into Korea and Vietnam, the Soviet Union forbore to send soldiers of its own. And when the Soviet

Union sent its army into Hungary, the United States held back. In 1967, when the Soviet-supported Arabs clashed with American-backed Israel, the two power nations opened direct conversations to assure each other that they did not mean to fight. The smaller nations, not possessed of the means of ultimate destruction, have not experienced this inhibition, and most of the violence in the world of the 1960's has been in the pattern of insurrection or civil war, where the bloodshed may be terrifying and the suffering great but—unless the great powers are drawn in to manipulate one side against the other—the threat to world peace is not paramount.

It is the power nations which have worked out the rules of limited war and have learned to live by them, keeping the balance of terror ever in mind. And since intergovernmental wars are instruments of national policy, the first restriction is political. The West may fight to curb Communism or contain its spread in certain sections of the world, but it cannot fight toward the goal of absolute destruction of Communism or the armies that support it. Nor can the Communist powers wage war for the purpose of absolute destruction of capitalism, because such religio-political goals tend to generate total, unrestricted war. These nations know, when they send weapons and advisers into an area of tension, or even commit their own troops to the battle, that there can be no expectation of ultimate victory. They have instead, in one manner or another, made it clear to their enemy that they have imposed specific limits upon themselves and that they do not intend to go beyond them. In fact, making the enemy understand the limits a warring power has set for itself is the key to limited war and therefore the key to survival in the nuclear age.

It is now established, for example, that the great nuclear adversaries will not fight on each other's soil. And a clear effort has been made to confine the conflicts between them to a single country, recognizing supply lines, training zones and neighboring states as sanctuaries. Even in the prolonged agony of the Vietnam war—despite some statements on both sides that might read to the contrary—the goal remained negotiation and not victory; and each step in the American escalation of that conflict has been carefully announced and kept to set objectives.

Americans tend to look upon war as a great moral struggle and are apt to be more receptive to the idea of outlawing it than of merely restricting it. If a war does not involve some high and all-encompassing ideal such as freedom, democracy, a war to end war, Americans are reluctant to go into it. If it does involve such a cause for them, then it must be fought with all-out effort toward total victory in the most effective, fastest possible way. It is hard for

8

them to find a place in such "wars of high purpose" for negotiated peace. The very term seems to mean compromise, "appeasement," and one does not compromise with the devil.

Thus it follows that restraint in warfare is so contrary to the American moral outlook that this new age of limited war requires not only new methods of fighting but profound changes in American attitudes. It was this conflict of attitudes that swept the United States when American troops were increasingly committed in Vietnam. For, like the war in Korea, which gave Americans their first disturbed understanding of present-day limited war and was perhaps the most unpopular war in the nation's history, the war in Vietnam was antithetical to the American emotional feeling about war.

To the Communist nations, limited war has an altogether different dimension. To begin with, under their rule there is little public questioning of national policy or the goals of leadership. There are few clarion calls across the country demanding that the government either get on with some war or get out of it. In fact, inspiring and supplying "wars of national liberation" which they intend to keep as limited wars has been a declared national policy of the U.S.S.R. for years. In 1961 Nikita Khrushchev announced: "There will be liberation wars as long as imperialism exists, as long as colonialism exists. They are revolutionary wars. Such wars are not only permissible, but inevitable. ..." And in 1967 his successor Alexsei Kosygen confirmed this. In the turns and twists and feints of these wars, in the maneuvering and bargaining, and above all in the long periods of waiting that are part of them, the Russians and the Chinese are temperamentally far better prepared than the Americans to wage them.

But time and the lengthening number of wars which have been fought throughout the world since the *Missouri* have established such a pattern of tested, often symmetrical, restraints that in 1965 a writer for the British *Economist* could excoriate India and Pakistan for failing to observe them with this comment on the new age of warfare: ". . . Both India and Pakistan have shown themselves inexcusably irresponsible in failing to follow the rules of international confrontation in the nineteen-sixties. This no doubt sounds fiddling: war is war, and if you are going to get there, who cares how? But it is not. The last ten years have taught the world a lesson about how to behave in the grey area between diplomacy and military action. It is only by attending to the rules of escalation, as the Americans and Russians have painfully worked them out, that full-scale war can be avoided. The first of the rules of confrontation is that one should make one's objectives clear, the second that one should do the least that is necessary to achieve them."

9

Only in this age of no-surrender and no-victory could these become the basic rules of warfare. And just as bizarre is the way in which these wars are now expected to end: not with declared cessation, not with gatherings of hostile men around conference tables making long, unacceptable demands on each other as they did in the Korean War, but by the simple process— expressed by a new military term in most unmilitary language—of letting a war "just peter out."

II

What Is War?

T HE WARS OF our time are a legacy of the wars that have gone before,
but their undeclared and inconclusive character gives rise to the question: What is war? At least a hundred definitions have been written, perhaps
the broadest being: "*War is a violent contact of distinct but similar
entities.*" * We live in a world so violent, a universe so violent, that this
definition might include the greater portion of man's experience: the "battle
of the elements" in which we live, the turbulence of mountains rising out of
roiling seas in that primeval world which was our home before man had a
backbone or woman had a breast; the far collisions of the stars whose echoes
touch us in ways we do not even know. It would include the competition-
unto-death between the phyla of living organisms over the past five hundred
million years, and even the microscopic wars within the human body when
cell does violence to cell and life goes down defeated by malignancy.

Insects make war and birds will fight for territory. Among our closer
cousins, the mammalian animals, the predator will kill for food and the prey
in self-defense—though seldom will they fight to the death with those of their
own kind. Among the rare species that will kill within the group is man, that
human being who was created in the image of his God and yet is the most
murderous of animals. And from the drives that lead him to such killing,
when they prove stronger than his need for order and self-preservation, comes
human war.

"*War is the use and predominance of material force in the conflict*

* Quincy Wright: A *Study of War.*

between the various human nuclei." * By this definition, war began perhaps half a million or a million years ago when the species *Homo sapiens* emerged and human societies were formed—societies more sophisticated than the pack or patriarchal family that had gone before. These were no longer herds or roving bands, arboreal travelers or ape men. They were our primate ancestors—those agile, hairy creatures with the great big brain. They had stone tools with which to dig, stone weapons with which to hunt and kill. They killed animals for food; sometimes they killed each other. These were men at their most primitive.

Ten thousand years ago all men were "primitives." They lived in clans or slightly larger tribes, and they were bound together by blood relationships and by a language and a set of habits they had formed against the wild world all around. In our time less than five percent of the world's three billion population are in this sense primitive, and in another hundred years, perhaps, all will have vanished. And yet they live in us.

Like them, we have a sense of inner group: a tribe, a nation. These fellow men we must not kill. Like them, we have our neighbor groups, half-understood, uneasy allies. With these the law prevails: an ambush for an ambush or the fair exchange, my spy for yours. The tribal man looks on the outer world with fear. He stays aloof unless his territory is invaded or the pressures of his own expanding tribe force him into another's land. Then he prepares himself for war and killing; murder is sanctioned. And so with us.

Man was a hunter, it is likely, before he was a warrior. The weapons and the tactics he first used for war were those he had observed in other predatory animals and that he himself had practiced in the hunt: he lay in ambush, pounced, thrust with his spear or swung his club, and then withdrew. The animal from which he learned has but one "law of war"; it follows from instinct, behavior patterns which evolved to ensure the survival of the individual and of his species. But man has long been conscious of his motives; the pattern of his social behavior has been learned in a long childhood and adolescence. Nevertheless, much of the animal remains.

As the lion must prepare himself before the spring, the dog snarl and bare his teeth before the fight, so does man before he goes to war make fearful noises and take a stance peculiar to the occasion. The normal urge to cling to life and to preserve the lives of others of his species must be overcome; he must create within himself a new condition in which the drive to kill, the willingness to be killed, take precedence. Today the brass bands of the parade to war have been discredited, but young men who are forced to become

* A. C. F. Beales: *The History of Peace.*

soldiers still must practice making blood-curdling noises while running at a dummy enemy. In this we do not differ from the most primitive man.

Peter Matthiesen in his *Under the Mountain Wall* describes a battle that he witnessed between the neighboring tribes of Kurelu and Wittaia in a hidden valley of New Guinea, where men still live in the Stone Age.

▶ At dawn that morning the enemy [Wittaia] began chanting and the chant, *hoo, hoo, hoo, ua, ua,* rolled across the fields toward the mountains. The fields were tattered still with mist, and a cloud hung on the valley floor, submerging the line of trees at the frontier. A man ran past the wood [and] cried out urgently, his voice a solitary echo of the wail from behind the mist. The call was taken up and trailed off northward to the villages of the Kurelu. . . .

When the main body of the Kurelu had gathered—over one hundred men—the Wittaia stood upon their ridge and danced and shouted insults and the Kurelu answered, brandishing their spears. . . . The light of the sun flashed on breastplates of white shells, on white headdresses, on ivory boars' tusks inserted through the nostrils, on wands of white egret feathers twirled like batons. . . . A flurry of arrows was exchanged, the armies withdrew, regrouped, [and] the Wittaia again began a chanting, heightened by shrill special wails used little by the Kurelu: *Dtchyuh, dtchyuh, dtchyuh—woo-ap, woo-ap, woo-r-d-a, woo-r-d-a—* And the Kurelu answered: *Hoo-ah-h, hoo-ah-h, hua, hua, hua,* like a pack of wild dogs.

More companies came swiftly from the rear positions to join the force, bare feet drumming on the grass . . . and the advance warriors swept forward as the Wittaia came on to meet them. ▶

Thus our forefathers may have prepared themselves for war while men still lived in tribes. And ritualistic warfare such as this had a special social function: it strengthened the inner unity of the clan. In prehistoric times those tribes who forged ahead were often those who had been most stimulated to invention by contact with their enemies, and whose sense of inner unity was most heightened by this distinction between the "goods" within the tribe and the "bads" without. Those more peaceable, on the other hand, were often overrun, absorbed, or driven to the least desirable pockets of the earth.

This utilization of war as a consolidating social instrument has sometimes been practiced in civilized communities too, consciously or unconsciously, by ruling groups or men. But among civilizations it has been less successful. The most aggressive and warlike civilizations have often had the shortest lives and left the least for their successors.

"War is the use of organized force between two human societies pursuing contradictory policies, each seeking to impose its policy upon the other." * By this definition we limit war to an activity of civilized man, a creature very recent in the world's history. There are those who blame warfare—modern, civilized warfare—on man's basic animal nature and primitive inheritance. Man was a weapon-user, they say, even before he truly was a man, therefore he always has used weapons, always will, be it the humerus bone of the lesser antelope, the iron sword, the muzzle-loader or the hydrogen bomb. Others hold that it is not man himself who is at fault when he makes war, but civilization. These are the followers of the "noble savage" school, somewhat old-fashioned now, since their source is the Age of Enlightenment rather than our post-Darwinian Age, which conjured up the sanguine picture of "nature red in tooth and claw." They say that at the dawn of history man was pure, and every little baby who comes into the world is innocent. It is civilization, somehow, that makes him greedy, cruel, self-assertive and fearful; it is civilization which has perverted the natural man into the war-maker.

And it is true that civilization changed the face of war—just as it changed the berry-hunt into the time of plowing and of reaping, changed the grass hut or the hide tent into the brick-walled city, changed the ghost-tree into the ziggurat, and the long tale told by firelight into the history of kings stamped on clay tablets or inscribed on stone.

No longer in the marshy regions of the great river valleys do naked men dart at each other with the fire-hardened spear, thrust and retreat. Now they have leather armor, helmet and shield, and metal-tipped pike; they march in order, tightly packed. City fights city, and the men who fight are conscripts, trained for the job. Nomadic tribes sweep in upon the city-states, give battle, plunder, and are thrown off. Next time they win a foothold, win a city and a civilization, found a new empire in the ruins of the old.

The glory of ancient Mesopotamia, in whose shadow we still live, lasted three thousand years. In the first flowering of their culture, these early people of the Tigris and Euphrates valleys built a complicated and successful social structure, invented among other things the wheel, the plow, the arch and the refinement of metals, and they evolved a calendar, a numbers system and a system of writing. But when war took precedence over their other arts and sciences, their "time of trouble," in the Toynbee phrase, had come. In the ninth century B.C. the Assyrians took over the rich valleys, and among these

* Hoffman Nickerson: "War" (*Encyclopaedia Britannica*).

conquerors from the north the art of war had been perfected.

For eyewitness accounts of war in primitive societies we can rely on contemporary observers who seek them out in the last lost corners of the earth. For such accounts of eyewitnesses to war in early civilizations we have the records of the men themselves, for they were written down on victory inscriptions. Such is the account of the Assyrian conqueror Ashurnasirpal, written in the ninth century B.C.:

> ► I stormed the mountain peaks and took them. In the midst of the mighty mountain I slaughtered them, and with their blood I dyed the mountain red like wool. . . . I carried off their spoil and their possessions. Their young men and maidens I burned in fire. The heads of their warriors I cut off and I formed them into a pillar over against their city. I flayed all the chief men who had revolted and I covered the pillar with their skins. Some I walled up within the pillar. Some I impaled upon the pillar on stakes. . . . ►

Such monuments to victory are not uncommon among civilized men. In the earliest written record of civilized war ever to be found—an inscription carved some fifteen centuries before the building of Ashurnasirpal's hideous pillar—the scribe includes the fact that the skeletons of the vanquished were piled upon the plain "in five separate places." And twenty-two centuries after Ashurnasirpal, Tamerlane, that limping Tatar from Samarkand, made pyramids of the skulls of his victims, who numbered, after the sack of such thriving cities as Baghdad, as many as a hundred thousand. Today in the wasteland stretch along the border of Yugoslavia and Bulgaria tourists may visit such a tower of skulls where the last fifty-eight remain of nearly a thousand heads taken from defeated Serbian rebels by the Turkish Pasha of Niš in 1809. In the twentieth century such atrocities are not displayed. Mass murders are done in secret, the corpses tumbled into hasty trenches and covered over, or fed into ovens to be burned. The murder of half a million Communists in Indonesia in 1966 was hidden from the world by censorship.

If man is conditioned by his animal past, what animal drives are these that produce such human actions? Where in the animal world do we find creatures in the mold of Ashurnasirpal and Hitler? Somewhere in the history of civilizations—in the long evolution from animal to primitive to modern man—the human being has achieved the capability to be inhuman on the grand scale.

* * *

15

The drives that bring on civilized wars are very different from the more basic drives of animals. An animal, alone or in a pack, may fight by instinct to defend his territory or his status in the pack, appease his hunger or win a mate. And primitive men may take to warfare under the compulsion of the tribal mores which were developed in the evolution of the clan. But civilizations are not animals or primitives. In civilized societies abstract ideas and learned behavior patterns have superseded animal instinct and the mold of the clan's fixed customs. It is through these complex behavior patterns and ingrained ideas that a civilized government can lead a large, disparate population into war.

Whereas an animal may fight for food, the individual civilized man does not take arms in search of his daily bread. But the press of overpopulation, underemployment, economic stress in general, may make him receptive to quite different calls to war: calls in the name of a religion, national honor, defense of homeland or the freedom of mankind.

Some naturalists say that animals will fight for mates, and there have been wars fought by civilized man for just this reason. The rape of the Sabine women was the most famous case, but woman-stealing, like slave-raiding, was a cause for war in many early communities, and until recently the promise of authorized violation of captured women was used openly to recruit fighting men. To this very day it is a persistent dream of soldiers that the women of his own society, whom he has left behind, will grant him their favors when he returns a hero. But this is hardly a primary cause for modern war.

The spirit of adventure in modern as in primitive man has often made him open to the call to battle. But this applies to times when war is not too dangerous and relatively few are killed. When war becomes less glamorous and less pleasant—as it has done since the age of gunpowder and the universally conscripted army—the call to high adventure loses much of its force as a drive toward warlikeness. It has been said, too, that the citizens of some nations fight because they are innately violent and enjoy the act of killing. But as Frederic Wertham pointed out, "Soldiers in modern armies do not fight because they have sadistic impulses; they fight because they have been drafted."

Fear, the terror of the unknown, is a breeding ground for war, for fear is not a quiet emotion. It is not suffered alone. It cries out and quickly spreads among others. "Whom man fears," said Ovid, "he longs to see destroyed." And in our own time President Kennedy said of the warlike tension between the Soviet Union and the United States, "We are both caught up in a vicious and dangerous cycle with suspicion on the one side breeding suspicion on the

16

other, and new weapons begetting counter weapons." As Thomas Fuller wrote, " 'Twas fear that first put on arms."

But far more important in civilized man than the drives for food or sexual dominance or for adventure—or even the actions that he takes through fear—are the drives incorporated in the civilized state itself. These are the drives for territory and for dominance, for preservation or self-defense, and for independence on the part of the oppressed.

Conflicting claims to territory—in civilizations as in animals and birds—have often been a cause for war. Men will almost always fight, and fight at their most determined, to defend a territory they consider theirs. But wars for the expansion of these claims—rather than the mere defense of them—have been far more frequent among civilizations than among primitive societies. As Quincy Wright in his monumental *Study of War* observes: "Civilized statesmen go after territory as civilized businessmen go after money, without direct consideration of what they are going to do with it when they get it."

The drive to dominate is as prevalent in civilizations as it is within the barnyard or the herd, where strength means dominance and dominance means order. Civilized wars, both international and internal, have frequently been fought for dominance, though for long periods they may be checked by the expedient of a balance of power. Without this balance, dominance brings violent reaction from the dominated sooner or later, and history is full of slave revolts and peasant uprisings, of cities challenging the rule of kings, religious or national minorities battling their oppressors, and—most notably in the two decades since World War II—colonial peoples fighting for independence from their colonizers.

Civilized man has developed to a high degree the reliance on abstract ideas as a potent drive and invitation to make war. Man as a social animal has been developed by civilization to the point where for "society" he will "fulfill his duty" and go to war for such abstractions as religion, patriotism, or for a purely cultural idea like democracy or Communism. When such ideas have permeated a civilization, the leaders of that civilization and the populace itself will go to war to spread them with the notion that they are actually benefiting those other populations whom they are forcing to accept them.

The history of civilized war is nearly as long as the history of civilization itself, perhaps six thousand years, and there has been a fairly steady technological progress in the means of waging it. Different civilizations have developed differing techniques, but their similarities are greater than their differences.

17

All are built upon the heritage of the primitives who went before them: the disorganized onrush into the disciplined advance; the thorn hedge into the stone-walled city fortress and the corresponding development of battering rams and catapults and then the mobile shieldworks to protect the demolition crews, the batteries of long-range guns, the bombing plane, the anti-aircraft and the ground-to-air, the air-to-air, the anti-missile missile, and so on.

A brief summary of this complex development, interwoven as it is with the development of all the other aspects of our history, cannot do more than give an indication of the changing techniques of waging war and underline the point that, though our current history is full of violence, it is no more so than the history of civilizations out of which ours grew. Many societies have contributed to the art of war. To the Sumerians' first civilized army with its leather-armored spearmen, the Hyksos added the horse and chariot. The Assyrians, specialists in war, inaugurated the regular standing army with an infantry, a cavalry and a corps of siegework engineers. The Greeks introduced the disciplined infantry of the citizen-soldier used in a phalanx charge, and the Romans improved on the phalanx with the more flexible formations and better weapons of their legions' hardened footsoldiers. It was Roman engineering, too, that raised the art of siegecraft to a level not matched until the seventeenth century.

The early medieval period, following the disintegration of the empire, was an era of armored cavalry. The Roman legions in their dying stage had been overcome by the mounted charges of barbarian horsemen, and the armies of the petty dukedoms into which Europe split were feudal levies of small groups of knights sometimes supported by a rabble infantry. But in the later Middle Ages, when feudalism lost rigidity and the Church much of its moral authority, mercenary soldiers took the place of vassal knights, and battles became more prolonged and dangerous, less chivalrous. Disciplined infantry—exemplified by the English longbowman and Swiss pikeman—was reintroduced to fight alongside the armored cavalry. It was at about this time, in the fourteenth century, that gunpowder was first used in battle—ushering in the era of modern warfare.

The increasing use of gunpowder, not only as a siege weapon to blow up ancient walls but in artillery that could be moved about the field on wheels, made the bowmen obsolete. Both infantry and cavalry took to the use of firearms and, in time, the pike was replaced by the bayonet, and the musket-with-bayonet became the almost universal weapon. The changing social structure of these centuries encouraged the increasing use of footloose mercenary soldiers who had no permanent commitment to any lord or king or

18

Church and who became, by the middle of the seventeenth century, almost unmanageable paid thugs. It was with armies such as these—savage, undisciplined, living by looting—that the Thirty Years' War was fought in a hideous mélange of religious and political battles. One third of the German-speaking people died as a result of that war.

Men were left exhausted and revolted by the atrocities of such wars. A wave of new thought, of humanism and a respect for moderation, washed over Europe. It coincided with the strengthening of the kings' power and a growing sense of national identity. Under the absolute monarchs of the seventeenth and eighteenth centuries the hordes of hired soldiers were replaced by small permanent armies loyal to their sovereigns. These brightly uniformed, strictly disciplined professionals advanced in formal order into battle, armed with musket and bayonet, and their ultimate ideal was the "perfect volley" fired in unison from an unflinching line or square. Such highly trained small armies were too valuable to waste, and warfare became less destructive, more a strategic game. Fortresses grew elaborate screening trenches and outworks, and the besieging of them became a highly technical and cautious matter. War, indeed, was a form of sport, following the current ideal of reason and decorum, and warfare was an instrument of politics in the adjustment of territorial claims. It was an era of moderation and it did not last; within these kingdoms were the seeds of discontent fed by the great disparity between the lives of the ruling aristocracy and the people of the land. The driving force toward self-rule by the populace, the ideal of democracy, swept aside the notion of moderation.

In 1793 the French Revolutionary Government passed the first universal compulsory-service law in history, and with the resultant mass army of raw recruits the tactics and strategy of warfare changed. Armies of mobs fought the trained professionals, and the disciplined line could no longer hold fire for the perfect volley. Under Napoleon these citizen armies became mobile, adept at long marches and surprise attacks. Battles were no longer games but heated charges of shouting men supported by artillery and maneuverable cavalry. Numbers became important; Napoleon led more than half a million men to Moscow.

The American Civil War was the first of the industrial wars, making use of railways, steam engines and the telegraph, and it was the first in which the rifle was widely used—increasing the range of infantry fire to six times what it had been with musketry. Against rifles, close infantry formations and massed cavalry charges became too costly; tactics shifted to the defensive with an emphasis on entrenchment and delay. From this was born the strategy of attrition, although this was not fully recognized for half a century. For while the technicians of the military—as technology advanced in every field—improved the rifle from the muzzle-loader to the breech-loader, to the magazine and finally the machine gun, the armies of Europe were still patterned on the Napoleonic structure with its cult of the offensive and reliance on great numbers.

In 1914, when the precarious balance of European powers collapsed under the drive of rampant nationalism, gigantic armies—each of nearly two million men—faced each other with the fixed idea of gaining a rapid decision through the neo-Napoleonic tactics of artillery bombardment, swift maneuver and overwhelming numbers. Within six weeks they found themselves stalemated in entrenchments that stretched from Switzerland to the North Sea. Through four years of this trench warfare, with the use of machine guns and heavy artillery, of battles fought with guns on armored tanks, of the first use of high explosives dropped from planes, and of great massive charges "over the top," they did no more than slaughter their soldiers and tear up the earth. At last even these mighty nations could not sustain this terrible attrition any longer. With the final collapse of Germany the war ended. But men's disillusionment and disgust did not last more than two decades.

In 1939, when the ideal of nationalism had swollen to totalitarianism and dreams of world domination once again, the German armies launched attack with the conviction that surprise, extreme mobility and superior firepower could overwhelm the enemy before entrenched resistance could be formed.

Before the time of World War II the modes of European warfare, which had developed from their ancient Asiatic roots into the capacity for total and near-totally destructive war, had spread around the world. Western civilization was now dominant—in Asia, Africa, America—and the convulsions of Western man at war were felt by every world inhabitant.

The technological ingenuity of the West, adopted also by such countries as Japan, produced machine-age war. No longer merely the steam engine or the crude Gatling gun, but the internal-combustion engine, which could put cavalry in armored tanks and even infantry on wheels, and add the airplane to the artillery support of troops as well as for bombardment. The increased power of the engine made it possible to combine speed and surprise with heavy protective armor for all types of vehicles and planes and ships. Communications could be kept by wireless radio, and radar made it possible for shells to home in on their targets and for defenders to detect an approaching enemy at undreamed-of ranges. Rockets were used as guns and then as missiles, and unmanned airborne bombs sufficient to destroy a city block were launched from a hundred miles away.

For the first time the manufacture of such weapons was as important as the use of them in the field. The economies of whole nations became accepted military targets, and civilian noncombatants were as vulnerable as soldiers at the front. Surprise, speed and maneuver; heavy firepower and protective armor; battles in city streets and over miles of deserts, on sea, and sea-to-shore and in the air—all were part of the last total war.

Man, the evolutionary miracle, equipped not with the bones of antelopes or feathered arrows but with seventy-five-ton tanks, massed heavy bombers, napalm and long-range missiles, fought fellow man—soldier and civilian without distinction—and turned vast farmlands into scorched earth, cities to fields of stone. Ashurnasirpal killed in his thousands; twentieth-century man in his millions. Sixty million people died in World War II. It culminated in the destruction of two cities by a new weapon, the latest technological advance of the advancing centuries, the release of atomic energy in an explosive charge. Sixty-eight thousand noncombatants were killed in Hiroshima, thirty-eight thousand in Nagasaki, and the war ended.

The date marked a new departure in civilized war: new tactical and technological advances in the means of waging it, and new limitations on its conduct and its aims. Since that time men no longer declare war or make an end to war. They simply war. Ours is an era of mass violence that goes by the name of peace.

It is fundamental to the human mind to try to find order in the diversity of the material universe and impose a pattern on seemingly random happenings in history. It does not satisfy us simply to list the armed conflicts that have taken place since 1945; similarities of motive, date, geography are recognized; causes and effects leap to the mind. But wars are as individual as the nations and the men who engage in them.

We may discern a pattern of a sort in recent history: the stages of the Cold War from the immediate post-war years when there was still hope for international cooperation, through the period of vital confrontations between East and West, the period of fearful stalemate and the growing effort toward coexistence; the early rash of anti-colonial wars and the utilization of them by the Communists; the ever-growing number of terrorist activities, guerrilla challenges and violent coups in the new and undeveloped nations. In 1966 the United States Defense Department estimated that there had been 164 of these insurrectionary outbursts in the previous eight years, and they seemed to outline a future pattern of worldwide violence less terrifying, perhaps, than the chilling confrontations of the Cold War, when (as during the Cuban missile crisis) the safety of the whole world seemed in peril, but full of misery and blood. But there is danger in oversimplification at the expense of small, disruptive facts. Perhaps the only simple formula is that war breeds war.

There is similar temptation to put wars into categories so that we can call things by their names and thus control them. But every act of organized violence has its own rules and characteristics and it is impossible to squeeze wars into convenient pigeonholes—though many an expert has given this an earnest try. Indeed, for the fifty-odd wars since 1945, more than twenty categories have been mentioned by everyone from Nikita Khrushchev to Robert McNamara. And insurrections "seem to exist in an almost endless variety of forms," as Samuel P. Huntington remarked in his *Changing Patterns of Military Politics,* "and the temptation to catalog them is virtually irresistible."

When we do resist this temptation, we can only say that, very broadly speaking, in most cases the wars since 1945 have been between the forces of a recognized government and those of insurgents or guerrillas within its territory—often with the aid of outside governments—seeking self-determination or a revolution. But in each of these conflicts the background differs and the men who fight them act in accordance with their own conditioning, their ethnic mores and national dreams. The uprising of the Hungarian people against their government in 1956 scarcely resembles the rebellion in the Dominican Republic in 1965, yet both were armed challenges to governments deemed unrepresentative. The struggles to end French domination in Indo-China and Algeria, both anti-colonial and fought for the right of self-determination, were as different as are Asia and Africa in mood and incident. In men at war, as well as men at peace, there is an infinite variety.

The proper study of our warlike era, then, is war—not in its massive impact, but in the details of what it looks and feels like in all its unpredictable and fateful manifestations. And we can see it best through the eyes of trained correspondents who report not only on the background of the war, its strategy and progress, but on individual incidents in individual encounters—on men as they react to violence—and thus illuminate the dark heart of the tragedy.

Whether two hundred thousand people are massacred in twenty years of insurrection and brigandage in Colombia, or two British commandos are shot dead in a skirmish in the Dhubsan Wadi of South Arabia, the reality of violent death is much the same to each of the victims. When the Cold War touched and briefly flared in Quemoy in 1958, the self-limitations of the confronting powers had little meaning for the sixty-five Chinese civilian islanders who were killed in six weeks of shelling. And the 33,629 American soldiers, sailors and marines who fell in battle in Korea were not concerned at that moment with the question of whether they died in a police action or an all-out war.

Soldiers in the midst of battle must fight without restraint, no matter what their government's foreign policy, for here they are confronted with the brutal and immediate choice of who kills whom. And though there are many instances of soldierly compassion for the enemy as well as for the men in one's own platoon, these do not spring from any faraway political considerations. An ambush is an ambush, and a firefight a desperate matter of win or lose, whether within the context of a local terrorist action or an international conflict on the widest scale.

To the noncombatants caught in the locale where the killing is, a limited war is indistinguishable from a total war. The planes sweep over or the patrol moves through; the huts are burned; the city street is shelled, the buildings crumble, people die and rot beneath the rubble while their families search for them. To those sitting by the ruined houses, or moving along the torn-up roads away from the noise of guns, or slowly starving in the stony places to which they've fled, it looks and feels like war, no matter what the name.

There is a Roman maxim, "Who desires peace, let him prepare for war." But Captain Liddell Hart, writing in this era of H-weapons, points out that what is necessary now, if we wish for peace, is to *understand* war. This understanding may come through a study of the basic causes and the history of war. But a more immediate and deeper appreciation may come from the experience of war itself, of men in the context of war situations. We know the Trojan War through Homer's close descriptions of the men who fought on the plain of Ilium, how they acted and what they thought of themselves and of each other, how one man fought reluctantly, with a true heroism, and another sulked.

In a war situation we see men's qualities more clearly than in peacetime. The quality of heroism is associated with war, perhaps because within the context of daily living such acts of selflessness—which are the dream of every boy and man—can be postponed, whereas in war's short periods of climax there is no time lapse between now and imminent death. Brutality and sadism are wartime qualities too, not because men are never brutal or sadistic in times of peace, but because the very purpose of war lifts the restrictions on these manifestations of our worst nature.

Thus we see war, and understand it, when we see the actions of men at war and hear the sounds they hear—the noises made by guns, mortars, falling bombs, or the words of dying men. We see what they see, smell what they smell—corpses rotting in the flower beds of city parks, or frightened prisoners crowded in an airless room.

Many of the small encounters in the more than one hundred instances of war and warlike violence since World War II reveal the sights, the sounds, the feel of war—the actions and the thoughts of men at war—in much the same repetitive terms of war's repetitive situations. But each was fought within its own milieu: the aura of Kipling still clinging to the desert warfare in South Arabia, the atmosphere of Conrad's *Heart of Darkness* evoked in the Simba terror in the Congo.

A sensitive reporter of the scenes of war sees not only what men do and how the war is fought, but senses as well the flavor of the time and place. With him we watch and listen, feel ourselves close to the fragment of the war that he has come upon, that touched him and that he photographs or writes about. Through him we gain an understanding of these wars of our own time.

MEN AT WAR

A SECTION OF PHOTOGRAPHS

Battlefield aid station, Vietnam.   *Larry Burrows*

British soldiers advance through a village in Yemen.   *Terence Spencer*

American Marines charge into action in Korea.   *David Douglas Duncan*

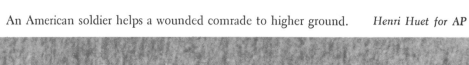
An American soldier helps a wounded comrade to higher ground. *Henri Huet for AP*

A British lieutenant protects a wounded soldier in Aden.   *Associated Press*

Under fire in a rice paddy.   *Henri Huet for AP*

Suspected fifth-columnists are executed by the Nationalist Chinese . . .

as Shanghai falls to the Communists.   *International News Photo*

In Vietnam a medic carries a wounded child. *Paul Schutzer*

In Venezuela a priest helps a dying soldier.   *Hector Rondon, La Republica, Caracas through A.P.*

Turkish Cypriots await a Greek attack. *Dominique Berretty*

American Marines advance past their own dead. *David Douglas Duncan*

Chinese Communists surrender to an American patrol in Korea.   *Hank Walker*

Hungarian security police shot by revolutionaries in Budapest.   *John Sadovy*

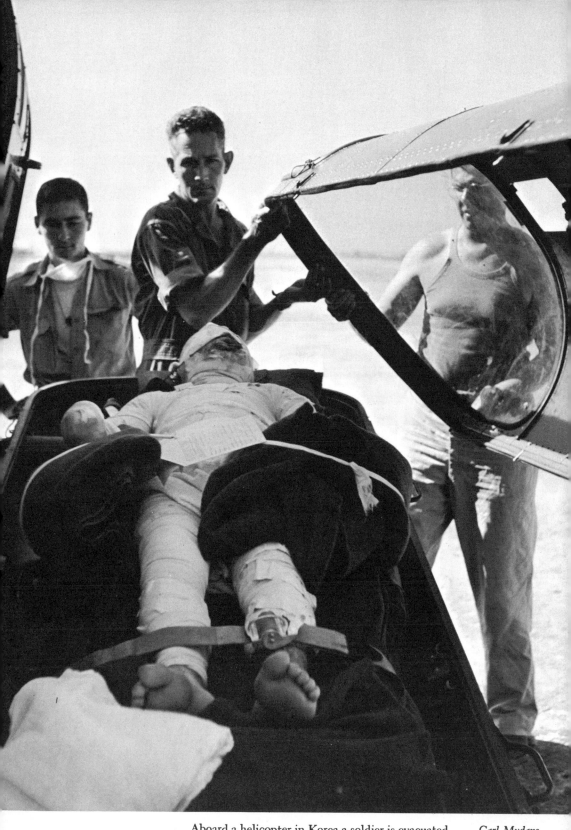

Aboard a helicopter in Korea a soldier is evacuated. *Carl Mydans*

In a helicopter in Vietnam a soldier dies. *Larry Burrows*

American Marines retreat from the Yalu River. *David Douglas Duncan*

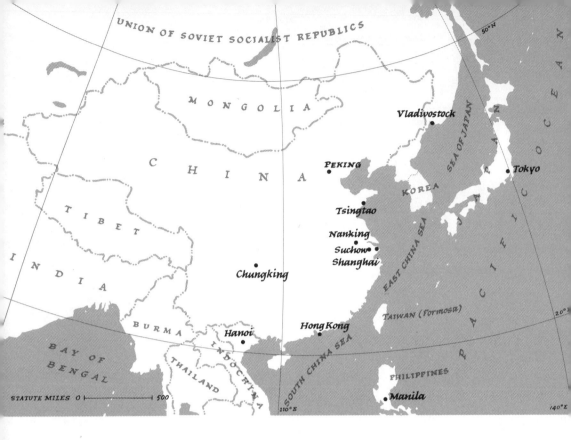

III

Civil War in China

(1945-1949)

THE FIRST CONFLICT in Asia to grow out of World War II was the Chinese civil war. Here the Japanese surrender and withdrawal of her troops in 1945 brought the conflict between the Kuomintang regime of Chiang Kai-shek and the Chinese Communists under Mao Tse-tung—by then almost a quarter of a century old—to open warfare as the Communists strove to gain the arms of the defeated Japanese and Chiang moved his troops in to prevent them. The Communists had at their backs the bases and supplies of the Soviet Russian army which had come to retake Manchuria at the end of the war. The Kuomintang forces were supplied and airlifted by the United States, which had supported them during their war with Japan.

By November 1948 the Communists had gained such force that they had encircled Peking and were ranging well south of the ancient capital. On the Shantung Peninsula they had formed a great arc around the old treaty port of Tsingtao and were closing in to take its formidable naval base so strategically placed midway between Shanghai and Mukden. Here, since 1945, when the Japanese surrendered its modern docks and installations, the United States had maintained its Western Pacific fleet. But now, unless it too were to become engaged in the war in China, the time had come for it to give up the facilities.

I had come there Thanksgiving week to cover the evacuation of foreigners, and I was staying at a little Dutch-owned hotel which stood just above the harbor. Its proprietors had already gone and most of the Chinese staff had disappeared after them. The dining room was closed, the stoves in the rooms were no longer fired, and we all gathered in the dark lobby to eat and to share the only source of heat in the hotel, an old Dutch stove that we stoked with coal ourselves.

Very few guests remained, and the half-dozen or so I joined around the stove in the lobby that morning might have been the last of them. They were all missionaries and they had lived and worked in China most of their adult lives. In the past few days they had come by ricksha and on foot from the interior, and now they were on their way out.

We were waiting for breakfast and we all sat idle and silent, gazing out the windows at the frost-covered roofs below us that slanted down the hill to the harbor. At the end of the slope were the waiting ships that would take us all away, and beyond, just a few miles off, was a fringe of islands. These— although it seemed incredible—were already in the hands of the Communists.

Behind me someone spoke and I turned back into the dark room. An old man in a long Chinese gown sat swaying slowly in a rocking chair. "Well, it's all over," he said. He brightened a little when he saw he had my attention. "Not much more we can do," he added. Then he leaned forward as though to confide in me. "You know," he said, "two weeks ago a Chinese soldier came into the mission compound and lived with us for a few days. He was the son of our wash amah. We've known him since he was a boy. A Christian. The last year or two he's been a radio technician with the Chiang Kai-shek forces. One day he said to us, 'What am I? I am like all other Nationalist soldiers. I have three choices. I can desert and try to flee south with my family. I can remain here and wait for the Communists to come and shoot me. I can travel north now and join them; and when they come in my family will be protected and cared for.' The day we all left for Tsingtao he brought us food for our journey—and then he went north to join the Communists." He sat nodding at me for emphasis, and then he added: "It wasn't much of a choice—under the circumstances."

By then Mukden had fallen and the weight of the Communist armies was pressing heavily toward Nanking, nestled in the great bend of the Yangtze which flows through the heartland of central China. "Manchuria is a limb that has been amputated," a Nationalist government minister said as November was nearing its end. "The body can live, despite amputation. North China is another limb, and even that can be sacrificed. But central China is the Nationalist heart—and if the heart is pierced, the body dies."

Hsuchow was the key to Nanking and the Yangtze Valley. Its history dates back to the time of the Emperor Hsia Yu, 2205 B.C., and since that time emperors and warlords have considered the battle for Hsuchow the climax in every change of dynasty. There is an old Chinese saying: "Hsuchow is the place military experts must take to control everything in the sky." Now again it was to play such a climactic role. Half a million men on each side had joined to give battle there. It began in early November and lasted thirty-eight days. It was to prove the last major engagement of a war that not only would involve our generation profoundly, but would change the course of history.

Only a few Western correspondents reached the fighting fronts of this decisive battle. One of them was Robert Doyle, who sent the following dispatch on November 21, 1948:

▶ The fine loess dust on the rutted dirt road from Hsuchow to the front, twenty-five miles to the east, was churned by our jeep into a long brown cloud which hung in the still air. We could hear the distant thump of artillery and the crunch of aerial bombs. Ahead and in some hills to the south, puffs of white billowed where shells and bombs found targets. In a village which had been retaken from the Communists the day before, an old peasant woman squatted at a roadside pond whacking at her laundry with a wooden paddle. Behind her on the mud wall of her burned-out hut the Reds, before they were beaten back, had splashed slogans in white paint: "Fight to Nanking!", "Land for the Tillers!", and "Capture the liar Chiang alive!"

We were met on the open road by a huge, red-cheeked adjutant who swung down from a truck loaded with heavily armed soldiers. He would escort us to the command post of Lieutenant General Li Mi, commander of the Thirteenth Army Group. He pointed north toward a hill rising like the hump of a razorback hog out of the fields. The truck wallowed off the road through a shallow ditch and followed a telephone wire stretched across the parched, lumpy land, already sown with winter wheat.

On top of the hill we shook hands with General Li Mi in front of his command post—a crude lean-to fashioned out of wooden poles covered with kaoliang stalks. He waved us to a rock ledge in front of the lean-to and said, with a grin, "Come sit with me on my sofa." General Li apologized for the roughness of his quarters. "Every day I move," he said. "We have no time for luxury." Li wore a padded private's uniform and a private's winter helmet with the earflaps drawn up.

On an order from the General, a soldier brought us yellow pears, as large as grapefruit. As we ate, the General traced the central China battle on the palm of his hand. Twelve miles eastward his old comrade, Lieutenant General Huang Po-tao, was encircled in an area three and a half miles in diameter around the rail town of Nienchuang. In eleven days of fighting Huang had lost forty thousand troops. From his position north of the Lunghai railway, General Li was punching east to relieve Huang. In a parallel position south of the railway, Lieutenant General Chiu Ching-chuan's Second Army Group was also pushing east.

On Li's left flank, to the north, were four Communist columns under Red General Chen Yi. Chiu's right flank to the south was menaced by another eight columns of Chen's troops. Ahead, Li and Chiu faced three strong Communist defense lines between them and the beleaguered General Huang. "This is the bitterest fighting I have ever experienced," said General Li. "I have orders from the Generalissimo to advance at any cost. Communists we have captured say they have been told to fight to the death to hold the line." In eight days Li had advanced ten miles. He had lost two hundred officers, more than eight thousand soldiers.

As Li talked, a Chinese air force Mustang, humming along in the fading twilight, nosed over and swooped down on a village three miles east. A few seconds later we heard the sharp chatter of machine guns. "That village is my objective tonight," said Li. "When the sun is down my artillery will open up and then the infantry will move in."

When the sun had dropped below the horizon and a white ground mist had crawled slowly up the valley floor along the black line of the Lunghai railroad, Li telephoned an order to his artillery commanders. Within a few minutes two spots in the valley blazed with the flash of cannon fire; tracers from the 37-mm. guns on Li's tanks cut red streaks through the blackness as they arched in a slow trajectory like monstrous lighted clay pigeons. Less frequently the huge muzzle flash of 105-mm. guns ballooned from the plain, hung for an instant, then blinked out. After an hour, the barrage slowed down. "Now the infantry," said Li. "Come, we will eat."

Our jeep trailed behind the General's as we ground in low gear across the rough ground toward a village headquarters less than three miles from the front. Jeep lights flicked on and off as the drivers tried to avoid the deeper holes. An elliptical orange moon popped over the horizon. As we neared the village we passed an artillery position. The dark forms of tanks loomed up against the sky. A 105-mm. gun directly in front suddenly cut loose, its red flash silhouetting for an instant the crouched figures of the gun crew. A pungent smell of gunpowder rolled over the jeep. General Li leaned out and said quietly, "Careful, careful, we are passing under your muzzle."

Li's headquarters were in a mud hut within a mud-walled compound. Outside the door a soldier hunched over a twig fire, drying his cotton shoes. Inside the hut at a table, the commander of Li's Eighth Army bent over a map. Two candles stuck in their own wax at the corners of the table were the only light. Li waved us to seats around the table and called for food.

Shortly after we began eating, an orderly called General Li to the phone. He talked for a moment in a low voice and returned to the table. In the candlelight the lines on his youthful face—he is forty-four—had sagged. He stared at his rice bowl, then explained quietly that he had just had word of a radio message from his friend General Huang. "The trap is closing," said Li. "He must have help soon. We must reach him in two days."

At the meal's end the General escorted us to our hut, apologizing again for the rough quarters. Through the bright moonlight, Chinese air force planes droned continuously overhead, some with bombs which dropped with a heavy concussion, some with supplies to be parachuted to encircled General Huang. Artillery, which was dug in behind the village, kept up an intermittent fire—first came the muzzle blast, then the scream of the shell overhead, then a distant crunch as the shell exploded.

Shortly after midnight, the brittle crackle of small-arms fire welled out of the distance, slowly drew closer. The adjutant roared with laughter at our nervous inquiry. "*Pu-yau-chin, pu-yau-chin*" (No matter, no matter), he said. "Do not worry. This happens every night. The Communists are counterattacking but we will stop them."

At the first light of dawn, soldiers carrying huge bowls of steaming rice cautiously picked their way down the trench-laced narrow streets. A donkey hitched to an ancient wooden-wheeled cart, loaded with shining black 105-mm. shell cases, munched slowly on hay.

Inside the headquarters hut, as Li splashed water on his face from a basin, the adjutant said the General had had a good night. He had been able to sleep from midnight until three in the morning. Over breakfast the General explained disconsolately that he had not been able to take his objective. Although a thousand shells had been poured into the village, the Communists had held their line and mustered enough strength to send a counterattack within a mile of the General's headquarters. "We will take it today, though," he said with determination. "We must."

We left him that morning to return to Hsuchow to board a Chinese air force C-46 on a mission to air-drop ammunition and hospital supplies to General Huang Po-tao. Nienchuang, Huang's headquarters, nestles close to the smashed Lunghai railway. The village has a heart-shaped double wall and a double moat. The southern section of the town was burning and all nearby villages were heaps of wrecked houses. Trenches webbed out from Nienchuang like some scabrous disease infecting the good earth. All around the village, crumpled parachutes from previous drops sprinkled the brown countryside. As the C-46 captain came down to two thousand feet to drop his supplies, Communist guns in positions within a mile of Nienchuang opened up on the plane but fell short of the mark.

That night we heard the melancholy news that Huang Po-tao's moated walls had been pierced. ►

After that, the Nationalists were cut into smaller and smaller pieces. Stocks of food and ammunition dwindled. By mid-November only air-drops which droned up from Nanking with food and bullets kept the Nationalist forces in the fight. Then bad weather cut the air-drops to a trickle. The Nationalists slaughtered all their horses for food. They ate green grass, the tiny green shoots of winter wheat. Then they ate the bark from trees. The first of the season's heavy snows blanketed the brown fields. Bitter cold came and the soldiers who could not squeeze into the meager mud huts in the villages froze. "What do you have to eat?" the Communists yelled across no man's land. In front of their lines they tethered fat pigs in full view of the hungry Nationalists. "Don't fight on," the voices called. "Come on over to us. We will feed you and protect you. If you stay there you will die. There is no escape."

One general, Sun Yuan-liang, escaped in beggar's rags. And General Li Mi himself, having led a last charge as his Thirteenth Army Group CP was being overwhelmed, broke through with only a dozen men and, donning civilian clothes and disguised as a cigarette-paper merchant, rode through the Communist lines in a wheelbarrow. By early December whole units of the encircled forces were going over to the Communists with their weapons. Of all the uncertainties of war, the uncertainty of loyalty had become the most frightening.

General Robert Soule, whom I had known as an infantry colonel during the war in the Philippines three years earlier, was now military attaché with the United States embassy in Nanking. He had on his wall a great map of northern China marked with the fighting fronts and the units engaged, and that day when I visited him I began to copy onto my own map such information from his as might serve me when I went forward into the fighting area.

The General stopped me. "If you're going up there," he said, "don't count too much on what you see here." He waved vaguely at his map. "We keep marking it up, but almost all our reports are from Chinese sources and very few of them are dependable now. These positions," he said, running his finger along a crayon line, "are shown here as unbroken defenses. But they're not that at all. There is no line. Just units, mostly independent of each other, and we're never sure they're where they say they are—or even whose side they're going to be on next."

I had never before known a military campaign like the one I found in the vast wheatlands of Anhwei, which stretched out from Pengpu. General Soule had prepared me to expect no line, but my earlier experiences in military engagements had fixed my thinking and I had, in fact, continued vaguely to visualize some sort of intermittent defense perimeter. Instead, I found the defending troops rolled into small, independent forces, dug in here or coming to rest there or moving on again, out of communication with their command, bumping into friendly units or the enemy and bouncing off again as aimlessly as amoebas in a puddle.

54

Somewhere on those great prairies the evacuated Hsuchow garrison, clumped with forces representing three separate army groups, was encircled and reportedly fighting its way south toward still another group, the Twelfth, which had come out of Hankow in support of the besieged garrison and was itself encircled. Small remnants of these groups, together with various other units in the area, confused and increasingly dispirited by rumors of defeat, were the amoebas.

Into these we drove, my young interpreter, Li, and I, twenty miles north of Pengpu. We had been carried to the end of the line at Chai Pai Chia in an armored train, our party increased by one, an English-speaking major who had been sent by headquarters to help us with our mission and who was eager to accommodate us when we told him that our goal was an area of combat. He persuaded the railroad command to provide us with a truck and driver and we headed out through the wheat stumps, across trackless flatlands. Next day I wrote the following report of what we found there:

▶ A smoke-smudged horizon bent around us and out there somewhere heavy guns thudded and soon we began to pass villages where there had been action. The villages were all small ones, rising like tiny atolls in an ocean of stubble, most of them completely destroyed by flame and shell, their bleak adobe-mud huts tumbled and scattered about.

Those villages that were not destroyed were full of troops and around each was a circle of spider holes, dug deep in Japanese fashion. Soldiers standing in these holes up to their chests frequently challenged us, and then passed us along into the hamlet. Late in the day we entered the village of Chiang Chia Hu. It was crowded with soldiers, some of them busily extending a network of trenches that wound through the thin alleys and under the houses. Every hut was packed with troops, and against the adobe walls rough lean-tos made of kaoliang reeds sheltered more men huddled in the cold.

Only a few villagers remained, running at the call of each imperative military voice, their houses commandeered, their heaps of straw being chewed away by the artillery horses, and their rice and vegetables and whatever livestock they had left disappearing into the cooking pots that boiled and simmered wherever rifles were stacked and men squatted by the heat of the smoky fires.

The village had changed hands a couple of times in the course of that strange warfare, and the experience had left its mark on the few survivors we found there. "Who is better?" Li asked one of them, "the

Nationalists or the Communists?"

"Both are good," the farmer answered quickly. "Only the people are bad."

When we were introduced to the commanding general and had photographed him, I asked if we could remain for a few days and cover his troops in whatever action might develop. He was an expansive man and he threw his arms in a great arc as he invited us to share his hospitality. And I began at once to document the scene of the encampment in pictures as a prelude to what might later follow.

After a while, though, the major, coming out of the headquarters hut, motioned me to join him and we walked over to Li.

"Now we must go," he said when we were all together.

"Go where?" I asked quickly.

"Go back to the railroad," he answered. "The truck is waiting for us."

"But we're not going back now," I said in astonishment. "The whole point of our coming here is to see some action. The general has invited us to stay as long as we want."

Li stood silent and the major shook his head. "The general misunderstood you and now we must go," he said. "This is a poor village. There is no place for you to sleep and the food is very bad. It is better for you to go back to Pengpu."

"But we're here to cover a war," I protested. "I don't care about the facilities! Let's talk to the general again."

"If we don't go now," he replied earnestly, "we'll miss the train, and no one knows when the next one will run."

"But I don't want to go!" I exclaimed. I was annoyed.

"Please," he pleaded. "We must go. We cannot stay."

I persisted. "But why?"

"Because," he answered slowly, and now plainly in anguish, "this general . . . these troops. Today they are Nationalists. But what they will be tonight or tomorrow . . . I cannot promise." ▶

I made a show after that of taking a few more pictures. But sometime before dusk we were back in the truck, rolling toward the railhead.

Two days later, back in General Soule's headquarters, I was told that the unit we were with had "disappeared"—into what fate we could only guess.

After Hsuchow's fall, the Communist armies, swelled by the defections of the Nationalist forces, swept over China. During the summer of 1949 all of the south fell. In December of that year the Nationalist government fled from the mainland to Formosa, where it was protected from Communist pursuit by the U.S. Navy. Eight years to the day after the Japanese made the attack that led, in 1945, to her unconditional surrender, the civil war which racked one of her conquerors came to a standstill—not through an armistice or agreement of any kind but simply by pause. Ever since then, each side in China's civil conflict has stood in arms against the other, one on the mainland, one on an island off the coast, each having vowed to launch—sometime—renewed attack.

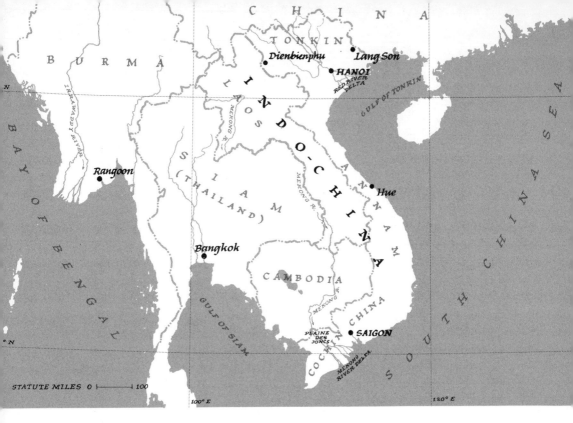

IV

Indo-China:
The Fight for a Lost Empire
(1945-1954)

THE WAR which had prepared the ground for Communism to sprout and flourish and finally overrun all of the Chinese mainland had similarly nurtured a longing for independence among the colonial people of Southeast Asia. The first of the anti-colonial wars to spring up in this area was that in Indo-China, and by the time the Free French forces entered there after the Japanese collapse in August 1945, France had already lost her Asian empire.

This was not yet clear to the French, and at the time they were quite sanguine about the prospects of reestablishing their colonial rule. As for the Indo-Chinese, they had behind them a thousand years' experience in opposition to invasion and subjugation.

For more than half a century this rule by foreigners had been personified by a French admiral in a starched and beribboned white uniform, surrounded by the traditional pomp and flourish of a colonial empire and supported by armed troops who marched to parade every day, their cadenced step and martial music ringing along the quiet tree-lined streets of Saigon. When the Japanese took over the colony in 1940, they chose to keep this white façade of French authority in order to free their own troops and administrators for duty in other parts of their suddenly acquired empire. The Vichy French accepted and played this role as though they didn't see reality, but the Indo-Chinese saw the situation clearly.

The day before the Japanese surrender, two planes made parachute drops over Indo-China, one in the south near Saigon and one in the far north. Out of the one in the south jumped Colonel Henri Cédile, who was to be the new French commissioner for the southern region; he and his two companions landed in a rice paddy and were seized forthwith and turned over to the Japanese. Major Pierre Messmer and two aides, who landed in the north near Hanoi, were treated by the local people themselves, who put them in prison and fed them poison, killing one of the aides. Thus did the Indo-Chinese reject the first attempt of France to return her rule to her richest colony. It was a dramatic symbol and a harbinger of the nine years of conflict that were to follow.

The Indo-Chinese nationalist underground had been active since the late 1920's, and during the war they stepped up their sabotage and terrorism against not only the Japanese and French but also against any collaborators who supported them. In the north especially, the movement had grown to such proportions that in the summer of 1945 it engaged the full attention of a Japanese division in Tonkin. Earlier, in 1941, the guerrillas had consolidated themselves into a nationalist party and had taken the name of Viet Nam Doc Lap Dong Minh Hoi—the League for Independence of Viet Nam. Its popular contraction was "Viet Minh." The week the Japanese surrendered, the Viet Minh gathered at Tan Trao, north of Hanoi, and formed a provisional government. They changed the name of Annam—which means "pacified south"—to Vietnam, the ancient name their country had borne before the

Chinese conquered them more than a thousand years earlier, and they swore themselves to independence.

The Allied Plan for Indo-China, worked out at the Potsdam Conference, took little notice of the Viet Minh dream. Instead, the country was divided into northern and southern zones. The Nationalist Chinese were given the responsibility for restoring law and order in the north, while the British were given the same assignment for the south, but their interpretations of "law and order" were quite different. The Chinese dealt with the insurgents' provisional government as the only existing authority, and disarmed the Japanese. The British saw their role as the protectors of French interests. They treated the Vietnamese nationalists as the enemy and disarmed the partisan units, while they released the French troops who had been interned and kept the Japanese fully armed to aid them against the local people. By late September the Viet Minh's Saigon government had been crushed in a bloody coup and French colonial rule had been reestablished.

The Viet Minh, even though scattered in the south, could still command a powerful guerrilla force. They had lost their Saigon headquarters, but they had a base among the rural Vietnamese that was almost impregnable, and from there, behind the lines of the French outposts and probing columns, they carried on their war.

"Many people think it is impossible for guerrillas to exist for long in the enemy's rear. Such a belief reveals a lack of comprehension of the relationship that should exist between the people and the troops. The former may be likened to water and the latter to fish who inhabit it." This familiar dictum of Mao Tse-tung's was so well followed by the Viet Minh that in a few years even the French admitted that, although they ruled by day, the Viet Minh ruled by night. And in many areas the majority of villagers, passively tending to their farms while the sun shone, became guerrilla fighters after dark.

When Mao wrote his essay "On Guerrilla Warfare," in which these lines appear, he based his theories on the experience of the Chinese Communists who fought a hard-pressed war of skirmish and retreat against the Japanese long before the full-scale civil war with the Kuomintang. But the concept holds and has been adopted by every insurgent movement in the many "wars of liberation" that have been fought since World War II, for guerrilla warfare is essentially political. The name was coined to fit the bands of Spanish irregulars who harassed Napoleon's armies in the early nineteenth century, and the science of it was elucidated by T. E. Lawrence during the Arab revolt against the Turks in World War I. The pattern tends to follow a slow growth

60

from acts of sabotage and terror to guerrilla hit-and-run engagements to conventional battles and full-scale war. In every occupied country in World War II, the partisan fighting units of the underground employed harassment and some guerrilla raids, but only in Yugoslavia and Indo-China were they able to progress successfully to full-scale war.

Mao wrote of guerrilla warfare as a prolonged struggle, fearful of neither time nor space because, being political, the goal may take decades to reach and, being irregular, has neither front nor rear nor long lines of supply. The tactics, he said, should be those of "making a noise in the east but striking in the west," and "avoiding the solid to attack the hollow." His strategic formula he set forth in the "16 key words," which are: "Enemy advances, we retreat; enemy halts, we harass; enemy tires, we attack; enemy retreats, we pursue." Soon to these sixteen he added another vital six: "Lure the enemy to penetrate deep."

As with all underground movements, the Viet Minh attacked not only the French but any who collaborated with them. Vietnamese who were suspected of sympathy with the French, who held any sort of office in rural or village government, or who even accepted French money were marked for murder. The aim was not merely to punish those the Viet Minh considered traitors, but to encourage active cooperation among the others. In the cities, especially Saigon, the killings were less discriminatory. There were some selective murders of collaborators, but more often bombs were thrown into a sidewalk café or left to explode in a crowded street. The purpose was to show that the Viet Minh were everywhere, even within the enemy stronghold. And inasmuch as a wavering population naturally gravitates to the winning side, this sort of terrorism had its successes.

French announcements of new victories in the field or claims of political success were often countered by daring acts of terror within the very complex of French military might. I witnessed a demonstration of such daring during the night of March 17, 1950, and wrote of it at the time:

▶ The American destroyers, the *Stickell* and the *Anderson*, were tied alongside each other among the French warships, sloops and gunboats at the French naval dock on the river in Saigon. Just across the street from them were the French naval headquarters and the grand mansion of Admiral Paul Ortoli.

On the admiral's expansive lawn, with lovely flame-colored trees and manicured flowerbeds, the fanciest of French cocktail parties was being given by the senior French naval officer, Far East, and his staff for the senior American naval officer, Far East, and the officers of his glistening destroyers. At sundown a French naval band marched in and positioned itself near the French tricolors flying at yardarm above the gathering of starched white uniforms and the darker flowered gowns of the ladies. Champagne glasses in hand or quickly placed on the lawn, the officers jerked to attention as the band played the French, Vietnamese and American national anthems. The colors floated slowly earthward. Outside the compound's massive grilled-iron gates a small knot of Vietnamese watched silently. The show was not theirs. Neither were the other elaborate activities earlier in the day: the protocol visits, marching sailors and clanging bands. It was easy to be carried away for long moments amid the pomp and elegance and imagine oneself in an era already dead.

But as dusk began to fade into darkness, the officers and their ladies climbed into sleek, low-slung French Citroëns to be driven up the tree-lined streets to a variety of other parties. And on the outskirts of the city, barricades were being lowered across the main roads and the soldiers and police who were to spend the night in their thirty-foot-high concrete towers were hauling their rope ladders up after them. For at this hour the power of the country was changing hands; in Indo-China the night belongs to the Viet Minh.

At 7:30 that evening, five American sailors from the *Anderson* were leaning across a bar with cognac before them, absorbed with the difficulties of conversing in their faintly remembered high-school French with a graying-blonde French barwoman. At the sidewalk tables outside sat a score or more of French sailors and a few Foreign Legionnaires. Across the square, which was crowded with strollers, was the Continental Hotel where the American admiral and his staff had rooms.

The crack of the grenade was sharp and the puff of smoke was small. It fell clear of most of the drinkers, wounding two French sailors and a Legionnaire. It killed two passing Vietnamese and injured half a dozen others. The police arrived in weapons carriers, their sirens wailing through the streets. They were businesslike and practiced as they collected the wounded and the dead and carried them away. There was no questioning at the scene of the attack. No one hoped to catch the grenade thrower.

At 11:20 the streets were almost empty. The first of the firing began with two heavy crashes. At our hotel six blocks from the river we knew it was mortar fire. Then we heard bursts of automatic weapons, then more mortars. They were coming in on the riverfront where the ships were lying and we ran toward them. The area was blacked out and the ships were dark, with only their red battle lights showing. A few police and men of the naval guard were taking cover, crouched behind trees and the wall to the admiral's garden. We heard another mortar smash nearby and then the sound of falling metal and shattered glass. The machine-gun bursts had increased but there was no return fire from the ships; the mortaring was coming from a densely populated Vietnamese area just across the river. The whole attack lasted not more than twenty minutes. Then there was stillness in the dark heart of the city. The Viet Minh had shown their strength and had faded back again among the people. ▶

The war was more than four years old when I went along on a French offensive into the delta regions of the Plaine des Joncs, a vast territory of marshes, rivers and creeks, stretching westward beyond Saigon to the Cambodian border. The Viet Minh had made it their stronghold for control of the southern military sections west and south of Saigon, and it was the command center from which the terrorist attacks within Saigon had been directed. This was to be the biggest French offensive against this major Viet Minh complex in a determined effort to wipe it clean. Ground troops, naval gunboats, amphibious tractors and air support units would make a coordinated assault. "The attack will operate like a fisherman's net," the briefing officer said. "We shall drive the Viet Minh into the center of our net—and pull the cord. And this time, maybe—" he shrugged—"we shall have them."

My report of that operation follows:

▶ We took off from a base on the Saigon River, our small pontoon plane rising over the city in dawn darkness. Then we banked sharply toward the first streaks of morning light and in a few minutes the Plaine des Joncs began to stretch below us, looking more like an ocean with patches of grass and jungle floating upon it than a land with lakes and rivers. But the illusion vanished as we flew westward, for now a great grassland appeared below us. And around it in a giant circle curved a broad band of blue smoke against the sparkling light of the new day. The operation had begun; the troops and the craft upon the rivers and creeks were sweeping the area with fire. Now and again we could hear the report of guns above the roar of the engine.

"The net," the pilot yelled at me. "It is being laid." We descended into the net: seventy miles west of Saigon, our "Sea Otter" glided down

63

upon the Cai Rung River, a sluggish coffee-colored waterway which smelled of the fetid decay of rich jungle and marshes. A small riverboat met us and I was put aboard an LCI, the command ship for the river sweep. It turned upstream full power, sailors and ground troops poised along its railings with their guns covering the shores which slid past us. The river was broad, and it was continually fed by countless other streams which the French call *rachs,* the Vietnamese term for "small waterways." Along the banks of these *rachs,* sometimes in the open, often hidden in an overgrowth of man-high jonc grass, bamboo groves, banyan and mangrove trees, live the people of this great marshland. Their simple bamboo and straw huts are clustered usually in twos and threes, or in small villages of a dozen or so houses. They live on the fish they catch, and from the small garden patches they have retrieved from the swamps. Chickens, ducks, black pigs and water buffaloes live with them, and white silky egrets and scarlet and black broadbills and snakebirds rise from their land. All the houses we passed were empty, but they had not been empty long. Wisps of smoke trailed up from smoldering fires under cooking pots, and wash hung on bamboo poles.

It was dusk when the LCI turned its blunt nose into the shoreline and came to rest noiselessly for the night on a little mudbank. An infantry unit was bivouacked along the river and there were other craft drawn up in the tiny cove. Among them were two LSTs, the floating homes of two battalions of 350 men each. Fifty amphibious weasels were parked on the shore among the trees and vines. The French Foreign Legionnaires who operated them had stretched their mosquito nets and shelter halves beside their vehicles and were already settled for the night, engaged in the countless chores of a military encampment. Some butchered pigs and ducks and chickens; others cooked or tended fires. They cleaned their weapons and sewed up rips in clothing and belting; they smoked and talked and bathed and sang; they dealt strange games of cards with soiled packs, and some played schoolboy tricks on others. The chatter of their voices rose in a polyglot, and the flash of faces and bodies was in variegated blacks and browns and whites. This was a gathering of men from many lands, French, German, Moroccan, black Senegalese, Algerian, Equatorial African—different in race, in tongue, in religion, in a hundred cultural mores. When they laughed or sang or told their stories, when they butchered their pigs and flipped the entrails into the river and paused to watch the fish rise to them, when they adjusted and sighted their weapons, they revealed their differences. Bearded, soiled, sun-beaten men, they had but one quality in common: they were all fighting men and killing was their business.

In our phase of the operation next morning, two infantry battalions, mostly African Goumiers, were working from both sides of the river, flushing the marshes. The weasels had already disappeared across a neck of land to cut off the Viet Minh escape, and the air arm was now overhead to provide intelligence and attack power. As our river course paralleled the troops', we heard bursts of rifle and machine-gun fire, and an extending smokeline marked the advance of the Goumiers across the marshes. Slowly another band of blue smoke was curving around the horizon.

A small picket boat came alongside our LCI and I was invited down into it. It had a crew of one French officer, two French noncoms, and two Vietnamese boatmen. We skimmed off at once, outrunning the command ship, and turned into a small stream. Our Bren-gunners fixed their shoulders against the stocks of their mounted weapons, and the tenseness of alert settled over the crew. We were moving slowly, with caution. Thick jungle, tall palms and clumps of bamboo stood on the river's banks. A tiny flotilla of ducks came eagerly toward us, and then as though judging us better, turned quickly away. The war and the shooting had moved off and the silence which had settled over us was disturbing.

A clearing appeared around a bend, and there were three small huts. The Bren-gunners sighted their weapons on them as we idled along the embankment. The lieutenant reached for a grenade, and motioned the coxswain to move off. As one engine quickened he tossed the grenade into a dugout, and behind us a column of water and hyacinth shot into the sky. The native boat settled into the muddy foam. "It is not good for the people who live here," the French officer said. "But if we leave them their boats, the Viet Minh will use them to move ammunition and supplies. Small boats are the motor cars of the Plaine des Joncs."

We passed a house on which we could see some posters. The lieutenant studied them through his field glasses and muttered, "Viet Minh." Then the squint-eyed French noncom at the forward gun fired a burst into the marsh. "Men," he said, as our engine speeded up and someone hurled a grenade ashore. As we sped away we watched a clump of mud burst into the air.

Twenty miles up the river, I went ashore and joined a unit of Goumiers led by a French captain. For hours we walked through the marshes and along the dikes, keeping our voices low while the pointman ahead advanced with caution. "Soon, very soon," the captain told us. "The Viet Minh will be squeezed and we will have a fight."

The houses we passed now were of reeds and leaves, built high upon skinny poles. The chickens and pigs were still about, but as from all the other houses we had seen, their owners had fled. Goumiers looked over each house we passed. When they decided that the Viet Minh had used them—if there was too great a rice supply, or any ammunition or pamphlets—they put the torch to the house.

At midafternoon the pointman came running back to the captain. The head of the column had exchanged signals with the Legionnaires. This meant the closing of the net and we quickened our pace to make contact. Overhead, French fighters were providing reconnaissance and communications for our converging forces. We could hear shooting in the distance.

Then we sighted the advance troops of the Legionnaires and soon we joined forces and went on together, tightening our circle as we pushed in toward the center of the ring. Late in the day we passed a headquarters unit of the Legionnaires at rest by the trail, some of its men beginning to set up a bivouac for the night. Our captain stopped and talked with their officers. Then he waved to us and started off again, leading his little column into an overgrown rubber plantation. When we caught up with him he gave us a particularly French look of gloom.

"The mission is accomplished," he said. "The drawstring has been pulled. *Alors!*" And he waved his hand, pointing through the rubber trees.

There we saw standing in a circle of misery and fright, a little group of Vietnamese women and children. As we walked up to them, the captain pointed again at the cowering group. "*Une victoire magnifique!*" he said with bitterness. "A splendid victory. As always, the army of the Viet Minh caught in our net!" ▶

In the four years that followed, the French increased their efforts and the Viet Minh increased their strength. Though Ho Chi Minh was the architect of the Viet Minh, the military genius behind the guerrilla was General Vo Nguyen Giap. A master of organization, he built his forces into three complementary groups: the regular guerrilla army, the regional units of full-time guerrillas, and the "popular troops"—those men and women who were peasants by day. With the victory of the Communists in China in 1949, he had gained a common border with an ally, and now he had the backing and supplies he needed to increase his regular army to conventional fighting strength. By 1954 he had at his command seven full divisions of some ten thousand men each and was ready to take the offensive. Again, political considerations played a major role. The people of France, so far away, so dedicated to their concepts of national and individual liberty, and restive under the costs of the war, were agitating for an end to this oppressive conflict. Under this pressure the French generals elected to make a stand. The place they stood was Dienbienphu, an isolated outpost in a shallow basin surrounded by hills.

On March 13 the Viet Minh opened their attack. The fighting on both sides was fierce, determined, full of heroic deeds. It lasted eight bloody, screaming weeks, until the final French defender was overrun May 7. Meanwhile representatives of interested governments were meeting in Geneva for a conference about the Indo-China war. The settlement they arrived at was a recognition of an independent state of North Vietnam, with its capital at Hanoi. The south was to remain in association with the French Union. The dividing line partitioning the country was the 17th parallel.

Even before this international agreement, the French command in the northern area had turned to the task of withdrawing and consolidating its remaining forces. It was not an easy task. Three weeks after the fall of Dienbienphu, an armored column was sent to extricate the garrisons from two French forts in the Red River Delta. Correspondent John Mecklin accompanied the column. This is his report:

▶ The two forts, one at Doai Than and the second at Thanh Ne, both lying within a fifty-mile radius of Hanoi, had long been at the eastern end of the line of Franco-Vietnamese control. Gradually and irresistibly the Viet Minh had been pinching these strong points off as a woodman cuts rings around a tree to save himself the trouble of chopping it down. The technique has been effectively used throughout Indo-China. First the branches begin to wither as the Viet Minh tighten their political and military hold on the surrounding villages. Then snipers and road mines make the patrol contacts between fortified posts, and between the posts and the villages, more and more hazardous, until finally they cannot be carried out without an increase in their military strength. One by one, the patrols cease visiting the villages and one by one the local Saigon government representatives vanish, and finally the Red cadres take over.

By March the garrison of fifty Vietnamese troops at Fort Doai

Than, and of sixty more at Thanh Ne, had been wholly immobilized, futilely sealed in their earthen pillboxes, their mission of protecting the countryside and collecting rice a joke. As they did at Dienbienphu, the Viet Minh have dug trenches into the fort's defenses harassing the garrison with small arms and mortar fire, and heckling and unnerving the Vietnamese troops with propaganda.

The men inside, like the villagers outside, know that the Communists can attack and overrun the posts whenever they are ready to. Even more humiliating, all this has been accomplished by the Viet Minh "regional" troops, rather than by the regular guerrilla army.

The French say the two posts are not cut off. But the cost of fighting their way in with the monthly supply convoys has become so expensive that not for more than a month have the French put a convoy through.

The mission therefore was to withdraw the two garrisons and destroy the two posts: "A consolidation for offensive action elsewhere," was the French phrase. The job was given to Lieutenant Colonel Jacques Navarre, and to rescue the 110 men of the Doai Than and Thanh Ne posts, he collected a force of 200 vehicles, with 15 tanks, and 2,000 men, including two battalions of infantry. Considering that the adversary would be barefooted peasants armed with mines, rifles and a few mortars, this was a formidable force.

Just before eight in the morning, word was passed that the first leg of the road had been cleared of mines and the column got underway. The road was badly pocked with saucer-shaped holes, filled in with fresh brown dirt where Viet mines had just been removed, and across the paddies in a wavering green light we could see the peasants already at work, some of them with small Vietnamese flags on sticks to deter fire from the convoy. In a few paddies already harvested there were beds of deep purple flowers in lovely contrast to the deep green of the unharvested rice.

The column ground through a series of villages, raising clouds of choking dust, blanketing food markets and settling on thronging crowds of peasants in conical straw hats and brown shirts and black pants. Seldom did any of them look up at us.

The first of a number of halts that would bedevil us the rest of the day stopped us when one of our trucks was blown up by a mine. More than half our column had passed over it before it exploded. While we waited, a peasant in a roadside paddy, up to his knees in rich black mud, guided his primitive wooden plow drawn by a water buffalo. And a pregnant woman with a dirty bare-bottomed boy plodded by with a flock of geese. A pair of peasants trotted past with a brace of squealing pigs suspended from a bamboo pole. Not one of them looked at us.

Now, one of our artillery batteries has opened up somewhere along the convoy and the shock waves crack across the paddy fields. The word is that there are snipers ahead. We pass an outpost called Dong Qui Thou, a typical strong point with a square brick watchtower, three or four concrete pillboxes and revetted mortar positions. We learn that the road beyond it has been closed for months. In another quarter of a mile, our convoy is blocked by gaping trenches, eight or ten feet wide and ten feet deep. They are spaced over a couple of hundred yards. And in another couple of hundred yards we can see two concrete bridges. The approaches to both of those have been dug away, leaving the bridges suspended in midair like stranded ships.

Near the bridge, a group of laughing Vietnamese soldiers, some in wet uniforms, some stripped to undershorts, display a collection of captured rifles and grenades, and handfuls of Vietnamese money bearing Ho Chi Minh's picture. They also have a couple of black sacks, shaped like inner tubes, which the Viets use to carry their rice in. On the far bank of the stream a soldier in an American helmet kicks over the mangled body of a Viet Minh soldier. A captured rifle goes off by accident and roars of laughter follow, especially from the soldier who was very nearly hit in the head by the slug. A Vietnamese captain stops for a chat. He says his battalion had a fight here an hour ago. His men surprised a company of Viet Minh. "We killed fifteen," he says in a professional way.

Our tanks now are moving awkwardly around the trenches to take fire positions, and bulldozers and a gang of two hundred Viet Minh prisoners move in to repair the road. The prisoners have picks and shovels and work in a close-packed, sweating mass. All at once a tank opens fire at pointblank range. It is shooting at a clump of huts across the stream. "Why?" I ask. "We want to make sure there are no Viets over there," the tank commander answers. Soon the huts are burning. As we watch, I see a sign nearby. It reads, "Expeditionary Force: Don't kill. Don't rape. Don't burn. Don't arrest young people." Now mortars suddenly explode in the tree-shaded village in billowing bursts which obliterate the straw huts in fire and smoke. They are Viet Minh mortars. Our batteries reply with a roar and silence them.

At one o'clock the first elements of the column reach the Doai Than post. The garrison is loaded upon trucks and heads back along the road.

The engineers haul down the French and Vietnamese flags from the flagstaff on the brick tower. Then they begin to plant explosives. While we wait, we see signs of the siege everywhere: rusted barbed wire, overgrown paths, Viet Minh trenches dug just outside the fort. Then the column pushes on.

Just beyond Doai Than, a Viet Minh sniper picks off a Vietnamese sergeant in the turret of his tank. Nearby are the overgrown walls of a Christian church which was destroyed years ago when the Viet Minh had unchallenged control of the region. Near the church, suddenly, a North African rifleman is killed by a mine. And moments later the Viets again lob a few mortars at us. The French retaliate by plastering another village. Behind us we hear an explosion. The engineers have blown up the post at Doai Than.

We reach the post at Thanh Ne and the garrison there too is loaded on trucks and the fort mined and abandoned. At last we turn back and late in the afternoon we have again reached the Dong Qui Thon post. Here a line of trucks carrying the sixty men from the Thanh Ne garrison stop. They have carried away what seems like every removable object in the fort—tables, chairs, sleeping mats, chunks of salvaged corrugated iron roofing, battered pots and pans, even a couple of ancient bicycles with no handlebars. A small group of Vietnamese women, giggling and excited, reach up to their men. They have not seen them in a long time. And when the men dismount, the women, still giggling, run after them.

Then behind us, in the distance, we hear another deep explosion. We feel it underfoot. And there is another, and another. We watch a column of brown smoke snake along the horizon. Thanh Ne has just been destroyed.

Our mission has been accomplished, and by late evening, most of the column has returned to base, leaving the men in Dong Qui Thon—the new end of the line—to wonder when they too will be "consolidated," or be ringed and left to wither and die. ▶

V

Greece: A Classic Insurrection

(1946-1949)

A S IN INDO-CHINA, the civil war in Greece was fought by guerrilla soldiers from their base among the people they controlled. In Europe as in Asia, a new kind of fighting man had emerged from World War II. After the panzer divisions and the steel-helmeted automaton-soldiers of the mechanized blitz, after the fleets of bombers streaking the skies in mile-wide swaths and the impersonal unloading of destruction on whole cities at a time, came the small band of irregulars, the ragged ill-armed figures in the forest or the craggy hills. Most of the time they were invisible: hiding beneath the water of a paddy field or behind the rocks of a desolate countryside—or in the dress of the ordinary villager, looking with blank eyes at the soldiers who sought them out. To citizens of wealthy, well-armed and well-governed nations they seemed more picturesque than dangerous. But they have been responsible for most of the armed conflicts throughout the world in the past twenty years.

In China, Indo-China, Indonesia, Palestine, Algeria, and Cuba, insurgents using guerrilla tactics won their political objectives. And even where the guerrillas were defeated—in such places as Malaya and the Philippines, Cyprus, Kenya, and the Congo—it was at the cost of prolonged military effort and some political concessions. Today in Asia, Africa, and South America they pose a threat to every government which is faced with a strong-willed faction bent on change.

The civil war in Greece, the home of classicism, was a classic case not only of guerrilla warfare but of the involvement of the rival powers of East and West in support of the rebels and of the governmental counteraction. As in most insurgencies immediately following World War II, its roots were in the partisan organizations of the underground who resisted foreign occupation; and in its post-war growth it set the pattern for the Cold War confrontations that were to follow. Its stakes were the control of a war-worn, weary people and the strategic land they called their home.

Peace had come to Europe three months earlier than it had to Asia and it brought different problems with it. In Asia the new world created by the Allied victory was surging with anti-colonialism and the awakening of nationalism, while in Europe the victory over the Nazis produced not only a divided Germany but a whole continent divided by the growing rivalry of two victorious powers.

The reactions of these two great powers to the end of the world war were widely divergent. The American impulse, in the first happy days of victory, was to "bring the boys back home" and to reject all haunting thoughts of future wars. The governmental policy in 1945 was to establish some world authority which would rest on close cooperation between the United States and Russia. This dream was possible because of the facts of America's geography and history, in which she had a great advantage over the Soviet Union. Bounded by two oceans and two friendly neighbors, she was secure; not in over a hundred years had foreign soldiers set foot on her soil. The Russians, on the other hand, were burdened by a history of invasions—first from the East and later by a succession of strong European armies—and she was suffering from the devastation wrought by this latest war. Over the centuries she had acquired an almost pathological fear of the powers beyond her own frontiers. Thus she sought to create a shield of dependent states around the motherland and to pursue the old-time czarist program of territorial expansion.

This obsessive need to protect herself was sometimes obscured by her crusade to spread a Communist regime throughout the world, but in Europe in 1945, it was the fear of the outsider that most influenced Soviet foreign policy. Even in the earliest months of the war, Soviet troops had entered and subjugated the neighboring states of Estonia, Latvia, Lithuania and the Karelian peninsula of Finland; by the last months they had taken control of Rumania, Bulgaria, Hungary and Poland and achieved agreements with pro-Communist governments in Yugoslavia and Albania.

In the Balkans, only Greece was able to resist the Soviet encroachment. And thus it was in Greece that a bitter internal conflict grew into the Cold War's first real confrontation. The Greek civil war was fought by Greeks and on Greek territory; neither the Americans nor the Communists supplied more than arms and advisers to the men who fought. But the real issue of that war was into which of the two great ideological camps the Greek nation—and others after it—would fall.

Late in 1940 Mussolini had invaded Greece and for five months of fierce resistance and inspired counterattack the people of Greece and their small army relived the glories of their ancient military past and drove the invaders back. But in April 1941 the Germans took over from the Italians, and for the next three years the defeated Greeks lived under Nazi occupation. Of the underground organizations formed to harass the Germans, the National People's Liberation Army, known as ELAS, was the most militant, and because of this received not only Allied arms and ammunition but also the attention of trained Greek Communists who took over its leadership. And by the last months of the war, when the Germans withdrew, the ELAS had grown strong enough to contest the post-occupation Athens government and the British troops which supported it.

This was the start of a civil war that lasted nearly five years. The ELAS lost the first round, fought in the streets of Athens, and withdrew to the hills where they established a network of guerrilla strongholds and a base of support among the isolated villagers who felt no loyalty to the Athens government. Many young peasants willingly joined the ELAS units while many of their elders supplied them with intelligence and funds and food out of real sympathy with their aims. This sympathy was nurtured by the Communists' promises of a better life for the peasants—a propaganda line that was reinforced by a stream of radio broadcasts beamed at Greece from the neighboring Communist countries to the north. By the end of 1946, when the second round of the civil war broke into intensive fighting, Yugoslavia, Albania and Bulgaria were sending arms and ammunition to the rebels as well as propaganda aid, and they had set up training schools and rest camps for Greek guerrillas inside their borders.

Early in 1947 the Greek National Army launched the first of its all-out but inconclusive offensives. For nearly two years they followed the same plan: a slow sweep from the south to north in an attempt to bottle up the guerrilla units and force a fight. Always the guerrillas slipped away from them, either into their mountain hideouts or to sanctuary across the borders of Yugoslavia and Albania. Each winter, when the government had given up the chase, they filtered back and slowly expanded their territory of control. Now they used terror with their propaganda, destroying villages which had received the loyalists, commandeering supplies from unwilling peasants, abducting young men for their army. In 1946 the guerrillas had about 2,500 soldiers; two years later there were nearly 25,000 and they were ranging over an ever-wider area, seizing whole towns and holding them for several days, plundering, burning, murdering and kidnapping. Tens of thousands of Greek children were carried off to the neighboring Communist states. Thousands more were orphaned in the fighting and had fled to the protection of the cities.

Late in 1947 the rebels formed a "Temporary Democratic Government" and though it was clandestine, its headquarters hidden in the hills, it had determination and a powerful leader in the romantic guerrilla figure, "General Markos." The national government, full of self-seeking and inept Athenian politicians, had neither of these things. And the British, who had helped to form that government and to support it, could no longer carry on alone against the Communists' pressure. Early in that year they had turned to the United States, putting the burden of this military and economic aid on their stronger ally. The American reply to their appeal marked a startling departure from traditional U.S. foreign policy. President Truman, enunciating what was to become known as the "Truman Doctrine," committed the country to active confrontation with Soviet aims.

American military aid and advisers, including a commanding general, poured into Greece in 1948, and the sweeps against the guerrilla strongholds were stepped up. In the summer of that year the National Army caught up with the rebels in the Grammos Mountains and forced a fight and won it. But thousands of guerrillas got away across the Albanian frontier and within a month were back again. The war went on.

By September 1948 the people of Greece had suffered through eight years of war and occupation and civil war. The marks of this were clear to correspondent H. G. Kippax when he sent the following report:

▶ Not until you leave Athens does the war seem real. Even in Konitsa, the battered, beautiful little town up in the north near Albania and within sound of the battle, each day's events seem to plod as patiently as the mule trains that go up to the fighting in mountains behind, and there is time for cups of coffee and afternoon siesta. The war seems a long way off.

But not as far, not as impossible, as it seems in Athens. In the violet twilight of the capital, gaiety, a sea of lights and prosperous city sounds froth around the monstrously opulent Hôtel de la Grande Bretagne and overflow into Constitution Square, whose every coffee table is occupied and where waiters sweat to deliver orders and even the beggars smile. The scene mocks reality. It seems to defy explanation. Let one of the British colony tell it.

"It's a mess," he says, "but the Grande Bretagne isn't Athens, and Athens isn't Greece. There's no war here—the war went with the Communists to the hills.

"Don't think there aren't Communists here, for all that. General Markos has only about twenty-four thousand men, and only one in three of those is worth anything to him. But the Communist Party has about two hundred thousand members. . . ."

A thin girl-child, barefoot, miserably dressed, offers a bunch of flowers and awaits refusal with patient, irresistible eyes.

"They're the ones who lay the mines and sabotage the trains and roads and ports and murder whom they can—Ladas, the minister of justice, for instance, as he was coming out of church last spring."

The flower girl watches you, and the very resignation in her eyes is a clue. You buy the flowers and talk to her. She is thirteen. Her father? "Kaput." Her mother. "Kaput." Her home? In Thessaly—burned down during a raid. And now? She lives with her sister. Her sister is seventeen; had a good job but lost it. Now she doesn't work but she makes more money. You guess the rest.

At a table nearby, a young bootblack is gazing down toward Churchill Street. His eyes are as bright as a bird's; his box and his brushes are beside him, and in his hands he holds and fingers quite a thick wad of notes. He talks to himself, he laughs. . . .

The bootblack is a well-known character; not mad, you understand, but his mental balance a little disturbed after he saw the Communists throw his father into a burning vat of oil.

Journeying north, terror and poverty loom ever larger. At Ioannina, in Epirus, the effects of civil war can be seen. They can be seen in the hundreds on the roads leading from the south—old men and youths, women and children, all driven by fear and fire from their farmlands, the precious strips of earth that have passed from father to son for generations and are only a little less dear than life itself. They straggle on, their goods on their backs or on mules, in little family and village groups, driving a cow or two and a few goats before them.

One is Mr. Tsika. He is a gnarled old peasant and he can remember the Turkish wars thirty-six years ago and thinks they were no worse than this. He carries himself well and shows the world no suffering. Yet a month ago, while he himself was away, some of Markos' men came down to his village. "They shot my sons. They said they were monarchofascists . . . and they took away some of the other young men . . . and a girl or two went as well. . . ."

Mr. Tsika looks thoughtful, and from somebody else you learn: "He *knows* the men who did it. He knows their families and their faces. Some day he will meet them. Then he will try to kill them. This civil war has started feuds that will last for generations." The war is all around Ioannina and yet the town itself holds little feeling of tenseness. There is a general siesta in the afternoon, and at night the coffee tables along the lake are crowded with townspeople and soldiers, talking, listening to bands playing American jazz tunes, talking—talking politics, local politics. . . .

A score of miles away, or less, the guerrillas will be mining the roads, mining the crops, raiding a village or two. They mine the road from Ioannina to Konitsa, some thirty perilous miles of potholes and bumps, every night, and every day the mine-detecting squads go out ahead of the convoy and clear a way for it.

The guards plod up the steep, difficult track leading out of Konitsa to the mountains with the mule train. They are cheerful, brown-skinned lads who carry a rifle or a tommy gun in one hand and a walking stick in the other. They seem carefree enough, but all the time they are watching where they put their feet.

The officers are from the brigade, on their way up to see the attack planned for that night. At the head, straight as a pine, rides Brigadier Katsias, a tough, grim, likable old soldier who has fought Italians and Albanians and Germans and Bulgars and who thinks the Communists the scum of Greece. It is a peaceful, beautiful scene—goat-bells tinkling from the valley, snow on the mountains, sunshine and shadow flecking the rocky path.

The battalion is five thousand feet up, precariously astride a razor-ridge that points like an arrow across the valley toward the rebels on the mighty and almost impregnable Kleftis. Through binoculars the enemy can be seen fleetingly on Anonymon opposite. Anonymon is the dome-shaped mountain just below Kleftis which the battalion is going to attack. From down in the valley the Greek artillery keeps up its pounding, and the battalion mortars in front of the battalion commander's headquarters, a pine-logged eyrie on the highest point of the ridge, also hurl an occasional shell across the two miles of valley.

The sun goes down gloriously behind mountain peaks as forbiddingly beautiful as anything in Switzerland, the shellfire becomes less and less frequent. In the foxholes they are having their evening meal—American rations mainly—and not very popular at that. The walkie-talkie operator calls methodically, monotonously. The stars come out. The battalion sleeps.

It comes to life again just as the first pale streaks of dawn are appearing behind Kleftis. Fires gleam, and there is a stir in the foxholes. Mess tins clink. The stir becomes a bustle and the silence is broken sharply by commands.

It is time to begin.

They come tramping in single file up the track past battalion headquarters. They go down the precipitous slope toward the valley, down toward the base of Anonymon. The thud of feet dies in the distance.

The sun comes up at five, and the artillery springs to life, snarling like dogs awakened. The troops are at the "start line." From Anonymon firing breaks out as suddenly as the rattling of summer rain on a tin roof. The attack has begun. The Greek infantry can just be seen pushing up through the pines, then they disappear. The intensity of the fire increases; enemy mortars open up; the first messages begin to come back from the company commanders.

The sun climbs. At battalion headquarters they have coffee, bread and cheese at seven, coffee at nine. Katsias has asked for air support. It arrives with a roar at 9:15—two Spitfires screaming down on Anonymon with rockets and 250-pounders. Great puffs of white smoke mushroom and sprawl on the mountainside. The Spits circle and dive again.

The first of the wounded begin to come back....

The Spitfires return to divebomb Kleftis once more. Again and again they dive, screaming down to within a few hundred feet. The battle sways in the sun. Then, almost as if by agreement, the firing ceases. Katsias grunts, drops down behind his map and orders coffee. The counterattack has been repulsed.

The Brigadier returns to Konitsa in the afternoon. All is still quiet. It is siesta time—in Ioannina, in Athens, on Kleftis—and everywhere the Greeks—Nationalists and Communists alike—are resting, and the war seems far away; everywhere, that is, except on the bare, sun-browned peak of Anonymon, where feverishly, sweatingly, they get ready for the new counterattack that will come that night. ▶

Attack and counterattack continued for seven months and, had Communism been the monolithic structure it was then pictured, would have gone on much longer despite American aid and a new determined command for the National Army. But in the summer of 1948 the Russians broke with Yugoslavia, and although Tito continued to give dwindling aid to the Greek guerrillas through the early months of 1949, in July he closed his borders to them.

In Indo-China the victory of the neighboring Chinese Communists had opened a sanctuary and a supply route that gave new life to the Viet Minh guerrillas; in Greece the closing of the Yugoslav border meant an end to such assistance and, very soon, the end of civil war. With their main source of supply and sanctuary gone, with many of their sympathizers disaffected and their recruitment fallen off by half, and with the replacement of their brilliant pro-Tito leader General Markos by a hard-line Communist, the guerrillas made a fatal change in tactics. When their Grammos bases were attacked again, they were forced to confront the enemy in conventional battle and they lost. Those who were left of their scattered units retreated across the border into Albania. It was from there that they proclaimed the end of the hostilities.

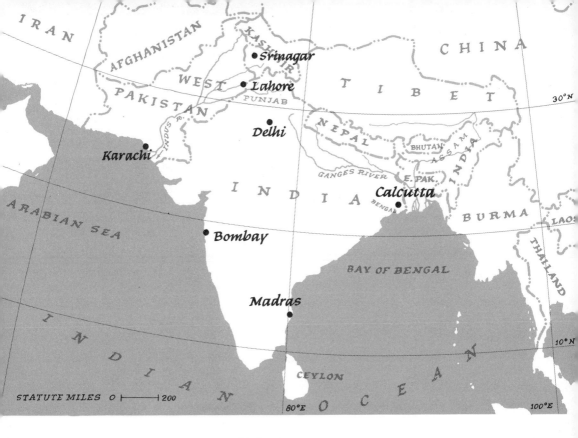

VI

The Partition of India

(1947-1949)

GREAT WARS give birth to new countries as well as sometimes killing off the old, and the peacetime birth is often no less violent than the
wartime death. After World War II, the new nations of Pakistan and India
were created by the division of the Indian subcontinent; and in the Middle
East four sovereign states were carved from territory that had once belonged
to the Ottoman Empire. Of these four, the granting of independence to Syria,

79

Lebanon and Jordan from their European mandates brought no strong reaction. But the birth of Israel on Palestinian land was cause for a series of fierce new conflicts. And the sundering of Pakistan from India was accompanied by wholesale murder.

Half a million people died in the rioting and upheaval that attended the partition of India in 1947. This statistic carries little impact in a world accustomed to mass murder, especially as it must be qualified by the statement that the figure is a guess, an approximation; nobody knows how many people died by violence in those few months. But in one of those riots, when a mob broke down the flimsy door of a home in Delhi, a tiny, terrified six-year-old girl darted out with her baby brother in her arms. She reached the middle of the street before the human pack closed in on her and left her dead. This we can feel.

The human beings who made up this mob were Hindus, followers of a religious faith noted for tolerance. The victims were Moslems. Their latent mutual hatreds, flaring from time to time in acts like this, go back nearly a thousand years to the time when, in that startling burst of military and religious energy, the faith of Islam swept out of Arabia to reach as far as Europe in the west and China in the east. Over the centuries, successive waves of these Mohammedan peoples filtered around the Himalayan barrier into India, and in successive conquests culminating in the Mogul Empire set up a virtual rulership over the subcontinent.

The people of India whom they dominated were themselves a mixture: the product of the ancient Indic civilization that flourished along the Indus River in man's earliest historic period, and of the nomadic Aryans who came upon them from the northern steppes about 2000 B.C. The Aryans brought their own religion and their concept of distinct class separation which became known as caste. And in a thousand years or so the agricultural Indic people and the pastoral Aryans fused to produce in Hinduism the world's oldest existing faith.

In modern Hinduism the Aryan's original four castes have split and proliferated into some three thousand. And the Hindu concept of an all-pervasive, all-embracing One—a single Divine Source from which all life is drawn and with which all aspire to unite—is worshiped through thousands of different deities and ritualistic practices. The karmic law of man's responsibility for his own destiny through an almost endless cycle of earthly lives dictates that in every incarnation men find themselves at different levels of their age-long paths toward union with the One. Therefore some Hindus may worship God through highly refined ascetic disciplines while others enact childlike ceremonies almost as though playing dolls with the fanciful images of their gods. All are acceptable, and there is no need to rub against the yoke of caste or the temporary inequalities of this present life. For such reasons have the Hindus become known for their passivity, and Hinduism the religion that not only tolerates but incorporates into itself many gods and tenets from alien faiths.

Only the warlike Moslems, fanatically dedicated to their one God, Allah, refused this sort of assimilation. Before Allah, all who believe are equal, and it was the duty of the Moslems who invaded India to attempt the conversion of the non-believers whom they overran. Their austere form of worship was the extreme antithesis of the Hindus' multitude of ceremonies in their households and their gaudy temples, their loud processionals through city streets or to the holy waters. Where the Hindus were merely passively receptive, the Moslems proselytized. And in their zeal to destroy false idols, they plundered the Hindu temples. Even today the memory of that violence is bitter among Hindus.

Many Hindu preachers, however, sought to bring Hindus and Moslems closer together and to draw on the best of both their faiths. In the sixteenth century a Hindu sect was founded whose members, like the Moslems, were sternly monotheistic, puritanical in their mode of worship, and determined to break down the barriers of caste. These were the Sikhs. Their founder was a gentle and enlightened thinker, but over the years Sikhism changed and became a militant sacred dynasty which fought the Mogul power and in the eighteenth century established an anti-Moslem warrior kingdom in the Punjab.

The Moslem rule in India lasted some five hundred years, until the world-conquering British with their thirst for trade encroached upon that power and, in the nineteenth century, when the British Crown took over from the British East India Company, established the authority of an English "raj" over the dozen provinces of British India and "paramountcy" over the rulers of some hundreds of princely states. During that time the Moslems and the Hindus had not really intermixed, though thousands of Hindus had been converted to the Moslem faith; rather, two parallel societies existed side-by-side, with the Moslem population predominant in the far north, the Hindus on the rest of the subcontinent. In this way the basis for two separate nations was laid down.

The British brought many Western concepts into India—in communications, government and law. Through education on the English pattern and in the English language they introduced the Indians to Anglo-Saxon attitudes in morals, taste and politics, and they produced an Indian bureaucratic class who soon took advantage of this learning to organize themselves for more say in their government. In 1885 these Western-educated men formed the Indian National Congress, designed to speak for Indians of every caste and religion, but which in fact was predominantly Hindu.

The Moslems, who constituted less than a quarter of the population and who had been slower to take advantage of the proffered education in foreign ways, feared that the new Hindu elite, if given power, would try to run the country for Hindus only. In 1906 they formed the Moslem League as a counterweight to the Congress party, and in 1909 they persuaded the British to give them separate electorates in the legislative councils. Communalism thus became a major factor in Indian politics. And in 1940 a meeting of the Moslem League committed itself to the formation of a separate Moslem country to be called Pakistan—Land of the Pure.

During World War II the Indians—Hindu and Moslem alike—increased their agitation for independence, demanding that the British "quit India" even though that might precipitate a division of their country. By 1945 the British were willing to agree, though how to go about it seemed an almost insoluble problem. But as proposal after proposal failed, the last of the British Viceroys finally announced that on August 15, 1947, power would be transferred "to some form of Central Government . . . or in some areas to Provincial Governments, or in such other way as seems most reasonable." The tone, close to despair, that haunts this statement reflects the concern of those Englishmen who loved India. The Congress, too, was loath to give up its long dream of a united, independent India, but against the determination of the Moslem League there was no hope for it. Partition was the only answer, and a line was drawn between those provinces who chose to be included in the Moslem state of Pakistan and those of the new Indian Republic.

The provinces of Sind, Baluchistan and the Northwest Frontier chose Pakistan. Those to the south chose the Indian Union. But Bengal and the Punjab, where the population was more mixed, were divided between the two. Rioting had already broken out before the day of independence; now it reached full scale. In Bengal and the Punjab—and spreading out with each new tale told of atrocities, and each new act of vengeance—Moslems killed Hindus and burned their homes; and Hindus turned on Moslems with a murderous rage. Refugees from both sides fled toward the safety of their own people and were set upon and slaughtered or died of starvation or exposure on the way. Some fifteen million people were uprooted and impoverished as the new nations struggled to survive.

Even in Delhi, the capital of India, the hatred flared. More than a thousand people were killed in the rioting there. On September 10, 1947, correspondent David Douglas Duncan was preparing to leave India for Egypt when he heard the sound of machine-gun firing slam across the garden behind his hotel. He sent the following report of what he saw when he rushed out into the stifling morning heat:

▶ Housetops were black with people, all looking in one direction and yelling. The distance was still too great to tell whether this mob was Moslem or Hindu, since it was on the boundary between neighborhoods of both faiths. The trouble center was directly ahead. Across the center of the road a horse cart was burning oilily. I wondered whether the driver had saved his horse before they fired the cart. I had almost passed by when my guts contracted with nausea. "God, he's still in it!" The driver had been killed at the reins and was now burning with his little cart. He was crouched as though trying to hide under the floor boards, so small that he must have been just a boy.

The crowd was mixed Hindu and Sikh. They were armed with the strangest assortment of weapons I had ever seen. This was a mob with no predetermined intentions. When we first walked down that street it was not even a mob but simply the menfolk of one neighborhood brought to their doorways by fear. They, too, had heard the firing and now rumors had just warned them of imminent attack from the adjacent Moslem quarter. Their first response was that of brave men. Each grabbed whatever household article might best serve for a weapon and rushed out to join his neighbors in the street. There was neither organization nor leadership. They only knew they were in peril.

Looters started breaking into shuttered shops whose Moslem owners had just fled. At first, only boys pilfered. But then, seeing mere children stagger away under such prizes as office chairs, wall mirrors, stems of bananas, fans, and even small safes, temptation shattered all restraint of the squeamish, young and old alike. Except for shouting as the doors came down, there was no mob feeling other than to loot and burn. Then the Sikh arrived.

Dressed in faded khaki shorts, an old sport shirt half-open down his chest, a turban and sandals, he dashed from one gang of looters to the next. Nearly a thousand men were either in the streets or their doorways. Shouting exhortations, he ran through them all. Strangely, for a Sikh, he was unarmed. But here was leadership.

Over the swooshing sound of flames and the snapping crackle of sparks as power cables burned through, the tone of the mob noise changed. Individual voices disappeared. Under the herding of the Sikh, separate bands of looters merged into one. Once it started moving as a whole, he would leave a gang and—churning the air with his arms that they were to follow him—hurl himself into another group farther along the street. Soon the Sikh had hundreds of men moving down the streets into the bazaar intersection. The fourth street lay empty and deathly quiet. It led to the adjacent Moslem quarter.

The intersection was now jammed with men. Most of them were Hindus, with only an occasional Sikh waving his sword overhead. The majority had no idea of what was actually happening. These were clerks, small merchants, government workers, schoolboys. One man, wearing only a loincloth and with his head totally shaved except for a wild-looking topknot, ran by, screaming, punctuating his screams by sliding the back of his wrist over his open mouth as in Western movies. He disappeared into the front of the mob, threshing the air with an ancient sword. Someone nearby grinned and explained that he was a milkman.

The Sikh stood shouting for a moment from the pedestal of the intersection's clock tower, then leaped down and charged into the deserted street, where he began tearing at a doorway with his bare hands. Behind these doors were Moslems who had not escaped.

The doors came off their hinges. A tiny six-year-old, hugging her baby brother in her arms, darted into the street. Hockey sticks, bamboo poles, hatchets, spears and swords flashed and fell, to rise again and again and again. Only an animal voice and smell filled the morning, for the mob sound turned deep, crushing all other feeling beneath it. The child sank in the middle of the street, her arms thrown protectively over the body of her brother. Swords and war axes flailed their bodies and, in a frenzy of madness, the ground around. Then they found her twelve-year-old brother and her sister, her mother and grandfather. They found the little neighbor boy next door, and both his parents. Each made the same heart-bursting sprint. The young reached the middle of the street. The old fell in the filth of the hard-packed earthen sidewalk. Their murderers had no idea of anatomy. Instead of piercing the brains or hearts, giving them a merciful death, the mob simply butchered and beat them to pieces. The two boys, despite having their heads and arms and legs nearly severed from their bodies, were still alive when their executioners left them.

A new sound arose. Someone had finally seen the police patrol, now slowly advancing upon the intersection from a side street. The Sikh was already upon the clock-tower pedestal judging the distance and time that separated those quietly moving men from his riot. They drew nearer. I counted seventeen men, each with his rifle slung backward over his shoulder. They were *talking* their way down the street, into the heart of the riot. Murdering men filled the intersection. The patrol kept advancing. The Sikh jumped down and raced again into the body-strewn street. Then, just as breakers eventually crash upon a beach, swirl around rocks, and retreat back into the sea, so did that mob of men when they knew it was finished. As they swept back out of the narrow street, they too broke and parted around what now lay crumpled in their path.

I talked to the constable in command of the patrol and learned that he had moved through the heart of the trouble zone where I first heard the machine guns. He had fired five rounds to restore order.

A choked cry spun me to face again that narrow street. Holding a dinner basket in one hand, the father of the tiny girl stood among the mutilated bodies of his family. He had returned from some all-night job, knowing nothing of the trouble. As I started back from the intersection where the police and military were now taking charge, I heard the sobs of the father following after me. ▶

The fear and hatred generated by such scenes as this poisoned the relations between India and Pakistan from the beginning. Most of the rioting took place in Bengal and the Punjab where the boundary cut through mixed communities. But the war which followed grew out of the situation in the princely state of Kashmir where the population was predominantly Moslem but the ruler a Hindu maharaja. It was the maharaja's choice to which country Kashmir would accede, but before he could declare it, Pathan tribesmen from northwest Pakistan invaded the Vale of Kashmir. The maharaja fled to the south, acceded Kashmir to the Indian Union, and called on the Indian government for help. In October 1947, Indian troops were flown to the trouble zone and cleared the tribesmen out. Pakistan responded by sending soldiers of its own, and for fourteen months the two young nations fought for control of this beautiful, strategic state.

In January 1949 the United Nations arranged a cease-fire and recommended a solution through a plebiscite by the Kashmiris themselves, but India could not agree. Over years the U.N. has reiterated this suggestion without success, and twice the smoldering hatred flared into fighting. So far the fighting has been cautiously controlled—the sort of wary sparring that takes place between men who know the horror of a madness that has escaped control—but as yet Moslem Pakistan and Hindu India have not found permanent peace.

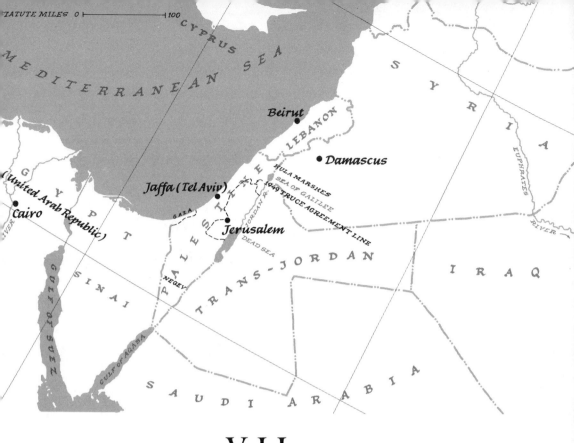

VII

The Struggle for Palestine

(1948-)

ABOUT TWELVE HUNDRED YEARS before the birth of Christ, God said to
Joshua: "Arise and go over this Jordan into the land which I do give
the people of Israel. . . . From the wilderness and this Lebanon even unto the
great River Euphrates, and unto the great sea toward the going down of the
sun, shall be your coast." And Joshua, leading the twelve tribes of Israel,
descended from the rocky wilderness where they had wandered forty years

87

since their captivity, and after many battles took the land and gave it "for an inheritance to Israel."

The dwellers in the land of Canaan whom the Israelites displaced were Semites like themselves, tribal prople living in petty kingdoms—the distant forefathers of many in the Arab nations who are the enemies of Israel today. Some of those early Canaanites the mighty men of Joshua killed, some they enslaved, but some they lived beside in peace, their sons and daughters intermarrying. And the relationship between the Arabs and the Jews, through these three thousand years of history, has been more amicable than hostile until very recently.

Among the Canaanites who were left to dwell peaceably by the invading Hebrew tribes were those who inhabited the city of Jerusalem. It was not an important city, though a very ancient one. Its history dates back to the Stone Age, when wandering Semites from Arabia settled and built a little hill fort on the rise between the Kidrun and the Er Rababi valleys. Its significance was in its site, poised on the watershed between the desert and the sea. The two great trade routes from the nations of the north down into Egypt passed either side of it: the trans-Jordanic caravan track to the east, the maritime way along the coast. Its early name was Uru-Salim, City of Peace, but in the nearly forty centuries of its history the city has endured over twenty sieges and blockades and two long periods of desolation after destruction by foreign conquerors.

King David took the city in 1000 B.C. and made it the capital of his united kingdom, bringing there the Ark of the Covenant—the compact between God and the children of Israel. And there his son Solomon built a temple to be the spiritual center of the Hebrews. The temple was destroyed, rebuilt, destroyed again. Only one small section of a wall remains, the "Wailing Wall," where, whenever they have been allowed into their holy city, Jews have come to pray.

Palestine takes its name from the Philistines, the "people of the sea," who settled along the eastern Mediterranean coast soon after the invasion of the Israelites. Before that time, the land had been under Egyptian domination, and since then nearly every civilization of the Middle East has overrun it. Assyria, Babylonia, Persia held it before the Greeks came, in the fourth century B.C., and the Romans after them. Under the Romans the final revolt of the Jews against foreign occupation was led by the Hebrew nationalist Bar-Kochba, whom some called the Messiah. After his heroic stand was broken, in 135 A.D., and his followers killed, Jerusalem was destroyed once more, its site plowed over, and a new Roman city built from which the Jews

88

were excluded, although believers in the new Christian sect were welcome. The Christians had opposed the claims for Bar-Kochba's messiahship and consequently the rebellion that he led. From that time dates the tragic enmity between these sister faiths. The numbers of the Christians had been growing and their influence spreading, both in Palestine and in Rome, and in the fourth century Christianity was made the official religion of the Empire. Until 636 the Holy Land was under Byzantine Christian domination and the Jews were excluded from Jerusalem "for all time."

Early in the seventh century, in a thriving market city on the caravan routes of western Arabia, a new religion was born. Its prophet was Mohammed, and the Way of Islam that he taught was based on what he had learned from Jews and Christians who came traveling along those routes. The One God, Allah, whom he preached, was the God of Abraham; Moses and Jesus were His prophets as was he—the prophet who had been chosen to bring the word of this Judaic God to the Arab world. In the earliest years it was toward Jerusalem, the central shrine of his new revelation, that Mohammed turned when he prayed. And at his death, in spirit or in fact, he visited the Holy City and from there made his ascent to Heaven.

With startling swiftness this new religion swept east and west, its armies conquering whole civilizations as they went, and in 637 these Moslem Arabs, under their inspired leader Omar, overwhelmed the Byzantines and entered Jerusalem. Unlike other conquerors before and after him, Omar spared the city and gave protection to its people and its churches, granting safe conduct to his enemies to move out. For most of the next thirteen centuries the country that God promised Abraham and gave to Israel for an inheritance was ruled by Moslems, and King David's city became a center of Mohammedan pilgrimage.

Christian and Jewish pilgrims also came there in great numbers until, at times, they dominated the population. But when a new faction of the growing Moslem world, the Seljuk Turks, took over the Holy Land, Jerusalem was barred to Christians. The reaction came in the eleventh century when the First Crusade, that motley army out of Europe, swept through Byzantium and entered Jerusalem and sacked it, killing Moslems in their mosques and Jews in their synagogues, until they walked knee-deep in blood and corpses.

The Christians had held Jerusalem less than a hundred years when the diverse units of the Moslem world were reunified under Saladin, who retook it in 1187. From then until World War I, the Holy Land remained in Moslem hands—under the Mamluks of Egypt from the thirteenth century and the Turks of the Ottoman Empire from the sixteenth. But with the weakening of the Ottomans, Europeans once again took interest in Palestine, this time for reasons of power politics rather than crusading zeal. By now the Ottoman hold was tenuous and its authority undermined by wandering Bedouins and other Moslem groups conspiring to create an independent Arab national state. Turkey had allied itself to Germany, and British, French and Russian armies ringed its falling empire. In 1917 the British army occupied Jerusalem and three years later, as the spoils of war were being handed out, the League of Nations assigned the Mandate of Palestine to Great Britain.

Up to this time, the Jews in their wanderings had found the most sympathy in the Eastern and Moslem world. The Diaspora, the scattering of the Jews, had begun with their exile in Babylonia in the sixth century B.C. Though some had returned to rebuild Solomon's Temple, many had remained in Mesopotamia. And with the failure of Bar-Kochba's revolt in 135 A.D. and the decimation of the Palestine Jews, the political cohesion of their nation ended. By the fifth century the center of Jewish population had shifted eastward and the wellspring of their cohesiveness was less that of a homeland than of a spiritual community. Babylon became the guardian of Judaic learning and tradition.

During the Roman occupation many Jews had also traveled west; many were Roman citizens of high standing and there were Jewish communities in every large European city. But with the growth of Christianity and of feudalism, Jews were increasingly restricted and their dark age of persecution and ghetto life began. By the seventh century they were being forcibly converted and in Spain the practice of Judaism was forbidden on pain of death. It was the Arab invasion of the "Moors" that brought salvation and a flowering of Jewish culture in the Western world until the First Crusade brought a reaction and an excuse to turn upon the Jews. In 1096, in a hideous perversion of religious zeal, whole communities in the Rhineland massacred the Jews among them in the first of a long, long series of atrocities, pogroms and expulsions which culminated in the attempted extermination of all Jews in Nazi Germany.

During the nineteenth century there had been a change in the Western European attitude toward Jews. Many were assimilated into the national life; many rose to eminence in fields that had been barred to them before. But to some gentiles, the Jew thus seemed a threat to their own ambitions, and when economic times were bad, it was convenient to find the Jew at fault. The roots of modern anti-Semitism grew from these vague fears. And to many a Jew who had attempted to adapt himself to the life of these Western nations and found himself once more rejected, the obvious solution was the creation of a Jewish homeland where he could build a nation of his own. From this reaction grew the movement known as political Zionism. The tragedy was that the rebirth of Jewish nationalism, so long dormant, coincided with the growing nationalism among the Arab peoples of the eastern Mediterranean.

In World War I the British had encouraged the revolt of the Arabs against Turkish domination, promising them an independent state whose territorial outlines were ambiguously drawn. At very nearly the same time the issued a statement, known as the Balfour Declaration, in which they informed the Zionists and the world that the British government favored the establishment in Palestine of a National Home for the Jewish people. Already the immigration of European Jews to Palestine had greatly increased; and when the Nazis came to power in Germany, the need for a Jewish haven became imperative. The Arabs, however, had been frightened by the influx of foreigners into their lands, and in 1936 they rebelled against the situation with a general strike and acts of sabotage against British authority, as well as armed attacks on Jews. The rebellion was put down, but in 1939, on the eve of war and with a pressing military need for Arab friendship, Britain announced severe restrictions on Jewish immigration and purchase of land in Palestine. Thus during World War II and afterward, millions of Jews were trapped in Europe and murdered, or condemned to a life in displaced-persons camps.

After the war the conflict over the land of Palestine, which had become endemic sub-warfare between the local Arabs and Jews, broke out afresh. The British, desperately trying to negotiate between the rival factions in their Mandate, turned, in 1947, to the United Nations, which voted to partition Palestine. Britain announced that all her troops would be withdrawn by May 1948, and with that warning both sides prepared for war.

Five Arab countries ringed the disputed territory, each with a standing army equipped with surplus French and British armaments. They had pledged to intervene in case of partition, some speaking of "a war of extermination" and a "momentous massacre," but they were weak internally and the only truly competent and experienced troops they had among them were those of the Arab Legion of Jordan. The Palestinian Arabs themselves were split into factions and had been demoralized and virtually leaderless since their rebellion in 1936.

The Jews, who constituted about one third of the population, were, in contrast, well organized and experienced in government—through the Jewish Agency, their self-rule organization of the Mandate period—and militarily.

91

Their army, the Haganah with its Palmach elite corps, was now underground, but it had been created in the 1920's and was strengthened by veterans of various Allied armies of World War II. It was equipped with armaments procured and smuggled in by its agents in various European countries and America.

As the British withdrew, Arabs and Jews rushed in to fill the vacuum, and the fighting became intense. On May 14 the Jews proclaimed the independent State of Israel; on May 15 the Mandate ended and the armies of the Arab States joined in a concerted drive on the new nation. Within a week the Israelis had turned back the Arab invasion from the north and, farther south, were fighting desperately to hold their quarter of Old Jerusalem and keep open the roads that led to the city. During that week, correspondent Eric Gibbs was with the Haganah forces on both fronts as they fought for the Holy Land. Following are his reports:

▶ Beneath a burnished sun shines the Galilee Sea, a polished turquoise oval set in the golden hills. In the distance is the Mount of the Beatitudes and beyond, on the far horizon, rises the majestic, snow-topped Hermon. The fire-blackened blot in the foreground of this peaceful landscape is a Renault tank. From the battered treads a long barbed-wire strand still trails to the spot where last week this Syrian tank breached a double fence and crashed into the Daganiya kibbutz, the oldest in Palestine. Without artillery, the kibbutz defenders stopped the tank at close range with a Molotov cocktail which set it alight. From the blackened tank leads a fire trail through the grass where a Syrian soldier in flaming agony tried to escape. The trail ends in the charred torso, with the spinal column sticking up, squatting on its haunches and stinking to the high, blue Galilean heaven.

This tank and this body mark the high-water line of the Arab advance on the northern front. Now the invading tide has ebbed to the borders and beyond. Even native Arabs have completely vanished from all of northern Galilee. In their thousands they streamed from the Safad front, abandoning the Citadel Hill and fortress dominating the town. Village after village of stone houses and reed huts lies deserted, and in the malarial Hula swamps the Arabs' water buffaloes graze untended.

High above this Hula valley stands the three-story concrete Fort Nebi Yusha, topped by a watchtower. It is a formidable position, dominating the communications of the whole area. A month ago the Palmach lost twenty-eight men in a vain attack on the fortress. Last week they made another night attack, firing all they had at the fort, but even heavy projectiles just bounced off the concrete walls. Jewish saboteurs crept right up to the fort and laid a heavy charge. The explosion not only failed to breach the wall; it also failed to draw any response from within the fort. It was only then that they realized that it was completely deserted. The Arabs had abandoned the key position of the whole of Galilee without a fight.

Through field-glasses from the fort roof, I could see a small group of Lebanese soldiers beside a gun which fires an occasional shell. And across the valley Syrians have four field guns on a hill. But there are no signs of armies massing for attack. All along this northern front, Arab activity is limited to occasional gunfire sniping or aerial bombing. At dusk, accompanied by Palmach officers, I joined a small party of men going into Lebanon to clear Arab villages near the border. The head of this commando unit was a Jew, but all the others were Arabs who have been secretly cooperating with Palmach and play a useful role, as they know the country so well and generations of brigandage have given them a natural flair for such marauding operations.

The Palmach commander in the area has been a Haganah member since he ran messages at the age of twelve. Now twenty-nine, he is the muscular, blond, blue-eyed type of Palestinian emerging here in sharp contrast to the dark Semitic features of the Jews from European ghettos. Natives of this type are nicknamed *sabra*, Hebrew for cactus, not only because they are indigenous, but also because of their tough, prickly character. Led by such men, the Palmach *esprit de corps* is very high, and they have good reason to feel proud. The first big impact of the Arab armies has been met and thrown back in most places. The Jews have largely won the battle of the Palestine frontiers. But the battle of Jerusalem and its approaches is another matter, and we hear reports from the south that desperate Jewish attempts to open and keep open the Jerusalem road around Latrun are costing a heavy blood price. ►

A few days later, on May 25, Gibbs visited that front, saw the battle for himself and sent this dispatch:

► The real battle for Jerusalem is being fought fifteen miles from the city at Latrun where the hills suddenly rise from the hot rocky plain. Here the road from Tel Aviv branches northeast to Ramallah in Jordan and due east through a narrow defile to Jerusalem. In between these two

93

branches are the dominating heights for which men have been fighting and dying since wars began.

In Ajalon Valley just east of Latrun, Joshua commanded the moon to stand still until the Israelites could avenge themselves upon their enemies. The moon was not so obedient for the Israelis. By choice the Jews fight only at night, and it was bright moonlight when they launched an attack to dislodge the Arabs from dominating positions around Latrun's Trappist monastery. But by dawn they had not reached their objectives. The moon and sun went their relentless, uninhibited way, and the hot glaring day found the Haganah units still in the dusty plain, firing from a cover of scattered rocks, fighting off repeated Arab counter-attacks as well as millions of vicious sandflies called *barhas*. As the sun's burning disk rose in the sky, the scorching east wind added to the miseries of the Jewish soldiers, especially the newly arrived immigrants from central Europe, who are unused, as the native *sabras* are, to these stony desert conditions.

Twenty-five-pounders and mortars, as well as guns from Arab armored cars, poured hot metal into the scorching plain. Haganah officers who had served with the Jewish Brigade in wartime, listened grimly to familiar British commands given in a cool, clipped English voice over an Arab intercom. With deadly precision, in sharp contrast to normal Arab inefficiency, the Legion laid down heavy fire on the Latrun plain. All day the battle raged. Arab shells set alight the tinder-dry wheatfields as effectively as Samson's fire-tailed foxes in nearby Timnath. Hunger, and particularly thirst, clawed at Jewish throats and stomachs. At last, evening brought welcome darkness and some relief.

In this, probably the biggest battle of the small Palestine war, the Jews have somewhat improved their position on the plain but have not yet captured any of the main objectives essential if the Jerusalem road is to be opened and kept open. Though they control most of the New City and are still clinging to their quarter in the Old, they are themselves cut off from essential outside food and supplies. And though the Old City's fall might be more of symbolic than strategic importance, nevertheless it would underline the gravity of the whole Jewish position in Jerusalem. ▶

While Eric Gibbs was writing this of the Old City, correspondent Donald Burke entered that part of Jerusalem with units of the Arab Legion and, on May 29, sent the following dispatch:

▶ The fight for Jerusalem resembles a concentric ring puzzle with the heart a gradually diminishing area wherein the Jews are hanging on against high odds. Surrounding them within the Old City walls are Arab fighters and civilians, and outside the walls on three sides are Haganah fighters who in turn are surrounded by Arab forces closing in.

At first glance Jerusalem seems in festive spirit. Gay flags flutter from many building tops—American, British, French, Ethiopian, Vatican. But these are merely highly colored hopes that they will escape deliberate firing. Overhead, Jerusalem's famed graceful swallows dip and glide, but the newcomer notices their sudden, frantic flight when the firing breaks out.

As we approached the Old City, down from the Mount of Olives, Jewish snipers in the tall Tiferet Synagogue snapped a dozen shots our way, keeping us down behind stone walls, and at the foot of the Mount we rested briefly in the Church of Gethsemane, sprawling on the cool flagstones. Directly before us were the gnarled olive trees under which Christ underwent His agony, and in the background a few hundred yards away was the Old City wall over which the sounds of firing came as in Jerusalem's agony the Arabs fought the Jews.

By now the Arabs hold all of the Old City except a portion of the Jewish Quarter. There are two Arab fighting forces: the irregulars, garbed in a wild variety of semi-uniforms and carrying assorted weapons including daggers; and the crack, disciplined Arab Legion in khaki battle-dress with green or checkered *kaffiyehs* on their heads. Their job has been to batter the Jews into submission, and to accomplish it they've taken positions along the city walls from which they keep up an almost constant fire.

In the last few days, the battle has become more intense. When we arrived the Jews were confined within an area slightly larger than eight hundred square yards and undergoing constant pounding. They were replying with semi-automatic fire, though evidently they had nothing bigger. Their main vantage points were two synagogues, the Tiferet, which has been abandoned some dozen years, and the Ashkenazi. Tough Arab squads, working their way through rubble as tangled as Stalingrad's, had laid charges close by the Tiferet's walls, blowing holes in it until now it resembles a Dali-like nightmare with gaping walls and shattered dome.

House after house in the area is similarly blown apart or crushed in by explosives, and still the Jews hold on. The main thing in their favor is a labyrinth of underground passages through which they move from house to house, popping up here or there. This morning I crawled through an abandoned section of their Quarter, scrambling over mounds of rubble, bending low to creep under earth-filled doorways to enter smashed houses. Every house and corridor had been hotly contested. Broken bureaus were jammed against boarded windows to make sniper nests; household belongings lay smashed underfoot—family pictures, dishes, a pair of imitation silk panties, lay mixed with spent shells.

The Jewish firepower has dropped off sharply in the past days. Friday the Arabs intercepted a radio message to the Haganah fighting outside the walls: "Unless you rescue us we will have to surrender." The Arabs sent a loudspeaker unit into the area asking the Jews to surrender on honorable terms, the surrender signal to be five tracer bullets. But although their position is hopeless, no tracers were shot off.

The Jews are suffering, but the Arabs suffer too. Saturday, as we walked up the steep Old City streets, we passed a stolid Arab housewife walking toward the emergency hospital. Her fighter son had been injured the night before. As we passed, a neighborhood barber approached us coming down. Seeing her, he lifted his two hands slightly, turning them outward in a hopeless gesture. More than anything I have seen, this despairing movement of the hands meant death. For a minute the mother's scream cut through the boom of the artillery in the background.

Yesterday the Ashkenazi Synagogue, a last Haganah stronghold, was attacked and shattered. Attempts to parachute arms and ammunition to the beleaguered Jews had failed. Now only a few straggling shots came from the demolished quarter.

Shortly before ten o'clock two ancient rabbis, stumbling and slipping over the piled rubble and clutching their velvety black robes about them, picked their way from the Jewish Quarter and walked slowly up the street skirting the city wall toward the Zion Gate. In the still morning air they waved their white flag with pathetic strength.

Arab Legionnaires spotted them from their outpost and brought them in, hustling them through several small old gates and along winding alleyways until they finally delivered them at the Armenian schoolhouse. Here, in a basement room, they were received by the Legion commander, a calm, efficient Transjordanian major. One rabbi, a Sephardic, sat straight and tall, his turban-like hat squarely on his head. His right cheek was covered by a large gauze bandage and his long grey beard hung below his chest. The other was an Ashkenazi rabbi, wearing a round, undented, black felt hat. He sat hunched low on the schoolbench, his head bowed, and swayed slowly from side to side as he chanted prayers of lamentation. They had come to offer surrender.

The negotiations were not easy. After the rabbis' first visit, they returned with Haganah personnel able to speak for the fighting troops, and later with the head man of the Quarter, Mukhtar Weingarten, who was accompanied by his daughter who is a nurse, a limping Haganah officer, and a young Orthodox Jew with a wound in his right arm. Calmly, quietly, the Arab commander laid down generous terms to each successive group, and after each conference the Jews were escorted back to their Quarter again. Trundling Jews through the Old City was a dangerous business since the local Arabs are inflamed against them, but the tough, disciplined Legionnaires effected it with a minimum of trouble.

After the Mukhtar conference the Legion threatened to renew their attack if the Jews did not return within an hour, but it was not until 4:30 that the surrender terms were finally agreed upon. Until the last moment the Mukhtar and the Haganah commander haggled over each surrender clause, even winning some points from the Legion commander who bent over backward to be fair. Despite their defeat, the Jews did not seem forlorn, but rather like people who have lost one round in a championship fight.

When the papers were signed, we followed the Jews along the wall into their Quarter, cutting across an open stretch under the guns of the Haganah fighters entrenched in the towering Church of the Dormition. We went slowly, fearing boobytraps and mines, through twisting streets and alleyways, clambering over the rubble of stones and roofing metal which had been blasted from the ancient houses, sometimes threading through passages as dark as tunnels. Every house was damaged to some extent, and as we approached the concentration point for the Jews, the smell of death came strongly into the narrow street.

Finally we cut through a door-like opening into a small courtyard. There were congregated the Haganah's fighting men, their khaki uniforms too long worn and their faces exhausted. Piled in one corner of the court was a small collection of their arms and ammunition. In the background by the walls and in the doorways the civilian Jews were clustered. Their eyes looked vacant, ringed with fatigue, in the bright sunlight. They seemed almost a race apart from the Settlement Jews; they were for the most part from old Orthodox families and they wore ear locks and flat black hats.

Without much ado the Haganah soldiers were taken off as prisoners of war, to be lodged temporarily in the Old City's prison. The civilians and the wounded were to be given safe conduct to Israeli territory. As the families gathered, the open space became a turmoil. They milled about, carrying an amazing array of bundles and small possessions: bedding, a box of cornflakes, bag of matzos, lamps. A mother screamed when she thought that she had lost her children. A shaggy-headed idiot girl plucked at herself spasmodically and shivered when she heard distant gunfire.

The Legion commander went quietly through the throng, reassuring the women and children but quickly weeding out the able-bodied males to be taken as prisoners. At six o'clock the civilians, with the Legion guarding them, started toward the Zion Gate, where they would be turned over to the Haganah. Laden with bundles, herding their children, they crowded down the narrow, cobbled lanes, jampacked from wall to wall. Slowly they filled the open area by the gate and pressed against the barbed-wire barrier. As darkness fell, there were some 1,500 with their ragged bundles.

Then as we stood there in the deepening darkness, the Haganah forces outside the city walls opened their loudest and most desperate attacks on all the city gates. The refugees dropped their bundles and clung to the ground. It was a brief and final effort, and as the shooting tapered off we were able to see the Jewish Quarter alight and burning in the darkness. ▶

The United Nations, having been responsible for the partition, tried to prevent the war and then to mediate it from the beginning. A U.N. representative had overseen the surrender of the Jewish Quarter, and the Truce Commission had called for a cease-fire on all fronts. The night the cease-fire was to go into effect, correspondent Eric Gibbs visited the sector between Jewish-held Sarafand and Arab-held Ramleh to see and hear the outcome of the U.N. appeal:

▶   Shortly after nine p.m., when the cease-fire was supposed to begin, I crept out toward the forward Haganah post. The way led along the bottom of a thistle-filled ditch beside the main Jaffa-Jerusalem road and then across a plowed field. The zenith was dark and starry but the western horizon still glowed faintly and must have silhouetted me as I walked over the ridge, although I stooped as low as possible. An Arab bullet came whistling close. I dropped to my stomach and looked at my watch. It was 9:30.

My Haganah guide went ahead and then called back, "Pssst, pssst," for me to follow. I was glad to reach the relative shelter of a shallow pit ringed with sandbags and defended by Haganah men armed with Bren guns and Sten guns and wearing British-style helmets. From an orange grove about a thousand yards away, the Arabs began firing sporadically. Sometimes a red tracer floated lazily through the air, seeming as harmless as a Jaffa orange. A revolving searchlight at the Arab-held Lydda airport periodically swept the no man's land and we all crouched lower to the ground to avoid being caught in the glare and perhaps shot by a quick-fingered Arab sniper.

The Jews did not return the fire, but, obeying the Israeli government's order, simply stared into the eerie darkness which might contain a creeping Arab. In theory the Jews are not to resume fire till they have received an order from the government. But Jewish rifles, Bren and Sten guns are all cocked against a sudden attack, and I doubt if they would await Ben-Gurion's O.K. ▶

The May cease-fire appeal was not accepted by the Arabs, but after twelve more days of fighting, both sides were ready for a truce. The Israelis were nearly out of ammunition, and the Arabs, having been halted almost everywhere, needed to pause and make appraisal of the situation. In early July the fighting broke out again, but ten days of Israeli victories, including the capture of the Lydda airport and the securing of an open corridor to Jerusalem, once more brought both sides to the negotiation table. It took the United Nations almost eight months to achieve a settlement, but in February 1949, Egypt and Israel signed an armistice agreement, and the other Arab nations followed Egypt's lead within that year.

The land of the new Israel was less than a quarter of that promised Joshua but far more than the Arabs had hoped to yield. The boundaries cut across communities, separating farmers from their lands and the Old City of Jerusalem from the New. In the almost twenty years since then there have been innumerable border incidents, bombings and raids on villages and kibbutz farms, and two brief full-fledged wars. The United Nations stationed truce observers and emergency forces in the areas of most tension over the years, but in the twentieth century A.D. no more than in the thirteenth B.C. is there peace among the nations in the Promised Land.

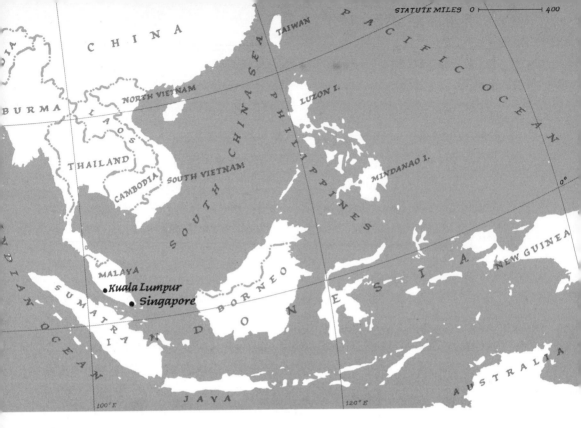

VIII

Malaya: The Long Emergency

(1948-1960)

I N 1947, AS THE Cold War developed, Stalin resurrected the Comintern—
the international Communist organization which had been disbanded
during the war—under the new name Cominform. This new body met for the
first time in Poland late in that year, and was told that the world was now
divided into two hostile groups and that the time had come for all colonial
peoples to "expel their oppressors." More explicit orders were given to the

Communists among the delegates at the Asian Youth Conference held in Calcutta in February 1948, and shortly after that, almost simultaneously, insurrections were inaugurated or intensified in Indonesia, Burma, Malaya and the Philippines.

Because the people, the leaders and the history of these countries were very different and because the governments which opposed the insurgents followed different tactics at different times, the patterns of these rebellions also differed widely. In Indonesia the insurgents suffered from a plethora of leaders, a lack of sympathy among the people, and no anti-Japanese resistance army to be taken over. Their uprising lasted little more than a month. And when the call of the Cominform reached the Burmese Communists, the country was in such chaos that it had little effect. Not only was there a split in the Party itself—between the "Red Flag" Trotskyites and the "White Flag" Stalinists—but many of the tribal minorities in the country, such as the Karens, Shans, Kachins, Chins and Mons, took up arms to fight for their own autonomy within the Union of Burma, which had been granted independence by the British only a short time before. Of all these simultaneous rebellions, that of the devoutly Baptist, severely anti-Communist Karens presented the sharpest challenge to the government, far outshadowing the efforts of the White and Red Flag Communists, who by comparison were not a major threat.

In Malaya and the Philippines, on the other hand, the insurrections lasted many years and in both cases came close to success. In both there were cohesive anti-Japanese guerrilla groups with whom the Communists could work, and although one was anti-colonial and the other an anti-governmental movement, in both large segments of the population suffered from legitimate grievances with which they could identify.

The situation in Malaya had its peculiarities, for here in the only land that is both part of the mainland of Asia and at the same time part of the vast archipelago stretching into the South Seas, lived five million people in one of the most extraordinary multiracial societies on earth. Separated into national realms of Malays, Chinese and Indians by walls of race, language, culture and religion, they passed unseeing through these barriers in their everyday lives, never quite recognizing whatever might lie outside their own community consciousness. The Malays' roots in the country go back to ancient times; the Chinese and the Indians have been there, in any numbers, only within the past hundred years. When the British took over the peninsula during the nineteenth century they found the production of tin and rubber so rewarding and the Malays so unwilling to meet the labor needs of both, they encouraged the immigration of Chinese to work in the mines and imported Indians as tappers on the great rubber estates. By 1940 these *nouveau* aliens outnumbered the indigenous people nearly three to two. However, the Malays are an inherently gentle people, non-political, unambitious, unacquisitive, and they seemed unconcerned by the stream of foreigners who steadily exploited the country's natural resources and grew rich on them while the Malays themselves shrank proportionally within their country's population and became the farmers, indentured to Chinese and Indian moneylenders by usurious loans. And since the Malays had no business traditions, the Chinese took over the lower and middle layers of the country's business and crowded the British at the tycoon level until it was said that Malaya was a cow which the British held for the Chinese to milk.

In 1942 the Japanese occupation forces found the inequalities of this multiracial society ready for their purpose. It was the Chinese, whose cousins in the homeland had for years been fighting the Japanese, who formed the Malayan People's Anti-Japanese Army and fought a guerrilla war against the occupation forces with some American and British help. Therefore the Japanese did all they could to stimulate the latent jealousy and hatred for the Chinese among the Malays, using the latter to help them fight the guerrillas, urging them into bloody vendettas and communal battles with the rallying cry, "Malaya for Malays." A by-product of this was the awakening of the Malay people to the possibility and hope of independence.

Between the time of the Japanese collapse in August 1945 and the return of the British colonialists, the Communist-led Malayan-Chinese had made a bid for the control of the peninsula, and for the next two years they contended with the British for political power. The appeal of their cause was a call for independence, the source of their strength the post-war economic chaos, and their weapon strikes. But by the end of 1947 the economy was improving, half the mines were again in operation and the plantations were enjoying the prosperity which came of a worldwide demand for rubber.

With the call of the Cominform, the Communists retired to the jungle, updated their old name of Malayan People's Anti-Japanese Army to the Malayan People's Anti-*British* Army and organized themselves into small terrorist bands.

Terrorism, as it was employed by the MPABA, is a specific branch of modern warfare. It has been called the weapon of the weak because it is most often used by those attempting to seize power from an established government, and it goes hand-in-hand with propaganda in an attempt to win the uncommitted populace. If that populace is well and strongly governed, these twin weapons have small effect. But in a nation weakened by war, or when the governing caste has lost touch with the people—whether it be a colonial power or a native oligarchy—terror, often the first step toward consolidated guerrilla warfare and the establishment of a revolutionary government, is a potent instrument of war.

Its use is nothing new. But in our post-war era it has been perfected. Terrorists operate within the structure of a partisan movement, and terror was used by the underground of many occupied countries both in Europe and Asia during World War II, while the terror of reprisal was used against them. From this bitter training ground came many of the guerrilla-terrorist movements immediately following the war. And since then, schools for terrorists have graduated thousands to ply their trade on every continent.

Wars between nations are primarily dualistic, but the wars between factions to control a nation's government are at least tripartite, for they involve not only the forces of the established government and the rebels, but also the people whom they both seek to dominate. For a revolution—whether it be Communist-led or not, and whether an anti-colonial struggle for independence or an anti-governmental uprising—is fundamentally a contest for the minds and bodies of the people among whom the insurrectionists make their base. On them they must rely for their intelligence, supplies and new recruits. And since they are self-appointed spokesmen for these people— whether their final aspirations are in actual accord or not—their primary object is to take political leadership and ingratiate themselves with the populace through propaganda and good behavior. As long as they have full support, there is no need for terror. But if there is rival leadership among the people, real or potential, it must be eradicated—publicly and dramatically—not only to stamp it out but to put fear into the rest of the community and to demonstrate guerrilla power.

The technique in every country is quite similar. A raid is made on a small village in the night. The mayor, the schoolteacher, or someone who has helped the government is singled out. His hut is burned, his family killed, and he himself is hauled away or murdered on the spot. Later his body is discovered with the message of the terrorists pinned to it: "Traitor."

Although the instrument of terror may be used directly against the enemy in a more conventional and less selective way, this calculated, almost surgical terrorism which operates against the people among whom the terrorists live is far more deadly. The Greek terrorists in Cyprus, for example, murdered three Greeks for every two non-Greeks. In Kenya, the Mau Mau slaughtered seven hundred Africans as against twenty-one Europeans in the first year of their anti-British uprising. And in Malaya the Chinese guerrillas likewise turned their terror on their own people, killing more than twice as many Chinese as all other nationalities.

These small guerrilla bands—which numbered, in the early months, as few as a dozen men—relied almost completely on the Chinese squatter-farmers living along the edge of the jungle. Therefore they preyed on them, demanding food and abducting men into their bands as they carried on their war. The fighting and the terror spread across the country like a rash, in small, quite separate eruptions almost impossible to eradicate. In June 1948 the British recognized the magnitude of their problem and proclaimed an "Emergency," attacking the guerrillas both with counterterror and on the broad political front.

Though in the long run it was through political rather than military means that peace was brought to Malaya, the British relied at first on force, developing a technique of pinpoint counterterror raids against the widely scattered small guerrilla bands. Such an attack, typical in very nearly every aspect of the first months of that long-drawn-out warfare—hideouts, informers, surprise, and brutality for brutality—took place in July 1948. Correspondent Roy Rowan accompanied the "killer squad" involved, and described the attack in his dispatch:

▶ A line of red tail-lights strung out along the highway ahead of us blinked off. Tires crunched in the gravel as the convoy of jeeps and weapons carriers edged to the shoulder of the road and stopped. There was no moon, and jungle sprang up thick and black on both sides of the thin highway. Carbines and Tommy guns scraped lightly against vehicles, and sneakers scuffed on the macadam as Captain Stafford assembled his "killer-squad" in the dark beside the parked convoy. We were a mile southeast of Kajang and twenty miles east of Kuala Lumpur. It was four in the morning.

The squad moved off down the road. Occasional flashes of heat lightning caught the black-shirted men and held them silhouetted against the sky for an instant, and then they disappeared into the blackness again.

Burly Bill Stafford, once a Shanghai policeman, had become a legend in Malaya. The Chinese called him "Tit Soo Pah," Chinese for "The Iron Broom." As chief of the Selangor CID, he had tackled Communist terrorists according to a simple formula: when the Communists organized "special assassination gangs," Stafford countered by forming a "killer-squad" of his twenty toughest detectives, comprised of Malays, Indians and Chinese—some formerly Communist guerrillas and bandits themselves. In the past two months his "killer-squad" has caught more terrorists than any other police or army unit on the peninsula. Now they were out to catch Lau Yew, one of the leading Communist guerrillas in Malaya.

"I don't trust that bastard," Stafford whispered to his Chinese sergeant. He motioned at the little unarmed informer guiding the squad. "Watch him," Stafford said. "If you think he's pulling a fast one, plug him." He was simply repeating his standing orders for handling informers, whom he considered a necessary evil. Ordinary citizens were too frightened to give the police or the army any information on terrorists, and both forces rely heavily on informers, paid piecemeal for their work: 1,000 Straits dollars ($450, U.S.) per terrorist taken, and 200 per firearm confiscated.

The squad stopped. Coconut-oil torches carried by rubber tappers on their way to work flickered dimly along the road ahead. Stafford signaled his squad into the jungle.

For an hour the men, stooping and squeezing and cutting, worked their way through a dense thicket, hooking their carbines on vines and tripping over tangled roots as they pushed on toward high ground. Moist ferns brushed coolly across their faces, and dead branches snapped under their feet. A cock crowed faintly from distant squatter huts. "You've got to be a crazy bastard to do this every night," Stafford muttered. Then he looked ahead as though he were taking a sighting, and said, "I think the bloody bloke's lost," and he motioned again toward the little informer, who walked slightly crouched and clearly frightened. Stafford held up his hand, and everybody stopped. "We'll wait here till dawn," Stafford said, and the men squatted down to rest.

When the stars faded and pink light streaked the morning sky, the squad reached a ridge half a mile from the road. Thick clouds of mist rolled up from the valley below. Then, on a signal, the men grabbed their rifles and followed quickly after Stafford and the informer who had started down a steep slope into the mist.

The informer picked up a narrow path which opened into long, slanting rows of rubber trees. The trees had been freshly tapped and white driblets of latex oozed from spiral cuts. Stafford quickened the pace. "These bloody assassination blokes never stick around much after dawn," he whispered back at me. "They may be back in the jungle now, or on a raid of their own."

The rubber plantation ended abruptly on the rim of a basin-shaped hollow which was blanketed with yellow kunai grass. At the bottom were three dilapidated board shacks. A shallow stream cut through the hollow close to the shacks. The informer was nervous. He pointed to the center shack where we could see a woman puttering over her morning chores.

The squad spread out and Stafford led them cautiously out of the plantation and down into the open ravine. The men, creeping now like black cats in the deep kunai grass, moved slowly toward the house. It was nearly seven and the sun showed brightly over the hill. A light breeze swept the ravine and rustled the grass.

The woman suddenly rose up straight and shrieked an alarm. Three men burst from the house. Two waved revolvers and the other carried a rifle which he dropped as they wheeled and fled toward the opposite hill. The sharp crack of carbines firing in rapid succession resounded through the ravine. A piercing scream was followed by more rifle shots. Then it was quiet, as still as if all the life in the little hollow had suddenly ceased.

Stafford popped up behind the house and broke the silence, barking fast, hoarse commands to his men scattered over the ravine. They yelled back reports. Two terrorists were dead, and the man who had dropped his rifle, captured. Six women and another man were also caught. The detectives were bringing the prisoners forward. Stafford was hurrying up the hill where one victim lay face down on the pathway. It looked like Lau Yew, but he wasn't sure. Blood dripped from the dead man's neck and hands and trickled onto the grass. And there was a gaping hole smashed into his forehead. A Luger pistol lay on the ground beside him.

The detectives dragged the dead men feet-first down the hill and deposited them in the bottom of the ravine. The handcuffed prisoners, stunned by the lightning attack, huddled trembling around the bodies, while some of the squad hastily hauled uniforms and documents, maps and rifles and sacks of ammunition from the shack.

A detective recognized Lau Yew's wife among the women. "See if that's her old man," snapped Stafford. Several men forced the cowering woman close to the corpse. Blood still dripped from an ear into a pool on a canvas mat. The woman stared blankly at the body and then nodded her head slowly in assent. They shoved her back with the other women.

"All right," yelled Stafford. "Let's burn this place and get out. There may be more of these blokes around here."

Two detectives, sweating in their black uniforms, held lighted tapers to the palm-thatched roof, and in a minute or two the wind carried the fire all over the building. Thick, yellow clouds of smoke billowed out of the house and rose in a column from the ravine.

Elated by their catch, many of the squad gathered and rapidly recounted the raid as they watched the guerrilla headquarters burn. The sun was hot and the ravine, ringed with rubber trees, looked radiant and lush. Stafford said that he was glad that he hadn't brought the Gurkhas. "They're bloody good," he said. "But my men work better alone."

The men were packing up to leave when an outpost sentry saw a man dash through the thicket. He fired at him fast and then the whole hollow suddenly exploded with the blasts of Bren guns and Sten guns and rifles. We were now receiving heavy fire and Stafford and the detectives sprawled on the ground and crawled with their faces pressed hard against the turf, heading for the brook. Bullets splattered the dirt all around us and sizzled through the grass. Two hand grenades exploded. A third bounced harmlessly on the ground. The men wiggled through the water and burrowed into the deep kunai grass on the opposite bank of the stream. There they stopped and returned the fire. Then they moved farther into the cover of the grass. From there I looked toward the prisoners and saw that five of the six handcuffed women had been caught helplessly in the grazing crossfire and lay crumpled on the ground near Lau Yew.

Groping their way across the ravine on their hands and knees, Stafford's men tried to regroup. The shack was still burning, and beyond it we could see about thirty guerrillas sliding down the hill to positions behind it.

Suddenly a police vehicle came grinding up behind us along a narrow track. Stafford had sent six men for it just after Lau Yew had been shot. Instantly he seized the opportunity for a bluff. Yelling out to his men, "Here come the Gurkhas! Here comes the army!" he started forward, firing rapidly. His men took up the cry and began the movement of a counterattack, blasting with carbines and Tommy guns. Gradually the firing subsided until only sharp reports of single shots echoed in the hollow. All at once, it was quiet. The Communists had gone.

"That was bloody promiscuous shooting," Stafford growled. He took one more look at the hill behind the smoldering shack. Then he turned and signaled to his men and started back over the track. "Now," he said, "let's really get the hell out of here." ▶

Responding to attacks such as this, the Communists reorganized themselves, changed their name once more—to the Malayan Races Liberation Army—and deployed their forces in larger units, attacking in terror squads of up to four hundred men, though their total number never rose above approximately eight thousand in the entire country.

In 1950 a "village resettlement" program, which moved the sympathetic Chinese farmers into guarded camps, cut the guerrillas from their bases of supply and compelled them to operate as they had done before, in tiny isolated bands. And in 1952, when the British announced a plan for gradual self-government, they were deprived of their main propaganda point. The first Malayan general elections were held in 1955, and independence within the Commonwealth was granted two years later. Thereafter the MRLA, deprived of their main source of supply among the villages and of their appeal among the people as a whole, dwindled to a few hundred stragglers deep in the jungles of the north. The threat was ended, and in 1960, twelve years after it had been declared, the "Emergency" was officially called off.

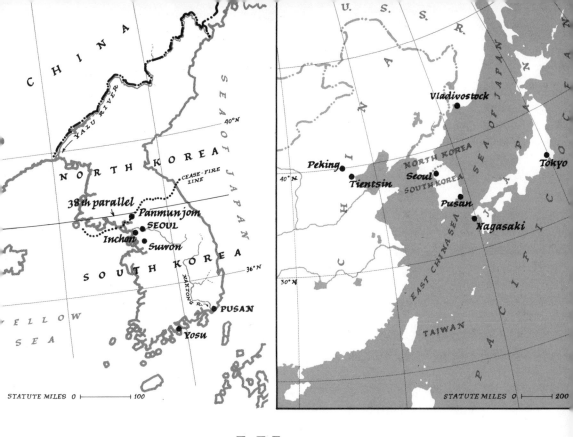

IX

Police Action in Korea

(1950-1953)

IN KOREA the confrontation between Communism and the West reached open warfare through a miscalculation. This turbulent country, misnamed "The Land of the Morning Calm," lies at the apex of her stronger neighbors, China, Russia and Japan, and her history has been one of a succession of invasions and foreign domination. For more than a thousand years she was subject to Chinese influence, but early in this century she was taken over by the Japanese, whose harsh rule made of her a serf-state. In 1945, when she was at last "liberated," as the action was then described, she almost immediately became a subject-state again, for now she had been split between Russian and U.S. control at the Yalta Conference. And even as the Japanese armies were being expelled from her land, those of the Soviet Union and the United States took facing positions, sealing the country in halves at the 38th parallel.

The division of Korea and the confrontation by the two superpowers which followed are especially notable for the lessons they taught. These lessons were many, but the first was that the West must make its intentions clear as to where it would stand and what it would defend, for into those gray areas not carefully defined came Communist seepage—both political and military.

In Europe the policy of containment, put forward by the Truman Doctrine in 1947, had helped to make clear the areas which the United States intended to defend. And the NATO pact of April 1949 drew, in effect, a defense perimeter, the violation of which would draw massive retaliation.

In Asia, however, partly because of the uncertainties of the four-year China civil war, such a perimeter had not been made clear. Early in 1949, General MacArthur attempted to remedy this by stating publicly: "Our defense line runs through the chain of islands fringing the coast of Asia. It starts from the Philippines and continues through the Ryukyu archipelago which includes its broad main bastion, Okinawa. Then it bends back through Japan and the Aleutian Island chain to Alaska." By this description both Korea and Taiwan were left outside the defense line. And as though in confirmation of this exclusion of Korea from the areas of American paramount interest, withdrawal of U.S. troops from South Korea continued— despite clear indications of planned Communist agression—the last of them leaving in June 1949.

Early in 1950 the U.S. State Department adopted MacArthur's perimeter with reservations, indicating that those areas west of the line might also be defended by the United States in concert with the United Nations where the governments under attack requested help. But the situation was left ambiguous, and to China and Russia these statements and actions seemed to mean that the United States did not consider either Korea or Taiwan to be worth fighting for.

It was a jolt, then, a major surprise, to the Soviet government when, in June 1950, her satellite North Korean troops walked into South Korea and the Americans turned back from their withdrawal to stand and fight, bringing the

United Nations with them. In this it might be said that the United States was guilty of threatening the peace, for within the now-understood rules of modern limited warfare, any unexpected military action by either of the two superpowers threw their precarious armed truce off balance and carried the adversaries further into conflict than they meant to go.

The steps, then, which led to the Korean War, a war which was to be a most significant event in the development of great-power post-war strategy, were the consequence of a misunderstanding of intentions, a miscalculation.

In July 1948 the South Korean Government had been established as a republic under President Syngman Rhee and the American forces had begun their slow withdrawal from the country, turning over their air bases and ports to the new government. Only advisory officers were scheduled to remain to help build the South Korean army. Unlike its counterpart in the north, which had been trained and prepared by Soviet advisers almost since the division of the country in 1945, the South Korean army had as yet little training and even less unity.

In the context of this disparity, the word that filtered back to Seoul in October 1948 of a mutiny in the army units stationed along the southern coast had a more than ordinarily disturbing impact. The revolt was Communist-led, and although it lasted only a few days, the brutality of the mutineers and of the government soldiers and police who put them down cast a long foreshadow and provided a preview of the kind of war that was to come to Korea twenty months later.

The revolt started in the seaport town of Yosu when a major of the Fourteenth Regiment of the new national army was arrested on suspicion of Communist activities. What the major had to say under questioning was enough to decide his superiors to ship the whole regiment off to the island of Cheju-do as a matter of quarantine. But before this could be done, forty soldiers of the Fourteenth rose in the night, October 19, killed their superior officers, and persuaded the rest of the regiment to follow their lead. Then, joined by many civilians who either were sympathetic to the Communists or merely shared the ordinary Korean's hatred for their police, they overran Yosu, murdering the police and city officials and hundreds of townspeople who were on their list of anti-Communists.

Next day they commandeered a train and went north twenty-five miles to the town of Sunchon where they fought their way in against the opposition of loyal government troops and city police, cut off communications with the outside, and announced that all of South Korea had been taken over by the People's Republic of the north. Then for two full days they plundered

111

Sunchon and terrorized its people. Three days after the revolt began, reinforcements of government troops attacked the rebels, who then withdrew, taking their weapons and supplies with them into the countryside. I entered Sunchon with the assault units, and that night sent the following report:

▶ The city stank of death and was ill with the marks of horror. Corpses lay in the gutters, and no one walked in the streets except heavily armed loyal troops. It seemed a deserted city until we got to the playgrounds of the local agricultural school. There we found everyone who was left of the people of Sunchon. On the expansive grounds sat all the men and boys waiting to be screened by the police for loyalty. And lined up on the roadway were the wives and mothers and sisters watching their men.

When I arrived, four young men, presumably found disloyal in this hasty questioning, had been separated from the rest and stripped to their undershorts, as were all those whose answers did not satisfy the police. They were on their knees, begging for mercy, while policemen beat them with clubs and rifle butts. One had his hands up in the symbol of prayer. Suddenly those hands were crushed into his mouth as a rifle butt smashed out his teeth.

Two men with clubs stood behind them, beating the kneeling group over the heads and backs until they had to pause for breath. In front of them a policeman in black glasses and a Japanese helmet danced crazily, uttering staccato barks. Alternately he spun his carbine butt forward and smashed a kneeling man in the face, then twirled the gun muzzle downward and feigned shooting. Finally he charged like a goat and smashed the steel helmet into the begging victim's head. After their beating, these four, like all the others whom the police suspected, were taken to the Sunchon primary school and shot.

I left and drove back through the town. Now I knew why it was deserted and why the corpses lay unclaimed. I saw the reason for the brutal retaliation, also. The bodies lay just as they had fallen when they had been slain by the rebels—in heaps with their hands tied behind their backs. In the police compound there were eighty-seven corpses flung into two piles, some of them civilians, some police. By the river and at the edges of the paddy fields, bodies lay tumbled grotesquely down the embankments. Others were burned into charred masses on the streets or lay alone outside the looted shops and homes.

During the first terrible days of Sunchon's carnage, no relatives dared to claim a body for fear that doing so would identify the living with the dead and thus bring quick retaliation from either the Communists or the government. Later, when it was safe, women streamed away from the big playground to poke among the heaps of bloated dead. When they found theirs they were at first cautious. Then, it seemed, stoical. But at last the tears came and they were hysterical. ▶

In the months after the uprising at Yosu and Sunchon, Korea seethed beneath the surface, erupting now and then into more bouts of slaughter, especially along the line of separation. Despite this, the United States withdrew the last of its military forces in June 1949. And though it strengthened its efforts to train a South Korean army, it had not yet armed and fashioned it into an effective fighting force before the Communists struck. In June 1950 the North Korean forces crossed the 38th parallel and began the invasion of South Korea.

The war was already ten days old when American troops, hastily gathered from occupation duties in Japan and rushed over to bolster the crumbling South Korean forces, met the invaders. I joined them that day on a winding, yellow, muddy road, the ancient highway running from the southern port of Pusan to the edge of China at the Yalu River. For the past five years the road had been cut off at the 38th parallel, and now the North Koreans were coming along it, cutting it shorter piece by piece.

I was sharing a jeep with several other correspondents, driving north in search of the first engagement, when we met a South Korean cavalry unit coming toward us at a gallop. As they passed us some of the riders shouted in English, "Tanks! Tanks!" Then their horses skittered off the road as a jeep came roaring up behind us, speeding north. In it we had a glimpse of an American bazooka team and we followed. The first monsoon rains had come and now the drizzle changed into a downpour. All around us clouds closed in, black and foreboding.

We caught up with the bazooka team on a rise when their jeep stopped and spun around and the men spilled out and ran crouching into a bean field. Again we followed, as more jeeps came piling up behind us and more men came running into the fields and crawling through the green vines in the drenching rain.

One bazooka team sprawled for action on a small knoll. Off to their right were the straw-thatched huts of a little village and above them, looking oddly out of character, the spire of a Christian church. Then suddenly, straight ahead, black as the storm and apparently sitting there all the while, we saw a tank astride the railroad track, its cannon slowly sweeping us in a semicircle,

113

cold and implacable, like some monster in its squat deliberation.

We flattened into the mud, although I was so startled I thought for an instant that the image must have been conjured from the storm. The bazooka men, though, were better trained and more sensible. They took the tank under fire. The charge was laid exactly on the target, spilling off the turret with a blood-red splash. Seemingly it accomplished nothing. "Get in closer," voices urged, and the men crawled forward and fired again, their aim equally true and the effect equally futile.

Now a second tank came crawling up the track. The bazooka team took them both under fire and both tanks returned the fire, one of them shooting its cannon and the other its 50-cal. After a while I saw some of the bazooka men running, bent almost double, carrying a body. "They got Shadrick," one of the men said in terrible surprise. "He's dead!"

The rest of the bazooka men were retreating from the field toward the road. "Where are you going?" we asked, astonished at the withdrawal.

"We're out of ammunition," one of them answered. "The charge we've got don't do a thing to those tanks anyway."

And so we all withdrew, bowling back along that road in the black rain, peering around us with that unpleasant feeling that comes when you don't know where the enemy is and expect him at the next turning.

By the time we found the battalion command post, the blackness of night had taken over from the blackness of the storm. Men were digging in around the building and some artillery pieces were being placed below it. In my first dispatch from the Korean War, I wrote about that night. It was one of many like it in those early weeks of slow withdrawal when the Americans were driven southward, their tiny forces frankly offered as a sacrifice to buy time until reinforcements arrived:

▶ The battalion CP was in a shabby schoolhouse on an eroded hill. Despite the heavy downpour, the windows had been removed to prevent injury from flying glass, and the wind and rain beat against grotesque draperies of Korean clothing and bedding hung in the open frames. Inside, the room was soggy, littered with wet clothing and shoes and stacked with weapons. On the desk was a map covered with red and black crayon markings. It had been rubbed into a reddish black smooch, for all day the battle lines had been changing.

Lieutenant Colonel Harold Ayres, commander of the battalion, leaned over it. Beside him his sergeant was on the field telephone. He had been hand-grinding it for more than an hour, but he had raised no one. Ayres poked the yellow end of a wet cigarette between his lips. Suddenly the sergeant shouted, "We've got contact!" The colonel dropped the cigarette and said quietly, "Fine, sergeant." A major took over the telephone. "Baker company calling," he said to the colonel. "They have some stuff stored two miles up the road. They're asking permission to send a party out to fetch it." Ayres fingered a ring. "Tell them negative," he said. "We haven't got even half that distance."

Three dripping soldiers were led in. They told their story in jerks. They belonged to a forward battalion, the most advanced American unit. Their whole outfit had been overrun, they said. These three had got through. They knew nothing of what had happened to the rest. The major got on the phone again. "This is a message to all company commanders. Be alert and in your holes. A minimum of movement in the rear—and none whatsoever in front. There may be troops coming through your lines and they may be friendly. Be aware of this."

The colonel bent over the major. He whispered, "Contact each company commander and tell them rations are being distributed." The major ground away on the phone. "One ration now being distributed for tomorrow. ... Negative. Negative. It's not for breakfast. It's one ration for breakfast, lunch and dinner. Tell the boys to save it. We may lose contact with them by morning."

Now there was great activity in the schoolroom. Men were packing. No word had been passed, but everyone knew what was happening. We were being enveloped. We abandoned the post and moved southward in the black, heavy rain. ►

A few days and a few miles farther down that muddy road I stopped at a medical aidpoint, and afterward sent this report:

► The lieutenant was barefoot when he walked into the dressing station, and he pointed to his feet with a raucous laugh. Then he sat down on a broken bench and wept. Near him a surgeon was bandaging a man's chest. He stopped when he heard the lieutenant cry. He asked the sergeant, "See if you can get some hot water and soak that officer's feet." The lieutenant raised a yellow face and shouted defensively, "It's not my feet, doctor. It's here. It's here," and he jabbed a clenched fist at his heart. "They were my boys, doctor. They were just kids. This is the third time in three days and nights we were surrounded and cut off. The body and the mind won't take it, doctor." The medic was directing a corpsman who was probing the boy on the litter with a plasma needle. "It's been rough, lieutenant," he said soothingly. The lieutenant's voice rose. "Rough? That's not it, doctor. It's those kids. Four of them. Our orders were to fight our way out and leave the wounded. One of those kids looked at me as we were leaving, doctor. His belly had been blown open. I handed him a grenade and took off. If I had more guts I'd have shot him myself." ▶

In the months that followed, the encircled and battered units were reinforced. A tenuous United Nations line was slowly extended across the peninsula, and the North Koreans were beginning to give ground under heavy attack. But each mile taken from them was a fight for hills and ridges which largely comprise the territory of Korea. One August morning in that first year of the war, the North Koreans were emplaced on top of a ridge on the Naktong River front. U.S. Marines were sent up there to take it away from them. It had no name on their maps, so they christened it No Name Ridge. Correspondent James Bell described the fight that day for that anonymous hill:

▶ No Name Ridge is a barren, useless place with a few scrub bushes and a patch of reddish soil in the center, the result of a landslide in some forgotten rainy season. To the right, a dark gully scars its side. To reach the top, one must first descend into the valley at its foot and then make the steep climb up.

Early one morning this week a U.S. Marine assault force prepared to storm No Name Ridge. For five minutes the height was pounded by U.S. artillery. Then for a quarter of an hour Marine Corsair fighter planes raked it with bombs, rockets and machine guns. After this there was another ten-minute artillery barrage; then the Corsairs came back over for final strafing runs.

As the Marines advanced down into the valley to make their assault on the ridge they were met with a hail of fire. From the left came the angry eruption of a machine gun, and another opened from the valley floor to the right rear. As the Marines started up No Name Ridge, more machine-gun fire, interlaced with mortar blasts, raked down on them from the top and burst around them as they moved up the barren face of the ridge. Everywhere along the assault line, men dropped. To continue looked impossible. But the line did not break. The casualties seemed unthinkable, yet the assault force never turned back. It moved, fell down, got up and moved again.

For more than an hour the assault force stumbled and struggled forward against a solid wall of fire. A Red mortar was knocked out by artillery, but the machine guns and automatic weapons continued without let-up. As the Marines neared the crest, their line ripped apart. The North Koreans rose from their positions and came forward throwing grenades. The Reds were cut down, but not before their grenades had done terrible work among the Marines. Their line wavered and paused; it withdrew a bit and waited. Then, with a final thrust, some ten Marines reached the northern crest. They never came back.

The assault force was ordered to withdraw. Men too exhausted to cry crawled back down the ridge with no name. For all their terrible sacrifice, the ridge was still in enemy hands. It became quiet. Medical corpsmen, leading stretcher-bearing teams of brave and unflinching South Koreans, began to cross the valley to pick up the wounded. They carried the wounded through the valley at the foot of the ridge and up a narrow trail to an aid station. I wondered if the stream of litter bearers would ever stop coming up out of that damned valley. I asked a corpsman who had just come off the ridge with a load of wounded, what it was like over there.

"Sir," he said panting, his fatigues dripping with sweat and his arms so weary they dangled at his sides, "up there there's a lot of shooting and a lot of hell. We are doing the best we can. We'll get 'em out." He couldn't remember how many trips he had made across the valley. He waited until his South Korean litter bearers had loaded the man they had just brought up onto a jeep. Then he shook himself, said, "Come on, characters," and started down the slope and up the bloody ridge again. The South Koreans, without a word, picked up their litters and started following him down again into this green, green valley.

I asked one Marine if he had been in the last war. He looked at me through bloodshot eyes and said: "No, and I wish I wasn't in this one either." ▶

The second assault wave carried No Name Ridge and the Marines continued to advance, slowly taking their objectives as they went. But the cost was terrible. The war did not turn and its costs did not diminish until the middle of September when, in a surprise amphibious attack, American forces landed at the port of Inchon, far behind the North Korean lines. Although this operation followed the pattern of such sea-to-land assaults perfected in the Southwest Pacific five or more years earlier, it was far more daring and therefore more surprising to the enemy. Inchon harbor would seem an impossible place to put a landing force ashore. Its tidal reach of thirty-two feet is one of the highest in the world; at low tide, miles of mud flats make an approach impossible and landing craft caught there between the tides become undefendable targets. Treacherous currents sweep the narrow channel that winds among small islands dotting the outer harbor. And the final transfer of assault troops from sea to land in the vital dock area must be made over a sixteen-foot seawall.

Inchon, Korea's second largest port and just eighteen miles from Seoul, the nation's capital, is guarded by a little island called Wolmi-do which sits about five hundred yards off the central port area and is connected to it by a concrete causeway. On the morning of September 15, 1950, the first assault wave landed on the bathing beach of Wolmi-do, and correspondent Frank Gibney went with it. The success of that first attack was vital, for, as Gibney cabled: "Worthless little island that it is, Wolmi-do commanded Inchon harbor. Enemy guns, even machine guns, from Wolmi-do could make a failure of any attempt to land in the port area; and U.S. guns mounted in Wolmi-do could ensure success of that landing. The proposition was simple: capture Wolmi-do fast or the landing fails."

The first wave to hit Wolmi-do was scheduled for 6:30 a.m. when the morning tide was high. The attack over the seawall in the Inchon dock area came just short of twelve hours later, timed to the swelling of the evening tide. Toward these vital hours steamed the assault fleet, 230 ships from four different staging areas, all converging in utmost secrecy, for surprise was a key to success. From the ship in which he sailed, Gibney sent the following report:

▶ A "Landing Ship Dock" is a hulking porpoise of a craft that looks like an oversized destroyer in front and a floating drydock from the rear. The day before the landing, the atmosphere aboard our LSD began to tighten. On the horizon, sharp eyes could see the silhouettes of other warships plowing toward the rendezvous: carriers, cruisers, destroyers and landing craft. "They're gathering," said the chief quartermaster. Just after midnight the alarm bell clanged over the loudspeaker system and a hoarse voice called the tocsin, "General quarters. Man your battle stations." Inside the ship was the pounding and scurry of hundreds of feet as the crew rushed to their posts. Above decks all was quiet and when the eyes got used to the dark one could just see the outline of the LSD stretching below from the bridge. From the huge gaping well deck astern one could make out the shapes of three large landing craft—the LSD's oversized brood.

By one o'clock we were edging our way into the black channel. For hours the convoy sliced through the dark glassy waters. Occasionally the dim rounded shapes of islands rose against the sky. From the shore no sound came. Shortly before three o'clock we saw bright distant flashes of gunfire and long seconds after the flashes came the soft muffle of far-off guns. The naval bombardment had begun. By four-thirty the sound of firing had risen to a loud and steady obbligato. In the distance a bright tongue of flame licked upward from the direction of Inchon. Dark outlines of buildings bulked behind it. South of the flames I could barely make out another black bulk. This, they said on the bridge, was Wolmi-do. Shortly after five the first hint of dawn showed faint and blue in the dark sky. The slender shapes of destroyers, like hounds closing in on their prey, sliced closer inshore through the green muddied waters, and the steady rumble of the guns from the ships grew louder.

Stumbling in the dark over the ship's gear, two lines of Marines groped their way aft from the troop compartments to the three landing craft. There were low curses as the men scrambled awkwardly down the ladders into the broad-bellied landing boats, their big packs dragging against the ladders. From somewhere I heard a young Marine voice say wistfully, "Three months ago I was so happy."

The water gurgled and rose inside the well deck and the choking fumes of exhaust swirled around us as the drivers turned the motors of their tanks over and the engines coughed and spluttered. "Lower the stern gate," barked the loudspeaker. The low barrier separating the well deck from the sea outside was slowly cranked down to a horizontal position. More water rushed into the well deck and, to the accompaniment of liberal cursing from exasperated petty officers, the young, not too experienced crews backed their craft stern first out of the well deck into the open sea. Their diesel engines revved and whined and added new noises to the overtone of naval battle.

The bombardment began to intensify. Like the sound of a door slammed in anger, the forward battery on the destroyer nearest to us opened up on Wolmi-do. The first round was followed by another and another. From below the horizon to the south came flashes of orange lightning, then long-delayed reverberations, as the cruisers joined in the bombardment. The destroyers farther in were wreathed each in an unholy nimbus of dirty gray smoke that rose from the orange flashes. The sound of slamming doors rose to a crescendo. The ships and their guns were all that mattered now, as they took on a baleful animal personality of their own.

Now Wolmi-do was smoking. The fresh morning sky was grimed with a rising pall. Two fires had already started low on the hillside. No sound or movement came from the island. Only once did a tiny crackle of machine-gun fire try vainly to stretch the impossible gap between it and its tormentors. Then a wave of smoke and sound engulfed the place where it had been and Wolmi-do was silent again.

It was six o'clock and the rocket ships went into action in an undulating wave of sound. Hundreds of searing rockets ripped through the air with a noise like tearing canvas. Clouds of smoke and earth billowed on the island. The land at the water's edge was no longer visible. There was only that low cloud of dirty smoke, blown slowly southward by the wind.

At 6:05, as the sun was spreading its light in bright corrugated streaks across the sky, the Corsairs came. Blue gull wings flashed down on the wooded hill, then wheeled sharply away again while ragged cylinders of smoke pillared upward from the flames the bombs made.

Love hour, scheduled for 6:30, was drawing near. The rocket ships, coming close now, were pouring pointblank salvos into the beach. At 6:29 nine more Corsairs dove down to lace Wolmi-do with rockets and machine-gun fire. Then suddenly, as they wheeled away, the roar subsided. At exactly 6:30 the boats put out for the beach. Our awkward craft floundered like mammals in an unfamiliar element. As we picked up speed, we braced ourselves and huddled down in the boat. From the beach came the crackle of small-arms fire, but no shots came our way. Suddenly, with less of a jar than I had expected, we hit the deep sand at the water's edge. The boat shuddered slightly, then grated securely on shore. The ramp went down and within a few seconds the first tanks were chugging their way across the scarred beach. Behind them the Marines worked desperately, unloading food and ammunition. Then they climbed up the debris-ridden slope in search of opposition.

There wasn't much opposition left on Wolmi-do. There wasn't much of anything left on Wolmi-do—whether buildings or trees or men. The smell of powder still clung to the island as tenaciously as the drifting clouds of dirty gray smoke. It hung over the shell holes and bomb craters in the sand and scrubby hillside, over the licking flames that crackled in the ruins of wooden shacks.

As I dashed up the slope of beach, I got my first look at Wolmi-do's defenders. Four half-naked North Korean soldiers, hands held rigid above their pinched, scared, sweating faces, stumbled out of the remains of one of their old shallow trenches at the command of their Marine captor. I talked to them in Japanese. They were almost incoherent with fear. "Are you going to kill us?" stammered one. When I said we wouldn't, he chattered back to the others and a little of the fear went out of their eyes.

I caught up with a tank which had rumbled on ahead of me just in time to see it fire two screaming rounds point blank into the mouth of a deep cave dug into a small hillside. Smoke and dirt spewed out of the cave's twin entrances. A muffled series of explosions rumbled from the depths; evidently some of the enemy ammunition had been stored there. Through the clearing smoke staggered a badly wounded North Korean soldier, blood-flecked arms raised high. After him stumbled another, then another. Amazingly, almost thirty men survived those pointblank rounds. In a thin line they staggered dazed into the bright early morning. Waiting Marines drove them down toward the improvised prisoner pen on the beach. Farther along the road a desperately wounded North Korean, his face blackened and bloody and both his legs crushed, waved his hands at the Marines approaching him. "Help me, help me," he said in Korean. Then, with his hands still outstretched, he fell back dead into the dust.

By eight o'clock a few scattered shots were all that remained of the battle for Wolmi-do. The island was pronounced secure. More than two hundred North Korean soldiers had been killed; their corpses strewed the scarred slopes of the hill or were scattered in the rubble of the ravines. One hundred and thirty-six had been taken prisoner. Only seventeen Marines had been wounded in the attack, none of them fatally.

By late afternoon the bombardment of the Inchon port area and the landing beaches had reached a climax and the waves of assault units tossed in their small boats, waiting to go in to the beach. The weather, which had been sunny all day, now turned black. A low cloud hung apocalyptically over the city of Inchon, and after the first assault waves had landed, a stinging rain swept across the harbor. Only in the west did the setting sun preserve a last patch of clear yellow sky.

I walked up the newly bulldozed road toward the causeway in the pelting rain and found the Marine battalion ready to jump off again. The tanks were already starting out, lumbering their cautious way toward the inferno at the other end. I climbed a small ridge and watched what they were going into. The scene over the new landing area blazed against the darkening sky like some brightly lighted Coney Island with its incandescent ferris wheel and roller coasters gone berserk. Flames leaped from the gutted buildings and edged the Inchon end of the causeway.

As the pall over Inchon thickened, the air became choked with fumes and cinders. Even on Wolmi-do the air was thick and oppressive, like the weight of a thousand sultry days. Yet, almost miraculously, the sky to the far west remained clear to the last. A Marine chaplain standing on the ridge with me looked awestruck at the peaceful yellow sky beyond the sea, then back at the smoke and fire of the near-night around us. "Heaven on one side," he said slowly, "and hell on the other." ▶

After their success at Inchon, the U.N. forces quickly recaptured Seoul, cut the North Korean army in two, and drove on north. By late November, American units had crossed the 38th parallel, swept into North Korea, and were probing gingerly along the Yalu River, which separates Korea from China. The war seemed to be coming to an end. Yet there was increasing apprehension. Reports were multiplying that Chinese soldiers had been identified among captured North Koreans. These reports were discounted in General MacArthur's headquarters in Tokyo. But a question continued to haunt the topmost war rooms and diplomatic conferences of the Western world: Would American military forces on China's border bring the Chinese Red armies into the war?

Something of this feeling of uncertainty was brought down to battle level as American soldiers fought along the river's edge and peered across it into an unknown land. Correspondent Roy Rowan shared this uncertainty when he joined a small reconnaissance unit on November 25, and later cabled:

▶ Our mission today in this freezing Yalu River gorge was to "feel out the enemy." I was with "Task Force Cooper," commanded by an aggressive young major named Carroll Cooper. He had a reinforced company of 360 men, bolstered by tanks, light artillery and heavy mortars. Late in the morning, moving through a bitter-cold canyon separating Korea from China, we reached a little town called Posong-ni, fifteen miles west of Hyesang-jin. The men were bundled in clumsy winter clothing and were inching cautiously along a sheer rock wall which towered five hundred feet above them. Far below was the ice-clogged Yalu, its emerald water twisting through a great gorge like a cold green snake.

When I reached Task Force Cooper, it had been advancing for three days, fighting and shoving back a stubborn Communist band, about two hundred strong. As they retreated through the gorge, the enemy burned bridges and blasted gaping holes in the cliff which tumbled over the road, to slow the attackers' pursuit. But this morning the Reds were lodged firmly in Posong-ni and were making their first stand. "I want to get some of those fellows," Major Cooper said tersely when I met him on the road. "And I don't mean dead either," he added. "If those men are Chinese, I want to know how many more there are ahead of us."

On the way out to join Cooper's outfit, I had seen some lonely footprints in the snow marking a trail across the Yalu in a few spots where it had been frozen solid from bank to bank. They could have been left by Communist couriers, soldiers, or by mere farmers. Nobody knew. But the day before, back in the cluttered Manchurian village directly opposite Hyesang-jin, we had seen a few Chinese soldiers. Dressed in faded yellow and blue quilted uniforms, they were just lolling leisurely about the river bank, enjoying their strange immunity.

Major Cooper's mortar crews were pumping white phosphorous shells into Posong-ni. Dense clouds of white smoke billowed up from the buildings in town. From beneath the smoke came an answering crackle of small arms as the Reds raked our exposed road with fire. Now we could see some of the flimsy frame houses at Posong-ni break into a blaze, but there was still no sign of the Reds pulling out. Many of them were concentrated around a yellow brick tower which rose up behind a sharp bend in the Yalu. From its top they had a clear field of fire on Cooper's men who were hung up on the cliff above them. A projection of land jutting into the river from the Manchurian side of the boundary concealed the base of the tower. "I think that tower's in Korea," shouted Major Cooper. "Tell the seventy-fives to nail it."

A loud blast, and another and another suddenly rocked the squat, brick structure. There was a small Chinese house perched atop a Manchurian knoll directly in front of the tower. When shells exploded there, a farmer and his wife dashed from the house and burrowed into a haystack to hide. "I guess that old geezer and his missus figure we've just declared war on China," laughed Major Cooper. "But to fight a war around these parts, you really need a squad of lawyers traveling right with the infantry."

The seventy-fives silenced the troublesome tower and we moved forward again. Two hundred yards ahead, the road tunneled through a large rock outcropping. We made a dash for the tunnel. From inside it, Major Cooper watched nervously while his assault platoon crossed a small tributary below. The bridge was burned and the men crawled on their hands and knees over charred timbers embedded in ice. It was deathly still in the little town just ahead. Even the buildings seemed to be burning silently. Then the whole gorge exploded with the sound of machine guns, burp guns and carbines firing together. The assaulting platoon moved swiftly across the snow-covered fields to the first line of houses. A startled herd of black pigs scurried past them in the opposite direction. The firing sputtered. Then it died. It was suddenly quiet.

Late that night I saw Major Cooper back at the Seventeenth Regiment headquarters. "We've got the town secured," he said. "But those Reds backed away from us again. And this time, I'm afraid we can't chase them very far. We found that the road crosses over into Manchuria just half a mile past Posong-ni." ▶

The next day, November 26, Rowan left the forward area. That night the Chinese army swept into North Korea with two hundred thousand men, hitting the American forces with massive assaults, encircling them and trapping them along that frozen northern front. Their attack caught the United States Eighth Army completely by surprise, despite the constant air reconnaissance by an air force which had control of the skies. Later, Rowan sent this last paragraph to update his dispatch. It read:

▶ Task Force Cooper and the Seventeenth Regiment are among the American troops now cut off by eight Chinese divisions. ▶

After this the United Nations fought Chinese as well as North Koreans until once again the opposing forces faced each other at the 38th parallel. After two years of negotiations, a truce agreement was signed on July 27, 1953, and a buffer area established between their lines. Yet there has been no peace. From time to time they ambush each other and trade violence. But it is significant that they still meet for talks, as well, strident and unpleasant as those talks sometimes are. It is a situation typical of our times, when stalemated warfare can fade into stalemated peace and violent words give pause to violent acts.

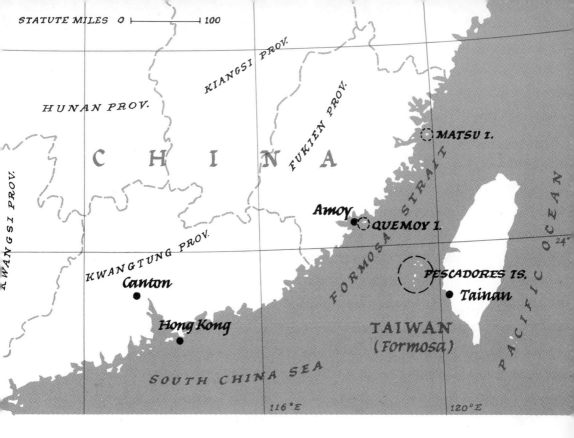

X

Quemoy-Matsu: The Siege

(1954-1958)

THE ISLANDS OF Quemoy and Matsu serve no significant military purpose. Yet, step by step, in a series of confused political and military
developments, these islands became a center of conflict between the United
States and Communist China and, in 1958, brought these two powers to the
brink of war.

When the Nationalists were driven from China in December 1949, their

125

government and that part of the army that could break away from the Communist forces fled to Taiwan, more than a hundred miles from the mainland, but continued to hold several groups of islands that lay along the China coast and on which they had garrisons during the civil war. The United States, having backed the Nationalists and protected their flight, committed itself to their defense on Taiwan. But U.S. defense of Quemoy, Matsu and the other offshore islands was never declared outright and came of a gradually shifting position.

In 1950 President Truman announced that the United States "will not pursue a course which will lead to the involvement in the civil conflict in China." But after the outbreak of the Korean War he sent the Seventh Fleet to patrol the Taiwan Straits, declaring that U.S. policy was both to keep the Communists from taking over Taiwan and to prevent the Nationalists from returning to the mainland. In 1952, however, the presidential campaign raised as a major issue the restraints placed on the Nationalists, and soon after Eisenhower became President he "unleashed" the Nationalists and removed the restraining order given the Seventh Fleet.

Next year, in September 1954, the Communists began their first heavy shelling of Quemoy. Three months later the United States signed a mutual defense agreement with the Nationalists, committing itself only to the defense of Taiwan and the Pescadores, and "such other territories as may be determined by mutual agreement." Later the U.S. Congress gave the President authority to use U.S. military strength "as he deems necessary for the specific purpose of securing and protecting Formosa (Taiwan) and the Pescadores . . . and related positions and territories now in friendly hands."

Late in August 1958, Radio Peking formally proclaimed that Quemoy-Matsu would be assaulted as a prelude to an attack against Taiwan. Until then the shelling of the little islands had been sporadic. Now it grew heavier; on August 24 the Communists fired forty thousand rounds on Quemoy and at the same time opened up their first intensive propaganda barrage. By radio and through amplifiers beamed across the water, they alternately coaxed and warned Quemoy's hundred thousand defenders: "Come over to the People's side and you will be rewarded. Taiwan has no means to help you now. End resistance and return to the fatherland or you will be destroyed." And when the voices stopped, the guns boomed out. It was the beginning of the Quemoy-Matsu siege.

The siege, unlike any other form of warfare, focuses upon an immobile point, the fortress. No matter how the battle sways or what techniques are used, it is always here—at the embattled fort—that victory must be gained.

The art of siegecraft dates back to that time when men first took a stand and faced their besiegers from behind earthen embankments or city walls and battlements of brick and stone. In the twentieth century great sophisticated fortresses have been built. Those at Verdun, whose fortifications date back to Roman times, were refashioned through the years to cope with changing warfare, and in the First World War held back the Germans in ten terrible months of siege, and cost in combined casualties an estimated one million men. By World War II, modern mobile warfare dealt with the fort by simply by-passing it as the panzer divisions did the Maginot Line, the most elaborate fortress of our time.

Despite the evolutionary changes in the fort, siegecraft itself has changed remarkably little through the ages. Every trick of battle has been used to overcome the fortress: bombardment, frontal assault, cunning and treachery, science and engineering, blockades to starve the defenders, words to seduce or frighten them, and finally, when all else has failed, the poised weapon of time which in the end determines whether the besieger or besieged has the fortitude and resources to outwit the other. All of these were used in the siege of fortresses Quemoy and Matsu.

Neither Quemoy nor Matsu was a fortress when the attack began. It was never intended that a stand be made at these islands. Unlike most other fortresses whose sieges marked high points in history, Quemoy and Matsu were not selected because their terrain and their location were advantageous to the defenders. In actuality, they were very nearly the opposite, for Quemoy lies just outside of Amoy harbor, less than three miles off the Chinese mainland. And Matsu, with an area of only twelve square miles, is less than ten miles from the Communist coast. By any sensible rule of present-day warfare, they are undefendable.

Yet slowly, almost imperceptibly, over the years the conflicting interests of China and the United States had become focused on these little spots of land. Late in August 1958, as the Communist barrage intensified, Nationalist supply convoys attempting to bring relief to Quemoy were beaten back and President Eisenhower ordered the Seventh Fleet to escort them to within three miles of the beleaguered island. The basic issue, the President declared, is "that armed force shall not be used for aggressive purposes. . . . There is not going to be any appeasement." With this the conflict, born almost of happenstance and the vague shiftings of national policy, suddenly hardened into a major confrontation from which neither power could disengage itself with grace.

In September the barrage grew into one of the most intense and longest-sustained artillery bombardments ever directed against a single objective. In one twenty-four-hour period the Communist batteries fired sixty thousand rounds from three hundred guns. The island was so small and so close to the mainland guns that every part of it was raked by shellfire. The landing beaches and the air strips were torn up and Quemoy's food and medical supplies and ammunition dwindled. Her casualties waited day after day to be evacuated. Her forty-four thousand civilians went underground. And while part of her troops manned their posts, waiting—as the calls from shore and on the radio taunted "We are coming, the landing is imminent"—the other part dug deeper and deeper and fashioned more steel and concrete into their defenses.

One murky night that September, a Nationalist convoy sailed west from the Pescadores Islands toward the China coast, carrying supplies and four hundred Chinese Nationalist reinforcements to the island. It consisted of an aging LSM, two gunboats and a minesweeper. For two nights Communist gunfire had driven it clear of Quemoy before it could accomplish its mission. Now on the third night it was trying again. This time correspondent James Bell went along and reported on his experience:

▶ The troops we had aboard were tired. They had spent the two previous nights unsuccessfully trying to get ashore on Quemoy. Now they lay in the dirty well of the battered ship surrounded by such unmilitary items as their personal puppies, bananas, pineapples, and huge, bright tin washbasins which could easily alert air observers. As we left the dock, they wore resigned looks. It would seem likely to them that they would spend the war cruising nightly between the Pescadores and the approaches of Quemoy. And such a prospect was not a happy one, for Chinese are notoriously bad sailors.

At about a quarter of the way to Quemoy, the weather grew foul and the sea roughened. Our old LSM bucked and rolled, at times attaining alarming lists. After it was dark, we began to encounter an amazing amount of shipping. One craft, a brightly lighted Norwegian freighter just out of a Communist port, passed us silhouetting a warship, perhaps a cruiser belonging to the Seventh Fleet. It grew colder and the men in the ship's well huddled together, chilled by the seaspray and the prospect of lurking Communist torpedo boats. By midnight we were approaching Quemoy and the artillery air bursts we had been watching as faint lights in the sky, now drew closer and could be clearly seen as Tatan Island and Little Quemoy and the south coast of Quemoy proper were taking their nightly lacing. Six miles southeast of Quemoy we dropped anchor in a line with the escorts ahead. Then three small landing craft approached our LSM, trying in the rough seas to hold fast and take men and supplies aboard. But the rising, foaming sea was wicked, and the loading over the side into the pitching boats went slowly. An order was being shouted to fall to and get on with the unloading when at that moment the Second Naval Battle of Quemoy broke out. By then half a dozen of us correspondents and twenty Chinese troops had made it into one of the boats, and as shooting flashed all around us we cast off and turned into the slopping seas.

The Communist navy had been lying in ambush on both sides of our convoy. Why our radar had not discovered them has not been explained. At any rate, they waited until the landing procedure got nicely mixed up and then opened fire from both sides. And were it not for the lethal implications to one floundering about in the well of a landing craft with five other newsmen and twenty Chinese soldiers, the night-battle display might have been a beautiful picture, something like Japanese fireworks. The sky was lightly overcast and a misty, milky light from a half-moon filtered through. Somehow it all cast a mood that this was a night for murder. Blood-red tracers raced and skipped across the sky, finally slowly floating and fading like spent skyrockets as they sought their targets. Brilliant diamond-bright air bursts from artillery batteries on the Communist-held Weito Peninsula to the east rained shrapnel upon the Nationalists' naval units. And the roar of Communist and Nationalist engines melded into the roar of the Nationalist three-inch guns and the chatter of the 50-caliber and 20-millimeter weapons from both sides. The range was short and the action confused, and we zigzagged through it, the skipper of our craft doing a remarkable job of sweeping in and out of the action without getting touched by even the ranging machine-gun fire. Several times we had to run down between the Nationalist and the Communist units, all of us crouching in the well of the violently pitching boat. And all the while the Communist artillery was pounding the Quemoy complex with air bursts.

In our landing craft we felt as big as a whale sticking out as a prime target. But there was really nothing to worry about, even though tracers often seemed to be seeking us out. Our plucky little Chinese coxswain kept his head, watching the course of battle, refusing to allow his gunners to fire their two 50's and give our position away, and skillfully staying out of the line of fire. In the end, the Communists never got a chance to line

129

up a torpedo run on the LSM, and in their gunfight with the minesweeper and the gunboats they were too busy to bother with small fry like us. By dawn the battle was over and the Communists had disappeared.

The Nationalists say they sank all the Communist vessels except one which fled. Maybe so. But I saw no explosions indicating sinking ships, though from where I sat, you couldn't see the whole battle. One Nationalist gunboat was hit below the waterline by a torpedo and was lying so low her numbers were partly obscured. I could see wounded on her decks and the crew jettisoning shells to cut the load. I watched as she was taken in tow heading back to the Pescadores.

Regardless how many ships the Communists lost, they accomplished their purpose. For the convoy's mission was foiled. Only twenty troops and a handful of correspondents got ashore. ▶

What the violent siege had done to the island of Quemoy and to neighboring Little Quemoy was reported by James Bell later. This is his story:

▶ Summer had broken, and the slim cedars along Quemoy's roadways bent before the first buffeting gusts of autumn. In the fields, the silver, feathery heads of *mao-tsao*, a grain used for fuel and fodder, swayed like the plumes of medieval knights. At night the moon brightened the island, and the pearl- and coral-colored bluffs loomed like phantoms above the beaches, pounded by a foamy sea. In other times it was the loveliest of sights. But this year autumn on Quemoy was a nightmare.

In three weeks a quarter of a million rounds of Communist artillery fire had raked the island. Roads were slashed up. Entire rows of cedar trees were blasted away. Quemoy City, scarcely scathed when I last visited, bared its broken walls and windows. Fewer civilians and more soldiers padded through the streets, and the cheerful horde of children was gone. Parents kept their kids indoors or underground, and civilians, who once seemed amused at the sight of the long-nosed foreigners, now pass quickly and silently. Sixty-five civilians have been killed on Quemoy and at least another two hundred wounded. Military casualties exceed one thousand.

At Kuning-tou, which means "ancient peace," on the northwest tip of the island, I found a village of two thousand people virtually deserted. On an earlier visit the streets were full of children, pigs, chickens and ducks. Now the pigs snort angrily in their concrete pens, the chickens scatter hysterically at the slightest noise, but the villagers are gone from dawn to darkness in search of safer places.

The harvest season is at hand, but there are no farmers in the fields. Only several hours before I arrived, a hunk of shrapnel had blown off the head of forty-year-old Li Wen-pi as he tried to lead his horse to safety. Even in the late afternoon, when no shells were falling, Kuning-tou's deep, dank underground shelter was crowded. The Communists are calculating their artillery fire to harass Quemoy's nerves—there is always fire at mealtimes and just after bedtime. Any crossroads is an unhealthy place to pause.

Lialo Beach, where the convoys come when they can, was pock-marked with shell holes. At one end a battered LSM, its back broken by Communist artillery, lay dead in the shallow water. With bluffs above eroded by wind and shellfire, the area looks like a valley of the moon. You feel appallingly naked as you drive along this lonely shore—watched by the tense eyes of the Nationalist soldiers dug into their caves, and by Communist eyes, natural and radar, on the mainland, only a few miles away. There is no cover here.

Scattered over the pitted landscape are white, blue and red para-chutes from the latest air-drop. Cases of food and medical supplies are strewn about uncollected by the island's defenders. Amphibious tracked vehicles piled high with oil drums still have not been unloaded, forty-eight hours after their arrival. The 53rd General Hospital has been hit repeatedly by shots aimed at the Nationalist convoys and planes. All the patients have been put underground.

On a visit to Little Quemoy Island a mile away, I found scarcely any man-made thing standing. There are only skeletons and scattered bones of houses. Kai Chai-tin, the island's civil-affairs director, says he believes there are two houses which have not been hit by a single shell but he couldn't find them. Neither could we. Strange to be looking for a house that had not been hit on an island whose population prior to the opening of a savage artillery attack was 5,789.

At Tungning, which with the neighboring village of Wushia was home to 1,042 human beings, there was virtually nothing left. In the village square the goals of a basketball court were shattered and dropped desolately down like a chicken's wrung neck. Wandering through the village, stepping over rubble and broken furniture, I was surprised to find that one commercial enterprise was still going. Yen An-tien is still selling cigarettes, tinned food and stationery in the back room of his shattered

131

shop. You climb over broken bricks at the entrance, push aside a child's broken tricycle and a couple of torn shoes, and you find Yen in a dark, damp back room, still open for small transactions. Business, he says, isn't too good these days, but what else is there to do?

Ten thousand rounds per square kilometer have forced Little Quemoy's population to live underground like animals. Only those soldiers and civilians with most urgent errands leave their dugouts and caves and trenches. Gradually villages have been evacuated and civilians have burrowed into hill caves.

At Hu Chin Tou, where the flag still flies defiantly, one feels closer to Communist guns than anywhere else in the complex. Through powerful glasses you can see the dragons' teeth and barbed wire of beach defenses on the mainland. If you look carefully you can spot a dozen camouflaged gun positions. I saw a couple of white-shirted farmers who appeared to be pottering about the field but by and large the villages, obviously hard-hit by Nationalist counterbattery fire, appear as deserted as Little Quemoy's. But you know there are thousands of Communist soldiers in that seemingly deserted landscape. And you know they are watching you with powerful glasses too. ▶

After the intense bombardment of 1958 the Communists' shelling tapered off and its pattern became erratic. At times they announced "suspension of fire" and the shelling ceased. At times they simply withheld their fire without announcements. But over the years they developed a pattern of firing every other day—"out of humanitarian consideration," they explained. And more recently even this alternate-day bombardment has become non-lethal. Ten years after the climax of the siege, on every odd day of the month, precisely at seven p.m., the Communists fire off one hundred non-explosive shells loaded with leaflets. As soon as the last shell falls, teams of Nationalist soldiers rush about and pick them up. Then they return the fire in the same fashion, shooting their own propaganda to the mainland.

But with more than eight hundred Communist guns zeroed in on Quemoy, the Nationalists continued to dig deeper and deeper into the rocks and the ridges of the island. Today Quemoy is one of the most fortified and formidable fortresses in history, and there seems little chance that the Communists can take it by assault. So the weapon of both the besieged and the besieger has become a question of time—who can outwait the other. And in the artillery exchange of propaganda, each adversary declares that time—and the changing world—is on its side.

THE BATTLEFIELDS

A SECTION OF PHOTOGRAPHS

Amphibious assault: Inchon Harbor, Korea.   *Hank Walker*

Infantry sortie in Vietnam.   *Larry Burrows*

Artillery barrage on the China mainland from Quemoy.   *John Dominis*

Untenable jungle outpost: Americans abandon a base near the Laotian border. *Howard Sochurek*

Guerrilla territory: a Greek gendarme observes a vital road contested by rebels.   *John Phillips*

Viet Minh territory: a French soldier guards the infiltration road from China.   *Carl Mydans*

In the hills of Magallal, Yemeni Royalists wait to ambush an Egyptian supply column.   George de Carvalho

Guard tower in Indo-China: Cambodian soldiers protect the road to Saigon. *Jack Birns*

Guard post in Egypt: a British soldier scans the road to Ismailia. *Carl Mydans*

Greek farmers near the Yugoslav border post a guard against guerrillas.   *John Phillips*

Moslems in western Algeria guard a French farm from guerrilla attack.   *Howard Sochurek*

British soldiers fire a Javanese village.   *John Florea*

An American column rests by a burning Korean farmhouse.   *Carl Mydans*

In the Sinai desert Egyptian planes strafe an Israeli column. *Israeli Government photo*
At Dienbienphu, Viet Minh artillery hits the French trenches. *French Service Presse Information*

Robert Ellison—Empire for Time

Sandbagged American artillery base near the Cambodian border, Vietnam.

Indian troops haul their transport up a Himalayan mountain road to face the Chinese Communists.

Larry Burrows

Through a jungle swamp an American tank moves up to guard a vital road from the Viet Cong.   Co *Rentmeester*

A helicopter skirts a cloud of fire.   *Larry Burrows*

A cluster of huts burns in a cloud of smoke.   *Larry Burrows*

Night artillery in Korea.   U.S. Army photo by Wayne Wiedner

Night patrol in Korea.   John Dominis

Amphibious vehicles and trucks race supplies over a Quemoy beach.   *John Dominis*

Israeli tanks advance into battle in the Sinai.   *Paul Schutzer*

French parachute attack on a Viet Minh supply center near the Chinese border.

XI

The Algerian Problem

(1954-1962)

T HE ALGERIAN PROBLEM—as seven years of armed rebellion, terror and counterterror, murderous rioting, systematic torture, and a French army revolt was called—was a three-cornered struggle born of a century of mistakes. Napoleon III saw the problem clearly when he said, "Algeria is an Arab kingdom, a European colony and a French camp." And ninety years later, in November 1959, correspondent John Phillips summed up the problem as it took shape in the fifth year of the conflict when he wrote:

"The French professional soldier in Algeria is painfully confused. On the one hand, most of the junior officers prefer Moslems to the Algerian French colonials whose mistreatment of the Arabs is largely responsible for the war. On the other hand, these same officers find themselves killing Moslems in part to restore the kind of "order" the *colons* want. Beyond this, professional soldiers confront a tragic possibility. After the defeat of 1940 and in Indo-China and successive withdrawals from Tunisia and Morocco, the French army feels it could not survive the shame of yet another defeat. As one ranking general said to me, 'If we are forced to abandon Algeria this is the end of the French army. The army will rebel.' "

Phillips, an American citizen, was born in Algeria and grew up in the midst of the hate between the European colonials and the Moslems. When he returned to cover Algeria at war, he saw the almost insoluble difficulties in many incidents. Of one such telling incident he wrote:

▶ The hopelessness of seeking a final military solution to the Algerian problem struck me hardest at the Foreign Legion post at Yakouren in the northern Kabylia. One evening the Legion colonel and I were alone in the mess having a nightcap when a sergeant came in. "He's talking now, *mon colonel*," the sergeant announced.

"Can he be seen?" the colonel asked.

"Seen, *mon colonel?*" The sergeant sounded puzzled.

The colonel nodded at me and casually replied, "Seen in mixed company?"

"Yes, *mon colonel*," the sergeant said. "The prisoner spoke of his own free will."

In the intelligence officer's tent a single electric bulb cast harsh shadows. The *fellagha* prisoner appeared to have a large welt under his right eye, but he seemed cheerful enough. He stood barefooted, his clothes tattered, scratching himself. Each time he brought his arms up his handcuffs rattled.

Here was the first live *fellagha* I had seen, a soldier of the nationalist liberation army, and I studied him carefully. The passive resistance of this single Arab suddenly became the passive resistance of all the Arabs I have ever known since childhood. It was not so much that he cringed; it was his slyness which struck me. I wondered how much the French officers understood him. Did they recognize the meaning of his shiftiness which made him seem almost an imbecile or a buffoon? The more he smiled and degraded himself, the more I became convinced that the French would get nowhere in Algeria with force.

"He says the arsenal is at Bou Nouman," the intelligence officer said. "That's where we picked him up three days ago." The colonel glared at the prisoner. The prisoner scratched himself and smiled. "Why did you wait so long to tell us this?" the colonel thundered. "I'll tell you why. So you could give your pals time to move the stuff, that's why."

"Ah *non, mon colonel*," the prisoner said. "This is not true. I swear to you. You'll see for yourself tomorrow. We'll find the arsenal."

"Empty," the colonel snapped.

"Not empty, I swear," the Arab replied with the utmost candor. "Full. Full of everything."

"You will guide us to the cache where there's eighteen hundred pounds of flour, won't you," the intelligence officer said persuasively, as if coaching an imbecile child.

"Yes, eighteen hundred pounds of flour." The prisoner smiled broadly.

Next morning I watched the prisoner, now wearing a pair of boots and carrying a heavy bundle, led at the end of a long chain to the helicopter for the flight to Bou Nouman. I hoped for his sake that the trip would not be for nothing. There wasn't room for all of us, so the colonel and I waited for the little Alouette to come back for us.

Bou Nouman is a village lost in the wilderness of Kabylia and we landed some miles away on a precarious mountain ledge where we waited for news, the colonel using a field radio to talk with his men in the village.

"They've found the arsenal," he told me. "Now they're looking for the food cache." In the distance I could see some of the Legionnaires heading our way. They were bringing with them everything they had captured. The arsenal itself, a concrete vault built under a house, had already been blown up. When the column came up to us, a Legionnaire emptied the contents of a single bag, all that had been found: a half-dozen ancient gunstocks, a hammer, a pair of pliers and two files.

The colonel stared at the old stocks lying on the ground. "Keep the hammer, the pliers and the files," he snapped. "Burn the rest." I admired his self-control.

The food cache had been located, the sergeant said, but it was empty. "I knew it," the colonel said with deadly calm. "That *fell* held out for three days to give his pals time."

I recalled that in the French Resistance it was said that a man had to hold out four days to protect his friends; among the Moslem *fellagha*, apparently, three days was considered enough. ▶

The Moslems of Algeria are for the most part the descendants of the indigenous Berbers, a fierce tribal people of Caucasian stock, and the Arabs who invaded the area in the seventh and eleventh centuries. It has been said by modern Algerians—European and Moslem alike—that there had never been a nation of Algeria before the French came there. But in fact the Berber tribes in this portion of North Africa combined to form the kingdom of Numidia in the third century B.C., and later the civilization of the area was able to produce such giants as the Christian theologian Saint Augustine. But from their earliest history the native people of Algeria were dominated, almost without pause, by Phoenicians, Romans, Arabs, Spanish, Turks and French. Under all of them they staged rebellions, were put down, learned to accommodate. And their own distinctive brand of clannish rivalry combined with an aloof passivity born of pride produced, by the twentieth century, a deep resentment and an uncoordinated spirit of revolt masked by a surface air of obsequious cooperation and humility.

The European colonizers of Algeria were, until 1962, citizens of metropolitan France, although perhaps three out of five of them were descendants of Italian, Spanish, Greek, Maltese and other immigrants from the Mediterranean basin. Some had been in Algeria for as many as four generations and, like the pioneers who opened the American West, developed the land at the expense of the indigenous population. Although in the mid-twentieth century there were only about one million *colons*, as these settlers were called, to eight million Moslems, the Europeans of Algeria—even so liberal-minded a one as Albert Camus—tended to see the country as predominantly European, with the mass of Moslems somewhat faceless in the background. The more racist or more insecure among them subjected the Moslems to daily humiliations and referred to them as *ratons*, little rats.

The third member of the triangle was the French army, instrument of the government of France, whose history in Algeria goes back to 1830, when it attacked the city of Algiers, which was held by the Turkish Dey, and took it in three weeks—only to spend the next seventeen years in a war against local Moslem leaders, and another twenty-five in warlike pacification. There were superficial reasons for the French attack on Algeria, but an underlying motive was the need to redress the defeats and humiliations of Napoleon's troops

169

fifteen years earlier and reassert the glory of French arms. As, more than a century later, the disaster at Dienbienphu was a goad to the French army officers in Algeria, so in 1830 they needed to prove themselves. They had not intended to take on the responsibility of the whole Algerian territory, but through a long series of unsuccessful military operations, shaky truces, and ventures into direct administration, the army was drawn deeper and deeper into Algerian affairs. Some of the military administrators were decent men. Some were brutes.

Marshal Thomas Robert Bugeaud, a blunt, patriotic soldier who became Governor General of Algeria in 1840, more than any other man was responsible for the three-cornered pattern of the social structure there for the next hundred years. His most recent combat experience had been in Spain, where he learned guerrilla tactics, and these he applied against the Moslems, not only in hit-and-run ambushes but in a scorched-earth policy and in indiscriminate reprisals against whole communities. When his men asphyxiated five hundred Moslem men and women trapped in a cave, the news reached France and was denounced in the Senate and by the press. The war was unpopular with Frenchmen at home, and this brutality disgusted them. Bugeaud's reaction—like the reaction of later French officers in Algiers after the systematic torture of civilian prisoners in 1957–58 caused a similar outcry—was to continue the practice, only to keep it secret.

Having destroyed the crops of the rebellious Berbers, cut down their trees, burned their villages and hounded them off their lands, Marshal Bugeaud encouraged the immigration of Europeans, saying, "Settlers must be put wherever there is good water and land. Don't worry who it belongs to." And many did make the fertile areas bloom again, some of them claiming that it had never bloomed before. By the end of the final uprising, in 1871, nearly one third of the cultivable land of the country was in European hands.

In 1845 there were some 50,000 Europeans in Algeria; fifty years later there were nearly 500,000. Known as *pieds-noirs* because so many of them had come barefoot and destitute from the poverty and civil strife of their own countries, they often settled in the cities rather than on the land. And the patois spoken in such low-income sections as the Bab-el-Oued quarter of Algiers was incomprehensible to most Frenchmen.

The period of colonization was a period of Moslem silence. Some Moslems adopted a French outlook and European ways, were educated in French schools and became prosperous. But the great majority degenerated into listless farm-laborers or drifted into the slums of the cities and became the "human dust," the ignorant and ill-paid proletariat. Not until World War I was there a stirring among Moslem intellectuals. Young Algerian workers and students who had served in the French army or worked as laborers in Paris were influenced by the Socialism of the 1920's to form, with their counterpart Moroccans and Tunisians, an Arab workers' union. At the same time, middle-class, French-educated Moslems in Algeria established an organization which denied there ever was such a "nation" as Algeria but urged the assimilation of Moslems into the French community. The third stirring was of purely Islamic nature, formed by men of religious learning to teach young Moslems that "my religion is Islam, my language Arabic, and my country Algeria."

World War II exposed Algerian Moslems to more positive ideas of patriotism and equality. Many joined the French army, witnessed its humiliation in the fall of France, and attached themselves to the Free French forces, while the majority of the *colons* followed Pétain in the early years. Allied soldiers stationed in North Africa brought talk of liberation and democracy, and the introduction of the radio into even the most backward Berber village and casbah warren carried news of Arab nationalism blossoming in the countries of the eastern Mediterranean. By contrast, the Moslems of Algeria, cut off from wartime France and denied a voice in their own government by *colon* intransigence, were living in desperate poverty and seemingly without any hope of change. In this atmosphere, the leaders of those early, tentative movements swung toward a more activist program.

On V-E day, May 8, 1945, Moslem nationalists paraded in the city of Sétif, carrying, among the flags of France, Great Britain, Russia and the United States, banners proclaiming "Long live a free Algeria." The police intervened, the marchers clung to their banners, shots rang out, and a riot started. It was an explosion of long-pent-up Moslem hatred. Without discrimination, infuriated gangs attacked Europeans with axes, knives and clubs. The madness spread from the city into the mountains to the south. Eighty-eight Europeans were killed and many more wounded, and the survivors, outnumbered seventeen to one, lived in a state of terror. The reprisal, conducted by the French police, the army and navy and the *colons* themselves, was even more indiscriminate and ferocious. The number of Moslem dead has never been truly counted and the estimates range from 1,000 to 50,000 killed in summary executions or by bombing, strafing or shelling from the sea.

During the next decade the remnants of those nationalists who organized the Sétif march regrouped and were joined by other Moslem leaders, now disillusioned in their hopes for recognition and assimilation by the French. Much of their activity was underground, and it came as a surprise to the *colons*, the French army and even the great majority of Algerian Moslems themselves when, on November 1, 1954, guerrilla bands struck simultaneously with separate acts of murder or sabotage in seventy different spots across the country. Most of these attacks were in the vicinity of the Aurès mountains, stronghold of ancient Berber tribes, and the organization and equipment of the bands were very primitive. But the very timing of the attacks showed a central organization; out of the various nationalist movements had grown the first consolidated group dedicated to achieving unity and liberty by force. Its name was the Front of National Liberation; its leaders were a group of nine young activists, and its fighting force was less than a thousand *fellagha*.

Within two years the FLN had drawn in all but one of the Moslem leaders in Algeria and was strong enough to reject the offer of Communist Party aid. Their 1,000 guerrilla fighters had increased to some 30,000 and the supply of recruits from among the originally non-committed Moslems was almost inexhaustible. They controlled large areas of the countryside, collecting levies and punishing collaborators through an underground administration, and they had forced France to commit an army of 50,000 to Algeria.

In 1957 they attempted to gain control of the city of Algiers through terrorism. The civil authorities turned over all security and police responsibilities to the Tenth Paratroop Division under General Jacques Massu, and the nearly year-long "battle of Algiers" ensued—a hideous contest between terrorist bomb atrocities and paratroop "rakings" of the casbah area, wholesale imprisonment, torture and execution of suspects and their sympathizers.

The systematic use of torture as a recognized weapon of war was defended by the army on the grounds that information gained this way often saved lives. But to the French at home, many of whom had suffered just such tortures in the Resistance, the idea of professional French torturers was too repugnant to be countenanced. The ugly facts were published and denounced, and as a result, a fresh concept of this branch of warfare was inaugurated in Algeria, that of "humane torture." The beatings, electro-burnings and half-drownings were not to be carried out in the presence of sadists or young soldiers, were to be applied so as to leave no trace, and were to stop as soon as the information had been given. However, since the published reports of torture had originally come from victims who survived, it was necessary in the cause of secrecy to shoot more prisoners. With these methods the paratroopers wiped out the terrorists in Algiers, and by the fall of

1957 had reduced the casbah, which had been their hiding place and base of operations, to a state of cringing cooperation.

Caught between pressures put on by European rightists in Algeria, French liberals at home, growing FLN demands for independence, U.N. condemnation of the war, and their own responsibility to work out a compromise solution to the problem, four French governments failed in a single year. The last of them, that of Pierre Pflimlin, collapsed under the threat of civil war brought by rebellious rightist colonials and French army officers in Algiers, thus ending the Fourth Republic and bringing Charles de Gaulle to power.

The new Premier seemed to have something for everyone. But with the referendum three months later, by which he was given an overwhelming mandate to form the Fifth Republic, he was no longer so much in debt to the rightists and rebellious officers of Algeria. He announced a plan of radical reforms to give the Moslem population political, economic and educational opportunities equal to the French. At very nearly the same time the FLN, which had grown, despite its defeat in the "battle of Algiers," to a well-armed force of some 130,000, moved its exile headquarters from Cairo to Tunisia and formed a "Provisional Government of the Algerian Republic." Made skeptical by years of French promises and rigged elections, they ignored the promises of the new program and rejected out of hand De Gaulle's high-sounding offer to negotiate a "peace of the brave."

Following the seemingly inflexible pattern of men at war, the General then launched the greatest offensive of the war with the avowed, if paradoxical, purpose of bringing an end to the war. This renewed attack in the countryside and on the rebel mountain strongholds lasted through 1959 and employed the bulk of the half-million French soldiers who by now were stationed in Algeria. The battered honor of the French army was at stake. But they were fighting elusive guerrilla bands and their dilemma was summed up in the despairing question the commanding general put to correspondent Phillips: "How can I win an Austerlitz against four men?"

The *colons* also saw their honor and their privileged way of life at stake. As De Gaulle's position shifted away from the concept of a "French Algeria" toward one of self-determination for all Algerians, they began to hiss his name as they had once cheered it. And when he dismissed General Massu, their hero of the battle of Algiers, they rose in a mob, clashed with the French gendarmes, and erected barricades in the streets. For the five days in January 1960 that became known as "Barricades Week," the army wavered in its

173

loyalties and the Fifth Republic hung in the balance. Then De Gaulle donned his uniform and spoke directly to the French soldiers in Algiers, commanding their loyalty and ordering them to dissociate themselves from the insurrection.

With that, the troops who had been fraternizing with the rioters allowed themselves to be replaced by units from the field, the barricades were pulled down and the rebellious *colons* dispersed. But it was not the last time that the Europeans of Algiers used riot as a weapon against the government. While De Gaulle searched for a road to peace with the FLN, the passions of the *colons* boiled up against him.

In December 1960 the extremists who were determined to "keep Algeria French" staged yet another strike and demonstration in the streets of Algiers. Correspondent Curtis Prendergast described the flavor of the city during these passionate uprisings:

▶ In front of iron-shuttered shops, knots of young Europeans gathered. Most were in their twenties, many black-leather jacketed. They looked tough and mean, spoiling for a fight. A few older ones had the sullen faces of workers. As crowds began to form, the gendarmes moved in to disperse them. They were seasoned, stockily built men, helmeted, booted, wearing long khaki overcoats, with rifles or sub-machine guns slung over their shoulders and gas goggles cupped under their chins. Ten companies of them were in town.

We followed them as they moved up rue Michelet, one of Algiers' main shopping streets. Many plate-glass windows had been broken and the debris of bricks, stones, and crushed glass had been ground into a chalky mud on the pavements, wet from this morning's rain. From ahead, as we rushed to catch up with the fighting, came great crashing sounds of gas grenades going off, shouts, more glass breaking. The air began to get rancid and our eyes watered uncontrollably from tear gas.

In front of the closed shops were remnants of barricades: packing cases, scraps of wood from a building under construction, a few paving blocks. Truckloads of gendarmes came slowly up the street to join the tanklike armored cars ahead. The men hunched under the canvas awnings of their trucks, their faces set against the booing and derisive whistling from angry Europeans standing in doorways or leaning over the iron-grillwork balconies above. Next to one shuttered shop a young girl of about twenty, her eyes streaming from tear gas, handkerchief clapped over her nose, took the handkerchief away for a moment to shriek,

"Murderers . . ." Her pretty doll-like features were twisted in rage. Then her mother took up the shouting: "Assassins! Assassins!"

At rue Michelet and boulevard Victor Hugo, which dips sharply downward toward the port and the lovely Mediterranean beyond, street fighting was going on. Two automobiles had been turned across the street to make a barricade. One, a cream-and-red sedan, was burned out. Behind it a crowd of several hundred young Europeans was gathered. They threw stones, chunks of iron, bricks, pebbles, at the gendarmes. On rue Michelet itself, tiles and flowerpots were crashing down. From a balcony above the palm trees an arm would appear and then something would come hurtling down, smashing lumpily on the street. In the ranks of armored cars, helmeted heads would duck inside portholes and the lids would clank shut. Then would come the drumming sound of stones hitting the steel sides. There were shrieks from the balconies: "*Salauds! Salauds!*" and "*Bourreax!* Executioners!"

Under orders not to shoot, the gendarmes picked up stones and threw them back. One broke from the uniformed ranks and stumbled away, his eye streaming blood. His comrades grabbed him and pulled him back around the corner.

Now the gendarmes tried a charge. Behind their screen of armored vehicles they made a rush toward the corner. There was a hail of stones, then a Molotov cocktail hurtling through the air, breaking on the pavement and bursting into bright orange flame. Everywhere was debris, remnants of grenades, broken glass, some clots of blood. The fighting swayed back and forth as the gendarmes charged and then retreated under barrages of stones. More Molotov cocktails splashed into flame and oily black smoke. Once again the gendarmes charged and this time swept ahead, down the boulevard Victor Hugo, scattering the crowd ahead while women shouted down insults from the balconies. On a high rooftop far ahead two men were silhouetted, throwing down huge chunks of tile.

A French official came up behind me, ducking, like all of us, under the overhang of balconies to protect our heads. His face was drawn and angry. "This on one side," he said grimly, "and the FLN on the other." ▶

This was the government's dilemma. But the stones and insults of a fanatic mob had not the weight of a seasoned guerrilla army and a Provisional Government that was recognized by eighteen nations. Early in 1961 talks

175

were begun with representatives of the FLN. It took a full year of intermittent negotiations till, on March 18, 1962, a cease-fire was signed and Algeria was promised self-determination.

All during 1961, while the peace talks were going on, rebellious high-ranking officers made desperate efforts to prevent what they considered the abandonment of Algeria and a shameful defeat. Under the leadership of their "Secret Army Organization," paratroop units of the French Foreign Legion seized control of Algiers on April 22 and held it for three days. In Paris, De Gaulle assumed emergency powers and denounced the rebel generals for their "odious and stupid adventure," and the great majority of the army in Algeria stayed loyal to the government. The OAS coup had failed, but their harassment continued, with bombings and assassinations both in Algeria and France, until it reached a peak in January 1962, when they proclaimed the "mobilization of all Algerians" to prevent a peace settlement. An amalgam of diehard French army elements and a hard core of about four thousand European extremists, the OAS was able to keep Algiers in a state of terror. Moderate Europeans were bullied into giving them support, and Moslems were indiscriminately attacked and murdered. The death toll ran as high as one hundred in a day, and for the first time in all the years of this vehement war Algiers became a truly segregated city, with the relation between the Moslems and Europeans one of open hatred, each afraid to venture into the sectors where the other lived.

The hope of the OAS was that they could goad the Moslems into acts of reprisal so that the French army might be forced to side with the dissident *colons* in order to prevent a slaughter of Europeans. But the FLN, so close to victory, managed to hold the Moslems in check. And the French troops were irrevocably alienated when, on March 23, a group of OAS terrorists in the poor-white section of Bab-el-Oued killed fifteen soldiers. The army sealed off the quarter and arrested some thirty-five hundred suspected terrorists. On March 26 the outraged OAS staged a demonstration, and on that day, one week after the cease-fire had been signed, correspondent Gordon Ackerman witnessed a final act of madness in this fury-ridden three-cornered war:

▶ It was the first sunny day in weeks, the beginning of the Algerian spring which has been sung by poets from Cervantes to Camus. With the formal cease-fire in effect, the army in control of the rebellious Bab-el-Oued quarter, and its European residents tired, hungry and discouraged, it was easy to believe that the Algerian nightmare was at an end.

At two o'clock we were standing on the balcony of our room in the Hotel Albert I, waiting for the start of what had been billed as "a demonstration of European students in protest against the treason of the Paris authorities." The students and their supporters were to march from the fashionable rue Michelet to the army barricades at Bab-el-Oued. And though peace was in the air, French army troops, comprised of both Europeans and Moslems, nervous, battle-weary, fresh from field combat, were on guard against a possible clash between the demonstrators and Arab bystanders. Hundreds of soldiers clutching machine pistols and automatic rifles lined the streets along the route of the march. A bright sun shone directly overhead and the sky was clear except for a pair of army helicopters circling low over the city.

By two-thirty the demonstrators had formed on rue Michelet and were quietly dispersed by two army squads. Then they came up the street under our window—some five hundred of them walking peacefully in little clots of five or ten. The majority of them were young people, students, boys and girls arm-in-arm, carrying French flags, some eating ice-cream cones. They weren't marching but simply walking, even strolling, like college freshmen on the way to a carnival.

Then almost imperceptibly a change came over the character of the demonstration and of the demonstrators themselves. Like the scorpions which infest the deserts of southern Algeria, this demonstration carried its sting in its tail. From far down rue Michelet we could hear the sound of singing. It was the "Song of Africans," the hymn of the OAS, and around the corner a corps of two hundred more demonstrators appeared. At their head was a band of fifty students carrying French flags and cans of aerosol paint bombs with which they sprayed the letters OAS on shop windows and walls. They were older than the students who had gone before and there were a good many women. They moved slowly and yet with a fearful kind of determination. They had a hard, frozen look of anger and hate. Men walked with their hands in their pockets, fingering revolvers, or reached periodically under their jackets.

Quite suddenly, the people who had been standing on the balconies around us and across from us disappeared, vaporized behind slammed windows and shutters. They knew better than we the aspect of imminent disaster in Algiers. The singing grew louder and wilder, almost incoherent. A French army ambulance sped down the street through the crowd in a vain attempt to break up the flag-bearers. Then the army halftracks which had been parked at the end of the street rolled heavily away and down a sidestreet in an attempt to head off the dangerous tail end of the demonstration, and were followed, inexplicably, by nearly all the troops stationed nearby, leaving only thirty very young, very nervous, very battle-weary soldiers on guard. Of the thirty, at least twenty were European, the rest Moslem.

The first shot seemed to come from a window on the top floor of a building at the opposite end of the avenue. Then we heard three more shots and saw a tiny circle of smoke drifting away from the balcony of an apartment. Instantly the window flew shut. Our watch told us that what happened next took seven minutes. It seemed like days.

A shot struck a French soldier just under our balcony. He dropped. The flag-bearers stopped singing, threw their flags aside, and began cursing a dozen soldiers who tried to surround them. Four marchers pulled revolvers from their pockets and began shooting.

Almost automatically, seemingly uncontrollably, reacting to conditioned reflexes learned on the battlefield fighting against the FLN, the thirty soldiers under our balcony raised their machine pistols to their hips, cocked them, and fired indiscriminately into the crowd a hundred yards away. Perhaps seven hundred rounds of bullets were sprayed into this gathering which was composed not of marchers or OAS sympathizers but simply spectators or shoppers who stood watching at the end of the street. Two minutes later more than fifty bodies lay on the sidewalk and pavement. The pistol-toting flag-bearers had fled and were either hiding in shops or firing back at the army from behind trees. Most of those who died were simply too old, too slow or too confused to get out of the way. An old man attempting to seek cover behind a parked truck was virtually cut in half by machine-gun fire.

For a moment there was silence, but the soldiers had not finished with their civilian enemies. They had stopped only long enough to let their guns cool and to reload with fresh cartridge clips. During the lull a woman ran into the street crying, "*Halte au feu, halte au feu.* These are French you're shooting! My God, we're French!" The soldiers ripped the empty clips from their guns, replaced them with new ones, and began spraying the street again. The woman stopped shouting. She stood up straight and then bent slightly backward and raised her hand to her hip.

In the next five minutes perhaps another thousand rounds poured down the street into the bodies and faces of those trying to carry away friends and relatives injured in the first skirmish. Now helicopters came and dumped tear-gas shells into the crowds, blinding those trying to help the injured and preventing others from finding places to hide. The woman who had cried *"Halte au feu"* was still standing directly in the center of the street. It was as if she were simply stretching or scratching her side. From beneath her topcoat, down her legs, and onto the sunny pavement flowed a broad river of blood. She bent forward again and her sunglasses began to fall away from her face. Once more she straightened, reached up and carefully replaced her glasses. Then she clutched her handbag tightly to her side and collapsed dead onto the pavement.

This scene from a nightmare was repeating itself a hundredfold at the opposite end of the street. It had turned into a slow motion mime of death. The soldiers did not run, advance, or seek cover, but simply emptied clip upon clip of bullets into the crowd. And the crowd itself was reduced to the dead, the dying, the crippled and the old.

The air rang with sirens and ambulances began arriving. The soldiers, simply for lack of ammunition, had stopped firing. Many in the crowd were choked with tear gas, but some began covering the dead with the tricolor flags of the marchers. We went down into the street. More than a hundred people lay between life and death on the pavement and sidewalks around us. Some staggered away by themselves, others were carried off by friends and relatives.

But equally tragic was the spectacle taking place at the other end of the street. There stood the thirty soldiers, and no appraisal of them, no matter how facetious it may sound, could be more accurate than that of a spectator who remarked, "They look like boys who have been caught smoking behind the barn." Their guns, steaming, lay on the pavement where they had dropped them. They were staring at them, speechless and dazed, and four of the men were sobbing. A crowd of a dozen Europeans grabbed one and began beating him and spitting at him. He made no attempt to stop them. ▶

"It is a strange peace," wrote a French journalist, "that begins by being more murderous than what was called war." But it was not yet peace. Two days after the massacre in rue Michelet, the OAS declared an "all-out war" against the forces of their own country. They continued their bombings and assassinations, but by their excesses they lost the sympathy not only of the people of France but also many among the French officers who had previously supported them, and the French community in Algeria. On April 8, French voters overwhelmingly endorsed the truce accord, and three months later a self-determination referendum held in Algeria revealed that a vast

179

majority—more than three hundred to one—of all Algerians were in favor of independence with close ties to France.

On July 3, 1962, President de Gaulle formally proclaimed Algeria's independence, but even this final victory for the nationalists—won after seven years of fighting, 150,000 of their number killed—did not bring peace. Instead it exploded in a sharp political conflict and a tragi-comic, seven-day, incipient civil war.

One faction in this confrontation was led by Premier Benyoussef Benkhedda of the FLN Provisional Government and included most of the leaders of the guerrilla army which had fought the French in the hills and cities of Algeria, as well as many a young "liberator" who had joined the army only after peace had been declared. The other group was headed by Vice Premier Ahmed Ben Bella, recently released from jail after five years in French prisons. Backing him were the general staff of the FLN army, including the chief of staff, Colonel Houari Boumedienne, whose headquarters were in Tunisia. They had at their command the well-armed, well-trained regular army troops who had been stationed along the Tunisian and Moroccan borders.

The conflict started when, shortly before the day of independence, Premier Benkhedda dissolved the general staff. Ben Bella denounced the action, and the general staff refused to be dismissed. They formed a seven-man Political Bureau to supplant the Provisional Government. A settlement was negotiated, and on August 7 the Political Bureau took over leadership of the new government. All was well on the political front, but many guerrilla leaders refused to accept the new authority.

The guerrilla troops had been divided into zones known as Wilayas, and as early as July, troops of Wilaya Four—whose zone was the central coastal region outside Algiers—had moved in and displaced the troops of the city's autonomous zone. Late in August, when the regular army attempted to return with their exile government—some filtering in small units into Algiers, some crossing in full formation into Wilaya Four—the ill-advised irregulars attacked.

Correspondent James Wilde saw the action in this brief, reluctant civil war from both sides. In his report he tells of the fighting both in the countryside and in the casbah of Algiers.

▶ After a series of false starts, antic tragedies and conflicting rumors, and despite massive nationwide demonstrations against it, fighting broke out in earnest late Tuesday morning in the rolling wheatfields between the small towns of Boghar and Boghari, a hundred miles south of Algiers.

Sitting on a hillside among the black tents of nomadic shepherds I saw the civil war begin. The sky was glazed hard blue. The air was bewitched with the smell of thyme and conifer and the light was hot, spiced, sparkling everything it touched. Two baby donkeys nuzzled each other nearby. In the distance the mountains were patched with trees.

Brown as the earth they sat on, the shepherds watched silently. Bleak-eyed hawks circled indifferently above. And below, black dots moved slowly amid the golden stubble, shooting at each other with pings, bangs, thuds, whooshes and coughs.

The events leading up to this were both comic and tragic. On Saturday two columns of Ben Bellist troops, each about three thousand strong, crossed over into Wilaya Four from the Sahara. About forty miles apart, they moved up the two roads leading to Algiers. Column one arrived at a village some miles beyond Boghar. Column two appeared near Aumale, a completely walled city that looks like a Saracen fortress. When they met the dissident troops of Wilaya Four, they fired into the air, embraced their adversaries as brothers, and then sat down together and had coffee.

Sunday afternoon a car backfired near the Algiers casbah, causing fighting to break out in this area for the second time in a week. Four days earlier I had been in the casbah and watched a small patrol in paratroop uniform moving warily through the dank, dark maze of streets. Their guns pointing roofward, they inched along with their backs pressed hard against the peeling, hunchbacked houses. Suddenly, from above, a gun was fired and a soldier slid down into the garbage-strewn cobbled street. The wounded man was dragged into a deep stone doorway where veiled Moslem women sat rocking back and forth and weeping, asking over and over in Arabic, "How can this happen? How can this happen?" For it wasn't General Massu's paratroopers or the OAS, but Algerian brother against brother.

Fighting had broken out early in the afternoon when a Wilaya Four patrol walking through the casbah was fired on from the rooftops. Fairly intense at first, the firing continued spasmodically late into the night. It was dirty fighting, against an unseen enemy, concentrated mostly in the legendary Pepe le Moko hunting grounds, a warren of rivulet-like streets, caves and tunnels. Until they were forced to clear off, Arab civilians sat packed around the coffee tables outside cafés in eerie silence, watching the struggle that was going on around them.

For a long time no one seemed to know who the enemy was. Finally a Wilaya Four officer announced that a battalion—five hundred men—loyal to Colonel Boumedienne had entered the city over the past few days disguised in civilian clothes. Serious fighting broke out when Wilaya Four troops, tipped off about this infiltration, tried to flush out the invaders. During the savage five-hour fight the Wilaya Four troops treated everyone as an enemy. One young carpenter was nearly shot in his workshop because he had a toy pistol. An incautious rooftop onlooker was shot and fell head-first into a huge basket of grapes. Walking through the twisting alleys, one had inquisitive sub-machine guns poked into one's stomach every few yards.

A few minutes before curfew time fierce fighting broke out around the Place du Gouvernement in downtown Algiers. Soon crowds gathered in front of the plush Aletti Hotel, which had been successively a play-place for French *colons,* the OAS headquarters, and a *pension* for Provisional Government ministers. Chanting over and over again, *"Seba snine barakat*—Seven years and that's enough!" the crowd of perhaps two thousand then marched toward the casbah. The Wilaya Four soldiers made no attempt to enforce the curfew, but merely faded back into the shadows, and with the streetlights turned off, the demonstrators soon became confused in the dark and the crowd broke up. ▶

This was the beginning of several days of demonstrations in Algiers and throughout the country, the people themselves attempting to avert a civil war, demanding peace and unity among their leaders. Under this pressure the rival factions arranged a cease-fire, but the fighting continued for a few more days. Correspondent Wilde was in the casbah once again on Sunday, September 2, and in the countryside September 4:

▶ The fighting in the casbah Sunday afternoon took place on the rooftops. It was bloody and chaotic. At least five men were killed and many others wounded within the first half-hour. Everything was banging off at once.

Then it suddenly became a bizarre passion play. Crouched beside a Wilaya Four patrol on a balcony, I heard them calling to the enemy by their first names. "Mohammed, stop firing. We don't want to hurt you. Don't you remember we had a drink together only a few hours ago?" Mohammed had apparently forgotten. He sprayed the balcony with his machine gun to the rhythm of the five-beat popular slogan which is usually chanted, "Ya ya Ben Bel la."

While this blind, dusty carnage was going on on the rooftops, thousands were demonstrating in the streets below. In the midst of the battle a group of veiled wailing women gathered in a small square and implored the men to stop fighting. They were caught by crossfire and one old woman was killed by a stray bullet, but the rest stayed firm. With arms uplifted toward the rooftops, they screamed, "Stop it! Shame! We have had enough!"

On Monday a ten-thousand-strong column of Ben Bellist troops crossed into Wilaya Four at Orléansville, halfway between Algiers and Oran. All Monday afternoon discussions went on between the commanders of both sides. They fraternized freely, ate together, drank together, and got nowhere. The arguments were always the same: "Dear brothers, we have orders from the Political Bureau to advance on Algiers...." "Dear brothers, we are very sorry, but we have orders from the Wilaya Four command not to let you pass." The commander at Boghari offered to fight a sub-machine-gun duel with his opposite number. The offer was declined. The commander at Orléansville sent a wagonload of vegetables to the regular army mess and paid for them himself. Fraternity was the password.

Like medieval armies, they lined up facing each other about thirty yards apart. With banners flying in the wind, they waved to each other from the forward skirmishing lines. Tuesday, however, the situation became tense. The invading commanders sent a message saying they intended to advance. The dissident guerrillas replied with machine guns. The civil war began.

As I sat watching with the nomads, I could see backstage. On either side of the range of hills the two convoys of the opposing forces were drawn up. The main road was still being used. A little girl in a red dress went to fetch water. A farmer was plowing his field. And nearly 2,500 Wilaya Four troops were moving into position. A jeep rolled up, carrying two men wearing black berets and the red armbands of Wilaya Four. The officer told me that the enemy was advancing and said quietly that he and his men would stop them. I went down the hill with him and, sitting in a trench with a Wilaya Four patrol, I watched a boy officer larking around, trying to steal the pistol of his commander so he could play with it. The "men" of Wilaya Four were more often boys. A motley collection of former guerrilla fighters and children, they were lightly armed. The enemy wasn't using any of his heavy stuff yet, so they were all joking and laughing. But they had no radio, no logistics, and little food.

An hour later, standing in a cornfield with the regular army forces, I heard the echoing rattle of gunfire coming closer. These regular army men, trained in Tunisia, were well-disciplined and well-equipped. They wore Chinese-made uniforms, carried Czech sub-machine guns and American water bottles, drove about in Skoda trucks and were well-supplied with Soviet artillery and recoilless weapons.

The sergeant in charge walked me up to a rise overlooking the battlefield and said: "We don't want to fight them, you know. We just want to go to Algiers." As he spoke, a burst of enemy fire kicked up dust puffs a few yards away. "You see," he said, "they are our brothers, but they don't understand. I have my wife and children living in Algiers whom I haven't seen in four years." For the first time I believed it when someone called them brothers. The firing was so close that he slowly and sadly took cover and ordered his men to start firing the 2-millimeter mortar and a couple of bursts from the 50-caliber Chinese-made Drush-kas.

The fighting had started, but it was obvious that the army was holding back its superior firepower and the greater bulk of its men. The serious fighting was going on at Aumale, and Wednesday I drove down there. I passed long, weary columns of soldiers in single line on either side of the road. Thinking that they were being relieved, I continued on about seven miles till the road dipped into a shallow gorge. Ahead it appeared deserted. It was only by turning off the motor that I realized heavy firing was going on, most of it small arms concentrated right on this strip of road.

I opened the door and made for a ditch with the unpleasant sound of hornets in my ears. The road suddenly came alive with soldiers, who rushed over to where I was lying and forced me at gunpoint to get up and walk over to the car. They were panic-stricken and hysterical. They ordered me to drive them "out of this dirty mess." I tried to explain to them that the car would be sure death and that standing there in full view was also ridiculous. At this moment one of them was shot in the leg. Instead of sobering them, it caused more panic. Seven of them packed into the car and forced me to turn around and drive off. As I turned, I heard a bullet strike the side of the car. The soldier sitting next to the righthand rear door groaned, sighed, and let his head rest on the back of the seat.

About a hundred yards farther on we came across an ambulance. I stopped and the soldiers got out. The man in the back didn't move. When I tried to open the door, I noticed a neatly drilled hole. A bullet had entered the soldier's right shoulder, pierced his chest and then his heart. He must have died a few minutes after being hit. No one would help me get his body out of the car. Several came up and just stared. All the clichés came true: the dead man's gun was gripped hard between his hands so that I had to pry open his fingers one by one. Then the gun was jammed against the car roof. He was terribly heavy, as dead bodies are supposed to be. When I finally managed to drag him out, the road was under fire. The ambulance driver helped me lift the corpse onto a stretcher and put it into the ambulance. Then he took off.

A few yards farther on, a gray, grizzled, stocky man stood in the middle of the road barely watching the lines of men passing either side of him. He wore a British-cut mustache and an officer's cap with a star and sickle moon emblazoned on it. His face was sagging with fatigue and full of bitter disgust. His men didn't even look at him. They were beat. At least a battalion trudged by in silence. Some just lay down by the side of the road, too tired to move any farther and oblivious to the gunfire which was catching up to them.

The officer told me the firing had begun at seven o'clock this morning. "They broke the truce," he said. He was withdrawing his men because they were finished. "They won't fight any more today," he said. Seven years with the Kabylia guerrillas, he'd fought the entire war against the French. "And now this," he said angrily. "It is all the fault of the Political Bureau. They have betrayed us. Well, they have their methods, and we have ours. This isn't finished yet. . . ." With that he turned and joined his beaten battalion marching off along the road into the hills. It was only then that I noticed he wasn't armed.

I headed back on a diagonal road leading to Boghar, forty miles away. I heard the heavy cough of the Chinese Drushkas several miles before I arrived. The positions hadn't changed since yesterday, but the fighting had. The air was filled with smoke and dust. No one was wandering about. The black tents had disappeared and no little girls in red dresses went to fetch water. Puffs of white dust kept rising all around as the Ben Bellists used their heavy artillery.

Standing by a huge concrete French water tower, I saw a patrol of Wilaya Four emerge from the brush. They approached with their fingers on their triggers. The bloodstains on my trousers and shirt made them suspicious. They looked very tough and fierce, but when they learned what had happened they said, "Thanks to God you were saved. Thanks to God you were saved," and put their arms around me half to console me and half to comfort themselves. Then they set off toward another line of hills nearby.

The fighting went on until late in the evening. Ben Bella arrived by French helicopter at about eight o'clock and scrambled about on his hands and knees between the lines, trying to get them to stop. Earlier in the afternoon he'd visited Orléansville and brought off a truce there. And at ten o'clock the firing ceased at Boghar. ▶

The civil war was over. Algeria was independent. And Ben Bella was Premier. He proclaimed the new nation to be socialist, neutralist and non-aligned, and he accepted continuing French aid as well as a $100 million long-term loan from Russia. But the country fell into economic chaos, the European *colons* who had run it left by the hundreds of thousands, and the Moslems were untrained to take it over. Ben Bella spent his energies in international politics, and in June 1965 Colonel Boumedienne took the government from him and put him away in a series of secret villas.

After achieving independence, Algeria developed a new three-cornered problem: its power was in its army, the third largest and perhaps the best equipped in all of Africa. And within the army a three-way rivalry grew among the old guerrilla chiefs, the Moslem military experts schooled and experienced in the French army, and the bright young Soviet-trained officers who understood the hundreds of millions of dollars' worth of Russian military equipment that had been pouring into Algeria since 1963.

All these dazzling missiles, tanks and planes gave Colonel Boumedienne a sense of power among his neighbors, but among the poverty-ridden people of Algeria, long sick of war, the feeling was that they had seven years of it—and that's enough.

XII

Revolt in Hungary

(1956)

"You can take so much and that's enough and you'll fight at any odds."
JOHN SADOVY, *Budapest, 1956*

F EW REPORTERS have been so prepared to see and feel and record an historic event as was John Sadovy when he entered Hungary from Austria in October 1956, to cover the uprising against the Communist government there. At thirty-one, he was a British subject who had won his citizenship fighting in the British army against the Germans who had earlier invaded his homeland, Czechoslovakia. To escape the Hitler Youth program he had fled

187

to Hungary and then to Yugoslavia. He stayed alive by working on farms and begging food, and he kept moving—just ahead of the Germans. In 1941 he found his way to Cairo on a fishing boat. Too young to be taken into the British army, he hung around units and did handyman's work. "It was clothes and food to me," he recalls. "It was a way to live." By the time his outfit moved to Italy and began to fight up the eastern seaboard, he had been signed into the ranks. He became a British army photographer. The only way to get good pictures, he learned, was to stay ahead of the infantry. Several times he fell behind enemy lines. He was captured in 1944 and got away. "By 1945," he recalls, "resistance, revolt and fighting was all that I could remember. My entire youth had been spent in this. It was the only world I knew. Like all of my generation in that part of Europe, I learned one thing that will never leave me: you can take so much and that's enough and you'll fight at any odds."

At the end of World War II, Stalin began the colonization of eastern Europe from the Baltic to the Balkans. Close to his own borders and as far south as Bulgaria, he was successful, but by 1956, as the Russians siphoned off food and resources from this captive area and met increasing hostility with increasing restrictive measures, an undertone of challenge to Soviet authority spread. Khrushchev, feeling the threatening pressures and fearful of open resistance such as had been shown in Yugoslavia, made his momentous destalinization speech in February 1956, and by condemning Stalin's acts of oppression, seemed to promise a new, enlightened rule and the return of dignity and freedom to a captive people.

In this, Khrushchev showed a remarkable misreading of the consequences. For it was the steps he took to alleviate the danger of soaring public resentment against the repressive regime of the Soviet Union that led to the open expression of that resentment, and this in turn to open revolt. It was Poland that rose first. And it was the success of this revolt that encouraged the Hungarians to think—and then desperately to hope—that they too could win their demands. But the conditions in Poland were very different from those in Hungary. The Polish victory was largely a consequence of two circumstances: the first was their history of extraordinary feats of resistance in the war against both the Germans and the Russians. In 1956 the Polish Security Corps was superbly equipped and trained and unquestionably loyal to the Polish leaders. And the Russians had no heart to face this kind of resistance again at this uncertain hour. The second circumstance was more important: it was the Polish Communist leaders themselves who led the demands for liberalization of Soviet repressive controls, and they held unbroken ranks. In Hungary it was quite the other way: the Communist Party leaders stood against the popular demands for liberalization of controls, and they had major differences over what the course of action should be.

Tamas Aczel, one of Hungary's leading novelists and a political writer, was present at the critical hour of the uprising of the populace in Budapest. He himself—until sometime during those early hours of revolt—was a Communist. He describes the failure of the Hungarian Communist leaders to understand the universality of the public demands, or even the substance of those demands. Imre Nagy was the one Hungarian Communist who had the trust of the populace: at that hour only he could lead them. Two hundred thousand people packed Budapest's Parliament Square that day, October 23, when the revolt turned to violence. As the people pressed upon each other, closer and closer, they began to chant: "Russians, go home. Russians, go home." Then they called for Nagy: "Imre Nagy. We want Imre Nagy." It grew into a din. "Imre Nagy. Where are you. Show yourself."

Aczel, a close friend of Nagy, realizing the gravity of the development, made his way out of the square, found his car, and drove to Nagy's villa in Buda. There were others already there on the same mission. "You have to go immediately," someone was saying. "There is not a minute to lose." Aczel's account continues:

▶ Nagy looked tired and irresolute. He glanced at me. "You have come from the square?"

I nodded. "Uncle Imre, the crowd is calling for you. For God's sake, why do you wait? If you do not start immediately, something awful is going to happen."

Someone said that it might already be too late and Nagy answered irritably, "How can I be late? Late for what?" He rose slowly to his feet. "Very well," he said. "I shall go. But I doubt that it will do any good." He turned to me. "Aczel, will you take me in your car?"

During the descent of the steep hills of Buda he was silent. Finally he asked, "How big is the crowd?"

"Tremendous," I said. "Perhaps two hundred thousand. More."

He said nothing until we had crossed the Danube and entered the crowds. Then, peering out of the car, he suddenly exclaimed, "Look! Look at that flag in the window!" It was the Hungarian flag but with the hammer and sickle of the Communist revolution cut out of the center. Nagy twisted around in his seat to look at other windows. "But all the flags are like that," he gasped. "What can be happening?" He took out his handkerchief to wipe his forehead, though the air was cold.

It was about eight o'clock in the evening when we entered the square and pushed through to one of the main gates of the Parliament. A young actor appeared on the balcony to declaim the famous poem: "Up on your feet, Hungarians, the country calls. . . ." And the crowd roared the refrain: "We swear, we swear by the Hungarians' God, that we shall no longer be slaves."

People made way for us and we went up the stairs and Nagy went through the door that opened on the balcony. I followed him, pausing at the door. The instant he showed himself the crowd below fell silent.

"Comrades," Nagy began. Then an incredible thing happened. From the dark, heaving mass in the square rose an inchoate cry of wrath. Nagy stopped, bewildered, as from one voice came the words, "We are not comrades."

Now, suddenly, everything was clear to me. Hungarians were finished with the old, discreditable, disreputable things; not just the Red army, the old Stalinist clique, but all the hackneyed falsities of Communism. Nagy was staggered. He seemed to hesitate and his eyes roved despairingly over the crowd, as if seeking a clue to its anger. Did he grasp even then what was really in its brooding mind? I don't know. All I am sure of is that at this instant of matchless opportunity, with Budapest waiting for a true signal, Imre Nagy made the wrong speech. He could have saved the situation. He might even have saved Hungary from Soviet power. All he had to say was, "Hungarians, go to your factories and occupy them. Take leadership in your own hands. I am ordering your army to supply you with weapons." That was what Gomulka had done only a few days before, in Warsaw, though under less desperate circumstances. Instead, Imre Nagy said: "My friends, go home now and leave everything to us."

Perhaps that was the only speech that Nagy could have made. Much as he loathed Stalinism, he was irretrievably a Communist. He was a Communist talking, he hoped, to other Communists, and because of his mistake the Hungarian destiny at that instant slipped irretrievably out of his hands.

Even as he fidgeted on the balcony, trying to fathom the reason for the crowd's disapproval, a man lurched up to me and seized me by the lapels. "Aczel," he gasped, "you must tell Nagy that the AVH is shooting into the crowd at the radio station."

I started for the balcony to tell Nagy. But just as I reached him, from somewhere in the dark square, cutting across Nagy's halting words, boomed a voice of fantastic power: "Citizens. To the radio station. The AVH is shooting demonstrators." ▶

The AVH were the Soviet-controlled Hungarian secret police. In opening fire on the unarmed demonstrators they were following the pattern of brutality with which they had suppressed the Hungarian people up till now. But this time the citizens of Budapest had had enough. When the news spread of what was happening, people from all over the city rushed to join the demonstrators, and units of the Hungarian army, sent to keep order, turned instead and joined the citizens. Russian troops were moved in to put down the rebels and were fought off by these Hungarian soldiers as well as hastily armed young civilian "freedom fighters."

The next day Imre Nagy was reinstated as Premier and his wavering government struggled to give concessions to the rebels. New political parties formed; free-speaking newspapers were published. For a few euphoric days it seemed that Hungary had gained a step toward freedom. Though Russian tanks and soldiers were still in the streets, it was against the AVH that the rebels turned their wrath. It was this hatred, so well justified and yet so terrible to witness, that correspondent John Sadovy captured in his photographs and in the words of his report of an attack on an AVH headquarters in Budapest on October 30:

▶ We were roving the town, looking at burned-out tanks, bodies covered with lime—trying to capture the horror going on. A partisan came along and said, "They are shooting on the other side of the city."

As we went we were passed by lorries packed with screaming women and boys with guns and revolvers. Guns they hardly knew how to use. As they went along they were jerking them to see how they worked. There were two or three of these lorries going into that fire. I later learned they were rebel reinforcements just picked up off the street.

We came into a square. There was grass in it and small trees. You could go for a walk there with your dog. We heard shooting. Then we saw a tank facing a large modern building at the end of the square. It was the AVH headquarters, someone said. The rebels were trying to take this headquarters. And the AVH were in there shooting at them from the windows.

My first instinct was to get behind the tank. There would be some shelter there and I would be close enough to take pictures. Halfway to the tank we found ourselves in the open park. Bullets began zinging past our ears. We fell flat on our faces. I tried to hide behind a young tree. I wished my tree were bigger and I tried to make myself smaller. I was still hoping to get behind the tank, but then it moved off. There we were, stuck, a half a dozen rebels and myself. It was not very nice there.

I started to crawl back through the park until I got to a shed and some bushes which provided cover. The fighting really began to flare up. People were dropping all around me. I crawled nearer and nearer to the building. There was great movement and activity all around me. White-coated first-aid people, mostly women, were coming and going, collecting the wounded. Then I noticed that the Red Cross people were being shot too. Now it was suicide to go in there. The women stopped going, and youngsters took over. They were magnificent—fifteen-, sixteen-, seventeen-year-old kids. They ran in there with no protection at all. A kid ran in, half bent over. He put a man on his back and dragged him to shelter. Now, many were at it. Young boys in two's, flat on the ground, some pulling stretchers, getting to the wounded and dragging them back. Nothing could stop them. One was hit. His partner dragged the stretcher with one end on the ground. It was incredible to see. Still they went out there. Some came back limping. Just kids.

A lorry arrived. It had ammunition for the tank. There was a scramble to carry the heavy shells—two or three to a shell, like people who haven't eaten for weeks scrambling for bread, with a fury and excitement. The ammunition was going to make a difference. They loaded the tank which went back and kept up a tempo of firing against the outside of the building.

Suddenly we saw a scurry of people. Then a tank, another tank, a third, a fourth—five in a row—flying Hungarian flags. Then there was a dead silence. No shooting, no shouting. A fantastic suspense. A feeling of what's happened now? Four or five minutes went by like this. Now there were more tanks coming and a mass of people tore off. They thought the tanks might have come to help the secret police. Nearly everyone who could run ran. Over the bushes, through fences, they went madly without thinking what they were going through—two hundred of them. I began photographing the people running over the fence and a Red Cross girl dragged me away, saying, "Don't run now, it's too late." She dragged me behind a car. Others were scrambling under cars, anywhere for shelter.

One of the tanks kept turning his turret 360° slowly, very slowly. And every so often I would be looking into the barrel of his gun. I had little confidence. I just calculated very simply that they might not fire.

They were four meters from us. Nobody knew what was going on. Then one of the newcomer tanks shot at the building and after a while the rebels on the ground began to move in closer. You would see three and four men lined up behind a tree. Then you would look again and the men were four bodies on the ground. A child couldn't hide behind those trees. But you could see the rebels gaining more confidence. Moving up. Now there was silence from the building.

I managed to get in front of the tank, flat on the ground. The heat of its gun going off was unpleasant, like opening the door of a hot oven. They were plastering the building wall. There was a thick tree there and a pile of something, I forget what it was, but I got behind it and stuck it out for a while and took a few pictures.

Suddenly there was noise of people running. They were running toward the AVH building. Now they were closing in fast. I went in with the first group. There were three of us together, myself and two German-speaking rebels. We met another group led by a man carrying a huge flag. "Come on, come on, we made it. It's ours," he was saying.

Other groups of rebels were coming in from the side, screaming. There would be no half measures here. Now there was only occasional machine-gun fire from the top floor. The tanks were still shooting and bricks fell from the building when the tanks blasted it. It was 3:15. People were still being careful. There were two burned-out lorries in front of the building with seven burned bodies under them. The people had crawled there for shelter and been caught. It was a mess in front of the building. At least thirty to forty dead were sprawled there. They got it going in, one after another. They were lying almost in line. When one was shot, the next one took his place. All dead now. Each of them silent. It was like a potato field. Only these were people instead of potatoes.

Now you could feel confidence sweeping the crowd. They advanced right to the main door of the building. The AVH began to come out. The first man to emerge was an officer, alone. It was the fastest killing I ever saw. He came out laughing and next thing I knew he was flat on the ground, his legs spread, dead as anyone could be. For an instant it didn't dawn on me this man was shot. He just fell down, I thought. Then the first group, the bravest of the lot, decided to go inside the building. They brought out a good-looking officer, his face white as chalk. He got five yards, retreated, argued. Folded up. It was over with him. They went back again and two came out together. There was a scuffle. An array of rifle butts, punching, kicking. Suddenly there was a shot. The two just dropped.

Six young officers came out, one very good-looking. Their shoulder boards were torn off. They wore no hats. They had a quick argument. "We're not so bad as you think we are. Give us a chance," they were saying. I was three feet from that group. Suddenly one began to fold. I hardly heard a shot. They must have been so close that the man's body acted as a silencer. Now they were going down the way you'd cut corn. Very gracefully. They folded up smoothly, in slow motion. And when they were on the ground the rebels were still loading lead into them.

They were all officers in that building. Another came out, running. He saw his friends dead, turned, headed for the crowd to take shelter among them. They dragged him out. He gave up with his hands up. Then he walked back six or eight meters. I had time to take one picture of him standing there, wind the film, the impact, wind film, he was down. There was something so dreadful about it. These people gave themselves up. They saw. They stood there and knew they were dead.

Then my nerves went. The tears started coming down my cheeks. I spent three years in the war, but nothing compares with this—so inhuman and so very correct, when you knew the background. The two extremes too powerful. No matter how you hate a man, you don't do this. It's worse than animal. I could see the impact of bullets on a man's clothes. You could see every bullet. Not much noise, they were shooting so close. Only by little signs you knew what was happening, then you knew with dreadful monotony. This was going on for forty minutes.

Then came a last scuffle at the building entrance. They brought out a little boy. They were carrying him on their shoulders. He was three or three and a half, with a sweet face, looking left and right. There were shouts of, "Don't kill him, save him." He was the son of one of the AVH officers. To see this little face after what you'd seen a minute ago brought it back. These were still people. It had been a bad dream and he woke you up.

Going back through the park, I saw the women looking for their men among the bodies on the ground. They lifted the flags that had been put on them to try to find their people. Then I sat down on a tree trunk. My knees were beginning to give in. It was from the weight of it. Like carrying something I couldn't carry any more. In some way one is responsible for what other humans do. ▶

For several days the Russians hesitated, reluctant to use raw power if the Hungarian Communists could control the revolution. But even as they announced that they were ready to negotiate withdrawal of their troops, Soviet agents were maneuvering the government's downfall and Soviet tanks and men were massing for a full invasion. On November 1, Imre Nagy appealed to the United Nations, calling for outside help, but, as before, he was too late. At dawn on November 4 the Russian tanks came rumbling into Budapest, moving implacably, the weight of a giant nation riding their guns, shooting down resistance until the last of it was crushed.

The Nagy government collapsed and Nagy himself was seized, imprisoned, and later tried and executed for "counterrevolutionary conspiracy." Two hundred thousand Hungarians fled into exile, leaving behind them three thousand dead and thirteen thousand wounded in their brief fight for liberty —and the survivors tighter than ever in the grip of Soviet power.

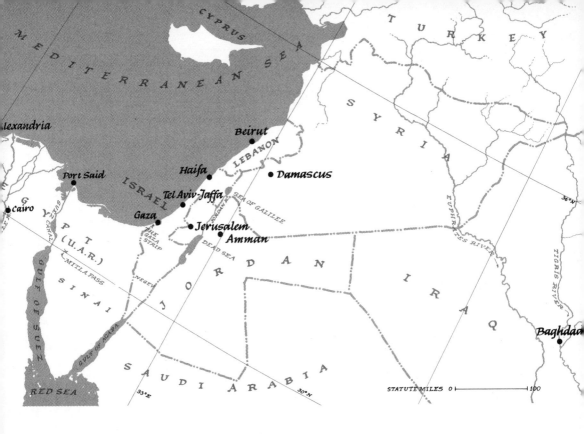

XIII

The Suez-Sinai Campaign

(1956)

T HE BLATANT USE of power, when it is successful, is never amusing. Only when the aggressors have been goaded into frenzied action and their elaborate plans are botched, does the situation take on humor. The pull and haul of conflicting interests in the Middle East after World War II was so fraught with irritations and frustrations for the countries of the West that sooner or later some ill-considered action seemed inevitable. All the big

196

powers had tried their hand at intervention there. But it was the French and British who passed the bounds of good sense in October 1956 and were made fools of by both their friends and enemies.

In July 1952 there had been a revolution in Egypt. Fat, dissolute King Farouk was out, and no one mourned for him. Clean, young Gamal Abdel Nasser and his idealistic officers were in. They hated Britain, but they talked the kind of government that was appealing to the Western nations as a whole. And to Israel, surrounded for four years by countries threatening her annihilation, it seemed that in democratic Nasser she might have a friend as a neighbor for a change.

These high hopes did not last. By 1956, Nasser, ambitious to make himself the leader of the entire Arab world, was playing on their anti-Western and anti-Israeli fears. His terrorist *fedayeen* were raiding Israeli territory and, having barred Israeli shipping from the Suez Canal, he was blockading it in the Gulf of Aqaba. Moreover, he was aiding the Algerian FLN against the French. He was pressuring moderate Arab nations to turn out their British friends, had compelled the British to remove their military base from the Suez area, and now was threatening to nationalize control of the Canal—the lifeline for British oil from the Middle East. Worst of all for the Americans, who were still mesmerized by the Cold War, he was accepting arms not from the United States but from the Soviet bloc.

The Americans found him very difficult to deal with. He insulted them at every opportunity, opposed the Baghdad Pact against the Communists which the U.S. had worked so hard to organize, attended the Bandung Conference which they frowned upon, and in the meantime asked them for a loan. Americans at that time were in the throes of moral rectitude: Nasser's acts were evil, but his need was great. Egypt was starving for lack of irrigated land and needed to build a high dam at Aswan. The loan, therefore, was offered. Five months later Nasser recognized the Communist Chinese, and the loan was abruptly canceled. That was on July 19. On July 26, Nasser nationalized the Suez Canal Company.

It was not the United States which found this slap most challenging. Its interests in the Middle East could not compare with the involvement of the French, the British and the Israelis. It was these three who hatched the plot that failed. Their target was not only the Suez Canal; it was Nasser himself, his downfall and political demise. Their timetable had been worked out with scrupulous care, but even for the most perspicacious statesman there are things unforeseeable lurking behind the opaque veil of time. And one of these statesmen, Prime Minister Anthony Eden of Britain, was ill to the point of exhaustion and beyond cool judgment.

The hope was that if the Israelis moved their army against the Egyptians in the Sinai Peninsula and dropped parachutists in the area of Suez, the British and French could step in as peacemakers before the United Nations had a chance to move. They could issue an ultimatum to both belligerents (Egypt, it was presumed, would fight) to withdraw their forces ten miles from the Canal. Then they could put their own peace-keeping soldiers in to occupy the zone. The timing was geared to the American elections on November 6, when their anti-imperialist ally would be too preoccupied to intervene. A solid plan. What was it that went wrong?

The Hungarians rebelled. The Israelis, already warned by the United States not to retaliate against Egyptian provocation, felt that the U.S., the U.S.S.R. and the U.N. would be too concerned with the Hungarian revolt to take note of what was going on in Egypt. Perhaps this was a naive estimation of the West's solicitude for freedom, but they were only the third party, lately drawn in, to the Franco-British plot, and had to do some thinking on their own. On October 29, so suddenly that they themselves had hardly time to know what they were doing, their army rolled across the border into Sinai and a battalion of their paratroopers dropped near the Mitla Pass, less than fifty miles from the Canal. They fought extremely well, and the Egyptians reeled. But they had jumped the gun by several days.

Very seldom is there such a thing as a "model military operation" in modern warfare. Many people called the seven-day Israeli campaign against the Egyptians in the Sinai Peninsula such a model of success, and it was indeed a brilliant execution of attack procedure. But there were mistakes made and there were extenuating circumstances surrounding the Egyptians' defeat. Although they had long built up their forces in the area, the sudden strike took the Egyptians, as it took the rest of the world, by surprise. And they had Britain and France to contend with in the Suez area itself just two days after the Israeli army swept across their border 150 miles to the east.

Nevertheless, the defeat was remarkable. The armies in the field were fairly matched in number—somewhat less than a hundred thousand men on either side—and in heavy armor. The Egyptians held well-fortified positions set behind minefields and barbed-wire entanglements. What the Israelis had, overwhelmingly, was spirit, especially among their officers. And this is what the Egyptians most vitally lacked.

The key to the Israeli victory, their secret weapon, according to one observer of the campaign, was "sheer effrontery." Their army's high command held to such dictums as, "Success comes when leaders lead instead of push-ing," "Leading means moving to the point of main danger," and "When in doubt, hit out," and their officers and men believed and acted on them. The results were that nearly half of all the army's casualties were among its leaders, that only one man was captured in the whole campaign and he was a wounded pilot who was shot down behind the enemy lines, and that the Israelis won their objectives—covering hundreds of miles of "sea sand" desert and rocky defile, fighting as they went—in seven days. Sometimes they drove right through Egyptian positions, running the gauntlet of their entrench-ments; sometimes they swirled around them using seemingly impassable tracks; sometimes they literally carried their bogged vehicles over miles of shifting sand. Theirs was the spirit of a citizen army with full faith in their command and the necessity of their cause.

Their cause was indeed urgent. For the eight years since her birth, Israel had been beset by hostile neighbors. Her frontiers had been drawn—some said with a heavy china crayon on a small-scale map—through a compromise of international argument far from the scene and the fortuitous positions of the rival armies when the cease-fire came into effect. Sometimes the boundary cut a farmer from his fields or a hamlet from its well, and this gave rise, especially along the Israel-Jordan line, to border violations, raids and counter-raids and clashes of patrols, growing more organized and vicious as time went on.

Israel's need to "make the desert bloom" in order to accommodate the flow of immigrants made it imperative that she have irrigated land. When she drained the Hula marshes near the Syrian frontier, the Syrians shot at the Israeli engineers and the settlers who tried to work the land. The settlers fired back. The indiscriminate firing grew, in time, to organized clashes, shelling and aerial bombing. Similarly, in the south, along the Israel-Egypt borders of the Gaza Strip and the Negev, Israeli settlers clashed with the neighboring Arabs, many of them displaced from their former homes in Palestine. In the early years these clashes were for the most part little skirmishes between patrols, but as the settlers moved south, opening new land with piped-in water, the raids grew bitter. Arab bands sneaked deep into Israeli territory and cut the water lines, stole crops and stock, harassed the farmers in the kibbutz settlements. The Israelis organized the Nahal, "Pioneer Fighting Youth," as part of their military forces to guard these frontier settlements and they became a dramatic symbol of the new Israel: bronzed young men and women fighting with one hand, farming with the other.

Thus did Israel see herself embattled on every side. Arab propaganda constantly poured forth threats to attack and overrun her, wipe the new nation from the map forever, and in 1954 Nasser, who had been preoccupied with internal problems, began to put into action some of the threats he had been voicing. All along, despite United Nations pressure, he had barred Israeli shipping from the Suez Canal; now he increased his harassment of it in the Gulf of Aqaba. In 1955 he organized the commando *fedayeen* to make raids deep into Israel, throwing bombs in the cities, ambushing vehicles along the open roads, murdering farmers, burning farms. Also he reinforced his troops in Sinai and the Gaza area until at one time he had some sixty thousand soldiers—a large proportion of his army—arrayed against the Israelis.

There were many clashes, and in 1956 the whole frontier was smoldering dangerously. In that year, too, the tension between Israel and Jordan had mounted almost to the explosion point. Jordan had massed her army near the border and was allowing Egyptian *fedayeen* to base their raids in her territory. On her invitation, Iraqi troops were moving up to her assistance in case of war, and in October she joined a military alliance with Egypt and Syria, the three armies to be under Egyptian command. The Jordanian chief of staff announced: "The day has come for the Arabs to choose the appropriate time to launch the assault for Israel's destruction."

It was instead the Israelis who "chose the appropriate time." Britain and France were building up their airborne armies in Britain's Cyprus base, and should their planned attack go through, then, as the Israeli chief of staff said, "We should be like the cyclist who is riding uphill when a truck chances by and he grabs hold."

In actuality, the bicycle got ahead of the truck by several days and the British and French were put in an untenable position. Nevertheless, they carried on, regardless of appearances. When the Israelis struck, the United States requested the United Nations Security Council to call for an immediate cease-fire, for withdrawal of Israeli troops, and for all U.N. members to refrain from introducing military goods into the area. The British and French, stuck with their plan, were compelled to veto this resolution. Moreover, they were forced by it to issue their own ultimatum to the belligerents far ahead of schedule. And since not even the handful of Israeli paratroopers were yet within forty miles of the Canal, let alone ten, the ultimatum had a very hollow ring. Next day, when their air-force units bombed Egyptian bases, any pretext that they were acting as peacemakers became downright farcical.

Meanwhile the Israeli bicycle was acting more like a tank with a souped-up engine that some daring youth had made to work through sheer determination. The call-up of the Israeli army had taken three days. All Israeli men and women undergo military training of at least two years and are on call for service wherever they may be. With this call, on October 26, 1956, they slammed their books shut, dropped their tools or left the plow mid-furrow, and reported to their units. Even the officers had scarcely time for briefing. But each had been trained to go it on his own. Thus it was an almost ragtag army that swept across the Sinai frontier just before nightfall on October 29. They seemed an amateur outfit, but their accomplishments were praised by the world's best professionals.

On the fifth day of the war, when the advance through Sinai had almost reached the Suez Canal, an Israeli battalion crossed the border of the Gaza Strip to the north. In the following report, correspondent George de Carvalho describes the exuberance—and the amateurish impression it produced—of the attack on the first Egyptian position at Ali Muntar, the primary defense point for the city of Gaza:

▶ At exactly six a.m. on Friday, November 3, thirty Israeli tanks clanked over a low crest, slamming shells in rapid fire, and headed over the wide open plowed fields straight for the Egyptian fortress of Ali Murtal jutting above the crest of the Ali Muntar ridge ahead. In the emplacements where they had waited and fired all night, the watching Israeli settlers of Nahal Oz, nearly half of them girls, let out a Hebrew cheer: "*Heydad! Heydad!*" Then the Egyptian mortars began kicking up around the tanks, and the settlers began firing again with their own American-made war-surplus battery.

Nahal Oz, which in Hebrew means Community of Courage, was a sitting duck amid the open fields, exactly 600 yards from the Gaza Strip border and 2,500 yards from the guns of Ali Murtal—just about top range for their artillery. The settlement was manned by a Nahal outfit of men and girls who guarded the border while they built the village and grew the crops. They carried guns on their tractors, dug slit trenches in the fields, and built a fortified emplacement between the border and their shrapnel-splashed huts.

On Monday, when the Israelis attacked across the Sinai border south of them, the settlers of Nahal Oz got word over their dug-in army telephone line and immediately moved into their trenches and began shooting too.

A young Nahal girl, Hannah Preer, told me afterward, "As soon as we got the word I began dropping shells into Ali Murtal right away." Hannah is twenty-two and a practiced mortar-gunner. "We kept it up all night, and every night, until now—four, eight, twelve rounds every few minutes to keep the Egyptians scared. We knew the army was busy in the south, and with five thousand Egyptians out there and us here alone, we just had to keep hitting."

Four days later, just before dawn, the tanks appeared, firing steadily as they crunched over the fire-blackened border strip. And then happened one of the most incredible things in this incredible war. About twenty silvery, mud-daubed Tel Aviv city buses drove up the dirt roadway a few hundred yards away and stopped in plain view of Ali Murtal. A blonde Dutch Nahal girl climbed out of her trench, Bren gun in hand, and laughed exultantly. "They're running excursions into Gaza already!"

Lean little Israeli troops, about six hundred of them, leaped out of the buses and loped across the fields in long, loose, fast-moving files. The Egyptians switched their fire from the tanks too late to get the buses which simply turned in a wide circle in the pasture and rumbled away as placidly as buses on Fifth Avenue. With no time wasted and no shuffling around, the troops headed over the mined border strip toward the enemy. In less than half an hour Ali Murtal fell, the Egyptians taking off on the run for Gaza. ▶

Gaza itself fell at noon that day, the fifth day of the war. On the sixth day the rest of the defensive positions on the Gaza Strip were taken and the whole enclave was in Israeli hands. In Sinai, forward detachments in the west were already overlooking the Suez Canal and in the south were heading for the southernmost tip of the peninsula and the fortress which guards the Gulf of Aqaba. It took another day and night, till the morning of November 5, to quiet that final outpost and complete the "model operation" of this little one-way war. Nearly 2,000 Egyptians had been killed to the Israelis' less than 200, and 5,881 prisoners had been taken to the Israelis' one. And the quantity of captured Egyptian war matériel was enormous: fifty million dollars' worth, including more than 2,000 vehicles, 200 pieces of artillery, 100 tanks.

On the day the Sinai campaign ended, November 5, British and French paratroopers landed at Port Said, and on the next their seaborne troops arrived. As usual with military operations which may seem bloodless when discussed in the chancelleries of safe capitals, the actuality of the Suez campaign was uglier than its conception. Correspondent Frank White found this contrast striking when he flew from the French-British base in Cyprus into Port Said on November 7, and sent this report:

▶ In Cyprus the impression was that it had been "an immaculate war." From the beginning the communiqués emphasized the small number of casualties, the deliberate effort to spare Egyptian life and property, the quick restoration of order. The three-day campaign against Egypt was an operation in which a task force of over one thousand British and French slammed into a well-armed strategic foothold and grabbed on. In the process it reduced a large part of Port Said to flaming ruins, cost a minimum of two thousand Egyptian and military dead, and left the remainder of the city's forty thousand population seething in the midst of food riots and smoldering hatred.

The contrast between the impression and the actual scene rose up for me when I alighted from a French plane just before noon on Wednesday. White, green and jet-black chutes still festooned Port Said's Gamil Airfield. Royal Air Force men had organized Egyptian work crews to clear the barbed-wire and oil-drum obstructions from the field. Bloodied but relaxed, British parachutists were well dug in. Their moment had come during and just after their drop. They had been nicked by machine-gun fire on the way down and then had regrouped and fought "the battle of Port Said cemetery."

The cemetery is a joint burial ground for Moslems and Christians and lies two miles from the Gamil strip on the main road to the city. Caught in a double envelopment, the Egyptian regulars took cover behind mounds and tombstones and fought back bitterly with mortars, machine guns and a few self-propelled guns. "They put up a bloody good fight," said a blond young paratroop lieutenant. "We had to go in and dig them out."

In one of the airfield's small repair buildings was a group of Egyptian prisoners. There were a couple of soldiers, one with a bandage around his head, eight civilians, and a tethered goat. The soldiers lay on rags in a dark corner, but one of the civilians came forward and wanted to talk in English. He said he'd been caught in the fighting at the cemetery where he and his brother and two cousins were burying his father. I asked him what he thought of Nasser and his chin quivered, his eyes watered, and he managed to square a pair of thin shoulders. "What do you think of Eden now?" he blurted. "Do you think he is a good man? Are you proud of him? Do you think we can fight the whole world?" The guards looked on coldly. Then one of them commented, "Civilians or soldiers, they all had guns when we got them."

The road into Port Said told some of the story of the struggle.

Slanting white sails of dhows sweeping across the inner estuary were etched against the background of a huge fire burning in the Esso refinery at the city's southern limit. Along the beach, row on row of German potato-masher grenades rigged as land mines sprouted like dirty vegetables. A burned-out self-propelled gun stood in the middle of the road and farther along two Egyptian ack-ack guns surrounded by empty shells peered out from the marsh grass. As we passed the cemetery where the fight had taken place the sweet, acid smell of death infected even the sea breeze.

Huge fires gutted the fashionable residential district just behind the waterfront. Because their solid structure offered the best protection for snipers, these buildings caught the brunt of the rocket and mortar attack, and driving along in the jeep I watched seven-story buildings waver and fall in on themselves, spewing up smoke and dust while telephone wires sprang into menacing tangles. In the poor quarter, one whole shanty-town district had been burned to the ground. Over an area equivalent to four city blocks, nothing stood higher than a mangled bedstead. Women were sifting ashes for anything they could find. I stopped and asked a survivor how many had died there. He just asked for water.

By Thursday, Port Said had been without food for four days. Shortly before dawn, people came down into the streets. Instead of being vague and remote, just viewing you coldly, their mood was desperate and hostile. By eight a.m. a crowd of over three thousand had surged into the market district. They charged a flour depot where hundred-kilo sacks were stored under sheds. Disregarding the guards armed with Sten guns, they pulled the sacks into the surrounding streets. Rifle fire broke out. A British tank lieutenant plainly did not like the situation and sent for orders. They were to break up the crowd. The muzzle of his great gun traversed and lowered like a big, annoyed, perplexed animal. But he didn't shoot. Not even a rifle. Instead he let women and children slit open the flour bags, scoop up double handfuls and run. Tragically, most of the flour sifted through their fingers. For blocks around, the streets were covered with the snowy silt.

The battle for food went on throughout the morning. I saw hundreds of men, women and children battling literally tooth and nail over a drum of half-putrid fish. British and French patrols were out, their tanks waddling through the streets, guns probing each side alley, but their potential menace seemed to scare no one. The struggle for food was more urgent. The crowds tore down the blinds of one shop after another, but they found little. A young man came over to our jeep. He pleaded:

"We're desperate here and everybody has a gun. Send somebody to make order." ▶

By late that afternoon, order was being restored. Supplies were unloaded for the populace from French and British ships, and toward evening the rioting and pillage tapered off. But the hatred for the conquerors did not diminish. Perversely, the defeated Egyptians seemed to think better of themselves, and of President Nasser, for their encounter with the Big Power nations. Correspondent Mohamed Wagdi, barred from Port Said by the occupying forces, entered the city disguised as a fisherman and talked to his fellow countrymen. Following is his report:

▶ The British hold their positions on the banks of Lake Manzallah, blocking any entrance to the city of Port Said, but they allow fishermen to come and go. However, as our small fishing boat approached, a helicopter flew low and looked us over carefully before waving us to proceed, and as we came ashore some were searched.

Nearby on a sandspit was a row of cottages, built of long reeds and slats of wood. Fishermen sat outside them, sipping their strong black tea. They talked freely. Every one had a story about how he fought the invading British and French. Every one remembered the number he had killed. "I was sitting right here on the shore of the lake with my rifle ready," said one young man with a long mustache. "The paratroopers began to come down. I killed twenty-five of them. But to tell you the truth, I fired at and actually killed only eighteen. The rest were drowned because their parachutes did not open. But I was ready to shoot them if they came up out of the water."

Another fellow squatted beside him sipping his tea silently. Then he looked up. "I fought them in the town," he said. "I was going out to sell my fish when I heard about them coming. I threw my basket of fish away and ran home and got my rifle. As I was going out, our street was blocked by a tank. I stood behind my door and started shooting. My neighbors did the same. When our ammunition was consumed we escaped over the roofs." Every one of these men is proud of what he did during the fighting. Their eyes glitter when they talk about it.

In the native quarter of the city itself, every other house has been destroyed or damaged. Many stand without balconies or windows. The whole scene is gloomy and depressing. Flies pile up on debris where human flesh is buried. Despite that, the inhabitants gather in groups, sit on the curbs and sip their coffee or tea. One wonders where they get their tea and coffee since all the shops are closed. But they want to indicate their passive resistance and non-cooperation with the occupation forces. There is a defiant look on their faces. Their presence in the streets in groups and sipping their drinks is in itself a form of defiance, since the British have repeatedly asked them to go back to work. British patrols go by in jeeps or on foot, but the inhabitants ignore them. They laugh or talk loudly as they pass, but rarely look at them.

The legend of another Stalingrad is growing up among the Port Said citizens. Four young men in *galabiahs* sat on the curb by the street. One of them showed his arm with a wound which he got from a bullet. They spoke of their glorious three days of fighting the British and French invaders. They told how they spent the whole time in the streets, never going home. They made it sound like an interesting game. "We were all in the streets," said a tall, lean fellow. "Their planes showed up overhead and started strafing us. We ran in the opposite direction. The plane made the turn and followed us. Then we changed our direction and ran back again. It was a kind of hide and seek."

With the same enthusiasm the group talked about their non-cooperation with the British. "Nowadays we sit down and do nothing," a young man said with pride. "The British tell us to cooperate with them, but we shall die before we do. We obey what our government tells us. We get word from Cairo now and then. We are advised to be patient and not to get excited. We are trying. You see us sitting in the streets and doing nothing." His eyes shone. "And we shall go on doing it!"   ▶

The United Nations came to the rescue of the defiant Port Said citizens. On November 5, in emergency assembly, they had established a U.N. Emergency Force to secure and supervise an end to the hostilities. And on November 7, Britain, France, Israel and Egypt all bowed to international pressure and accepted the U.N. call for a cease-fire. Two weeks later the first company of the United Nations Force arrived in Port Said, and in another month the last of the French and British troops withdrew from Egyptian soil. The Suez crisis, touched with human folly on every side, was ended. Only the withdrawal of the Israelis—still deep in Sinai—and the settlement of their differences with Egypt yet remained.

In March 1957 they did at last pull back behind those questionable borders that had been drawn in 1948. And Israel—that green and alien nation which Europeans had created on Palestinian soil—was once again encircled and harassed by hostile neighbors.

XIV

Yemen: The Battle for South Arabia

(1962-   )

IN SEPTEMBER 1962 a palace uprising in Yemen scattered or killed the royal family of Imam Muhammad al-Badr, and suddenly turned the world's attention to the fighting which was spreading over that ancient land. Few outsiders who learned of the new war could place Yemen very clearly in their mind's eye, nor could they recall very much about its history except, perhaps, to remember that it was the legendary land of the Queen of Sheba.

Its recorded history reaches back to the beginnings of the first millennium B.C., but its people, the Yemenis, had long receded from our evolving world and had hardly obtruded themselves beyond their own society since the Middle Ages. Yet the twentieth century, shrinking the globe and rushing like high water over its boundaries, swept into the Yemen conflict and turned it from a small war of tribal differences into another captive conflict of this generation: an international war-by-proxy, a war fed and supplied and inspired far from the hills and crags and blowing sands where the fighting was going on.

It is an irony that the outside world should have entered and extended the war there. The Yemenis have always distrusted foreigners. Many of their legends say there is safety in keeping them at a distance. And there is every likelihood that without foreign involvement, in this land where hate flares and dies with the course of the sun, this present conflict might have been resolved in months instead of years. But behind it there developed a fierce struggle in the Arab world between the Pan-Arab designs of Gamal Abdel Nasser and the resistance to them of King Feisal of Saudi Arabia. And the contending interests and influences of the British and the Russians and the Chinese and the United States were quickly drawn into it, giving the war global dimensions.

Egyptian troops joined the fight in Yemen almost as soon as it began, and by 1967 Nasser had nearly 60,000 soldiers in the field, for not only had he chosen Yemen as the battleground for a showdown in the Arab world, but he also saw his troops there advantageously positioned to challenge the fate of Aden and to harass the British, who had announced they would withdraw from their protectorate at Aden in 1968, thus relinquishing their last foothold on the Arabian Peninsula.

Yemen is a triangular land tucked into the elbow of the Arabian Peninsula. It has had, over the ages, an uncommon share of violence. It is a country where manhood is marked by the rifle which is habitually on a man's shoulder or within reach of his hand; nor is he often without his *jambiya,* a foot-long curved dagger which is strapped in a sheath on his stomach. "A Yemeni," it has been observed, "wears his weapons like men of other lands wear neckties." But they are not for dress. They have frequently found their mark, and they have punctuated the history of the land. Yemen's ruler Imam Yahyah was machine-gunned to death in 1948 with his grandchild in his arms. His son Ahmed the Devil, who spent most of his time, in spite of his great obesity, amusing himself with his forty harem women and his three wives, ruled by scimitar. When he felt that his tribal sheikhs failed in their obedience, he sometimes invited them to a great feast and then had them beheaded. He died on September 18, 1962, weakened by five bullets he received in an attempted coup. His son Badr had been the new Imam only eight days after that when Abdullah Sallal, son of a blacksmith, and a pro-Egyptian Yemeni who had become commander of the palace guard, turned the guns of his Soviet-made tanks on the palace in another coup. Badr escaped and fled into the mountains and rallied loyal tribesmen. Sallal, with Nasser's support, made himself President of the new Yemen Arab Republic. Thus began the present war in Yemen, in which more than a hundred thousand people—soldiers and civilians—have been killed.

The Yemenis on the side of Imam Badr are called Royalists; those fighting on the side of Sallal are Republicans whose tribesmen were soon joined by regular Egyptian forces. From the start of the revolution, the Republicans held San'a, Yemen's capital. Imam Badr, directing the war from mountain caves, swore to retake it.

Both Saudi Arabia, with vast mineral reserves on the Arabian Peninsula, and Britain, with its vital port of Aden, reacted with alarm when Egyptian troops poured into Yemen, and they in turn increased their support of the Royalists. Nasser retaliated against the British by stirring up and supporting South Arabian guerrillas within the neighboring British South Arabian Federation. Thus spread two contiguous wars. They were separate wars but also interwoven wars. And the fierce and internecine tribesmen in both were very much the same people who fight in much the same way, in the same cruel terrain of blowing deserts and moonlike mountains.

The Yemen war was five months old when, in February 1963, correspondent George de Carvalho, traveling by camel, donkey and often on foot, reached the Royalists. "Here in the mountains," he wrote, "only a thousand yards from the Egyptians, I met Captain Aly Achmed Almaydani, who has been fighting almost from the war's start." The young officer recalled how it began for him:

▶ "It was in the revolution's fifth day. Sallal had sent me with a planeload of troops to reinforce his garrison in Sada, in the center of northern Yemen. We went in an Ilyushin transport with a Russian crew. But when we flew over Sada, tribesmen fired their rifles at the plane. They had already taken the town and the airport. The Russians wanted to turn back, but I talked with my men and we decided to join the tribesmen. We forced the Russians to land. We burned their plane and sent them out to Aden. And we have been fighting for the Imam ever since." ►

Later, along the same front, de Carvalho found Sheikh Achmed Ibn Ali Ezedin, thirty-seven-year-old leader of Sirwah, bivouacked at his command post in the dry riverbed of a rocky wadi. He was gaunt and burning-eyed and profoundly committed to battle. It was at night and the Sheikh talked in his tent by lamplight.

► "When the Egyptians first came—two hundred men with six tanks—they were cocky men. 'We have come to help Yemen,' they told my brother, Mohammed, who was Sheikh then. My brother told them, 'We don't want your help or any foreign interference in our country. I'm chief here and I don't take orders from you.'

"The Egyptian commander told my brother, 'We are the strongest people in the Arab world and you must obey orders.' My brother said nothing. He took out his *jambiya* and stabbed the Egyptian commander dead with one stroke above the collarbone. The blade went all the way to his heart. There were nine Egyptian officers in the house and we killed them all with our guns and knives. Since then the Egyptians have come in force and the fighting has spread all over our country. Mohammed and my three other brothers have all been killed, and now I'm Sheikh. The Egyptians have tanks and armored cars and planes, and they have heavy guns that can shoot as far as a man can walk in five hours. We have only rifles and knives. But we will fight for vengeance year after year, and generation after generation. For every man killed, our women will give birth to two more. Eventually we will win because Allah helps the warriors of Islam against Egyptian dogs and infidels."

The Egyptian positions were very close and they kept firing brief machine-gun bursts during the night. At dawn they reached a sudden frenzied crescendo, hundreds of red tracers zipping overhead. The Sheikh grinned. "The Egyptians are frightened children shooting at shadows," he said. "By seven o'clock their planes will come from San'a." At seven sharp two Egyptian YAK fighters roared low overhead and dropped a string of anti-personnel bombs down the wadi and then circled back for a low strafing pass. They did no damage.

That night my guides and I moved around the Egyptian positions and headed west towards San'a. On the third night at midnight we reached Azzat village and the mud-house headquarters of Prince Abdullah Ibn Hassan, commander of the southeast San'a front. Just beyond was the Egyptian strong point at El Argoup, a massive bluff with sheer rock walls rising from surrounding ravines. In the morning we started toward it. Abdullah took rifle potshots at Egyptian tanks brazenly straddling the skyline. "A very dangerous position," he smiled. Then he said, "They have eighteen tanks and armored cars there. El Argoup and Jehanna, five miles beyond, are their strongest positions defending San'a. I have surrounded them both and am attacking them both."

Five hundred tribesmen in three separate groups had clawed their way up the steep ravine walls. Some wore khaki but many were fighting in the colors of their tribes, who dress in sarongs and turbans of eye-catching chartreuse, electric blue, flaming orange and shocking pink. They had been under fire all the way, but had managed to secure separate footholds. "Now we are going to charge and wipe them out," said Abdullah.

A mortar battery atop El Argoup opened up and fired at least six hundred rounds. T-54 tanks fired hundreds more—direct fire, pointblank at the tribesmen. Twenty Ilyushins, MIGs and YAKs, shuttled over all day and heavy bombs shattered and splintered the rock for hundreds of yards around. From the ravine below we could hear but not see the battle. The difference between the shattering reports of the Egyptians' barrages and the thin bursts of Yemeni rifle fire was dramatic. All day the tribesmen advanced only four hundred yards.

At dawn on the second day we began to climb ourselves. Soon we overtook about forty tribesmen crawling around three rock-roofed Egyptian machine-gun nests. Three dead Egyptians sprawled outside one of them which had been overrun and silenced. The two others, about a quarter of a mile apart, were burning out their barrels with belt-long bursts of fire at tribesmen less than a hundred yards away. Obviously the Yemeni were overrunning the Egyptians' first line of defense. They were pinned down but slithering around the rocks on both flanks toward a slight hill where three tanks were skylined against the blue.

My two escorts had been provided me way back at the start of my journey. "You are safe with them anywhere," I had been told. "They are very brave." Their names were Mohammed Ali Talib, who was twenty-six, and Abdul Wahab Mahmoud, a tiny fourteen-year-old, and they had been my companions of many days. We were lying in open ground, so we crawled forward about fifty yards and wedged into the rocks. The machine-gun bursts zipped over very high and we seemed safe enough as we watched half a dozen Yemeni leap up and run for the gun position, snap-shooting as they ran. The machine gun ripped at them and dropped one, but they kept going, and within seconds three Egyptians jumped out and tried to run. The Yemenis, only yards away, shot down all three.

Now the attacking Yemeni began crawling and leapfrogging slowly toward the hill. The tank guns swiveled around and slammed vicious airbursts all over the area. Suddenly Mahmoud, this little kid, jumped up and ran forward toward them. In each hand he had a grenade that he had taken from a dead Egyptian. "Get him back," I said hoarsely to Talib. "Let him fight," he said. But he went after him, crawling cautiously. The last I saw of Mahmoud alive, he was running madly toward the three tanks and they were firing both cannon and machine guns. Then I couldn't see the boy any more.

Later I found Talib again. He had been hit in the head and hurt badly. "It's not your fault," he gasped when he recognized me. After a while he spoke again. "Mahmoud was very brave." He had charged the tank with his hand grenades and was shot to pieces. Other tribesmen pulled his body back and then went after the tank and put it to flames.

Talib didn't speak any more. We were pinned down for many hours and he lay there, glazed eyes wide open, mouth frothing bloodily, but he stayed alive. When it was dark and we could move again, he was still breathing, but the Yemenis took his shoes and his dagger and rifle. I remembered how proud he was of his shoes and how he took them off and carried them in rough terrain to save them.

One of the tribesmen seemed to read my thoughts. "He doesn't need them any more," he said to me. During the night Talib died. ▶

In half a decade of battles, ambushes and erratic skirmishes like this, the war in Yemen was fought to a standstill by the tribesmen loyal to Imam Badr. The Egyptians, frustrated by years of a costly war they could not win, cut back their forces, gave up defending their extensive lines, and consolidated their positions along the coastal plain and in the main towns of the south, thus establishing a de facto partition of the country. In 1967, when the war with Israel began, they withdrew half of their troops from Yemen, and after that brief and devastating conflict they were compelled by the conservative and oil-rich Arab nations to withdraw the rest of their troops in return for a subsidy and a Saudi Arabian promise to halt their aid to the Royalists.

The war in Yemen reverted to an internal conflict and there was hope that a cease-fire might be arranged, but that would demand negotiations and agreement among the Yemeni, and, as in the past, such talks became "a dialogue of the deaf," as a despairing sheikh remarked. "Both sides talk but neither listens." Meanwhile the neighboring war for control of Aden continued in a complexity of disintegrating sheikhdoms and contending rebel groups.

As early as 1964, Nasser, stalemated in Yemen, had turned his attention to the training and support of terrorist organizations whose purpose was to disrupt the vital port of Aden with its naval base and nearby airfield and force the British to abandon their South Arabian protectorate. That conflict spilled over into the Radfan Mountains, which rim the Yemen border, and the battle that was waged there between British units and South Arabian guerrillas was interlocked with the war in Yemen, each of the belligerents supplying the other's enemy.

In June of that year, correspondent Jordan Bonfante reached the British forces who were battling fierce tribesmen known as the Red Wolves of the Radfan, sixty miles north of Aden. As the following dispatch he sent from there shows, he witnessed a war that was in many ways a throwback to the wars that Kipling saw:

▶ Packs grating against crumbling rock, hands reaching for tenuous holds, three hundred paratroops and commandos felt their way down the nearly sheer cliff. Two thousand feet below them at the bottom of a three-sided canyon was the start of a long narrow wadi of pleasant green flatland. It was a fertile pocket hidden like a Shangri-La deep in the tangle of the mountains and nobody knew what or who would be there. When they reached the bottom, the men advanced cautiously with guns at the ready.

For a while there was silence in the wadi. The riflemen, part of the British Third Paratroop Battalion and the Forty-fifth Royal Marine Commandos, had deliberately passed up the more attractive sloping route into the canyon in favor of climbing straight down the cliff face that closed it off. With that they had taken the enemy by surprise, but only momentarily. The Red Wolves of the Radfan were waiting in force. After a few yards, heavy rifle and automatic-weapon fire opened up on the advancing troops from a hilltop fort above their right front and from unseen nests in the flanking rock cliffs.

During most of the morning the expedition was nearly pinned down.

Red berets of the Red Devil paratroopers and floppy field-caps of commandos bobbed from cover to cover, darting from rocks to brush, advancing with painful slowness by force of machine guns and mortars. Signalmen panted under their heavy loads as they inched forward. Medics sprinted up to help the wounded. As a commando platoon scrambled over a wall, a marine rifleman from Liverpool was hit in the neck. "Sir!" the marine said to his platoon leader, and then he died in the officer's arms.

A lofting army scout helicopter carrying the Third Paratroop Battalion commander was hit fifteen times before it got fifteen feet off the ground. The helicopter plunged to a crash landing and the occupants leaped out and rushed to cover. On the ground a paratrooper ran to their rescue. He was wounded across the stomach and hit again in the knee as he tried to get out of the open.

Finally, with Hawker Hunter jet fighters scream-diving overhead and support artillery lobbing over the canyon walls, the enemy fire was lifted and the attackers swept over abandoned enemy positions. By then two men had been killed and five had been wounded. On the other side at least six of the enemy were dead. But by midafternoon the British troops were in control of the wadi Dhubsan, and they had cracked into the very core of resistance of the Radfan and had penetrated deep into a region so remote that there is no record that any Europeans had ever been there before.

The prize was a forsaken wasteland of desert and rock at the southern edge of the Arabian Peninsula. Barren dark hills rise out of the desert like whales' backs in a yellow sea. Silver oil-refinery tanks glitter on the sand like giant stacks of newly minted dimes.

The battleground is a forbidding range of other-worldly mountains. Red and black like the volcanoes that created them ages ago, as fruitless as ash, these craggy peaks of burnt rock sprawl formlessly over one of the most primitive and remote back corners of the earth. From the air the Radfan can look like so much scar tissue, the color of coagulated blood.

The rebellious Red Wolves are the diehards among the bellicose primitive tribesmen of the area. Garbed in turbans and *gutahs*, only a few hundred strong, they are as skilled in the use of firearms and the ornate curved *jambiya* daggers as they are instinctively expert at canny concealment and navigation among the countless caves and crevices of the red rock mountains they inhabit. They can hide so well in a rock-barricaded *sangar* that a patrol passing five yards away may fail to see them. And they are such savage warriors that they are capable of decapitating a fallen enemy at a stroke, as they did to two British soldiers a month ago at the start of the hostilities.

Pitted against the Red Wolves are some three thousand crack British troops of various arms, two battalions of the local Arab army of the South Arabian Federation which is still largely under the command of British officers, and an imposing air force of jet fighters, bombers, helicopters and other aircraft. All of them have converged into a dusty, sweating little war that has all the exotic trappings of a bygone age.

Britain, which has shed most of its nineteenth-century empire with uncommon grace, is defending it in the Radfan, one of her last colonial outposts. Here she is fighting what could be her last colonial war, a mechanized but vivid reversion to a Kiplingesque age of Arab Legions, desert rats and gunboat diplomacy. The pursuit of this British no-nonsense policy, in an Arabian Nights land of scorched desert, throbbing sun, moon mountains and camel caravans, has produced, on a small scale, faithful strokes of Victorian grandeur. Though the likes of the "Tins" and the "Blues" are only names fondly exchanged during mess gossip, other resonant regiments from Royal Scots to Queen's Royal Lancers are represented in strength. Officers of the Dragoon Guards lead convoys up the mined and sniper-menaced Dhala road. Gunnery specialists of the Royal Horse Artillery range 10-pounders onto rebel-ridden hills. At the camp of the battalion-strong King's Own Scottish Borderers, uniformed in shorts and tam-o'-shanters, it is bagpipes that sound reveille. And at the front, promptly in the afternoon at four, everything stops long enough for tea, served piping hot in tin cups despite blistering 120° temperatures.

"The British have a knack and a strange liking for messing about in nasty places," observes a senior British officer at Thumeir. "It's that sense that you mustn't let the side down. If we were so equipped, I wouldn't be a bit surprised to find that we dressed for dinner here."

Thumeir, a dust-blown tent encampment on a plateau at the edge of the Radfan, serves as an advanced staging base for the British Radforce operations. Its only edifice worthy of name is a gray stone fort garrisoning federal guard troops and it looks like a Beau Geste Christmas toy beside the roaring instruments of contemporary warfare. Ash-fine dust that can render a man anonymous in a few minutes blows as high as the surrounding hills when kicked up by incessant battle traffic. Convoys roll through from north and south. Tanks and Ferret armored cars rumble out to positions in the hills. Helicopters and other transport aircraft raise mushroom clouds of dust beneath them on the airstrip.

The only meaningful land communication across the bulk of South Arabia is the Dhala road, and that was where the Radfan war was provoked in the first place. This north-south route runs sixty miles from the coast at Aden to Thumeir, then another twenty to the medieval town of Dhala near the Yemen border. It is hardly a real road, just a way to get there.

Traditionally, the Radfani tribesmen have supplemented a meager living scratched from their barren land with professional brigandage. The rifle is the supreme status symbol. When they are not shooting each other over wells or patches of arable land, the Radfani take enthusiastically to raiding and banditry on travelers, even pilgrims bound for Mecca, principally on the Dhala road. This spring they were at it again, this time with far more than their usual gusto. Brigandage had turned into insurrection. Armed now with an abundance of automatic rifles and machine guns, many of them from Egypt, they put up roadblocks, then descended from the hills onto trapped vehicles or sniped from their hidden perches. With British mines hoarded since their capture at Suez in 1956, or simply a primed hand grenade under a rock, they blew up British and Arab civilian vehicles alike. Three British soldiers were killed by mines. The British have fought them back many times. What gained the Radfan conflict world attention this time was the decapitation of two British soldiers.

Provoked by the atrocity, the British intensified their military operations. The Dhala road was secured and turned over to patrols for surveillance. And shock troops began elbowing their way into the unknown rebel territory to the east.

Before they pushed off into the jagged, moonlit emptiness of the Radfan, their brigadier explained to his commandos what this operation was all about. "This is a small area, but a terribly important one to us," he said. "Much is at stake for us in South Arabia now, and if we prove ourselves here it will have a great effect on our whole position in the Middle East. Make no mistake about it." ▶

But it was beyond the power of the brigadier to change the course of history. The war in the Radfan was only an incident in the continuing conflict over the British state of Aden and the sixteen sultanates and sheikhdoms which made up the Federation of South Arabia. Britain's colonial past was dead—despite the dash and courage of her men in the world's "nasty places." In February 1966 the Labor government announced that Britain would pull her forces out of Aden no later than January 1968. Her problem, as it developed, was to find someone to whom she could hand the power of government there.

By the end of 1966 two rival nationalist organizations—the National Liberation Front and the Front for Liberation of Occupied South Yemen—had emerged from the welter of terrorist groups which had been indulging in indiscriminate killing as a means of gaining independence. In 1967, having won their point, they turned increasingly from terrorizing the British to fighting with each other for control of their government when the British withdrew. In September the flimsy Federation, which the British had stitched together and supported, finally collapsed. The sultans, sheikhs and emirs of the little member states evaporated into self-protective exile or were in the hands of the nationalists. And on November 28 the British High Commissioner pronounced South Arabia independent. The following day the British withdrew the last of their troops from Aden, and on November 30 a new nation, the People's Republic of South Yemen, was proclaimed, with the National Liberation Front the victor in the bloody internal struggle for power.

Thus while the war in Yemen still flared, the conflict in the South Arabian regions abated. But the internal problems of this vital area, which sits astride more than half the oil reserves of the non-Communist world, continued to be a center of international concern.

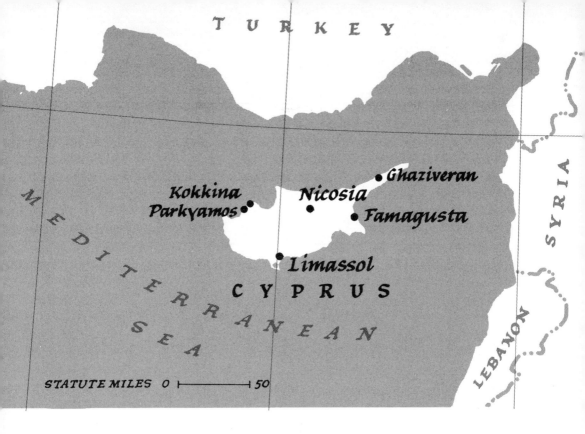

XV

Cyprus: "The Trouble"

(1963-   )

B RITISH RELUCTANCE to pull out of South Arabia was motivated by more
than national interest. As her power ebbed after World War II and
the tide of her empire receded, it left in its wake violent struggles among the
peoples who were freed of imperial restraints. Despite the delicate and sincere
efforts of the British to provide against disorder as they withdrew from those
lands, bloodshed and often chaos swirled in behind them. Often the causes

were deep-seated human conflicts which even today seem insoluble. Such was the case on Cyprus.

Cyprus is a sun-baked island standing high in the blue Mediterranean. Shaped like a cello, it is only 60 miles wide, and nearly a third of its 140 miles in length lies in the narrow strip that is its finger board. Through the centuries, Cypriots looking northward have seen the edge of Asia Minor only 40 miles away. And in these centuries the outposts of great empires have met on Cyprus, and the Cypriots have been molded by those who came—some with the sword and the cross, some with the scimitar and the faith of Islam—and left behind their culture and religion.

Geographically and strategically, Cyprus connects most logically with Turkey, yet there are 500,000 Cypriots with Greek origins, and only 100,000 with Turkish. And the island's ties with Greece, going back to the Mycenaean age, are far older than its bonds with Turkey. Almost all of Cyprus' history has been under foreign rule. After its long association with the Hellenic and Alexandrine Greeks came four centuries under Roman occupation, eight under the Byzantines, another three under a Frankish kingdom, and a hundred years of Venetian rule. The Turks are relative late-comers. They took Cyprus from the Venetians in the sixteenth century. The British got it from the Turks in 1878 when they secretly agreed to assist them against Russian encroachment and extracted the right to occupy and administer the island as their price. In 1914, when they went to war against the Turks, the British annexed the island, and in 1925 they made it a Crown Colony.

The surge for independence among colonial peoples after World War II swept over Cyprus too, and in the summer of 1960, after more than two thousand years of foreign domination, and after several years of futile counter-action by the British against the EOKA, the Greek Cypriot terrorist army, Cyprus at last won its freedom. The power behind this victory was a politico-religious leader, the young Archbishop Makarios of the Greek Orthodox Church on Cyprus. Almost immediately the independence of this new republic led to internal dissension; independence had a far different meaning for the Greek Cypriots than did independence won in any other anti-colonial war. For, once won, the goal was to give it up again in order to carry out the age-old plan of *enosis:* union with Greece, the motherland.

To the Turkish Cypriots, *enosis* meant surrendering their independence to yet another foreign power. They saw themselves threatened as a tiny minority within Greece; what they want instead is partition. "Makarios has offered us minority rights," Vice President Fazil Kuchuk, leader of the Turkish community on Cyprus, said. "But we are not merely a minority. We

219

are an ethnic community. We want to live as our own masters, not as servants."

This difference is what the present war on Cyprus is all about—this, and all those other differences which have come down through the centuries and have kept separate the Greeks and Turks who live beside each other on a small island.

When Britain agreed to withdraw from Cyprus, a constitution was worked out which carefully assured the Turkish Cypriot minority of their civil rights. In the constitution's "Treaty of Guarantee" the Turks were given a broad representation in the police force and the army, and a veto on all "important matters." Greece and Turkey and the United Kingdom, which retained military bases on the island, assured the "independence, territorial integrity and security of Cyprus." Archbishop Makarios became its first President, with Kuchuk the Vice President. In 1960, in the republic's first year, it proudly became a member of the United Nations.

But soon after the republic's birth the Greek Cypriots made it clear that they would demand that the constitution be revised, and early in December 1963 Archbishop Makarios presented thirteen revisions to Vice President Kuchuk, many of them curtailments of Turkish rights and representation. Kuchuk angrily rejected the revisions. Antagonisms sharpened and voices were raised in both communities. It is not clear who fired the first shots on the night of December 21, but Greek police in civilian clothes and Turkish civilians engaged in a gunfight in the Turkish quarters in Nicosia, and two Turks were killed and five wounded. Bitter recriminations swept through the mixed communities. Both the Turks and the Greeks began to organize themselves and prepare for their own defense, and on December 24, heavy fighting broke out in the capital. The constitution provided that 10,000 British troops remain on the island, along with 950 Greek and 650 Turkish soldiers, to keep the peace and enforce the constitution. Instead, Greek and Turkish troops joined in the battle.

Soon the fighting erupted in other cities, fragmenting them into enclaves of besieged and besiegers. And it rushed through the countryside, where in many small villages the people abandoned all their possessions to seek the shelter of larger gatherings of their ethnic groups. In others, the peasants turned their villages into stockades to fight off attacks. The desperate plight of one such village was reported by correspondent Rudolph Chelminski, who made his way into the little Turkish settlement of Ghaziveran while it was under a Greek Cypriot assault:

► Ghaziveran is a shabby crossroads hamlet some forty miles north of Cyprus' capital city of Nicosia. It has one main street at right angles to the road, the end of which peters out in a dirt track. There's one café there, a dirty little mud building with a Bel-Kola sign in front. Usually a dog is asleep in the dust. Roughly seven hundred people live there—no one is sure of the exact number, only that every single soul is a Turk. That is why war came to Ghaziveran last week.

When the nasty, brutal little bloodletting now known as "the Cyprus trouble" began, the fifth of the population that is Turkish acted with a unanimity that almost seemed a race instinct. They drew back— away from the Greeks, and into pockets of isolated but homogeneous humanity that really amount to herds.

Ghaziveran, one of the many herding places, had the ill fortune to lie between two Greek towns. To the Turks this meant they were surrounded. They threw up roadblocks, one at either end of the village. Protection, they said, from marauding Greeks. "Illegal gangsterism," said the Greeks, "arbitrarily blocking the main route from Morphou to Xeros."

At four a.m. on a cool, foggy Thursday morning two bands of Greek special police forces came to do something about it. Their men were well-armed and wore full combat uniforms complete with helmets and ammunition belts. Drawing up at a safe distance from either roadblock, they demanded through a bullhorn that the Turks get out of their positions and surrender their arms and clear the road. An hour and a half later the firing began.

By midmorning the village was completely surrounded. Behind an armored bulldozer parked on a dirt trail leading off the main road, a little knot of Greek fighters sprawled in ditches and behind sandbags. With no apparent object in mind, one man would open up with a rifle, aimed in the general direction of the village. From across the way other arms in the circle would answer him. Then, for perhaps thirty seconds, an angry chorus of popping, clattering fire would go chopping into Ghaziveran. From the woods and orange groves mortar shells arced in and landed with a distant thwunk, echoing powerfully across the fields.

The men defending Ghaziveran were a sorry lot, almost laughable, so pathetic were their means. Three of them stood behind a shoulder-high mud wall on the eastern edge of town, peering suspiciously out across the fields. Behind them chickens clucked and scampered nervously through the dust. One man's uniform was an old soccer jersey. Another

221

wore a motorcycle crash-helmet. The rest were bareheaded.

Around the corner, in the main room of an adobe house, a few dozen women, children and old men huddled for safety. One ancient, white-bearded man leaned for support on his vintage shotgun. Too old to fight, he apparently had been deputized to guard the women as best he could, should the Greeks enter the town. His eyes were full of tears, and he cried without a sound. In the back of the room a woman suddenly became hysterical and collapsed on a couch, ululating in long, repetitive phrases.

Niyazzi Hassan, the village leader, was a grim-faced, gray-haired man of about forty, who looked sadly incongruous in his crumpled suit and necktie. "The Greeks want us to give up our arms," he said through an interpreter. "That would be like dying."

The fire became even more intense, and all the women and children were ordered into the town's schoolhouse, Ghaziveran's one modern structure. Carrying wretched little bundles of bedclothes, they streamed from their hiding places up the main street and into the building's three main rooms. Bullets flew overhead and the frightened women literally dragged their small children across the dangerous open ground. Not a male was in sight, except for a few aged invalids or outright babies. Every single man was at the ring of outposts.

Inside the school the refugees huddled on the concrete floor, a great, seething mass of humanity crammed together. The air was dank and humid. No light penetrated, since all the shutters were closed in a pathetic, meaningless gesture of self-protection. Gay paper cutouts schoolchildren had done a few days before still adorned the walls. They were barely visible through the gloom. A steady note, the moaning of many female voices, rolled out through the three doors.

Outside in the street the scene was chaotic. A fresh volley of Greek fire cut through overhead. The more distant bullets whined and lost themselves somewhere in the distance, but the nearer ones cracked angrily like a vicious whip. A few stragglers danced crazily forward in terror toward the schoolhouse, not knowing which way to dodge for cover, since the fire came from all directions. From the edges of the town came the occasional whoosh of a bazooka being fired, then a rumbling explosion as the charge landed. Sudden bursts of machine-gun fire, gathering together in the same spot, meant that the Greeks had found a Turk in the open.

As night fell the Greek fighters slowly began talling back. But no

Turks left the schoolhouse and the men didn't come back into the village until daybreak. Then it was time to count the dead. Already by nightfall there had been two known dead, perhaps three. Now a jeep made its way to the isolated posts. They found the first of the dead in an orange grove. He was lying face down under a small tree, a youth about seventeen. In his deserted sandbag bunker there were a few empty cartridge casings and a dirty plate. Apparently he had taken a meal there. The dead boy's brother came with two friends and carried the body away.

Farther to the east there was another bunker on the edge of an open field, shouldering up on one side to a line of saplings. Three men lay dead there, one by the entrance, another perhaps five feet farther and the third about twenty feet away toward the town. Apparently the three had run out of ammunition and tried to make a break for it in broad daylight. They were cut down in their tracks by a crossfire which came from three sides.

As the morning sun came higher the women and children straggled out of the schoolhouse. Now they filled the street in a moaning, wailing mob, grieving for their dead, or simply weeping in their common bond of despair. Bare-bottomed babies took up the chorus.

In a few minutes a car came by, carrying the bodies off to a burial place. One old man watched with dull eyes as the vehicle drove past. He squatted on the ground, his body shaken with convulsions and his voice producing over and over again the rhythmic Ah-ha, Ah-ha, Ah-ha of a man in hysterics. He had lost two sons and a brother. ▶

Associate Judge Saleh Dayioglou, of the Cyprus Supreme Constitutional Court, sounded the fear and despair which had come of the communal killings: "Oh my God, oh my God!" he cried. "What can we do? What will happen next? We cannot give up our arms. We need them to defend ourselves and we don't even have enough to protect our people. Wherever Turks surrender and give up their guns our young men are kidnapped and killed, our women raped. What can the United Nations do? What can the world do to stop this slaughter?"

The United Nations was already trying. When the communal war broke out, the U.N. Security Council met in New York to consider steps necessary to place a peace-keeping force on the island, and its machinery was moving toward that end. Meanwhile the fighting continued—in the villages and in the cities, where Greek and Turk lived side-by-side in their separate quarters.

In the following dispatch, correspondent Timothy Green tells what it was like in the besieged Turkish enclave of Limassol when the Greeks attacked:

▶ For almost seventy-two hours this week the heaviest fighting that Cyprus has seen since her independence raged in the narrow streets of the seaport of Limassol on the south coast of the island. It was triggered off by the Greek and Turkish Cypriot communities contesting control of the ancient Berengeria Castle, overlooking both the port and the Greek and Turkish communities. Greek Cypriot police, aided by steel-helmeted men openly wearing EOKA armbands and backed up by three home-made tanks, also launched an all-out assault on the six thousand Turks surrounded in their square-mile quarter by the thirty thousand Greeks of Limassol.

The Nicosia-Limassol road that runs for sixty miles through lonely countryside and rocky, bare hills was almost completely devoid of traffic except for an occasional British army truck. Our car kept in tight convoy as we raced southward. When we reached the outskirts of Limassol, life seemed to be going on as usual. Stores and gas stations were open, people appeared to be going about their business as usual. But as we headed farther into town we saw only groups of men standing in bunches on street corners and doorways staring west. Some waved to us to stop, but we kept on going, twisting through back streets to avoid main roads which might have checkpoints.

Soon the streets were completely deserted. All houses and stores were shuttered and boarded up. Ahead came a crack of rifle fire. Suddenly we came out into an open space of a hundred yards between the houses where a narrow bridge spanned a small river. As we sped over the bridge, a Bren gun fired a volley somewhere to our right. Then our brakes went full on. Lying across the road in front of us were a series of plastic bombs with wires trailing to a house just off the bridge. We were running the gauntlet into the Turkish quarter and they had laid the bombs as a first line of defense. As we sat feeling very exposed out on the bridge, a man in a balaclava helmet and an old military greatcoat and toting a Sten gun waved us forward. We shot ahead and spun into a side-turning. We had made it into the besieged Turkish quarter. As we piled out of the car, Turks from nearby buildings shouted to us to keep low—"There are bullets flying everywhere"—and beckoned us into the shelter of the Turkish community center.

The community center, with a statue of Ataturk in front of it with the inscription "Turks, be proud, work and be truthful," had been hurriedly turned into a makeshift hospital and refuge center for people driven from their homes. A haggard, unshaven Turkish doctor greeted us. "My own clinic up the road has been attacked and captured by the Greeks. We have been forced back here with little equipment. Almost all our medical supplies are gone. We are trying to treat fifteen wounded men in here." One long room at the back of the community center was a sad scene of turmoil. At one end the pallid, injured men lay on tightly packed beds. In one corner nurses and another tired-eyed doctor were giving blood transfusions to an old man who had just been carried in. At the other end of the dimly lit room, two hundred women and children sat huddled on beds and chairs.

A man in a torn green sweater, with two grenades stuck in his belt, took us from the community center through a series of back gardens, shattered houses and holes torn in walls, toward the firing line. There in a narrow alleyway the Turks had thrown up hasty barricades of rocks, boxes, oil drums and an overturned cart. Behind each barricade crouched half a dozen unshaven men clutching shotguns and old rifles. One or two had Sten guns. "Many of these men do not really know how to use their rifles," said our guide. "They have just had them put into their hands." A man in a steel helmet and denims came running up the street clutching a red canvas bag in his hand. Behind the barricades he passed out new ammunition. Up at one end of the alley an ancient truck had been swung broadside as an extra defense. Two Turks slipped out of a doorway, trailing wires behind them, and, crouching down behind the truck, fixed a packet of four sticks of TNT to the back axle. "We shall blow it up if the Greeks try to come through," said one as he dodged back to cover.

A hundred yards away around a corner came a heavy explosion, and a cloud of smoke and dust rose into the air over the buildings. "That will be the Greek tanks moving in," said a Turk. "The Greeks have put armored plating around bulldozers and are using them as tanks. Come and see." He led us up a narrow dark stairway to the third floor of a bullet-riddled building. A Turkish Bren-gunner crouched in one room behind closed shutters in which he had cut a small hole for his gun. He pulled back his gun barrel and pointed out to a street just visible through a small grove of lemon trees. An ungainly vehicle was wallowing forward. It looked at best like a World War I tank, or perhaps an outsized kitchen range. It was in fact a bulldozer with a sheet-steel shroud all around it. A few little portholes had been cut in the sides and through those the Greek

Cypriots were firing machine and Bren guns and lobbing grenades. Farther up the street was another tank of slightly superior vintage. This one was composed of an old Sherman tank, tracks and chassis, on which a homemade turret had been erected. From the turret fluttered the white-and-yellow flag of Cyprus. Neither appeared to be equipped with heavy guns; rather they were used as armored personnel carriers. But the Turks were not deterred by these strange monsters rumbling up and down the streets. They had tied sticks of TNT to long poles which they maneuvered out of windows and into the middle of the street. Then they waited to detonate them if the tanks came too close. Evidently the tank drivers could see the bombs and they kept them at bay for the moment.

As the morning wore on, the tension back at the community center mounted. "Why don't the British troops come in?" asked one man, with a plaster on his forehead, as he kept guard in a doorway. "Why doesn't someone do something?" ▶

The British were making every effort to reestablish order, but under the terms in which they operated on the island they could not move to try to end the shooting while political discussions were going on between the Greek and Turkish Cypriot leaders. By the time they were empowered to act and had arranged a cease-fire in Limassol, sixteen Turks had died and thirty-five had been wounded in three more days of fighting in the city.

In the countryside small British patrols went shuttling between the combatants, talking to each side, listening, talking again, showing enormous restraint. But in the heat of communal hatreds they could make small headway, and only on occasion accomplished a brief local truce. On February 22, correspondent George de Carvalho accompanied such a unit and drew a picture of the manner in which it operated:

▶ One wild stormy afternoon a British convoy of two Ferret armored cars and two radio armored squad carriers with ten riflemen crawled up a winding dirt track in the north Cyprus hills to stop a Greco-Turkish gun battle.

Silvery sunrays glowed bright between huge black thunderheads billowing high in the sky. Lightning streaked out of the clouds. And between thunderbolts, thin bursts of rifle and Bren gun fire crackled across the gnarled green hills.

Laboriously the armored vehicles backed around right hairpin curves, climbing high above the green-black Mediterranean which

226

foamed against the rock-encrusted coast below. "Bloody mess this is," said a British major, glowering at the lovely rain-soaked landscape.

Several hundred Greeks and Turks along the ridgelines were shooting intermittently—ring ping tututut—across the mud-brown plowed fields, sloping green pastures, olive groves and cherry and almond trees already blossoming white and pink. Brief Bren-gun bursts spattered into the dirt track ahead. "Nice welcome," said the major glumly.

Stopping, he called HQ and said, "Sixty-three X-Ray. Sixty-three X-Ray. There's lots of shooting in the hills here, some of it our way. I'm investigating. Over." He sent one Ferret a thousand yards ahead and, standing silhouetted on the ridgeline, scanned the hills lengthily with field glasses.

Nothing moved except a few distant flocks of white sheep and black goats. From Kokkina, a Turkish village on the coast below, came the radio message: "One one tango. One one tango. There's heavy firing down the coast road. Situation getting worse. Over."

The major answered, "O.K., I'll come back down. Try to find the village headmen. I'll get them to stop the shooting—if they can." To HQ he reported, "Trying to find leaders with sufficient authority to order cease-fire."

At Kokkina a hatchet-faced village headman, Ali Riza, was waiting in a whitewashed coffee shop crowded with gun-toting excited village youths.

"The Greeks attacked us twice in the last month and now they've come again," he snapped. "They have five hundred men and more are coming. We have to shoot to stop them."

The major said, "Well, you stop shooting and call your men back and I'll get the Greeks to do the same. We must have a cease-fire by nightfall." "I will stop shooting if they stop," the headman said, "but we must keep our men out. If the Greeks get on top of those ridges they will fire right into our homes. We have three Turkish villages here with less than a thousand people and there are ten thousand Greeks living around us."

The major said, "All right, let's get the cease-fire first, then worry about withdrawal. Send word to your men within an hour: cease-fire at six-thirty. I will send someone to Parkyamos and get the Greeks to agree."

Sunset stained clouds purple as I drove with a captain and four soldiers in a Land-Rover along a tortuous coast road to Parkyamos.

Enroute we dropped off two Tommygun-toting messengers, who scurried up the hills with the cease-fire order. Rounding a corner, we saw in the dusky gloom a Bren-gun crew of four Turks walking single file. They dropped flat and we drove on.

A mile down the road, armed Greeks met us outside Parkyamos. The local organization boss, a handsome young schoolteacher who refused to give his name, complained bitterly: "This is the third Turkish attack here this month. The first time they killed one Greek and the second time they kidnapped fifteen hostages. We gathered all our men and they released the hostages. Now they've been shooting at us for two days and we are just standing here. Today they fired ten thousand rounds and we fired only ten or fifteen, to cover the withdrawal of some people pinned down by their fire."

He glared at the dark hills still crackling with gunfire: "If they keep shooting we will kill them all. We have gathered our men and we can wipe them out in twelve hours."

Suddenly Bren-gun bursts spattered down the road: the Turkish crew was opening up. We backed behind a sandbagged cottage. Furiously, the Greek leader snapped: "You say you've arranged a cease-fire at six-thirty. Well, it's almost six-thirty now. If they keep shooting, we will finish them off once and for all. We will not leave one Turkish house standing or one Turk alive."

Soothingly the captain said, "The Turks haven't had time to send word around to everybody yet. Set the cease-fire for seven-thirty and I guarantee they'll comply. We will station troops on both sides to make sure."

Scornfully the Greek said, "Your troops only make sure of trouble. Wherever you British go the Turks start shooting. Where do they get their Bren guns? Where do they get all this ammunition? If you didn't come, the Turks wouldn't have supplies and wouldn't dare make trouble."

The captain brushed off the accusation: "I cannot discuss politics. We were called in by your government to help stop the fighting. If you agree to the cease-fire tonight, we will try to get all the Turks back into their villages."

Grudgingly the Greek said, "All right, cease-fire at seven-thirty. Tell the Turks if they make more trouble we will kill them all within twelve hours. We are strong enough." Looking straight into the Briton's eyes, he added slowly: "And we will attack anybody who gets in our way."

Headlights on, we sped back to Kokkina, driving straight past the

Turkish Bren-gun crew. "The headman better get word to them fast," the captain said. In the coffeehouse he told Ali Riza: "You are in great danger if the fighting keeps on. For your own sake, you better stop shooting before seven-thirty. The Greeks have promised not to attack unless you keep firing."

"Promises will not save us," said the headman. "We must fight to save ourselves. We will stop firing, but we will not withdraw. If the Greeks get the ridges, we will be at their mercy and they will kill us all."

"Our troops will protect both sides," the captain said. "Don't worry about the ridges now, but for God's sake stop shooting." It was seven and shots still cracked in the hills. The headman sent out more messengers.

The captain ordered one platoon to make camp in Kokkina and another to accompany us back to Parkyamos. When the two trucks pulled up, the Greek leader said, "I'm sorry, but you must go. We don't want you here."

The captain replied evenly, "You complain that the Turks are shooting at you. We have got them to cease firing and—"

"Listen," the Greek snapped. A distant Bren gun was firing short bursts: tutut tutut tutut.

"It's not quite seven-thirty," the captain said. "We are ready to station British troops here for your protection. They can make sure the Turks stop firing."

Coldly the Greek replied, "We don't need your protection. We don't want you here. We don't trust British troops."

The tall, blond, blue-eyed captain stared at the tough, curly-haired little Greek. "All right, we will leave," he said. "It's about seven-thirty now. We will report to headquarters and to the press if either side attacks or breaks the cease-fire."

"Don't worry," the Greek said. "Just leave us alone. And tell the Turks we are ready to kill them all. We know how to die, but we also know how to kill."

Later, driving alone over the dark hills to Nicosia, I listened for the guns, but they were still. Village streets were empty and cottages shuttered. Nothing stirred except armed men at the roadblocks, Turkish and Greek, springing up as the car approached. Otherwise Cyprus was quiet—deathly quiet. ▶

In this our shrinking world, each act of violence is like a pebble dropped in a pond: widening ripples spread fear and immediate counteraction in distant lands. The small and seemingly insignificant decision of the Greek

Cypriots, in August 1964, to break the cease-fire at Kokkina and capture the little seaside village once and for all brought such reaction. Though Kokkina with its population of some seven hundred Turkish farmers is of little interest even on Cyprus, it does command adjacent beaches that are the only landing areas in this vicinity over which outside supplies can be received, and the Greek decision brought immediate reaction from the government of Turkey. Two days after the Greeks had seized a portion of the Kokkina beachhead, Turkish jet fighters bombed and strafed the Greek positions and a Turkish invasion force set out to sea. The Greek government announced that it would send its own armed forces to the island, and the Greek Cypriots warned that at the first sight of the Turkish fleet they would annihilate all Turkish Cypriots. Archbishop Makarios appealed to the Soviet Union for assistance, and NATO, with two of its own key members on the very edge of war, met in emergency session. Once again the United Nations summoned the Security Council to deliberate, in its dazzling skyscraper on New York's East River, over the problems of that little Turkish village on a Mediterranean beach.

In March the council had set up an international policing force, known by the piquant name of UNFICYP—United Nations Peacekeeping Force in Cyprus. And now the British soldiers on the island shared their unrewarding task with Swedes, Danes, Finns, Canadians, Irish and Austrians.

Meanwhile, correspondent de Carvalho's view of this reverberating crisis in world affairs was brought down to a smaller scale, which is what the reporter more often sees when he reaches what those personally involved feel is the heart of the matter—the fighting front. This is his report:

▶ By the time I arrived from Nicosia the Greek Cypriots had encircled the entire Turkish position at Kokkina and the Turkish air force had heavily hit the Greek Cypriot positions. Both sides were dug in or hidden behind sandbags in huts and buildings and were shooting at each other. As we approached the area, a Turkish Sabre jet swished over, and the Greek Cypriots who were accompanying us stopped the tour, saying it was too dangerous, so we went on by ourselves.

Traffic was spare indeed, with only a couple of military Land-Rovers on the highway. Vehicles parked off the road were heavily camouflaged or hidden under trees. Villages were deserted. At Parkyamos, now the last Greek village behind the lines, rifles and machine guns were crackling. We stopped. We could hear the exchange of bullets and the chattering of the command-post field telephones. A hundred yards beyond the last house in Parkyamos, a bunch of Greek Cypriot guardsmen manned a roadside position. They were relaxed because the bullets whipped well overhead, and they were eating watermelon and brown bread with bitter goat cheese when we came up to them. They stopped eating long enough to denounce the United States and NATO for permitting the Turkish air strikes. Across the road, littered with rubble, an armored car was on its side, charred and smoking, tires still burning, six feet away from an enormous bomb crater. Next to it a fat wounded pig writhed once or twice and then died.

We went on and passed more burning cars and then reached a white armored vehicle marked with a blue U.N. Near it were two personnel carriers of a Swedish peace-keeping battalion. They had come only this morning to try to organize a cease-fire. The Swedish major kept saying, "Stop shooting, for God's sake. Why don't you stop shooting?" And the Greek commander snapped, "The Turks are shooting at us."

After a while, when it seemed the shooting was letting up, we decided that we ought to try to cross no-man's-land to the Turkish side and see the miserable little village over which the entire current Cyprus crisis had flared. It was a dubious decision, for both sides were nervous and inexperienced both in the use of arms and in the niceties of the white flag. But with the decision made and with white shirts fluttering from the car windows, we took off from the command post, moving slowly and cautiously. The Greeks had promised not to shoot at us, and we hoped that the Turks wouldn't. A few shots echoed from the hills above us as we twisted and curved along the narrow car-wide coastal road. On our left was the blue Mediterranean, and on the other side the parched, lethal hills followed us steadily. Suddenly we came upon and passed an armored car. We neither stopped nor looked. Then almost immediately we saw an entrenched position ahead, and on a ridge a hundred feet above the road were half a dozen fighting men. "That's the last of the Greek positions. From now on it's no-man's-land," I thought. But no! They were Turks! As we rounded a curve, half a dozen Turks leaped up from the roadside and thrust rifles and tommy guns at us. They looked fierce. We braked hard and threw up our hands. "American press," we shouted. As some began to lower their rifles, we pointed to the white shirts. They downed their weapons and some broke into smiles and waved us on. One Turk shouted in English: "The civilized world has come at last."

Kokkina was now jammed with more than two thousand civilians from five neighboring villages which had been overrun by the Greeks.

The women and children had at first been crowded into the cottages and public buildings, but as the Greek artillery began to land in the village itself, the noncombatants had been moved to the hillside above, into shallow caves and behind rock ledges. We could hear them digging there, making the caves deeper.

In quite a different sort of cave, not a thousand yards from the front line, we found thirty or so young Turks in green fatigues. Their beards were five days old and their faces showed that they were exhausted. Some were asleep, snoring loudly at high noon. They were students from the universities of Ankara and Istanbul who had been landed clandestinely from small boats to give support to the local Turkish Cypriots. They had no legal business fighting in Cyprus, but they were passionate in their conviction that their cause was just. After five days of battle these college kids and the local menfolk had lost much ground, but they still held a beachhead at least two miles wide over which life-saving help could come. For the first time the Greek Cypriots, after eight months of overwhelming victories, were being held.

"We volunteered," one student told me earnestly, "to save our fellow Turks from annihilation." And as we left, another shouted after us: "Tell the free world we don't want war. We only want to save the Turks from genocide." ▶

Slowly, under the patient and often seemingly hopeless efforts of United Nations peacekeeping teams, the fighting on Cyprus was brought to a standstill and the shooting petered out. There was nothing certain about the peace. Both communities continued the arms race with open and covert aid from foreign powers. Turkey and Greece each escalated their legally permitted garrison forces on the island with illegal landings at night. And the hatreds and fears which brought on the killings have only been rooted deeper and made potentially more dangerous by those very killings.

A hope, of course, lies in United Nations, which, yet in its infancy and stumbling in its inexperience, had already accomplished intermittent truces in several tinderbox areas of the world. Perhaps in each case the belligerents were ready to end their fighting, and the importance of United Nations peacekeeping units lay only in that they provided the vehicle. In any event, they did bring about cease-fires, transient and threatened as such cease-fires may be. And on Cyprus, as in other embittered areas, killing gave way to argument, and time was given a chance to heal.

STREET FIGHTING

A SECTION OF PHOTOGRAPHS

Turkish Cypriots crouch under fire in the streets of Limassol.

Hungarian rebels cover a street in Budapest.   *Michael Rougier*

British soldiers search the alleys in a Suez village.   *Larry Burrows*

Stones in the streets of Algiers. French security forces hold back rioting *colon* extremists protesting Algerian independence. *Dominique Berretty*

Sticks in an Athens square. Greek police battle Greek rioters protesting British control of Cyprus. *Megaleconomou Photos*

Viet Minh bombing creates havoc in the Place du Théâtre, Saigon.

Colombian rioters burn a government building in Bogotá.

East Germans stone Russian tanks in Berlin.   *Associated Press*

South Vietnamese are killed by a Viet Cong bomb.   *Le Minh*

A sniper shoots from a building ledge in Panama City.   *Eduardo Martinez*

A sniper's bullet hits a Vietnamese soldier in Saigon.   *Howard Sochurek*

An American paratrooper runs down a rebel-held street in Santo Domingo.   *Arthur Schatz*

A Cuban rebel races through a burning government army post.   *Andrew St. George*

Moslem dead in the streets of New Delhi, the aftermath of Hindu-Moslem rioting.　　*Max Desfor, AP*

Colombian dead in the streets of Bogotá after police opened fire on student rioters.   *United Press*

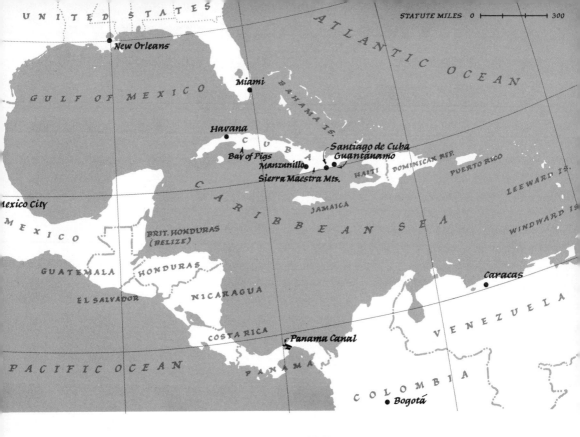

XVI

Revolution in Cuba

(1958-1959)

At the end of the last century, when the forces of the Spanish government were fighting the Cuban insurrectionists, a young British observer, Lieutenant Barnes of the Fourth Hussars, wrote a critique of that bitter struggle.

"The government forces in Cuba," he said, "were surrounded by fierce enemies. The countryside was densely wooded. There were no good roads.

This absence of communications had a most paralyzing effect on military movements; the mobility of the intangible enemy was, however, unimpaired. Moving swiftly by the tracks of the forest, the Cuban rebels harassed the Spanish columns and occasionally destroyed one. The Spanish held great numbers of towns and villages with strong garrisons and they defended or tried to defend long lines of communications. They treated the rebels as though they were merely agrarian rioters and attempted to subdue the revolt by quartering troops all over the country. But it was a war. And this the Spanish government would never recognize. After every petty guerrilla skirmish there were frequent executions and stern reprisals." These, he said, "threw a darker shade on the conflict."

More than half a century later, Lieutenant Barnes's report could, with only a few word changes, be placed in the record of how Fidel Castro fought his war against government troops—especially the British officer's observation that "the darker side of the conflict" came of "frequent executions and stern reprisals," for it was these in the end which turned the island populace from neutrality to active support of Castro, carrying him to victory with the same conspiratorial hatreds and individual courage which inspired their grandfathers to bring the Spanish down in 1898.

When Christopher Columbus arrived at Cuba nearly five hundred years ago, he called the island "the most beautiful land human eyes have ever beheld." Its balmy climate and rich soil lured Europeans to exploit its land and blackbirders to sail into Havana harbor with African slaves. On the backs of these wretched Negroes an elegant, sugar-based society came to flourish on the island.

While other Spanish colonies rebelled, Cuba remained quiet until 1868, when a planter named Carlos Manuel de Cespedes, crying, "Freedom or Death," inspired a ten-year revolt. Others followed, including the poet José Martí, who renewed the call for freedom and died fighting for it. He became Cuba's national hero. Spain declared that "Cuba shall remain Spanish though it takes the last man and the last peseta." And the Cubans replied, "We will be free, though we have to raise a tomb in each home." As the rebellion grew, the Spanish gathered the Cubans in huge concentration camps. In Havana province alone, fifty thousand prisoners starved to death.

American public opinion strongly supported the Cuban rebels and the United States sent a naval force to protect American lives and property. After the U.S.S. *Maine* was blown up in Havana harbor, the United States declared war on Spain and sent an invasion force to Cuba. The Spaniards soon surrendered and, in December 1898, relinquished all claims to Cuba. The United

States occupied the island for nearly four years, during which time a constitution was drawn up, largely modeled on that of the United States, and on May 20, 1902, Cuba gained her independence, although under the terms of the Platt Amendment the U.S. reserved the right to intervene in Cuban affairs and set up a naval base at Guantánamo. Cuba's first President, Tomás Estrada Palma, was elected that year and served his four years as an effective, honest leader. He died in poverty. After that, Cuba never knew an honest President. In the 1920's President Gerardo Machado coupled graft with terror. Known as "The Butcher," he rode in a $30,000 armored car and had some of his victims thrown to the sharks. He was unseated in 1933 after a revolution which cost twelve hundred lives. Seven Presidents followed him in seven years. All were dependent on one man-behind-the-scenes who rose in those years from orderly-room sergeant to king-maker—Fulgencio Batista.

Batista became President in 1940. He retired to Florida at the end of his four-year term to live in luxury on his graft. But in 1952 he led a military coup that deposed the current incumbent and, proclaiming himself Provisional President, he suspended the congress and wrote a new constitution. In 1954, as the only candidate, he was elected President. Under Batista, corruption became a way of government and Havana the Western Hemisphere's capital of lust and license. There were ten thousand harlots and as many panderers. Payoffs from prostitution and gambling ran into the millions. Batista's brother-in-law had charge of the slot machines.

Yet, despite corruption and license, Cuban economy continued to grow. Commerce thrived on the island and Batista's bribe of high wages to workers widened the consumer class and gave Cuba one of the highest standards of living in the Caribbean region. Batista used his labor bosses and they were good to each other. But honest men were revolted by his graft and his tyrannous rule.

Fidel Castro, a young lawyer who had run for congress in the 1952 elections which Batista canceled when he seized power, was only one of many who turned themselves toward ridding the island of "the Tyrant." Among those who felt as Castro did, and who later supported him when he built up his army in the Sierra Maestra Mountains, was perhaps as unlikely a group of conspirators as ever set out to overthrow a government. It included some of the country's top businessmen, bankers, doctors, lawyers and educators—precisely the kind of citizens who uphold governments, especially those under which they are so prosperous. The revolution that they envisioned proclaimed no social aims or radical changes in the economy. The early moves were plotted in the very best clubs and drawing rooms of Havana, and the revolutionary fervor grew not out of hunger but despite the handicap of a record prosperity.

These men were amateurs at making a revolution; and because they were, their final victory when Castro came to power cost them everything they had set out to win. Theirs was an almost personal revolt against Dictator Fulgencio Batista, whom they detested because he robbed Cuba of its liberty. In the beginning, Castro was just such an amateur as they. At dawn on July 26, 1953, he led a small unit in an assault on Santiago's Moncada military barracks and was overwhelmed by more than a thousand Batista troops. Castro's men were rounded up, seventy-five of them were shot, and Castro and his brother Raúl were tried and sent to prison. "It does not matter," Castro shouted at the judge. "History will absolve me." Two years later Batista declared an amnesty and both brothers were freed.

Fidel went into exile, first in the United States, then in Mexico, still dedicated to his revolution, which he named the 26th of July Movement after the date of his disastrous attack on the Moncada barracks. It was from Mexico that Castro set sail for the adventure which won him Cuba. On December 2, 1956, he landed with eighty-one seasick revolutionaries on the southern shore of Oriente province, six hundred miles from Havana. They were met by overwhelming Batista forces and only a dozen escaped capture or slaughter. Among them were Cuba's future leaders: Fidel and Raúl Castro and Ernesto "Che" Guevara, an Argentine doctor. These few remaining rebels reached their refuge in the Sierra Maestra, a region of sheer cliffs and impenetrable hills overgrown with vines and forest. From there Castro got word of his survival to a small underground of supporters, and in time weapons and food began to reach him both from Cuba and from abroad.

As the rebels' strength grew, Batista increased his military attacks on them; and his reprisals against those whom he suspected of supporting the 26th of July Movement, both in the cities and in the countryside, were carried out with incredible brutality and depravity. "It is government atrocities which are driving the people to Castro," an American political officer observed. "They are handing Castro a victory. If the government had surrounded Castro and left the people alone, Castro would have rotted in the hills."

As resistance spread, Batista's bullyboys enlarged their activities. They emasculated a fifteen-year-old boy accused of placing a bomb, and shipped the body back to his widowed mother. The chief of the Santiago police killed a businessman on the street and, as the dead man's wife ran to the body and wept, said: "Don't cry, madam. If you can't love him any more, you can love me." Later he caught up with Frank Pais García, an idealistic young teacher of twenty-one, head of the Castro movement in Oriente, and took him and the hardware-store owner who had hidden him, out back of the San Francisco Church in downtown Santiago and gunned them down. The next day the citizens of Santiago went out for seven days on a spontaneous one-hundred-percent strike. Eighty thousand people, nearly half of the city, turned out for the Pais funeral. "If the cops and troops move on us today," someone shouted during the funeral procession, "we'll attack them with our bare hands."

By mid-1958 Castro had a thousand armed men in the mountains, and an active underground of his 26th of July Movement permeated every Cuban city and reached into every hamlet.

In the last week of March 1958, correspondent Sam Halper, who had made contact with the rebel high command, was taken into the Sierra Maestra to visit Castro in his mountain lair. After passing succeeding tests at a number of military roadblocks, being transferred to a jeep and then to ponyback, and after being handed from guerrilla escort to guerrilla escort, Halper reached his goal:

▶ It was already dark when we came out of a thundering rain and stopped before a large barn made of palm fronds. Outside there was not a sentry, not a soul. Inside, the room was full of grandmas, wide-eyed children, kids wearing 26th of July armbands, a few fellows in uniforms, and there I saw Castro. He was a big man, over six feet tall, with a full, patchy beard so long that in moments of stress I later saw him take the ends in his mouth. He was talking and his voice had a curiously soft, almost womanlike tone as it droned. He was sitting under a dim kerosene lamp bracketed to the wall, rocking back and forth. Close around him kids sat on overturned five-gallon cans and listened to him, and old peasant women sat on benches and looked at him as though he were king. A couple of his troopers had transistor radios and they were turned on all the way, the noise blasting out. In the background, others played guitars. Marimbas shook, and girls dressed in their best for Castro's visit danced with boys wearing holstered guns at their sides.

A messenger came in with a package and Fidel opened it, took out what looked like a ballpoint pencil, and from the barrel unwound a typed message. He read this while a young man with a Christlike beard carefully shone a flashlight for him to see by. Eyes watched Fidel's every move, but he went on imperturbably, puffing at a cigar. He motioned me to a seat, looked at me with deep brown eyes and said: "You have come at the right time." When I told him I had made it in six hours, he laughed delightedly, cried the news in Spanish and said: "You have set a record." He asked me if I had eaten, and when he learned I had not, a middle-aged woman bustled off and soon in the kitchen I had a good meal of rice and meat served on a clean tablecloth. It smelled sweet and fresh despite the pigs and dogs grunting and snuffing on the dirt floor around my feet. After that I was given a bed behind a sheet-partition in the next room, and between the comings and goings of the women, I fell asleep to the soft voice of Fidel, talking on and on, answering questions and making declarations. It was like the rain on the roof. We marched early the next morning. "We are always moving," Castro later told me. "We have no encampment except for the night. No one ever knows where we are or where we are going. The physical exertion is good and we train by marching and fighting."

That morning the sun beat down on the rocky peaks, on the palm trees, on the long, straggling line of men walking over sheer trails cut into the gullies of the Sierra Maestra hills. *Guajiro* children in rags and torn shoes came out silently from the palm frond huts, stood in the doorways and watched. The soldiers looked up from their plodding and waved and the kids and their mothers and fathers waved back. Sweat poured down the rebels' faces, darkened clothes already stiff with the sweat of marching hundreds of miles, but they did not stop. Their order was ragged, they marched not like any army imaginable but more like riffraff, carrying their weapons every which way, but they marched without grousing, complaining or questioning.

In appearance Castro's army is the essence of a rabble in arms. They wear blue jeans, work-shirts, khaki pants, cheap green trousers, Truman shirts, Eisenhower jackets. Most are in semi-military dress if only for a forage cap, but no two are uniformed alike except that somewhere on each man is a red-and-black 26th of July emblem. Their weapons are corroding cow-plunkers, .22 target rifles, ancient double-barrel shotguns, Garands, Springfields, 1892 Spanish Mausers, a few .30-caliber machine guns. Nothing heavier. They wear sidearms—cheap, mail-order nickel-plate revolvers beginning to rust, and some businesslike automatics. On their backs they carry heavy packs—mostly produce sacks stuffed with a few clothes, a box of crackers, a few boxes of shells. And their waists are girdled with bayonets, hunting knives, frayed ammunition belts to which they tie two or three homemade hand grenades or Molotov cocktails made of beer bottles and cloth wicks.

There is not a single field radio, semaphore, walkie-talkie, field phone or anything resembling a modern communications device. All communication is by runner. Castro has no field company, no typewriters, no office. He usually writes lying full-length on a bed. Celia, his secretary, who on the trail is indistinguishable from any other trooper, carries a few letters in four or five plastic bags and regularly, usually at night, goes through them, rereading the little sweaty, folded slips of paper jammed with cramped writing, saving a few and crumpling the rest for burning. That is the army's complete record and file system.

At the end of a march the encampment is established in the most informal manner, each man hanging his hammock wherever his fancy takes him while the security outposts are set up with what seems a careless ease. In the morning the men normally get up before daybreak with no formal reveille other than the blaring of the transistor radios. They march an hour or two to get away from where they stayed the night before, then eat a breakfast which is actually a sort of brunch—maybe some dried shredded codfish, or bananas, or boiled yucca root, or raccoon, or boa constrictor. About midday someone may pass around canned condensed milk and everyone takes a swig or gets a little slice of a bar of sweetened guava candy. At night there may be rice, chickpeas or malanga root (the black bread of Fidel's revolutionaries) with some meat, all cooked in ten-gallon pails.

This is the army of Fidel Castro that after sixteen months threatens to topple the government of Cuba, whose forces are armed with some of the best military equipment in the world. It is in his men that Castro has his strength. Most of them are young—they start with downy-cheeked, girl-faced boys of fourteen and run to ripe old bearded men of thirty-one or thirty-two. The best of them—and they make up the majority of his columns—are the mountaineers of the Sierra Maestra. They are absolutely iron men. They will walk all day up and down the hills in the rain, ford streams, get over boulders, and if they have to run they will do that, too, and then carry dispatches all night. Latin American history makes you suspicious of liberators like Castro, but, hard-boiled as you try to be, you cannot look at his men and live with them without feeling that here is a storybook legend come true—that these are people willing to be killed for freedom.

As strong an asset as his army is Castro's relation with the people—the *guajiros*. When he appears, they put on their Sunday best and walk in front of him, peering. They carry their babies up to see the hero;

they bring presents and stand and look at him. He is almost always available to the peasants. He spends hours talking to them about their crops, their animals and their roads, and his doctors are always ready to treat them. There is no other legislative or judicial authority around; he is the ruler. A peasant will come up courteously, introduce himself and start to lament: "We have a difficulty; the neighbor's mule came into our malanga patch and ate many malangas." Castro hears them out and advises patiently. And his advice is the law.

The peasants repay him with complete loyalty. Castro knows when a government force is moving up as soon as it comes out of its compound. The peasants house him, feed him, and secrete him and his men. One day Castro talked about this to me. "If I were Batista," he said, "I would say to my soldiers, 'I will give you a million dollars, but surely, surely, whenever you go into the country don't take a man's pig or meat or house without leaving a bill on the table. You should always be the friend of the countrymen.' But Batista's men are directed by military minds. They are always too inflexible to cope with an irregular force like ours. Besides, his soldiers have nothing to fight for. They are not aggressive against us. Why should they be? No man wants to die for thirty-five dollars a month. If they had been fighting for an ideal, they would have defeated us thirty times." ▶

While he was still in the mountains, Halper met Andrew St. George, photographer-correspondent and veteran of many months with Castro's columns. He came into the headquarters camp with Che Guevara's "suicide squad" after a twenty-two-hour forced march and he was preparing in a few days to accompany a small guerrilla team on a daring raid. Their mission was to reach the main road leading into the port city of Manzanillo and there lure an armored car out from the city's garrison and blow it up with a jerry-made bomb. Its purpose was to demonstrate that the rebels were now in such strength that they could operate on the main highways and challenge Batista's heavy weapons. This is St. George's report of that mission:

▶ It was noon when the bomb was at last tested and ready. Guajiro and Cuco el Gatillo had contrived it from a dud that Batista had dropped in the mountains, and now it had been wired into a raw timber box no bigger than a beer crate. After it had been roped to the back of a mule, they started up toward the mountain peak where headquarters was that day. It was only seven miles away, but the climb up the ridges

255

through thick jungle and forest took them all night. The encampment had been astir several hours by the time they arrived, and when they unroped the box and lugged it carefully toward the commandant's shack, they got full attention from the revolutionaries. "Guajiro—the bombardier," someone shouted. "He's made them another present."

Commandant Fidel Castro lay propped back under the whirling bicycle wheel of an improvised foot-driven dental drill. One of Castro's bodyguards worked the foot treadle, and a guerrilla lieutenant was probing into Fidel's mouth. But when the commandant glimpsed the two bomb-makers out of the corner of his eye, he brushed the dentist aside and sat up quickly, exclaiming: "*Hola*, Guajiro! The thing is ready, eh?"

It was the first electric demolition device to come out of the Cuban rebels' jungle bomb shop.

"*Sí, sí,*" Guajiro said proudly. "This one goes into any roadside ditch, and press this little buzzer button here, and he'll blow up any tank—the biggest tank."

Now Castro has bounded out of his dentist's chair. "Bring it in," he shouts, waving toward his headquarters hut. Inside, the men set the bomb down on an old table and Castro, bending over it, cries with delight, "What a tremendous toy Guajiro has tinkered up."

The room is now filling up with troopers—his *barbudos,* the bearded ones. Castro squeezes the buzzer over and over, "*Tremendo!*" he shouts. "*Barbaro!*" These are his two favorite words of eulogy. Then he bellows, "Frances! Caballo! Escalona! Mario!" And lowering his voice, he commands, "Send them all up here."

"El Frances," a goateed, bare-chested student who just finished a year studying political science in Paris; Caballo Loco, a burly mountaineer; Dermidio Escalona, a skilled guerrilla-raid leader; and Mario Segundo, a strong, fun-minded Negro boy, have appeared. "It is a special mission," the commandant tells them. A map is found under Castro's crumpled sweater, and Castro's finger travels along it, down the mountain to the outskirts of Manzanillo. "Here," he says, and everybody crowds around and looks. Then the camp is astir, helping or watching those who are getting ready for the mission. Arms and ammunition, food—everything is hung on them. Then we are off.

We need no guide, for most of these men are veterans. All have boots, not rope sandals but strong work-shoes smuggled up from Havana. Among them there are five canteens, two borrowed Tommy guns with spare clips taped to the stocks. There is a sense of excitement as we start the descent to the plains, and Escalona, in a rare gesture among the abstemious rebels, passes around a pint of *aguardiente*, a raw, hot, canefield rum.

It is a long, fast, dark, circuitous march. The column thins out and works its way across the escarpments of the 6,500-foot Turquino Peak, and then down into the badlands of ridged hills and ravines. We pass from the murk of the jungle to golden bursts of afternoon light glittering on tall tropical grass in the interspersed clearings.

The bomb started the journey on Cuco Gatillo's shoulder, but gradually it is shifted among the men. Since each of them carries fifty pounds or more in equipment, the box is a burden. "Afterward," Caballo Loco says, sweating under the load of the bomb—"afterward" is the rebel term for when they have won. "Afterward, I'm going to make a box like this for Batista."

Suddenly the pointman stops the column. In the evening dusk we see a house far below us. "An informer lives there," someone says. We turn our route to avoid it. "Coming back," someone else says, "we'll stop off and see him. We have something to give that little *chivato*." A *chivato* is a goat that bleats.

At the first light of dawn we are among houses. It is a strange feeling to be among houses again. We are on the outskirts of Manzanillo. Our goal is the Carretera Central, the main national highway which leads into the port city.

Someone says, "We are nearly there!" And we hear a truck in the distance. Then Loco is alert. He points at a small house and runs for it. When I enter, it is nearly filled with *barbudos*. Escalona and Mario are already at the curtained windows, with guns ready, checking. Across a thin stand of orange trees there is a dark ribbon of road. Gatillo is out there, planting the bomb.

The house has a single room. Sitting on chairs in the center are its owners: a young married couple, two small children and an old woman—all shrunken with terror. The woman is sobbing quietly and the husband seems embarrassed at his helplessness.

It is now 5:30 and still half dark. At 6:00 every morning the intercity bus leaves Manzanillo and passes here about 6:10. The rebels are to intercept and burn it, and when the Manzanillo army command responds by sending out an armored vehicle to investigate, Gatillo will press the button. Riflemen have already slipped out and taken positions by the roadside. Escalona's Tommy gun rests on the windowsill and four more riflemen have taken firing position in the room.

Now we hear the clatter of the diesel engine of the approaching bus. Out in the road, Loco stands up straight, waving his automatic rifle. The bus brakes sharply. We can see the passengers thrown from their seats. In great fright they stumble from the bus and run madly. Loco shouts at the bus driver, who turns and opens the vehicle's hood and runs away too. Loco takes a small brown jug which has been hanging on his belt, puts his cigar to it and, when it begins to trail smoke, tosses it under the open engine hood. There is a small explosion and soon the bus is burning.

"Just like in the movies," says Mario Segundo, grinning when Escalona looks at him sharply.

Now everybody waits—seven, eight, nine, ten minutes, my watch says. But surely it is wrong. It is much longer than that. Then Escalona grabs Cuco's arm. "It comes," he says hoarsely. A moment later I see it too, a flat-headed green toad-monster wheeling down the road toward us at what seems like terrific speed.

"Ready, Cuco," says Escalona.

When it is fifty yards away, Cuco presses the button. He comes down on it with his whole plunging shoulders. Nothing happens! Cuco's arm is like a pump now; he presses the button half a dozen times while the vehicle rolls on untouched. Immediately its turret begins to turn, tracing a figure eight as the vehicle doubles back on the road and pulls up nose-to-nose with the burning bus.

Someone curses bitterly and Escalona spits sharply. A sense of urgency rises in the room. Impatiently Escalona rips aside the curtains and leans out with narrowed eyes. "The bastard is on the radio," he says in a tense voice. We all know what to expect now: truckloads of infantry.

There is a murmur of criticism about the bomb. "Why didn't it work? Why didn't it blow?"

"Shut up," says Escalona. His voice is so casual that I turn to him in surprise and see that he is smiling. "Watch out, everyone, I'm going to blast that wagon."

"At this distance!" Paneque is contemptuous. "With his side plating, even *my* gun couldn't—"

"Shut up," says Escalona again. "You don't understand. Caballo Loco is out there waiting for us to let him know what to do. We're going to tell him. When we shoot, that wagon will move, and when it does, it'll move over that box again. And when it does *that*, we'll blow up the bomb by firing on it."

Without waiting for a reply, Escalona leans out the window and fires a long blast in the direction of the scout car. Instantly the room explodes with the roar of Mario's gun. The report hits us like a sledge-hammer. Then the two Garands join in with ear-ripping "bangbang-bangbang," and Cuco's Thompson and Frances' carbine bark away. The room trails with the smoke, and the smell of cordite is sharp.

We see the scout car shake. It begins to creep forward. Escalona raises his arm sharply. A signal. All firing stops and the room is tensely quiet. Then he yells "Fire" and the house trembles with the blasts. Suddenly there is an *aaaaa*ᴬᴬᴬᴬᴬᴬᴬᴬʜʜʜʜʜʜ!, a breathtaking explosion. And a great shower of earth and gravel and smoke flies into the sky. The blast knocks the scout car sideways and it lurches and rocks dangerously, but through the plume of gray dust we see that it is upright and scurrying across an open field. The blast was an instant—half an instant—too late. Silence has entered the room. A wave of fatigue washes over everyone. Then Caballo Loco crashes through the doorway, breathing hard. "The trucks are coming," he gasps. "The trucks . . ." He is reloading furiously. Now everyone is in action, putting new clips into their weapons, unbut-toning the flaps to their ammunition belts, nervously shifting about the room. They all have the same kind of tenseness, the same look of the runner on the mark.

An army truck loaded with troops roars past the house. We are still invisible from the road, and for a moment there is indecision. Everyone seems riveted to the floor. Then suddenly we all burst out of the house, running for the trees, the palms, the brush. Within half a mile we are out of the housing area, but the cover is poor. Someone calls "*Avion*," and over us sweeps a slow spotter plane, the hated Beaver. It has seen us and is slowly circling overhead.

The word is passed: "Break! Spread!" The plane has alerted the infantry and now they are closing on us in a triangular sweep. We are caught between two skirmish lines of infantry. The firing swells. The rebels are answering. But now we are split apart and I have no way of knowing what is happening.

Crawling along the ground, I see someone rise ahead of me. It is Mario Segundo. He is firing in frantic bursts. His target seems very close. He takes a bomb from his belt and lights it and rises halfway to fling it in a wide arc. There is a dull boom and then muffled cries. He is lighting another. He rises again to hurl it, but instead he twirls wildly. He is hit. I crawl near enough to be sure, and I see his body twitching obscenely, again and again. A machine gun is raking him with repeated bursts. I crawl away, into the bush. There are other rebels in there too. I roll over and over, down a gorge. I half-rise and begin to run. The firing is dropping away behind me. Suddenly, looming in the sky above the gully, I see a wonderful sight—the top of a house. For an instant I am overwhelmed by a feeling of hope. I run right up the embankment and burst through an open door. I am in the kitchen. A bearded rebel is already there. He is gasping, pleading with his arms. He is breathless and cannot talk. I too cannot talk. There are two women and a sallow-faced man in his twenties and a teen-aged boy. They are pleading, too. In terrified voices they are saying: "Go! Please go! For God's sake, go! We will all be killed."

The *barbudo* leans against the wall, his body heaving. I lean against the wall, heaving too. We are desperate. We cannot catch our breath. We cannot talk. The *barbudo* points to his beard. He points to mine. One of the women exclaims. She whirls around. She is back with two razors. She runs to the sink and wets a dishrag. Frantically she wets our beards. We shave, we tear at the hair. Then the boy runs into the kitchen. He has some old clothes and two big straw hats. He is the only cool thinker in the house. Now they are all helping. They are ripping at our clothes, tearing them off. It is easily done, for our pants and our shirts are already in shreds. Out the door they push us. The boy is leading us. We follow him through the orchard, trying now to walk easily. The boy is dragging the rebel's rifle. "Get rid of it. Throw it over the hedge," the *barbudo* says hoarsely. But the boy holds on to it until we reach a straw pile, where he quickly hides it. Then he flashes a smile at me.

"*Rebelde?*" he says hopefully.

"*Photographo*," I say, but it is pointless; my beard is official rebel insignia, and I am too exhausted to explain. Besides, I realize he is a fan. He will be a rebel one day if Batista keeps it up. All these terrified people will be. It is in their eyes.

The firing has faded into the distance and the sounds of the planes are gone. The boy hides us in a stable, then in a well. In the morning he is back with more clothes. We look good enough now to move in the open, and the *barbudo* and I separate. I walk down to the Carretera Central. A bus comes along and I flag it down and ride all the way into town. But I keep thinking of those angry, terrified eyes.

Later I learned that Caballo Loco and two of Escalona's riflemen died that day, as well as Mario. But the rest of us escaped, and that was because those eyes were watching Batista's army from every side. And in those eyes are written the end of Batista's dictatorship in Cuba. ▶

Very few of the men who planned revolution with Castro or who helped him while he was in the Sierra Maestra survived in his revolutionary government. As early as April 1958, nine months before Castro's triumphant descent from the mountains, Sam Halper wrote:

▶ The day I came down from the hills and was preparing to leave Cuba, I had lunch at the Havana Yacht Club with one of Castro's underground men. He was questioning me on what I had seen in the Sierra Maestra, and he seemed at first to be elated at what I told him. But then he looked troubled. "There is an equilibrium of forces at the moment," he said. "But the potential for violence among Castro's followers is enormous. If Castro gets too big, he may not need us. He could be a man on horseback. I understand the subtleties involved in American restraint in intervening in Cuba on behalf of freedom-loving Cubans. Some of us who are supporting Castro are aware that the time might come when chaos will be of such a magnitude that you will have to intervene. I tell you frankly that we may not be in command here later." ▶

It was a tragically prophetic insight. Soon after Castro took over, it became clear that the freedoms he promised were hollow things, lost in the trickery of language, and that the victory of the 26th of July Movement, which had cost the Cubans eight thousand dead, had only brought another repressive regime and another dictatorship for Cuba. It was a different kind of repressive regime. Batista's goal was wealth and power; Castro was a revolutionary whose social goals, vague and unformed while he was in the mountains, became the goals of a Communist state. To reach them he needed uncontested power, and his rule, too, became oppressive. Once more there were crowded prisons, executions without fair trial, and a flight of refugees from the island.

Despite the early brutalities of the Castro regime—which were, after all, no worse than those of previous governments the United States had recognized—the U.S. as well as the governments of many South American countries looked on this new experiment in Cuba with friendly eyes, forgiving many things in the hope of a new era in the Caribbean. And in April 1959, when Castro visited the United States, it was made clear to him that Washington was prepared to give him economic aid. But he rebuffed these offers and on his return to Cuba announced the first of his sweeping agrarian reforms, which would involve the confiscation of U.S. property. By mid-1960 these confiscations had become so widespread that the Eisenhower administration retaliated by cutting off the import of Cuban sugar, thereby striking the Castro government a staggering economic blow.

Even more alarming to the nations of the Western Hemisphere than these signs of consolidating Communism within Cuba was the growing evidence of Castro's involvement with revolutionary movements outside his country as Cuban arms and Cuban-trained guerrillas began to show up in Panama, Nicaragua, Haiti and the Dominican Republic.

The Soviet Union, which at first had treated the new government with reserve, extended aid to Cuba and began to talk approvingly of the "national liberation movement" there. In 1960 both the U.S.S.R. and Communist China established diplomatic relations with the Castro government and Khrushchev promised military assistance against the possibility of United States intervention. Technicians from the Communist bloc began arriving on the island in significant numbers. In October, Eisenhower recalled his ambassador and imposed an embargo on most exports to Cuba, and in January 1961 he formally broke relations with Castro. The Cold War had swept into the Caribbean.

The refugees from the early Castro years had found asylum in other lands, especially in the United States, and among those who fled were many who had sided with Castro while he was in the mountains. Now disillusioned, bitter, and once again set on revolution, they were eager to reenter Cuba, join with those who they were convinced would rise to fight beside them, and overthrow the man who, in their eyes, had perverted their revolutionary ideal. Their ambitions coincided with the growing feeling within the Eisenhower administration that a Communist Cuba was a danger to the Western Hemisphere that could not be tolerated. From these combined interests came the botched attempt at counterrevolution that became known as the Bay of Pigs fiasco.

The threat of American intervention in Cuba which the Russians had noted, first took shape early in 1960 when Washington authorized the arming and training of a Cuban exile "army of liberation" under the direction of the CIA. The plan, which developed gradually throughout that year, was to mount a counterrevolutionary invasion from secret bases in Guatemala. The guerrilla band—which grew into a conventional force of fourteen hundred men—was to be supplied and transported with unofficial American aid, and their attack was to be supported by sixteen Cuban-manned American bombing planes. The question was left hanging whether more direct U.S. participation would be forthcoming if it was found necessary.

But before these plans could come to fruition, the elections of 1960 brought a change in American administration and Eisenhower was replaced by Kennedy. And when they became an actuality, the new young President had been in office less than three months and had not yet gained the assurance and the inner strength of leadership that would serve him so well in another and more serious crisis over Cuba eighteen months later.

In this instance he was troubled and uncertain, deeply opposed to subterfuge and masked aggression and yet unable to extricate himself from the already overripe operation he had inherited. Therefore the plan went forward limpingly. The President underestimated the number of invasion troops required for such an operation, overestimated the capability of the tiny exile air force, erroneously assumed that the landing would immediately stimulate wide support among the Cubans at home, and clung to his initial policy, which he made public before the invasion when he said, "There will not be under any conditions an intervention in Cuba by U.S. armed forces."

The invasion force, known as Brigade 2506, was doomed before it set out, on April 14, 1961, sailing from Nicaragua in five small freighters. The Brigade was to have landed on a beachhead a hundred miles east of the Bay of Pigs, but because the area was heavily populated, the more cautious planners under Kennedy, fearing civilian casualties, changed the location of the assault to the swampy and less favorable final landing place. There were to have been three pre-invasion air strikes by the exile air force, but after the first one, made while the transports were still at sea, President Kennedy canceled the follow-up bomb attacks. And the first strike, though it destroyed half of Castro's air force on the ground, alerted Castro to the danger and gave him time to round up and arrest some hundred thousand Cubans who might have joined the invaders. If there was any hope of a popular uprising, it died in Castro's swift preventive action.

The assault itself began just after midnight, Monday, April 17, near the resort town of Playa Giron. The invaders fought strongly, gaining their first objective and even seizing and bulldozing an airfield. But without the ranging firepower of their bomber force, which had to commute four hours from their base in Nicaragua, and without the help of U.S. jet fighter cover which they had expected, they could not long sustain their beachhead. And Castro's three jets, which survived the first bombing strike, sank or drove off the transports and supply ships. Trapped on the beachhead, short of ammunition and food, overwhelmed by the steadily reinforced numbers of Castro's militia, the counterrevolutionary fighters were driven back across the beach. Sixty-four hours after they had landed in the swamps of the Bay of Pigs, those who remained alive of Brigade 2506 were overrun and captured. Until the very bitter end they had believed that the United States would not let their invasion fail.

The Bay of Pigs fiasco staggered the United States. The young President, commenting wryly that "victory has a hundred fathers and defeat is an orphan," took full responsibility for the blunder on himself. But later, revealing how deeply he felt about this failure in the first months of his term, he remarked to his adviser Theodore Sorensen, "All my life I've known better than to depend on the experts. How could I have been so stupid, to let them go ahead?" In the next crisis over Cuba he was in full command, utilizing the overwhelming power of the United States with control and sensitivity to steer the nation through the most dangerous episode of the post-war world and avert the final agony of a nuclear war.

The threat which the Bay of Pigs invasion had presented to the first strong Communist bastion in the Western Hemisphere alerted the Soviet Union to both the dangers and the possibilities there. Not long after the American attempt to eradicate Communism in Cuba—as early, perhaps, as the spring of 1962—the Russians decided to place long-range missiles there. During that summer, reports of an unprecedented Soviet arms build-up on the island were delivered to Washington, and in August the CIA sent an urgent message to the President that "something new and different" was taking place. On August 29, photographs taken by a U-2 intelligence plane showed surface-to-air missile sites being built on the island, and although they seemed to be for purely defensive weapons, the President decided to put Moscow on notice with the statement that any evidence of "significant offensive capability either in Cuban hands or under Soviet direction" would give rise to "the gravest issues." Moscow replied that "armaments and military equipment sent to Cuba are designed exclusively for defensive purposes."

Nevertheless, the situation seemed alarming enough for President Kennedy to obtain congressional authority to call up 150,000 reservists, thereby warning the Soviet Union that he intended to take a very strong stand. Three weeks later, on October 14, the U-2's brought back the first photographs of actual Soviet missile emplacements. That week the tension mounted as more evidence came in to Washington of the arrival of jet planes capable of carrying nuclear warheads and of the installation of medium-range ballistic missiles with a striking distance of more than a thousand miles and of sites under construction for intermediate-range missiles whose targets might include most of the major cities in both North and South America.

On October 22 President Kennedy addressed the American nation—and, indirectly, the leaders of the Soviet Union—in a television speech in which he revealed American knowledge of the extent of the Soviet build-up on Cuba and pointed out that this rapid escalation of offensive military weapons had been carried on secretly and in direct contradiction to Soviet assurances. He announced that he was issuing orders for a naval "quarantine" of Cuba— which meant, in effect, a blockade to stop the flow of military equipment there—and warned that if the weapons were not dismantled and removed, the quarantine might be but a preliminary step. "It shall be the policy of this nation," he declared, "to regard any nuclear missile launched from Cuba against any nation in the Western Hemisphere as an attack by the Soviet Union on the United States, requiring a full retaliatory response upon the Soviet Union."

By this speech he simplified the growingly complex Cuban situation, bringing it to a clear-cut confrontation—the first in history—between two nuclear powers. For six days the world waited fearfully while the leaders in Moscow and Washington stood toe-to-toe and Soviet ships enroute to Cuba approached the American naval patrols. Would they accept the American quarantine, or would they try to break through?

The initial test came on October 25, when the first Soviet ship, a tanker, reached the naval picket line and was challenged by a U.S. destroyer. The captain replied that he was carrying no arms to Cuba. This verbal assurance was accepted and the tanker was allowed to pass without boarding. Both antagonists had given ground. It was an indication that the crisis might pass peacefully, and within a few hours twelve of the twenty-five Soviet ships on their way to Cuba were reported to be turning back.

The following night, October 26, President Kennedy received a long letter from Premier Khrushchev which made it clear that he was backing down. He wrote of his longing for peace and urged that both powers work to prevent the situation from getting out of hand. If the United States would lift the blockade and give assurance that it would not invade Cuba, he said, this could bring about an important change, for then there would be no need for the U.S.S.R. to give military assistance to Castro's government. The Soviet missiles would be removed. The crisis, he said, was like a rope with a knot in the middle; the more each side pulled, the more the knot would tighten, until it could be severed only with a sword. But if each side slackened, the knot could be untied.

Kennedy accepted this proposition, and two days later it was announced by radio from Moscow that work on the missile sites had been ordered stopped, the rockets would be dismantled, and ships were standing by to remove both the missiles and Russian jets from Cuba.

The crisis was over. And although Fidel Castro, having been ignored throughout this confrontation, refused to allow the United Nations to supervise the removal of the missiles, U-2 surveillance of the dismantling and U.S. naval inspection of the departing Soviet ships which carried the weapons away proved that Khrushchev was faithfully carrying out his commitment.

This, then, is how power nations behave in the cold dawn of a nuclear showdown, and the world learned a lesson. When it was over, President Kennedy wrote to Premier Khrushchev, "You and I . . . were aware that the developments were approaching a point where events could have become unmanageable." It is this awareness that enables powerful men with thermo-nuclear weapons in their hands to back away from victory. The President showed his perception of the rules of this kind of confrontation when he not only left a way open for an honorable retreat for his adversary, but stepped back a pace himself, committing the United States to a promise not to invade Cuba. Thus, when it came to the showdown, both sides acknowledged that the "ultimate deterrent"—so often spoken of—did in fact deter. And it demonstrated also that in this age when there can be no victor, it is just as true that neither adversary must be forced to acknowledge himself the van-quished.

Years after the Cuban confrontation, Nikita Khrushchev, now divested of his power and in retirement, looked back on those days of crisis and explained in a television interview for the National Broadcasting Company how he saw it. "Perhaps we shouldn't have done it," he said. "But if rockets had not been installed, would there be a Cuba now? No, Cuba would have been wiped out. And if that is true, it means that the transportation of rockets was justified. It cost us money, but we did not lose a single man.

"We took our rockets and bombers away in exchange for President Kennedy's promise not to invade Cuba. . . . And I am not ashamed of that. As the newspapers wrote, I made concessions to the American President and ordered the removal of the rockets from Cuba. . . . We must give credit to the United States, and first of all to President Kennedy, who also showed sense and coolheadedness. He gave us his promise to carry out his part and we carried out ours. And that's the way we liquidated the possibility of beginning a nuclear war. . . .

"So who was right and who was wrong. . . . We brought the breath of war closer. . . . We also demonstrated a clear understanding of when one can avoid war and solve a question by negotiation."

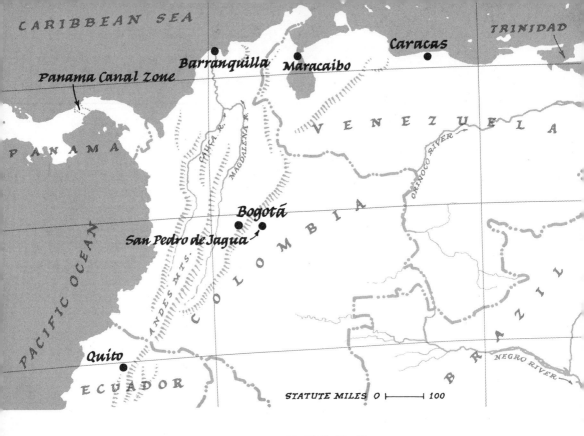

XVII

La Violencia in Colombia

(1948-   )

W ITH THE FAILURE of the attempted counterrevolution in the swamps of the Bay of Pigs, the United States lost her chance to establish a friendly government in Cuba. And when the Soviet Union was defeated in the missile crisis she forfeited not only a base for Communist weapons in the Western Hemisphere but much of her influence over the Cuban government. Communist China attempted to take her place, but the Chinese were so beset by internal problems that they could do little more than offer slogans in lieu of aid.

Communism took a new name in Cuba: Castroism. And Fidel Castro continued to attempt to export this particular brand of revolutionary activity to the countries of Latin America. His guerrillas operate in many countries, from Guatemala to Bolivia, but in none have they had much success. For although in many of these countries the economic climate is conducive to revolution, each has its own peculiarities of history and modes of behavior. In each, though the rebels may take on political labels or call themselves Communists—or even Castroites—they are apt to be stubbornly faithful to their own indigenous brand of mayhem and insurrection. The terrorism known as *La Violencia* in Colombia is a case in point.

In the spring of 1948 there was a gathering in Bogotá for the ninth International Conference of American States to discuss matters of high moment to the hemisphere: the charter of the Organization of American States and the future industrial development of Latin America and containment of Communism there. The visitors and delegates filled the city's hotels and overflowed as guests into many of the fine homes of Colombia's leading gentry in that mile-high, four-hundred-year-old capital in the Andes. The mood was festive, with flags flying and elaborate entertainments given by the wealthy families of the ruling society—that landed class which still lived by codes of formality preserved from the time the Spaniards had governed the land in the sixteenth to the nineteenth centuries. There was pride in that city and in the country, and by April 9, after ten days of talks, hopes were high and glasses were raised to a peaceful future in all the Americas.

Shortly after noon that day a light rain swept across Bogotá, wetting the columns of the Capitolio as most of the delegates were leaving for lunch. At very nearly the same moment, six blocks down the street, Jorge Eliécer Gaitán, a short, muscular lawyer with piercing black eyes, stepped briskly out of his office, also luncheon bound. An instant later four shots exploded behind him and he fell dying on the rain-splashed pavement.

Correspondent Thomas Dozier, who was in Bogotá covering the conference, reached Gaitán's crumpled body minutes later and reported on the killing and the disorders that followed. He was, of course, unaware that this single murder would usher in an era of violence of such astonishing savagery throughout the country that it would claim more than two hundred thousand lives in two decades of terror—with no end to the slaughter yet in sight.

Dozier's report that day follows:

▶   As Jorge Eliécer Gaitán, a rabble-rousing leader of Colombia's Liberal Party, crossed the sidewalk, a man with a pistol in his hand slipped up behind him and fired four shots into his neck and shoulders.

Like a man who has been bludgeoned, Gaitán fell, face down, and bloodstains widened on the sidewalk. A lottery vendor standing in the doorway dropped his book, grabbed the assassin and shouted: "This is the man." A café patron ran from another door and smashed a chair over the gunman's head. A clotting crowd tore off his clothes, pounded him with shoeshine boxes snatched from ragged urchins, kicked his face into bloody pulp. They knotted a tie around his neck and dragged him six blocks. All afternoon his body lay in the gutter before the Presidential Palace, while the rainwater made little whirlpools around his bare heels. Gaitán had been picked up and carried to the Clínica Central.

To Colombia's working classes, Gaitán had been an enshrined hero. For a month they had burned with resentment because the Conservative Party leader Laureano Gómez had kept him from being a delegate to the International Conference. Now they were enraged because they were convinced that the Conservatives were responsible for the shooting. As Gaitán lay on the surgeon's table, his hysterical supporters stormed the Capitolio, screaming, "Death to Laureano Gómez!"

Gómez, a rightist, Foreign Minister, and backbone of President Mariano Ospina Pérez, and president of the conference, was not there. But rioters poured in anyhow. They threw typewriters out of windows, splintered furniture and tore up records.

In midafternoon the word spread: Gaitán was dead. The mob, which had quieted under the efficient handling of federal troops, went mad. Its members stormed public buildings, set fire to Gómez' conservative newspaper, *El Siglo*, and hurled stones through the windows of the President's Palace. Across the city smoke swirled, and the thud of explosives could be felt. Gangs swarmed through the International Conference headquarters. No foreigners were injured, but the crowd's fury spread a chill of fright among the delegates and visitors. Federal troops and police were now powerless.

A few hours after the murder, I saw from my hotel the bodies of ten men and one woman lying on the pavement. They had climbed on one of the tanks that moved through the mob to defend the Presidential Palace, and government riflemen lying prone on the street popped them off at short range. One fell beneath the tank's treads and his head was crushed. It was not a pretty sight.

Tonight the rioting continues. Hundreds have been reported slain, and Bogotá looks more like a blitzed city than one that has been through a mere revolution. Buildings are burning and hundreds of stores have been wrecked and looted. Some have been dynamited into rubble.

When I walked from the hotel to the cable office, about eight blocks, I stumbled over bodies and debris. To escape soldiers' and snipers' bullets, I crouched in doorways and flattened myself against walls and dashed across exposed street corners. This city is in a state of frenzy. ▶

For five days the Bogotá riots raged. More than two thousand Colombians died there, great sections of the city were laid waste and a new word was added to the Spanish language: *bogotazo*—contagious mob fury.

It spread immediately to the countryside and throughout the land. Its causes at first seemed explicit enough. For generations Colombians have belonged to one of two political parties formed in the days of Bolívar, the Conservatives and the Liberals. The Liberals advocated limiting the Church in state affairs and called for a sharing of power between the central and local governments, while the Conservatives were clerical and centralist, but in modern times their differences have largely disappeared. In late years the two parties have been led by very nearly identical groups of landowners and industrialists, and have opposed each other simply to win political leadership and thus control the power of the country. This failure of the two parties to provide the people with a choice between differing political positions has brought no protest from the great mass of Colombian people because traditionally they have given their allegiance to strong leaders rather than to any political program. Today, however, membership in either party is fixed by hard and bitter hatreds perpetuated by memories of the terrible violence each party has suffered at the hands of the other, for the gun and the machete lie behind the Colombian ballot box.

Ever since Gaitán died that rainy afternoon in Bogotá, the killings and destruction have continued, although the emphasis soon shifted to the country regions of the Andes, where armed bands of brigands flourish in the roadless, almost impenetrable ranges and prey on the isolated villages tucked into the valleys. These villages are known by the name of the political party that once attracted them, and the bandits, too, call themselves either "Conservative" or "Liberal." But the designations are largely anachronistic and bear little actual relation to the nation's politics. The killings are so savage that the motivation for them seems to lie far deeper than in surface politics.

Typical of these bandit raids was the attack on a little town in a remote part of central Colombia in July 1951. Word had reached Bogotá that a band of brigands had struck the village of San Pedro de Jagua, killing twenty-four people and sacking and burning the houses. A small government expedition of seven civilians headed by Dr. Gonzalo Montes Duque, once an UNRRA doctor, was mounted to travel there to gather information on the problems of banditry and to distribute clothing, basic household utensils and medicines to those who had escaped. Correspondent Philip Payne joined the expedition, and after six days of traveling by Land-Rover, horse and mule, they reached the ruined village. Payne's story follows:

▶   Riding along a sheer mountain trail, we came upon a sudden clearing in the trees and saw the village of San Pedro lying below us. The first and continuing impression is one of desolation. The white adobe walls of the houses still stand, but the interiors are nothing but sad heaps of ash and cinder and broken roof tiles that fell in when the beams burned away. When we rode into the town, we saw that only the schoolhouse, the church and four dwellings were left unburned. In two of the still standing houses we found San Pedro's last living inhabitants—two scrawny dogs, too listless even to bark.

We dismounted and went exploring. A fused mass of broken bottles showed where the cantina had been. An orange tree standing next to a burned-out house grew green fruit on one side and scorched brown globes on the other. In the empty plaza lay the overturned harmonium from the church, and inside the empty church itself my footsteps echoed loudly. In the belfry, up two shaky ladders, I found three bells hanging. I rang them with a fingernail. They were sweet-toned and I wanted to pull the rawhide thongs leading down to the bellringer's platform, but it seemed inappropriate in this silent town.

Through the louvers of the bell tower I looked down across the plaza into the main street leading out of town, the route by which the bandits came marching the bloody morning of June 24. I could see the absurd little three-sided *trinchera*, the waist-high adobe wall with loopholes, set in the middle of the street. And then, as I gazed down upon the ruins, the story of the death of the village, recounted by the survivors, came back to me in detail. For a long time up there in the belfry I saw and even heard the violence of that day when the bandits came.

San Pedro was a Conservative village, they told me, but everybody got along with everybody, even with Carlos Londoño, the one village Liberal, who ran a small soda-pop bottling plant and was the town's leading businessman. This point was especially stressed to show me how peaceful the village really was. They had never been bothered by bandits, either. Still, nervousness had grown in San Pedro this year, and the citizens organized a raid-warning system among the outlying farmers. Anybody who saw bandits coming was to fire a gun. After that, the villagers hoped, the detachment of eighteen departmental police stationed in San Pedro would defend them.

Some did hear the warning shot at 4:30 on the morning of June 24. One was Carlos Londoño, whose big wooden house stands at the end of the street. He looked around and finally roused the police, half a dozen of whom wandered off with wavering flashlights to see what they could see. Señora Londoño told the maid to give them all a *tinto* when they got back. After a while the maid looked out to see if they were returning and saw instead men in military uniforms marching in columns of fours. She called out, "Here comes the army!" And Londoño, rushing to the door, exclaiming, "What army?" heard one of the marchers shout: "Don't shoot. We're the army. We've come to relieve the police."

The police patrol had just returned and taken positions behind the *trinchera*. One of them shouted, "Army, hell!" and fired a shot. In answer the bandits fired a heavy volley at the police, who fled without any further effort to defend the town.

The Londoños waited in their house, hearing the bandits marching past, then hearing the sounds of running feet, of rifle fire and of screams spreading through the village. A rifle butt thudded against the door. "*Virgen Santísima*," Londoño cried, "they are here!" And as the door was thrust open, Señora Londoño screamed, "Don't kill me, I'm a Liberal." A bandit holding an automatic rifle motioned them to leave the house, and the Londoños came out timidly, carrying their two children.

"Is this Fonseca's band?" Londoño asked hopefully. He knew Bandit Fonseca personally. He was a Liberal.

"No," the bandit said. "Fonseca's not with us. This is Bautista's outfit."

The prisoners were walked to the plaza, where other prisoners were being gathered, and then Londoño himself was taken to the comandante, Tulio Bautista, who was directing the attacks. He was a slim young man with well-formed features and a steady voice which carried authority, and he was dressed in good civilian clothes, a new poncho and fine leather shoes, unlike the rest of the bandits, who wore captured army uniforms and cheap canvas sandals.

The young comandante needed all his authority to keep his gang in hand. There were more than two hundred of them, mostly country boys, some as young as fourteen, and they had been marching toward San Pedro all night, capturing or killing all the families whose houses lay near the road. They carried Mauser rifles, machetes and knives. Their battle cry was *"Viva el Partido Liberal!"* And every man, woman or child who resisted or tried to escape they dropped with one shot or slashed and stabbed to death with their machetes and knives.

While Londoño showed his identity card to prove he was a Liberal, bullets were cracking all over town. A boy stepped out of a doorway holding up his identity card and a five-peso note. A bandit quickly dropped him with one shot, then bent down, grinning, and pulled the money from the dead boy's hand. When they found six of the police cowering in the coffee bushes behind the priest's house, they set up a cry of delight, yelling, "Come out, you bastard cops," and mowed them all down.

Londoño, having proved that he was a good Liberal, pleaded for the lives of his friends. Sometimes he was successful. Sometimes the bandits brushed him aside. They brought up the three sons of old Francisco Ruiz. "They are young," said Londoño. "They are *godos*, Conservatives," the comandante answered harshly, "they will grow up." And as Londoño argued and old Francisco continued frantically to beg, the three boys were executed before their father's eyes.

The shooting died down in the early afternoon. Smoke began to rise from the burning houses, and systematic looting began. In charge of the loot was Doña Edelmira, the comandante's girl. Slim, dark, darting Edelmira, in her man's clothing with two revolvers and a knife at her slim waist, made a lasting impression on the survivors. It was she who saw that no woman was raped or kidnaped, an exception that made San Pedro almost unique in the story of Colombian banditry.

Their killing, looting and firing of houses done, the bandits lined up in the plaza to drink up what was left in the cantina. Then they hauled the little harmonium out of the church, tried to play it, failed, and beat it apart with rifle butts. After that they found a Victrola, which, with stolen guitars, provided music for a wild dance in the plaza. Edelmira did not dance, and under her severe eye the bandits did not dare seek village women for partners, so the men danced together, one cavorting crazily in an old cassock he found in the house of the priest.

By midafternoon the dance was over and the stolen mules and nine selected captives were loaded with the loot. The bandits were ordered into formation and marched in good order out of town, leaving behind them smoldering ruins, twenty-four dead, and the destitute survivors to bury their sons and fathers in hasty graves and begin a straggling procession from the little village and quiet valley of San Pedro. ▶

From time to time a thread of reason can be found in the evolution of *La Violencia*. But, like the trails of the brigands themselves, it disappears as it is being followed. The *bandoleros* once murdered to avenge the murders of relatives and friends. Then they stole coffee and took property and became outlaws. In time their killings degenerated into acts of sadism, with brutality feeding upon brutality. Youths who had seen their mothers and fathers killed and their sisters raped returned the outrage with equal violence. And in a country where more than half of the people live in rural areas where the one-crop economy has never been able to provide a sufficient living, a farmer's son is often confronted with the choice of moving into the city to join the unemployed or staying in his native mountains with a brigand band.

Whatever the motivations these terrible killings may once have had, they no longer explain the continuing bloodshed in recent years. Nowhere else in the world today can such meaningless group violence be found on such a scale. The very terrain of the country lends itself to this. Often in the ridges of the Andes it is a full day's hike between two houses within hailing distance on either side of a mountain gorge. From their inaccessible hideouts the bandits sweep down on isolated hamlets or ambush buses on the lonely roads, murder without discrimination, mutilate the bodies and then, dragging away what they can carry and burning what they cannot, they climb back into their mountain lairs to rest until the dark urge again comes over them to descend upon the next village and repeat the carnage.

In the nearly two decades since the massacre at San Pedro, banditry has continued in Colombia, the bandit leaders taking over whole areas, sometimes fighting each other for territorial rights. Acquiring such names as "Sure Shot," "Black Jug" and "The Gnat," they live in the romantic image of the outlaw, but they are not Robin Hoods. They take from the poor as well as the more prosperous farmers, and they kill with the chilling skill of the degenerate.

In 1957 the Conservative and Liberal leaders, shocked at last into seeking some lasting solution to the violence, created the National Front, with the country's President alternating between the parties every four years from 1958 until 1974. It was an attempt to provide a sixteen-year truce—a time for the nation to heal. For a while the killings fell off, but in recent years the violence has increased again, some of it with a deeper ideological hue. And it has spread not only in the rural areas but into the cities as well. It is an endemic disease which solutions like the National Front only perpetuate, for Colombia's basic trouble is that the country is run by an establishment of wealthy and influential men while the vast majority of the population lives on marginal farmland in the rugged areas where the bandits flourish, or has been driven by hunger or by *La Violencia* itself into the slums of the cities.

This is the economic climate in which revolutions grow, and some of the well-known outlaws such as "Sure Shot" now boast of Communist backing. This is what Fidel Castro knows when he speaks of turning the Andes into the Sierra Maestra.

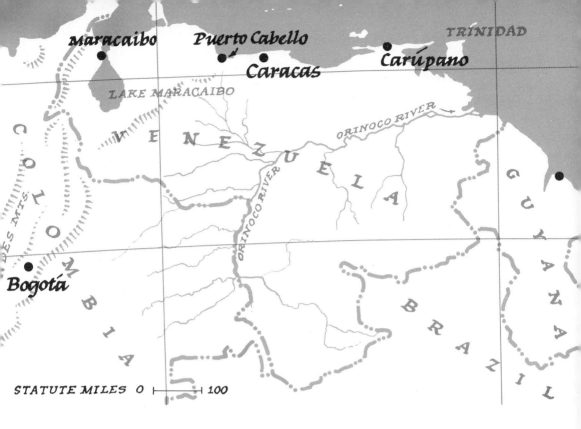

XVIII

Terror in Venezuela

(1961-1963)

I N THE TWILIGHT of Simon Bolívar's life, the great republic of Gran Colombia, which he had created after freeing the area from Spanish rule, broke into pieces. Gran Colombia was to have been a showplace of representative government for the rest of South America. It failed because the factions contending within it chose to use force rather than political means—thereby setting a pattern of power struggles among strongmen that has been followed

277

in many Latin American countries down to our day. In despair, the "Great Liberator" abandoned the goals that had been his inspiration. "Those who have served the revolution have plowed the seas," he said bitterly before he died.

More than a century later, in Venezuela, Bolívar's birthplace and one of the three countries formed from Gran Colombia, another kind of struggle developed which also set a pattern for the Latin American continent. For many years the country was dominated by local *caudillos* commanding private armies, but toward the end of the last century individual strongmen were able to consolidate their power and establish national armies to enforce their centralized rule. During the civil wars through which they fought to supremacy, the regional differences throughout the country were minimized; and under the oppression of their dictatorial rule, class distinctions of race and color tended to disappear. Thus when the last of these dictators, Marcos Pérez Jiménez, was thrown out by a popular uprising in 1958, Venezuela was more or less united, more or less classless, and more or less ready for a democratic government.

During the time of the dictators many students and intellectuals had gone into exile and there acquired ideas of modern government, both Marxist and democratic. One of these was Rómulo Betancourt, a Marxist-oriented student whose early radicalism matured into democratic liberalism as he gained experience and responsibility. He had been Provisional President, ruling through a junta, from 1945 to 1947, and in 1958 he was elected President for a five-year term beginning in 1959; during the last years of that term much of his effort was spent ensuring that the office would pass to the next President in an open and free election.

The forces that challenged this democratic process were not of the right wing and military cliques as they had been earlier in the nation's history, but those of the Communist Party and the Marxist Left with whom Betancourt had broken. Both sides saw the need for social and economic change. The income from Venezuela's fabulous oil fields had been stolen by government officials and the economy was stagnant. Thirty percent of the national income was enjoyed by three percent of the population. And around the dazzling modern city of Caracas there were rings of appalling slums. The struggle between the elected government and the radicals was simply whether the change would come through violent or peaceful means.

When Fidel Castro was in the Sierra Maestra, Betancourt supported him, and after he had made his victorious entry into Havana in 1959, the Venezuelans cheered him. He was received in Caracas with delirious acclaim as the man who had overcome the tyrant Batista as they had overcome Pérez Jiménez. But the Venezuelan leader's ardor for him cooled when, instead of following the road to democratic government, Castro chose the path of force and became a new sort of Latin American strongman. Bitterness replaced the friendship between the two, and when Castro began training young Venezuelans for violent revolution, sending them arms and calling for "another Sierra Maestra in the Andes," Betancourt broke diplomatic relations with Cuba and brought charges against Castro in the Organization of American States.

When Castro made Venezuela his special target, his revolutionary fervor inspired left-wing insurrectionists, composed largely of students, artists and writers, to build an extensive network of urban terrorists and rural guerrillas. Early in 1962 they staged strikes and demonstrations designed to discredit the stability of the Betancourt government. One of their major targets was the military establishment which they had been infiltrating. In May a marine detachment in Carúpano staged a mutiny which was put down in a day and a half. But a similar uprising on June 2, in Puerto Cabello, Venezuela's largest naval base, was better planned and involved more insurrectionists, hundreds of students rushing to join it. Again loyal army and navy forces were sent to confront the revolutionaries. The young radicals were as yet inexperienced in the use of terror, and the soldiers who were sent to face them were equally new to war. Correspondent Mo Garcia, arriving with a government unit, observed their confrontation:

▶ After two days of fighting here, the vultures are circling the skies over Puerto Cabello and the smell of the dead has permeated this old Spanish port city. Two days ago when loyal government troops engaged the rebel marines, some of the mutineers surrendered on first contact. One whole unit of fifty men gave up without an exchange of fire. And others, in small groups of twos and threes, entered private homes and asked for refuge and handed their arms over to the homeowners. But the rest have been fighting bitterly and holding out to the end.

On the morning of the second day I joined an infantry patrol moving through an area near the hospital and we came upon an earlier patrol which had been wiped out, literally cut to pieces. The vultures scattered as the soldiers went forward to regain the bodies, and suddenly the rebels opened fire, driving the loyalists off. The tanks with the patrol replied with their cannon, and a house farther down the road crumbled into dust. Then the patrol gathered up the dead. They were bloated and fly-covered. One of the soldiers paused over a swollen corpse. "I know

279

this lieutenant," he said. "I pity his wife. He was married only a month ago."

Wounded were being brought from a side street. One of them had a big hole in his chest. "Please don't let me die," he gasped. "I think I am going to die." The men carrying him reassured him, but they knew that a man with 50-caliber slugs in his lungs had only hours to live.

We moved on to the high school. It had just been captured and the building was in shambles. A soldier came out of the school with a large picture of Castro. He carried it over to an officer, who exploded when he saw it. "Put the picture of that son-of-a-bitch out there where we can show him what we think of him." The soldier propped it fifteen yards away and everybody opened up on it with a shattering blast.

Few of the men fighting on either side had ever been in battle before and the impact of seeing men slain for the first time showed clearly in their faces. They were scared and shaky. At one street corner a sergeant ordered a soldier to cross the intersection to signal another unit moving up a parallel street. The soldier stood mutely, not refusing, not going. Looking at the sergeant with imploring eyes, he said, "They are not there yet, sergeant." The sergeant pushed him, saying, "Don't be afraid, get moving. They are out there. Tell them we need their help." The soldier had moved only a few steps when the rebels opened up. He recoiled instantly, throwing himself back and cowering under a tank. "I'm not going," he said. Another soldier got up and ran, under covering fire, and reached the corner safely. The others were obviously relieved because they had not been ordered to go. No one said anything.

All that day the loyalists moved slowly through the town, systematically driving the opposition into pockets. Sometimes their tanks cleaned up the holdouts with withering, pointblank fire. Sometimes they took the marines and their civilian supporters at gunpoint when the insurrectionists realized that their revolt had failed and came out with their arms up. Some were wild-eyed and shaking, some defiant. One tough marine who had been roughly disarmed shouted, "We are fighting for democracy." A loyalist knocked him down with a rifle butt, saying, "Shut up, you son-of-a-bitch, and stop talking that political crap." And a student, about sixteen, who was captured with a machine gun in his hands, said, "Take it and do whatever you want with me. I've already killed seven."

An old man who watched nearby and saw the gathering of captured young men was unmoved by their fright or defiance. "They asked for it," he said. "They had no reason to join this thing. They're all young and they want to be heroes. Well, this is what they got out of it." ▶

By 1963 the terrorists had gained experience. A coalition of left-wing insurgents who called themselves the Armed Forces for National Liberation, FALN, were robbing banks, blowing up pipelines, burning newspaper offices and disrupting the normal life of the country. Their main target was Caracas, where one million of Venezuela's nine million people live, and their objective in this election year was to demonstrate that Betancourt could not control even his capital city, and to prevent an orderly election by frightening the people away from the polls.

As the year went on and the tempo of terrorism increased, a feeling of fright and frustration permeated Caracas. Hit-and-run killers shot down policemen at random. Arsonists fired a rubber warehouse, a paint factory, a section of the huge Sears, Roebuck store. Bombs were set off in midtown buildings and under bridges. Shootings resounded throughout the city, often accompanied by showers of leaflets mocking the government and threatening more violence. It became a common practice for the terrorists to spill tacks along the city's main arterial highway, the *autopista* that cuts through the heart of the city, creating such massive traffic holdups that the government finally forbade the sale of tacks without permits.

One noon in mid-September 1963, three months before election, correspondent Miguel Acoca was riding in a taxi in Caracas when the FALN was concentrating on that section of the city. His report on his experience follows:

▶ The people waiting for buses and taxis around the Plaza Urdaneta, which is festooned with a profusion of bright election posters, suddenly began to run. They ran with the tense and ungainly crouch of people fleeing bullets, and sought cover in the arcades around the plaza. Cars and buses sped for sidestreets. Horns blew. A bus driver abandoned his bus in the middle of the plaza. The policeman who had been directing the heavy flow of traffic vanished.

"They are firing," shouted a man hiding behind a pillar. Another man stood out in the deserted street and called up to an empty window. "María, María," he yelled. "Where are the children, María? Are they with you?"

"*Sí*," a voice screamed from above. "*Corre. . . .* Run."

"Let's get out of here," said Alfonso, my taxi driver. "The terrorists don't care what they do or whom they hurt. They like to burn cars."

It was noon in Caracas and fear was abroad. It was visible in the faces of the men and women peering from behind the pillars, looking out of doorways, peeking from windows. The only brave one was a boy about ten who continued to bathe in the plaza fountain.

The shooting stopped, and slowly people began to emerge from cover. Horns began to blow again and traffic moved slowly around the plaza once more. But everybody moved with caution.

Then there was a loud blast. It was a bomb. Again people abandoned their cars and everybody ran for cover. Again the plaza was empty—except for the boy bathing in the fountain. Then a car wove its way through the stalled traffic and leaflets were thrown out of it. They warned against going to the rally of the Acción Democrática, the government party, which was to be held at the bullfight ring.

It was quiet again, and after a little delay, traffic began to move, and people once again came out of hiding and there was a great rush for buses and taxis. They were all going home for lunch and they wanted to get off the streets. The taxi drivers knew this and demanded higher fares. "There are tacks on the streets of El Cementerio," one driver complained to a group of people trying to crowd into his cab. Another said: "They are burning buses in San Bernardino, and in 23 de Enero." The radios in the taxis were turned on full, blaring out the news of bombings, of bank robberies, of snipers shooting from buildings in many parts of the city.

My taxi turned out of the plaza and fell in with the traffic along Avenida Sucre. We saw a young man of about twenty get out of a car. Traffic stopped us behind his vehicle and we could see, as he dismounted and his coat caught on the door handle, that he had a revolver in his pants pocket. He wore lilac pants and a gray coat. We watched as he walked off, the telltale bulge showing as he disappeared into a building.

Moving along again in the heavy traffic, we heard a siren. It sounded closer and closer, and then a police car with police armed with rifles raced by us. Alfonso agreed to follow the police car. We raced along in the eddy it left behind, and in a little while it pulled up before a huge, middle-class apartment building. Other police cars were already there. Police with rifles and machine guns were standing around the entrance. Inside the building more police were crawling up the stairs, pounding on doors. An officer said: "Two young men and a girl forced their way into an apartment of an army officer, a lieutenant. He wasn't there. But they tied up his wife and took her husband's uniforms and his guns. That's all they took."

Back in the taxi, I heard the radio reporting that a new supermarket had been held up and set on fire. The employees had been herded together and forced to undress. Later, another bank was held up. All through the day there were reports of violence all over Caracas. The

FALN has terrorized the city to the point where people are afraid to go out at night. And with the election coming up in December, the killing and the bullying are bound to get worse. ▶

But three months later Rómulo Betancourt did hold his elections. In the last weeks before the nation went to the polls, two symbols appeared all over the country: the beard to represent Castro, and the pipe to represent Betancourt, for the President was an inveterate pipe smoker. And Raúl Leoni was elected to succeed Betancourt as President of Venezuela, ninety percent of the eligible voters dramatically appearing at the polling places throughout the nation, despite the FALN threats. What they said in the ballot boxes had become an election slogan: "Pipe yes, beard no."

Castro's setbacks in Venezuela and in other parts of Latin America could be viewed as battles lost, but they were only skirmishes in a continuing war. After President Leoni's election, guerrillas continued to operate in Venezuela, but on a much reduced scale, waiting a better opportunity in the future.

As Presidential adviser Milton Eisenhower said, "Revolution in Latin America is inevitable. Only the form it takes is uncertain." Che Guevara, once Castro's political theoretician, advocated one kind of revolution when he said, "Violence is the midwife of new societies." And to carry this message, Castro has exported transistor radios as well as guns to the farthest corners of Latin America and to Venezuela in particular. But the way of peaceful revolution which was chosen in the elections of 1963 has so far held its own. And President Leoni expressed his determination to keep his country on this path when he said, "Though we may have made a late entrance into the twentieth century, we now live in the serene conviction that we will arrive on time on the threshold of the twenty-first."

XIX

The Dominican Upheaval

(1965)

H ALFWAY BETWEEN Cuba on its left and Puerto Rico on its right lies
the divided island of Hispaniola. The western third of this island
belongs to the Republic of Haiti, the eastern two-thirds to the Dominican
Republic, and the sun-drenched hills of both countries, the clear green waters
of the Caribbean that surrounds them, are in sharp contrast to their gloomy
history and the shadow of uncertainty that dims their future. Whereas the

Haitian government is still in the grip of a dictator, "Papa Doc" Duvalier, the Dominican Republic has had four military coups, three junta governments and six presidents (two of them elected) since the assassination of their own strongman, Rafael Trujillo, in 1961.

At the time of that assassination, the Dominicans had not had a freely elected government in thirty-eight years. And before that—ever since Columbus discovered the island in 1492—it had known successive occupation, on and off, by Spain, France, Haiti and American Marines (1916–1924) and its history was full of upheavals, incompetent governments and near chaos. After Trujillo's death, the government was in the hands of Joaquín Balaguer, who had been puppet-president under him, until a seven-man council of state took over the preparations for free elections. And in December 1962, Juan Bosch, a mildly leftist, idealistic but indecisive man of letters, was chosen president by an overwhelming vote of the Dominican people.

An honest man but ineffectual politician, Bosch managed in seven months to lose the support of his backers, both in the business community and among the urban poor, because his unrealistic economic policy brought business to a standstill and increased unemployment. But those he irritated most were of the right wing and the ranking military men, among whom many still profited from the favored positions they held under Trujillo. They accused Juan Bosch of not being anti-Communist enough—an accusation given a semblance of reality both by his tolerance of leftist groups and by their own fear of Castroism, which could so easily be exported from their next-door island—and on September 25, 1963, Bosch was overthrown in a military coup and was sent into exile. A three-man civilian junta was selected to rule until the next elections, which were scheduled for September 1965. But even with the aid and encouragement of the United States, this triumvirate—which soon shrank to a one-man junta bereft of any but vestigial Dominican support—could not last the time allotted it.

The man at the helm of this wavering provisional government was Donald Reid Cabral, a businessman and, like Juan Bosch, honest but politically inept. By the early months of 1965 the country was suffering from a protracted drought, a disastrous drop in sugar prices and the continuing paralysis of ineffectual government. Various factions were vociferating against Reid's attempts to enforce an austerity program and reforms to remove the special privileges of high-ranking military men. The nation's two most popular leaders, ex-Presidents Joaquín Balaguer and Juan Bosch, were both in exile, and to the Dominicans it looked as though the provisional President planned to prevent their return in time for the elections. By April several military

285

coups were being hatched at a variety of camps and bases. In an attempt to test the rumors and clear the air, the President sent his chief of staff to an army camp, where three lieutenant colonels were reported to be plotting his overthrow. On April 24 the chief of staff drove to the camp alone, called on the suspected officers to hand over their commissions, and was arrested by them on the spot.

Some of the ensuing chaos came from the fact that Reid had precipitated the action several days before the stage for the coup was really set. But a more basic reason was that the rebels themselves were divided in their aims. The more conservative among them wanted to set up another military junta, under General Elias Wessin y Wessin, in preparation for elections. Others, especially among the junior officers, wanted a return of Bosch, whom they considered the legally elected president, and the reinstatement of the constitution of 1963, under which he had governed. This latter group had the support of the mass of urban civilians, especially in the capital, Santo Domingo. The former had the loyalty of most of the army, navy and air-force units.

By midafternoon that Saturday the pro-Bosch military rebels and their civilian sympathizers were broadcasting from several radio stations that the government had fallen, and in Santo Domingo crowds were running through the streets, attacking the hated government police, and gathering to demonstrate in front of the presidential palace, calling for Juan Bosch. Although the Wessin forces retook the central radio station and the government broadcast that all was calm, the younger rebels began distributing arms to all comers and the actual state of affairs was one of armed chaos.

When the "loyal" commanders of the army, navy and air force were called on to put down the revolt, they demurred. And by that non-action the provisional government was not so much overthrown as tossed aside; from the day the actual fighting began, on Sunday, April 25, the Reid junta was no longer a consideration. When, on that day and the next, the bulk of the regular military forces struck at the rebel groups in Santo Domingo with naval guns and strafing planes, they were fighting not for the return of the junta but against the return of Bosch.

The chaos had resolved itself into a civil war, and by the end of the month each side had a government for which it fought: the pro-Bosch group—because their indecisive President hesitated to return from Puerto Rico—set up a "Constitutionalist" government, first with the former president of the Chamber of Deputies as president, later with an army officer elected by the remaining members of the Bosch-regime congress. The "loyalists" operated under a three-man military junta—later to become a five-man "Government of National Reconstruction"—named by their commander, General Elias Wessin y Wessin. From the miasma of vague plots against an ineffectual government emerged the old familiar pattern of the Left against the Right.

Governments as well as individuals are inclined to see things in the light of their own fears, and there was nothing that the United States government feared more than a second Cuba in the Caribbean. As early as 1959 a Castroite group had made an abortive attempt to land in the Dominican Republic, and now the U.S. embassy in Santo Domingo had spotted a handful of Communists among the civilians of the pro-Bosch crowds. The U.S. Navy and Air Force were put on the alert. And when General Wessin, on April 28, admitted that his troops—the overwhelming bulk of the Dominican force—could not overcome the pro-Bosch rebels, the first contingent of U.S. military men, 405 Marines, landed in Santo Domingo.

The purpose of this first Marine contingent was to protect the lives of U.S. citizens. Although so far no Americans had been injured, hundreds of Dominicans had been killed in the tank and air attacks and the wild firing of the street fighting. Civilians of every nationality were in danger, and there was no authority left in the Republic capable of bringing order. The first Marines arrived by helicopter from an aircraft carrier late in the evening of April 28. They landed at a polo field near the hotel where American citizens had gathered, set up a perimeter, and sent a platoon to defend the U.S. embassy a mile away. Immediately they were taken under sniper fire and two Marines were killed. Next day 1,500 more Marines were sent to reinforce the first contingent, and the day after that, two battalions of paratroops.

By May 5 there were 19,363 U.S. soldiers and Marines in the Dominican Republic and, following a resolution of the Organization of American States, they had set up an International Safety Zone outside the rebel-held area of Santo Domingo. Then, inching forward street by street, they established a corridor through the city, linking the safety zone with the airbase where the paratroops had landed. It was a puzzling job for the North Americans. Having evacuated the foreign refugees who had fled to the safety zone, they attempted to bring some order to the city. But whereas the people whom they had rescued called them heroes, those in the rebel zone seemed to be blaming them for all that had happened. In the garbage- and rubble-strewn streets of the rebel area, young men with rifles and machine guns waved their fists and shouted, *"Fuera los Yanquis! Viva Bosch!"* A sign on a deserted square read: "The people defend their rights and will not be stopped by Wessin, the

Yankees, or death." And all through the city, even in the safety zone, hidden snipers shot at the Marines and airborne soldiers.

To the United States, which in the first week of its intervention had air-lifted more than twelve thousand tons of military equipment and was shipping in more than a thousand tons of food, all for the avowed purpose of keeping order and alleviating suffering, this seemed like Communist subversion. The Central Intelligence Agency produced a list of fifty-three Dominicans who had Cuban training or were "known leftist activists," and a young Marine complained to a correspondent: "We're here to fight the Communists, only I wish they'd let us fight. You train and train and train, and when there's action you want to be in on it." Another, absorbed in making friends with Dominican children, turned to observe: "These are good people. We're not going to let the Communists take them over."

As puzzled as were the U.S. soldiers, the great majority of the pro-Bosch rebels were equally dismayed. They did not consider themselves to be Communists, but supporters of a legally elected president. A rebel captain in command of a building where sniper fire was being exchanged with the Marines volunteered to an American reporter the information: "I am not a Communist, and no one I have here is a Communist." And at the Constitutionalist headquarters an earnest, rifle-carrying rebel student said: "When Juan Bosch returns we will all turn in our arms. Everyone knows that Bosch will fight Communism with social reforms."

Although the Dominican upheaval had started as a coup and developed into a civil war, the men who wound up shooting at each other were these two somewhat bewildered groups of men. On May 10, correspondent Mo Garcia crossed from the safety zone into the rebel-held area of Santo Domingo and sent this report of his experience:

▶ After dark the rebel zone of this city is eerie, quiet. There are very few lights, but as I was returning from the cable office to my hotel I saw a feeble glow through a window, and inside several men talking and drinking beer at a bar. When I went in, I saw they all had rifles, one of which lay on the counter, pointing at me; I decided to move around the end of the bar. One of them took out a revolver and the bartender asked him not to point it his way. I said I had moved to avoid freezing my eyes on the rifle barrel. They laughed and I joined the conversation.

There were five of them. They were rebels on patrol, members of the "Commando Luperon," which meant they had their headquarters on Luperon Street. Could I join them? Yes. We went outside to where a new white Chevrolet was waiting at the curb, and for forty-five minutes we cruised the jittery rebel city in the dark, crawling along at times, weaving around the smoking piles of burning refuse in the streets, racing across intersections down which firing might come. There were six of us in the car. The driver was a handbag manufacturer. I sat in the middle. The man on my right was a chemist, twenty-seven years old. He had on fatigues and a steel helmet and seemed to be in command. In the back were a university professor, a high-school teacher and a senior law student, all of them in their twenties. They carried San Cristobal .30-cal. rifles made in Santo Domingo.

We rode slowly along Hostos Street. The man on my right barked at the driver, "Race across this intersection!" After we reached the other side he told me, "The American snipers are there at Molinos Dominicanos. They have very good aim." The rebels were not very well organized. There was a discussion about the lights. "Every time you pass a checkpoint, flash your lights, then return to dim," the chemist told the driver. But the driver decided to drive with them on and dim them at the checkpoints.

Cruising slowly along the dark streets and speeding at the intersections, we passed a line of parked cars. The law student pointed them out to me and said they were recovered stolen cars. The rebels were cracking down on looters. Suddenly we heard shouts, "A theft! A theft!" I saw the glint of guns and helmets on men crouching behind parked cars, and three armed men ran toward us. We stopped and stepped out. All was confusion. Other figures moved up in the darkness and a mutual counsel was exchanged. A man said, "I was going to fire in the air." The chemist told him not to fire at anything unless it was absolutely necessary, and then to shoot first at the tires if the car he challenged did not stop.

There was no more talk, so we got in and went on till our blazing lights brought cries of "Halt! Halt!" and I could hear the click of rifle bolts being pulled back. It seemed very loud. Someone yelled, "Put out the lights!" The driver doused them without any questions, and we went on. The chemist said, "One cannot go around with lights on here." Someone in the rear seat said, "One cannot go up there. The yanquis are very close up there." And the chemist repeated, "One cannot drive with lights. This is a dangerous zone. The guards don't have precise instructions."

We crawled along in low until we passed the Constitutionalist headquarters, where the chemist shouted, "*Pueblo, adelante!* People, forward!" as we rolled by. Then he sat back and said, "If the President of the United States had been who he should have been—Kennedy—this would not have happened." We got back to my hotel just as shooting broke out around Barrio San Carlos, where the Marines are putting pressure on. . . .

Next morning around 5:30 heavy shooting and occasional dull thuds woke me up. The sun streamed through my third-floor window. I dressed and went out and walked through the fresh, cool air of early morning. There was a smell of smoke from the trash piles burning in the streets. In spite of the firing in the distance, the city seemed peaceful. Vendors were hawking fresh vegetables and cheese in the streets. On a tall building at a corner there was a sign: "Danger. The yanquis are shooting from Molinos Dominicanos." People hesitated at the corner and then ran across the intersection.

I was walking along General Cabral Street toward the river when someone ran up and shouted, "They have wounded someone! They have wounded someone! He's lying on the steps and no one can get to him!" I joined two others in a jeep for a fast ride toward the river, where we had to stop and go on foot. A young boy with us said, "We must go with our hands up." We went crouching along the wall and sniper fire crackled. I ran down the steps where the man had been hit. He was no longer there. Fire crackled again and I dashed into the customs warehouse at the riverside and saw a group standing around a wounded man. He sat bare to the waist on a swivel chair. On a desk before him lay a blood-stained khaki shirt. He had a makeshift bandage across his chest and over his left shoulder. The bullet had gone in the front, high, and come out the back. He perspired heavily. Flies landed on him and he said, "I am getting nauseated. *Ay, mi madre.*"

Did it hurt?

"Yes, very much."

He kept telling me, "You are a newspaperman? Tell the truth. Say what the yanquis are doing." His friends urged him not to talk because it weakened him, but he kept talking. "If Kennedy were alive," he said, "this would not have happened." ▶

The next week correspondent Garcia visited the rebel zone again, this time to talk to a U.S. Marine prisoner. With a rebel civilian guide in his car, he drove through a maze of barbed wire where the U.S. paratroopers had their checkpoint approaching the corridor, and while he got out to be searched, a soldier in a manhole inspected the bottom of his car. Then he was waved on through. After his interview with the captured Marine, he cabled:

▶ We stopped at a small, heavily guarded, orange-and-blue concrete building and I was taken through the door and into a narrow hall, where I found myself walking after a big, fat, barefoot man who was limping. The man was the Marine prisoner.

We went into a small room where the prisoner sat down in a rocking chair and two guards took positions behind him. Another guard sat at a desk in front of him, his sub-machine gun on the desk. The prisoner was stripped to the waist, from which hung a gray cotton shirt of the kind worn by laborers in the United States and the police here. He wore gray pants of the same material, with the right leg rolled up close to the knee. A red patch of mercurochrome showed on his calf. He smoked incessantly and seemed nervous—a big, two-hundred-pound, twenty-one-year-old boy with red hair, blue eyes, lots of freckles, and a roll on his stomach no Marine first sergeant would care to see. He was reluctant to talk, but after I identified myself he opened up a bit.

He said he was driving a semi-trailer truck with another Marine when they got lost. "We got lost and we got in an ambush. They ambushed us," he said. "I got out of the cab and jumped under the truck. I felt something hit me in the leg." The Marine with him had also jumped out. "He got behind the cab. I heard a scream. I tried to help him, but there was too much fire. My gun jammed. He fell across the bed of the truck. He was laying across the bed of the truck face down, and blood was running out of his shoulder. I seen him and I tried to get him, but I couldn't. There was too much firing. When I tried to help him, they took me away."

The room was very small and people were crowding around us. They all wanted to volunteer information. A woman who had brought the Marine his dinner and breakfast said his pants had been washed and she would iron them as soon as they were dry. She pointed out to the yard where they were hanging. I asked the prisoner how he felt and he said, "O.K., but I'm scared." He said he was getting good treatment, but he wished he had some books. "I asked my guard for a Bible."

A rebel soldier nudged me and said, "Ask him what he thinks of our movement. Ask him if he thinks we're Communists." But I said I couldn't do that.

When it was time for me to go, I offered to do what I could for the prisoner and he said, "Tell the American people I'm all right." I told him I would be glad to send a cable to his family, but he said, "Just tell the Marines."

When I left, a rebel sergeant offered to take me to see the dead Marine. I was surprised, but I got into a pickup truck with him and we drove very fast through the streets. The sergeant honked his horn in a fancy rhythm and blew on a police whistle as we sped along. Now and then bullets zinged near us and we could hear mortar shells exploding in the area. I was trying to make myself as small as possible when suddenly we stopped near the base of the Radio Santo Domingo control tower. An olive drab semi-trailer truck stood in the intersection. The rebel soldiers guarding it objected to our coming near, but the sergeant snarled at them and they backed off.

Sprawled on the platform behind the cab lay the dead Marine. His face was turning black and the flies were swarming over him. There was blood on his head and shoulder. Someone had stolen his shoes, but he had not been moved. The air was getting heavy, and in the oppressive atmosphere the flies were settling. It was going to rain. I looked at my watch; it was nearly noon. He had been killed at 4:30 yesterday. ▶

Twenty-six U.S. servicemen as well as some two thousand Dominicans were killed before the Dominican Republic's chaotic civil war congealed into a stalemate punctuated by sporadic snipings, bombings and political upheavals. By mid-May the Organization of American States had taken responsibility for bringing order to the country, and with the arrival of Latin American troops, the United States began pulling out its Marines. Slowly, patiently, over the next months, an OAS negotiation team worked out a compromise between the rival Dominican governments. The "loyalist" government was brought into line when the United States cut off the funds which had been paying its employees' salaries. The "Constitutionalists" gave up after the inter-American troops made a successful foray into the rebel zone to clear out snipers.

By September both sides had accepted an "act of reconciliation" ending the conflict and setting up a neutral transitional government under which elections could be held. Leaders of both sides were sent abroad to diplomatic posts, and the two ex-presidents, Bosch and Balaguer, returned from exile. In June 1966 the Dominican people elected Joaquín Balaguer over Juan Bosch by a large majority. "The people were fed up with violence," said one observer. And Bosch's name had been used too often in that period of violent upheaval.

The Balaguer government, like its predecessors, was supported by the United States and the OAS. And Balaguer—as did Bosch and Reid before they fell to military coups—chose a moderate policy and committed himself to reforms that would cut the privileges, the graft and smuggling, of the old Trujilloist officers. But such men do not give up easily, nor do the Communists whose leadership was forged and hardened in the battle of 1965.

The Dominican Republic enjoyed a period of peace—interrupted by occasional shootings, bombings and political murders—after the crisis of 1965. But in 1967 a prominent Dominican journalist told a correspondent: "Don't ever deceive yourself about momentary tranquillity in this country. This is a divided house we're living in. If you forget it, you are bound to make the wrong prediction about us."

THE WARRIORS

A SECTION OF PHOTOGRAPHS

Yemeni Royalists, the troops of Imam Badr.

American Marine reconnaissance group in Vietnam.   *Robert Sherrod*

Viet Cong weapons unit in Vietnam.

Venezuelan terrorist band in their jungle camp.   *Douglas*

Katangese gendarmes at the Stanleyville airport.

Anti-Castro Cuban guerrillas in a mountain hideout.   *Bohemia Libre*

French Foreign Legionnaires in Indo-China.   *Carl Mydans*

Anti-government rebel recruits in Guatemala.   *George Silk*

Simba rebels in the Congo.   *AP–Paris Match*

Hukbalahap insurgents in the Philippines. *Carl Mydans*

Turkish Cypriot irregulars in Cyprus.   *Dominique Berretty*

XX

Chaos in the Congo

(1960-1965)

W HEN EUROPEAN ATTENTION focused on "the dark continent" of
Africa in the mid-nineteenth century, King Leopold II of Belgium,
avid to join the grab for colonies, fixed his ambition on the far-off regions of
the Congo River, which had just been explored by Henry Stanley. Leopold
had written a sort of guidebook of colonialism for himself in which he
summarized some thoughts: "How to find people to civilize, to lead to

304

progress, while at the same time ensuring fresh revenues for ourselves, jobs for the middle class, a little activity for our army, and for Belgium as a whole a chance to prove to the world that it too is an imperial people capable of dominating and enlightening others." With these inspiring ideas he persuaded the Berlin Conference of 1885 to grant him the heart of Africa as his own personal property.

The Congo spreads over Central Africa for 900,000 square miles—equal to almost all of western Europe, eighty times the size of Belgium—and it was said that Leopold fixed its boundaries by "explorers' fatigue," the points at which his agents tired of walking, though actually they were limited more by the counterclaims of Britain, France and Portugal in the surrounding territory. It had been settled over the centuries by successive waves of popular migration, and by the time the Belgians pushed their way in, there were some fourteen million people of a variety of backgrounds sprinkled rather thinly through the rank equatorial forests and the vast wooded savannas of the plains. Some were grouped into cohesive kingdoms, some in more loosely knit and often warring tribes, some were semi-nomadic. They represented seven major "culture clusters" and spoke some four hundred different dialects.

Of all the things King Leopold had hoped to gain from colonization, he found most rewarding the "fresh revenues for ourselves" that he got from the Congo: ivory from herds of elephants and rubber from the stands of wild rubber trees. And when in 1892 he imposed an export duty on the ivory, he found as well the "little activity for our army" he was looking for. Arab slave traders in the area, whom he had used as local governors, objected to the tax, and there was brief, colorful warfare; but after that King Leopold ruled his "Congo Free State" uncontested by any but the local African chieftains.

The primary thing the King did not do was "prove to the world that [Belgium] is an imperial people capable of dominating and enlightening others." For one thing, the Belgian people and their parliament were not allowed a look-in on the King's African estate. For another, tales of his mismanagement there, and the suppression of the Congolese, theft of their land, "veiled slavery" of the native rubber tappers, and inhuman punishments leaked to the outer world. The Belgian parliament was roused to look into the King's affairs. In 1908 it took his "Free State" from him and formed instead a colony: the Belgian Congo.

From the beginning it was the wealth of the Congo that most absorbed the Belgians. The glittering natural resources of this dark land, they discovered, were far beyond the dreams of Leopold in his preoccupation with ivory and rubber, and they were diligent in developing them. By 1960 this vast colony produced some seventy-five percent of the world's industrial diamonds, as well as cobalt, copper, tin, uranium and gold, and it was the world's second largest exporter of palm oil.

All this had been developed and was controlled by a few private Belgian companies, great cartels that managed the Congo's economic life, the mining, agriculture, banking and transport. Europeans owned these giant combines and furnished the management and technicians; Africans furnished the labor. They did not mix. And the great majority of Belgians—those who had never seen their colony—had little interest in or sense of duty toward it. Many held stocks in the cartels which fed upon the Congo's natural resources, but so did many British and U.S. citizens. It was a business matter. Thus they were shocked, in 1959, to hear of rioting in Léopoldville and angry demands for independence.

When the wave of nationalism that swept Africa in the 1950's lapped at the Congo's borders, the colony was still administered paternalistically by just two men: the Minister for Colonies in Brussels and the Belgian Governor General in Léopoldville. No Congolese had risen higher than a minor clerk in his own government, and no one, black or white, could vote. The Belgian plan was to educate the Congolese gradually but on a massive scale, "bringing them up together" step by step, and there were twenty-five thousand schools throughout the country teaching the rudiments of reading and writing and preparing their students for simple manual and agricultural work. A very few were trained as technicians, schoolteachers and clergymen. Not until 1956 were there any facilities for higher education, nor were the Congolese allowed to go abroad to study. On the eve of independence there were fourteen Congolese university graduates—out of a population of nearly fourteen million.

Prepared or not, the Congolese longed for an independent nation of their own, though they were far from certain what kind of nation they really wanted. There were four schools of thought among them, forming four rudimentary political parties. The Abako Party, of which Joseph Kasavubu was the president, was primarily interested in the rights and liberties of the Bankongo people, inheritors of the culture and language of the ancient, semi-fabulous kingdom of Kongo. The Conokat Party of Moise Tshombe, top man in Katanga province, wanted a loose confederation of large semi-independent states under a titular central government, the power residing in the states themselves—especially that of Katanga, which contributed sixty-five percent of the Congo's wealth. The Belgian-sponsored National Progress Party was content to postpone the whole idea of independence for a while.

Only the party of Patrice Lumumba—the National Congolese Movement—wanted a strong, united, independent Congo now.

There was no time to resolve the conflicts inherent in these views. In Brussels the Belgians heard the cry for independence with a sympathetic ear, called a round-table conference, and gave the Congo representatives what they said they wanted: free elections in four months and independence six weeks after that—June 30, 1960. A vague, warm sense of brotherhood—and a reluctance to send their sons to war to keep imperial power—pervaded Belgium, while those who lived (and made their living) in the Congo felt that independence need not bring much change. The untrained Congolese would have to lean on them to run the mines and the plantations, the transportation and communications—even their government—as they had done before. The only army that they had was the 25,000-man Force Publique, composed of uprooted young Congolese who were quite literally whipped into shape by their 1,100 Belgian officers. Lieutenant General Emil Janssens, Belgian Commander of the Force, wrote on the blackboard of the officers' mess the sly equation: "Before Independence = After Independence."

Among the great mass of the Congolese, seventy-eight percent of whom still lived in the primitive bush and belonged to more than two hundred often antipathetic tribes, there was no sense of national identity nor any very clear idea of what independence meant. Some tribesmen believed the story that if a box were filled with earth, on Independence Day that earth would turn to gold. Some traveled from remote villages to camp beside the railroad tracks, thinking that independence would arrive by train. Some city workers thought their pay would rise as much as a thousand percent, or at least match what was paid to white workers.

There were some others with a clearer notion of Western ideology and institutions. These were the *évolués,* the "evolved ones," who had been brought into the European orbit and were a little better educated than the average Congolese, able to read and write, to hold positions as technicians or as clerks in the lower ranks of government offices or business firms, to educate themselves in the theories—if not the practice—of Western politics. They lived in the de-tribalized quarters of the larger towns, wore European clothes, observed and were infected by the white man's love of money and the things that it would buy, and had become increasingly resentful of white prejudice.

Of these *évolués,* numbering perhaps 150,000 throughout the country, no more than about a dozen had "evolved" to the point where they could exercise political leadership in the Western sense. In this process many had forfeited the protection of their tribal identity. By and large, the African is less self-centered than the Western man, less eager for material well-being, and less concerned with planning for the future than with the enjoyment of the present hour. He is less an individual—with both the lonely freedom and the responsibilities that implies—than a member of his tribe.

Thus in 1960 the Congo was like her own dark turbulent waterways, fed by many tribal streams, rumbling with the sound of distant cataracts, full of crosscurrents and isolated eddies. And on its surface rode these dozen "Westernized" politicians, skating about like waterbugs, changing direction without seeming cause, sometimes colliding, sometimes joining up in pairs or little groups to ride along together. Joseph Kasavubu, president of the powerful Abako, was presumed to be the nation's leader, but it was Patrice Lumumba, with the backing of most of the evolved ones and of an amalgam of small independent tribes welded together simply by his charismatic personality, who won the May elections.

By June the Congo had a parliament (though few of its members knew just what that meant) and the Belgians had selected Kasavubu to be president and given the premiership to Lumumba with his preponderance of votes. On Independence Day the streets were quiet, the people smiling; the tribal villagers were relatively calm, only a little frightened or exhilarated by they knew not what; the Belgians too were quiet in their handsome houses in the better parts of town, all set to carry on behind the black façade. Only some rude words by Lumumba jarred on the pleasantries of the official speeches.

One more day of stillness, then the explosion: with Belgian strictions gone, tribal hatreds flamed into warfare in the bush, rioting in the cities. Striking workers shot arrows at the Force Publique; the Force shot bullets at the crowd. The strikes spread and the rioting went uncontrolled. Then on the fifth day the Force Publique itself went wild. In Thysville and then Léopoldville the soldiers mutinied, disarmed their Belgian officers and, with their guns in hand, joined in the rioting. Europeans trying to flee the chaos were turned back at the borders and humiliated; some were killed. Belgian paratroopers were sent in to rescue them and repaid the blacks' atrocities with white brutalities.

In the disorder Moise Tshombe seized the opportunity to withdraw his Katanga province from the republic and declare it an independent state, while Kasavubu and Lumumba flew from one city to the next to try to stop the rioting and tribal wars. To gain control over the mutinous Force Publique, they promoted every soldier to officer's rank with officer's pay, and fired the Belgians they replaced. Sergeant Victor Lundula was made commanding general of this new army, with ex-soldier journalist Joseph Mobutu as his chief of staff. Then Lumumba turned to the outer world—first to the U.S., then to the U.S.S.R., then the United Nations—appealing for help in ridding his country of the Belgian troops and bringing order to the disintegrating land.

The United Nations responded with remarkable alacrity. Three days later, on July 15, the first contingent of U.N. troops arrived: 40 Ghanaian soldiers, snappy in black berets, followed by 600 tough Tunisians. The next day, contingents from Morocco and Ethiopia landed in Léopoldville. Within a week of the first call, 3,500 U.N. troops from African nations were in the Congo, spreading out to various trouble spots; 6,000 more from Europe, Africa, Asia and America were on their way. It was a truly worldwide effort, the largest in U.N. history, with thirty-five nations actively involved, fourteen of them sending fighting troops. American Globemasters brought in the Tunisians and Moroccans; Russian Ilyushins brought the Ghanaians. Thus they flew to the rescue from every side—bringing the Cold War with them.

Ralph Bunche, the U.N. representative in Léopoldville, declared that the U.N. force "could not use arms to wound or kill Congolese, for that would defeat its purpose"—which was to bring peace. But not every U.N. soldier understood this basic aim. One Ghanaian alighted from the plane that flew him in, waving his rifle, crying, "Who do we fight?" And a Guinean officer told his troops: "We're here to represent Black Africa and see the white man out."

Except for Katanga, the U.N. did "see the white man out," replacing Belgian soldiers with peace-keeping units. But Tshombe's seeming immunity from U.N. intervention encouraged others to establish "independent states," and when the Premier sent troops to put these movements down, the chaos in the Congo threatened to consolidate into an all-out civil war. Congolese army soldiers advised by Czechoslovakians fought Congolese rebels advised by Belgians; Ben Lulua tribesmen fought Baluba tribesmen; caught in the middle, small U.N. contingents were set upon and some were killed. One hundred thousand refugees fled from the hut-burning and indiscriminate slaughter into the bush.

The dozen politicians trying to run their wildly careening country denounced one another, plotted one another's murder, put one another under house arrest. Kasavubu fired Lumumba and the Premier in turn fired the President, but the bewildered parliament reinstated both. At last, in mid-September, Colonel Joseph Mobutu, chief of staff of the fragmented army, announced a military coup, suspended parliament and put Premier Lumumba under arrest. Then he ordered Soviet and all other Communist diplomats to leave the country.

Few wars are fought with armies neatly lined up facing each other, but the war in the Congo, with its roving bands of undisciplined soldiers carrying rusty Belgian rifles, its magic-ridden tribesmen armed with poisoned arrows and filed-down elephant guns, its secessionist provinces and political fratricide, all overlaid with the international conflicts of the thirty-five-nation U.N. force, was the least neat, perhaps, of any.

Typical of the confusion was the battle at the Ghanaian embassy in Léopoldville on November 25, 1960, as Lee Griggs described it:

▶ It was an unprecedented diplomatic situation that caused the violence in Léopoldville on Monday. Joseph Mobutu was determined to make good his promise to expel the Ghanaian chargé d'affaires Nathaniel Welbeck, who, by rights, should have been gone two months ago. He had refused to leave when he was declared persona non grata and his efforts to remain had been successful because Patrice Lumumba, although under house arrest, had Ghana's Kwame Nkrumah and the United Nations' Rajeshwar Dayal working hard on his behalf.

At eleven a.m. the Congolese Interior Commissioner, Jose Nussbaumer, accompanied by Security Inspector Henri N'gampo, walked past the skeleton U.N. Tunisian guard into the grounds of the Ghanaian embassy residence on "Embassy Row," which overlooks the Congo River's Stanley Pool, just above the rapids. It was a clear hot summer day and down on the riverbank two big crocodiles yawned lazily some fifty feet from the embassy door.

N'gampo remained outside and shouted threats: "Blood will flow here today unless he goes!" But Nussbaumer brushed past the Ghanaian escort police who guarded the door under United Nations orders. Then loud and violent words drifted out of the embassy windows: Welbeck shouting, "I am not home to you. This is my territory. You are a trespasser. Get out!" And Nussbaumer's answer, "You are too vulgar to be a diplomat. There's a Sabena plane leaving this afternoon at three o'clock and by God you'll be on it!"

As Nussbaumer stomped out of the residence, Welbeck came to the door and waved a red-and-white-striped Ghanaian fetish stick after him, shouting, "Get out and stay out!" Nussbaumer turned to shout back,

"I'll be here at three o'clock to see that you catch that plane." And promptly at three he did return to escort Welbeck to the airport.

Tunisian guards were slouching on the lawn and several urinated openly in the embassy garden. Suddenly shots rang out across the street and the Tunisians zippered their trousers and grabbed their sub-machine guns. But it was only the Congolese civilian police shooting a ten-foot boa constrictor out of a tree.

Again sharp words at the embassy doorway and Welbeck hollered, "I refuse to leave." With that, Nussbaumer called for Congolese army troops. But the United Nations, confident it could outbluff the Congolese, rushed 150 Tunisian soldiers to the embassy to reinforce the skeleton guard of twenty. They took up their positions in a solid phalanx surrounding the embassy grounds. It was now a quarter to five and the Sabena plane took off without Welbeck. As it roared low over the embassy, Nussbaumer glanced up, clenched his fists and swore. Welbeck emerged from the embassy door and shouted gleefully, "I'm still here!"

All this while, Security Inspector N'gampo had been smoking the raw marijuana that the Congolese call *bangi*, going behind a hedge across the street to light his little metal pipe. Now crazed with the drug, he screamed, "This is absolute provocation! We will kill him!" A hundred Congolese troops arrived with two armored cars and deployed themselves across the narrow street facing the embassy. Both sides were jittery, with the men on each side ready to open fire on command. N'gampo, by now a raving maniac, was pacing around in drugged excitement, shouting for violence, but for more than an hour no one made a move.

Lieutenant Colonel Joseph N'kokolo, commander of the Léopoldville army garrison, was in charge and at 7:40 he and four Congolese lieutenants started walking across the street to the embassy with the evident peaceful intention of negotiating with the Tunisian lieutenant commanding the U.N. forces. They were wearing pistols, but they were holstered. Suddenly N'gampo shouted hysterically: "Fire! Fire!"

The Congolese hesitated, but the tense Tunisians didn't wait to see. A sub-machine gun chattered. N'kokolo caught a burst that ripped open his chest and killed him instantly. His lieutenants ran for cover and heavy firing started from both sides. The troops were separated only by a narrow street with hedges on both sides, and N'gampo, still standing up and screaming for more fire, was hit and fell. He died two days later in the U.N. hospital.

The firing continued as it grew dark. At first it was heavy and

311

continuous, with tracers lighting the night sky and an occasional thud of shells from the armored cars. At eleven o'clock a truce team from the United Nations and the Congolese army set out to try to stop the fighting, but they had no radio communication with their soldiers and were caught and pinned down by crossfire two blocks from the embassy and had to pull back.

After midnight the shots dwindled to a dozen or so each hour as both sides lay low in the moonless dark. At dawn Mobutu agreed to withdraw his troops on the understanding that Welbeck would be flown out at once. And once again the cease-fire mission drove to the now quiet battle scene and entered the embassy. They found Welbeck in his bedroom, crouched between the beds.

As he emerged from the bullet-scarred residence, carrying his fetish stick and wearing his astrakhan cap, he managed a weak smile and called out: "I was in danger all night long. But I am moving only because my government asked me to." He disappeared into a U.N. Volkswagen and headed for the airport, leaving behind six dead and forty-one wounded—Tunisians and Congolese. ▶

This bit of senseless, almost ludicrous killing was but a tiny fragment of the entire ludicrous and tragic warfare in the Congo from 1960 almost without stop until 1965.

Premier Lumumba had been in protective custody during the incident of the Ghanaian embassy—guarded from both friends and enemies by U.N. troops. Late in November he escaped, but on December 1 he was recaptured and, now under Congolese army guard, was thrown into the Thysville jail, charged with inciting to army mutiny. He had indeed set Congolese soldier against Congolese, but the imprisonment of Lumumba's person did not stop Lumumbaism in the bush. His troops, supplied by Russian planes, increased their terrorism in the eastern provinces, and his vice president, Antoine Gizenga, established a Lumumbist administration in the northeastern capital of Stanleyville. The tribal warfare set off by this civil war increased until, at the time Lumumba was arrested, three hundred thousand Baluba tribesmen had fled from Lulua territory and were starving in the bush. At the peak of the famine, it was reported by U.N. relief teams, there were two hundred deaths a day—a secondary side effect of war.

Presumably it seemed imperative to Kasavubu and Mobutu to send their fractious rival to be jailed in some far place where his adjutants could get no word from him. They sent him to Katanga, to Moise Tshombe.

Correspondent Eric Robins, in a dispatch sent January 18, 1961, described his arrival:

► Prophetically, the Air Katanga DC-4 from Léopoldville flew into a crackling tropical thunderstorm as the pilot circled Elisabethville and cryptically radioed the control tower: "I have a precious parcel on board." On direct orders from Tshombe, the plane taxied off the runway away from the main apron and came to a standstill near a small hangar remote from the airport main building. An armored car pulled up and trained its cannon on the door of the plane.

Lightning slashed black stormclouds as steel-helmeted Katangese soldiers and police brandishing their machine guns swarmed round the airliner. And in this grimly Wagnerian fashion, the Congo's deposed premier, Patrice Lumumba, was delivered into the hands of his arch-enemy, Tshombe.

Swedish United Nations guards at the airport, tall and tough, stood by, shadow figures in the background, as Lumumba, blindfolded with a grimy bandage, his hands tied behind him, and roped to two of his political lieutenants, was directed down the steps of the plane. Within sight of a large airport billboard proclaiming "Welcome to Free Katanga," the trembling, stumbling Lumumba and his fellow prisoners fell to the ground in a hail of savage baton, rifle-butt and fist blows and kicks from a gauntlet of snarling Katangese.

One of the victims screamed loudly as the thunder rolled across the veld. And then, with the soldiers forming a screen of steel around the vehicle, Lumumba was flung into a Gendarmerie jeep and trampled on by his guards as he was driven away. ►

Premier Lumumba was murdered that day or the next. But not for a month was his death made public, and then Moise Tshombe, through his Belgian sycophants, announced that Lumumba and his companions had "escaped" and been attacked and killed by "hostile tribesmen" in an unnamed village.

Political murder now became the vogue, adding a new face to this multifaceted war. In the week after the belated announcement of Lumumba's death, twelve pro-Lumumba politicians were taken from jail in Bakwanga and beaten in the public square and seven of them were killed, while in Lumumba territory fourteen anti-Lumumba men, ten of them members of parliament, were similarly slaughtered. Piecing together all the dark rumors and murky incidents, one observer estimated that close to twenty percent of the Congo's parliament had been killed in the first year of the nation's life.

Belgians became fair game again; many were beaten or raped, and some were killed. In the streets of Léopoldville, running slashing knifefights between Africans flowed through the darkened native quarter in deadly silence, leaving some stunned, some castrated, some dead.

Like the running knifefights that flowed through the streets of Léopoldville, playing out tribal animosities and political hatreds—vicious, senseless, brutal, and inspired by fear as deep as childhood terror in the night—the war in the Congo flowed on through the years. To Baluba villagers it was the rush of Lulua tribesmen with spears and guns and whips made of bicycle chains, the hut-burning and slaughter and the flight into the bush, the gathering in makeshift refugee camps and the starvation and descent into cannibalism. To Europeans on the plantations, to the missionaries in the outposts, and to the Belgian civilians even in the towns, it was the horror of a drug-crazed gang of dirty soldiers appearing at the windows in the night, entering to humiliate and threaten, steal what they liked in the name of the Congolese army, promise protection and then leave—only to return to seize and mutilate and rape. And to the United Nations units it was the nightmare paralysis of soldiers sent to keep the peace who were compelled to witness, immobile, war's worst atrocities.

Frequently the U.N. soldiers were themselves the objects of attack. They were humiliated, threatened, beaten up, forced to take their shoes off and run the gauntlet of laughing Congolese until they dropped. And some were murdered. Thirteen Italian airmen flew into Kindu to deliver two scout cars to the Malayan U.N. outfit guarding the airfield there and the Malayans took their guests to lunch. Into the quiet mess hall came a leaderless unit of the Congolese army, drug-crazed and wild-eyed, looking for "Belgian paratroopers." They seized the Italians and, while the armed Malayans—bound by U.N. orders not to fire unless fired upon—looked on helplessly, clubbed them with rifle butts and took them off to the city jail. There they were murdered and cut into pieces, and the negotiable parts of their bodies were bandied about the town. The U.N. could do no more than reinforce the Malayan guard outfit, while the murderers moved on along the dusty roads, looting, raping and killing as they liked.

Nevertheless, by mid-1961 the U.N. had brought some peace to the fighting tribes and concord among the leftist and rightist factions of the central government. Warfare was at a lull. The primary problem now was to bring Katanga under the central government's rule. Early in the Congo Republic's history, the U.N. General Assembly had determined to "safeguard its unity, territorial integrity and political independence." The "unity" included the return of secessionist Katanga to the Republic. The U.N. Security Council later added that all foreign military and political advisers should be evacuated from the Congo and at the same time authorized its units in the field "the use of force, if necessary, in the last resort."

In September 1961 the U.N. commander in Katanga tried to implement these orders and deport the foreign mercenaries who were the mainstay of Moise Tshombe's independent army. They were surprised to find themselves in all-out battle with the Katangese Gendarmerie. The second Congo war—that of the United Nations *vs.* Katanga—had begun.

Describing it in a dispatch sent on September 21, correspondent Lee Griggs wrote:

▶ This is war of the worst kind, fought not with nuclear bombs and ballistic missiles but by two reluctant armies, both jittery in the extreme. It goes on chiefly in Elisabethville, capital of Katanga, which is now in the midst of sub-equatorial spring with flowers growing in the well-kept Belgian gardens and tidy African communes, and the Jacaranda trees in full, violet bloom throughout the city.

War broke out last Wednesday, after the United Nations made a massive miscalculation that it would be easy to take over Katanga and reintegrate it with the Congo in accordance with the Security Council resolution. The ease with which his forces of 4,000 Indians, Irish, Swedes, Malayans and Ethiopians had rounded up and deported all but 100 of the 400 white military officers and mercenaries who led the Katanga army had made the U.N. commander cockily confident.

In the first surge, the United Nations took the post office and the communications building in the center of the city and occupied the Radio Katanga building, where they calmly announced that they were taking over Katanga. They confidently figured that that ended it. But the Katangese made six furious counterattacks on the post office in the next four days and the fight for it has raged intermittently ever since.

The two armies avoid encountering each other most of the time. But when clashes occur, both sides shoot everything in sight that moves. Snipers are constantly active on both sides and hardly an hour passes without bullets whining overhead somewhere in town. Civilians stay indoors away from windows. Streets are deserted. Shops are closed tight, many with their windows pockmarked by bullet holes or shattered by grenades and mortars. Every day firefights break out in the afternoon and continue with only brief breaks all night. All the sounds of war are here—the whine of rifle bullets, staccato blasts from Sten and Bren guns, thundering bangs of bazookas and whistles of two-inch and four-inch mortar shells overhead and the earthshaking roars as they hit. Between outbursts, an unearthly quiet settles on the town, broken only by an occasional crowing rooster or barking dog.

It is at the Katanga Radio's one-story, yellow stucco building where casualties were heaviest. When the Katangese counterattacked there, the defending Gurkhas took a quick toll of twenty-five dead Katanga police and soldiers. Courageous Red Cross nuns braved repeated U.N. fire to go into the station grounds and toss the already rotting bodies into the building's cesspool as a crude grave, covering them with blankets. But for several days arms and legs, grotesquely stiff with rigor mortis, protruded from beneath the blankets. The stench was awful. Finally the Katangese managed to get to the scene and pour lime on the bodies and cover the hole with rusty metal sheeting. They leaned a cross against it, topped with a soldier's helmet and festooned with three gunbelts. A Red Cross doctor scribbled "Died for Katanga" on the cross, but an angry Belgian rushed up and wrote "Murdered by the United Nations" in its place. Then a U.N. patrol appeared and fired over the heads of the crowd to disperse them. ▶

The fighting in September ended in an shaky truce while both sides built up their forces and imported planes. New white mercenaries were brought in to replace the ones deported, and in December the fighting flared again. This time the United Nations managed a more decisive cease-fire and Tshombe—not for the first time nor the last—agreed to end the secession of Katanga.

But all through 1962 the province continued to operate as a sovereign nation with its own currency, stamps and border control. It also continued to keep for itself all of the taxes paid by the wealthy Belgian combines in its territory while Tshombe talked with the central government, made promises, reneged, over and over again. The U.N. and the distracted government, meanwhile, were busy putting down secessionist copycats in South Kasai and, much more ominous, in the Stanleyville area, where Antoine Gizenga, heir to Lumumba, had stirred up more rebellion.

At Christmastime the Katangese once more attacked the U.N. units in

Elisabethville. It was the third and final round, and the U.N. soldiers—
Tunisians, Ethiopians, Irish, Gurkhas, Sikhs and Indians, supported by Swedish jets—fought with a cold, efficient determination. In three days they
secured Elisabethville and took the surrounding area with its outlying towns
and rail points. The Katangese army was defeated; the few planes of its air
force were destroyed; Tshombe fled to Rhodesia and then into exile among
his Belgian friends.

The U.N.-Katanga war was over, and for nearly a year the Republic of
the Congo clung to the "unity and political independence" that the United
Nations had undertaken to safeguard.

The third war in the Congo's tangled history was an outgrowth of its
earlier wars, as wars are apt to be. The United Nations fought Moise
Tshombe to preserve the unity of the Congo and the authority of its central
government. But the Western nations of that international body much
preferred him to the other element disruptive to this unity, the neo-
Lumumbist left, which threatened to exploit tribal discontent. There had
been sporadic rebellions ever since independence. In the summer of 1962
alone, the army put down two revolts: in Kindu and North Katanga. And in
the spring of 1963 the province of South Kasai was "pacified" and thousands
of tribesmen massacred.

There were sound reasons for this unrest among the tribes. Since the
bright promise of independence, if life had changed for them at all, it had
worsened with the exodus of Belgian employers from the plantations, Belgian
teachers, Belgian nuns and missionary doctors from the hospitals. The "black
colonialists" of the swollen bureaucratic government had even less regard for
the tribesmen than had the whites, and they were aware of the gulf between
their life in the bush and the glittering life for the few in the capitals with
their big houses, shiny cars and cocktail parties on wide lawns. They knew
that a minor government official earned fifteen thousand francs a month
while a palm-nut cutter earned fifteen hundred. Men who had looked forward
to independence with shining hope, who had even cleaned up their cemeteries
in expectation of the resurrection of the dead on June 30, 1960, saw that not
only had the dead not risen but the living were hungry and their hopes were
gone. The independence that the politicians spoke of was to them a sham.

In September 1963 the first troubled news of unrest among the Bapende
and Babunda tribes of Kwilu province reached Léopoldville, only 250 miles to
the west, but no one in the army cared to go there. There had been three
more mutinies in the Congolese army, and pressure on the soldiers to go out

317

and fight did not seem wise. Nothing was done until January 1964, when a state of emergency was declared. By that time most of the Kwilu provincial government officials had fled from the terror or been killed. And in February the next rebellion stirred—far to the east, in Kivu, among the pygmoid Bafulero tribe.

The pattern of primitive unrest seemed much the same in all these tribal uprisings. But now another pattern became clear. Late in 1963 President Kasavubu had sent the unmanageable Congolese parliament home on enforced, indefinite vacation. Many of those parliamentarians of the Lumumba-Gizenga camp had gone, not home, but across the border to the neighboring Brazzaville Congo. There, with the help of friendly Soviet officials, they formed a "Committee of Congolese National Liberation." Soon the Chinese were advising them in a more practical way, setting up guerrilla training camps at Gambona on the Brazzaville border and at Bujumbura in the neighboring kingdom of Burundi. Lumumbist sympathizers and army deserters came to these camps in the hundreds. And it was not by chance that the sites of the new rebellions in 1964 were in Kwilu, which has access to Gambona, and in Kivu, on the Burundi border.

The Kwilu rebellion was exploited by a revolutionary genius, Pierre Mulele, ex-ambassador to Cairo from the onetime Stanleyville secessionist government of Antoine Gizenga. Mulele had been visiting in China and returned with a sure touch to play on the Babunda tribesmen he knew well, appealing both to their ancient superstitions and to their present-day frustrations. Soon the witch doctors were passing out "Mulele water" guaranteed to make rebel warriors safe from harm. "Bullets cannot hurt you," a captured Mulelist assured an interviewer. "They just go right through you and leave a little hole. But our poisoned arrows can kill you with a touch." They gave as reason for their war against the central government the fact that "the soldiers came to take the golden book away from Mulele. It was passed from Lumumba to Gizenga, who gave it to Mulele. The golden book contains all power. Nobody can rule the Congo for long without it. It has all secrets: who the Congolese are, where they came from, and how much land belongs to whom." But at the same time they spoke with quite astute political sophistication of the "profiteers of independence" who ran the government for their own private gain and must be deposed by the "popular will."

The outbreak in Kivu was taken over by another revolutionary, Gaston Soumialot, a mystic and the Lumumbist party's propaganda chief, who had set up the training camp in Bujumbura. His *jeunesse* rebels often went naked to the waist and wore fur bracelets and hats made of spotted feline fur. Their weapons were usually no more than spears and long bushknives, though they learned to make Molotov cocktails out of Primus beer bottles and occasionally used a kind of primitive muzzle-loader gun that they called a "poo-poo," which fired bolts and nails. The political message that Soumialot brought to them they sometimes sang in a primitive five-tone chant: "We love Lumumba. He gave us freedom. Tshombe spoiled it."

All this primitive innocence was belied by the sound guerrilla tactics followed in each rebellion after the National Liberation Committee had been formed. Phase one consisted of cutting communications by damaging bridges and ferries and burning every vehicle they came across. Phase two was the assassination of policemen and provincial officials and the destruction of all radios in the mission stations and on Belgian plantations. Neither Mulele nor Soumialot wanted to scare the whites out of their territories: they were needed for the economy and for education. But primitive savagery was not so easily channeled, and their control, once they got rebellion really rolling, was very tenuous. It could not hold the anti-white resentment from flaring into acts of sadism and slaughter.

Four years after independence, then, these two full-size rebellions roiled the nation, and more were brewing—in South Kasai, in North Katanga, in Kindu and in the vital Stanleyville area in the northeast. In June, with the last of the United Nations troops scheduled to leave, the Congo seemed to be drifting toward disintegration with no one to stop it. The politicians in the capital tried desperate measures to keep the country in one piece. They recalled Moise Tshombe from the European exile he had imposed upon himself after his defeat by the United Nations, and he became the head of a new "government of national reconciliation," calling for the "liberation of all Congolese patriots." These patriots included such men as Antoine Gizenga, who had been in and out of jail ever since the collapse of his Stanleyville government in 1961; Pierre Mulele, busy with his rebellion in Kwilu; and Albert Kalonji, self-styled "King of South Kasai," who returned to become Tshombe's agricultural minister.

But even with this governmental mixed bag of insurgents in nominal accord, the rebellions continued to grow. Gaston Soumialot proclaimed himself head of a "Revolutionary Government of the Western Congo." His *jeunesse* had taken the cities of Baudouinville and Albertville, and as they moved northwest through Kindu, thousands of local tribesmen joined them, taking the name of Simba, which means lion in Swahili. On August 5, spearheaded by some thirty slow-marching Simbas armed with religious wands, the rebels captured Stanleyville. There they surpassed themselves in terror and atrocities. One hundred twenty local officials and government representatives were executed publicly in front of the Lumumba monument and their bodies left to rot. The mayor himself was eviscerated while he lived and his liver and kidneys were eaten before his eyes.

The fall of Stanleyville sent shock waves through the capital. More than one sixth of this enormous country was in the hands of rebels or else so restive that the army was afraid to send its soldiers there. And although the insurrectionists fought under different names—Mulelists, partisans, *jeunesse*, Simbas—they all had a common enemy, the "black colonialists" of the central government, and they all revered one name: Lumumba. The terror of their magic "dawa" so infected the countryside that even the government soldiers panicked at their approach. Sometimes, to scatter the demoralized troops, they needed to do no more than telephone that they were coming.

With the United Nations gone, there seemed to be no one to stop the terror and the massacres. Nevertheless, resistance stiffened, and only a few days after the fall of Stanleyville the army retook Baudouinville and Albertville. And at Bukavu, the Belgians' favorite resort town on the shore of Lake Kivu, the rebels were thrown back by one determined colonel. On August 27, 1964, correspondent Jonathan Randal arrived in Bukavu as the army was mopping up the city and cabled the following report:

▶ The American-donated GMC truck braked to a stop in a cloud of dust in front of army headquarters, a former European villa at the end of one of the many fingers of land jutting into Lake Kivu. It was three p.m. Sunday. Half a dozen soldiers jumped to the dusty ground. Others pushed two rebel prisoners out of the truck. One prisoner, his hands tied in front of him, wore a dirty undershirt and dirty shorts. The other prisoner was completely naked. His hands were tied behind his back, his face was a bloody mess. He lay panting in the dust. The soldiers crowded around him, screaming at him. Finally one soldier found a dirty cloth and tied it around his loins. Then the prisoner was marched fifteen feet across the road to the edge of the bank which sloped down to Lake Kivu, twenty feet below. The soldiers were screaming ever louder and suddenly the naked prisoner was shoved over the bank. More than a hundred rounds were fired from automatic weapons. The prisoner's head bobbed up above the water near the bank, went under, reappeared, and disappeared for good. The firing was still going on. It stopped only when Colonel Leonard Mulamba rushed out of the staff meeting which was going on inside the headquarters and ordered the shooting stopped. A

320

minute later a soldier gave the other prisoner a cigarette. The electric charge of violence had been temporarily spent.

Tireless, calm, polite Colonel Mulamba saved more than merely a prisoner's life in a part of the world where human life is cheap. Last week he saved Bukavu from a massive rebel attack. In six days his troops killed more than a thousand rebels. For the first time in the Congolese National Army's history, troops stood and fought—and fought well. Admittedly the troops had their backs to the lake and few soldiers knew how to swim. But in the past they have thrown away their weapons and uniforms and joined the rebels. Mulamba's leadership saved their reputation and could well be the beginning of a new tradition in the Congolese army.

Mulamba deserves great credit, not just for beating back the rebels but for trying to maintain law and order, for trying to prevent reprisals against innocent civilians. The justice minister of Kivu had made a radio broadcast in which he said that rebels did not deserve a trial and should be killed immediately. Sensing the possible consequences of this open invitation to violence, Mulamba, driving an unarmed jeep, led a small column on a tour of the city. Rebel cadavers, many with their throats cut, baked and bloated in the warm mountain air. In the commercial section, which was worst hit by the attack and its aftermath, fly-covered bodies lay in the street among the looted goods. Here a body, there a hobbyhorse, a sewing machine, cheap steel footlockers, blankets. The rebels had started the looting and then told the population to continue the pilfering. Later the soldiers took over. From time to time Mulamba stopped the jeep, jumped out, disarmed the soldiers guilty of pilfering, and sent them back to army headquarters.

At a traffic circle a man ran out and stopped Mulamba's jeep. He said his brother had been arrested after Mass on Sunday, dragged out of church by policemen and hacked to death with machetes. Mulamba listened. Suddenly a green pickup truck used to collect cadavers for burial stopped in front of Mulamba. A desperate man, dressed in a dirty undershirt and pants, started screaming at him in Swahili: "They want to kill me because they say I am a Mulelist. But I am innocent. The policeman who arrested me is trying to settle a personal grudge." On and on he ranted with the conviction of a man who knew that by some odd quirk of fate he had come on the only person who could save him. He was on his knees in the back of the truck and Mulamba stood in the road beside him, his neat little mustache quivering with anger. Finally he

321

ordered the man released and sent a soldier to find the policeman who had arrested him. "You are to take this man back to his home," he said. "And I will have you executed if I ever hear of his being molested again."

When they had left, Mulamba turned to the men around him. "This is very dangerous," he said soberly. "Everybody goes around arresting innocent people. It is getting to be catastrophic. The whole population, which was with us, is going to be entirely against us if this goes on. It is very, very serious. You simply don't kill people *au hasard*. I do not understand." And then, still clinging to his extraordinary self-control, he sighed: "I have to do everything myself."

And it was true. During the wild three days of fighting Mulamba acted as his own sergeant, company commander, intelligence officer and community-relations officer. And afterward he stopped the looting and indiscriminate killing. It's a pity he is alone. ▶

Colonel Mulamba did have the assistance and advice of two experienced Belgian army officers. When Premier Tshombe took over the central government, he had immediately begun to build up a white mercenary force, as he had done when he was president of secessionist Katanga. By early November there were more than four hundred Belgians, South Africans and Rhodesians to bolster the morale of the Congolese army, and they were moving back along the muddy, potholed roads toward Stanleyville, as the Simbas had moved along them a few months before. The panic that had infected the government soldiers was now transferred to the rebels, and the army had no need even to use the telephone to announce their coming; as they advanced they could hear the drums beating out the news of their approach and the Simbas faded before them.

As they drew close to the rebel capital, the shaken revolutionary government broadcast the warning that it "could no longer guarantee the lives of Belgians and Americans" in its control. In answer to this threat—made hideously real by the stories of white survivors in other recaptured rebel cities—more than five hundred Belgian paracommandos, flown by U.S. Army Air Force planes, jumped into Stanleyville to rescue their compatriots. Even as they dropped to the landing area, the rebel radio went on the air for the last time: "This is the voice of the revolution . . . kill them, kill them all. Men, women and children, kill them all. Have no scruples. Kill . . ."

Fifty whites were killed in Stanleyville before the paratroopers could rescue them. But, as usual, it was the blacks who suffered more. Six thousand Congolese civilians had been slaughtered by the Simbas. And when the government column reached the city, the army's "killing machine," as the unbridled retaliation had come to be known, executed eight hundred Stanleyville civilians. Some six hundred Simbas or suspected Simbas had been killed in the brief fighting.

The fall of Stanleyville to Belgian paracommandos, American Air Force planes and the white mercenaries of the army focused attention on the new pattern of contending outside interests in black Africa. The mercenaries were supplied with Western matériel, and the rebels, now in retreat, were bolstered ever more heavily by Russian and Chinese equipment and political training. As the mercenary outfit known as Commando Five, led by that most success-ful outsider of them all, South African "Colonel Mad Mike" Hoare, pushed out along the red earth roads toward the last pockets of resistance, they found increasing evidence of stepped-up Communist support: Russian rifles and machine guns; Chinese bazookas, heavy mortars, recoilless rifles set on wheels like baby cannons; cases of shells still bearing the address: "Uganda Army H.Q., Box 20, Entebbe." Hundreds of tons of stockpiled arms and ammuni-tion brought in from bases in the Sudan, Uganda and Tanzania filled native huts and red brick warehouses in rebel headquarters along those friendly borders.

Poisoned arrows and poo-poo guns were replaced by anti-tank mines and 120-mm. mortars; the magic "dawa" of Mulele water and the pronounce-ments of the witch doctors gave way to a reliance on hard-headed training in modern guerrilla tactics. But with the change, the great mass of the Simbas had lost faith. As the mercenary columns pushed them back, their numbers dwindled. And although the remaining "partisans" fought with better disci-pline and tactics, their base of power among the people was disappearing.

By the end of the year the revolution had reached its dying stage. The potency had gone out of the Simba magic, and the Congolese were sick of the depredations and brutality of the rebels. In village after village the mercenar-ies were made welcome by the African civilians. On April 15, 1965, Colonel Hoare announced, "As far as I'm concerned, the war in the northeast is over." And by September the last rebel stronghold in the east, Baraka, smack on Lake Tanganyika with its water supplyway to Uganda and chockablock with foreign armaments, was taken by amphibious assault.

All the injustices and frustrations that had led to the desperate outbursts of the Bafulero tribe, the Bapende and Babunda, the Bakusu and Batetele, still remained. But the organizational brains that had channeled them into two years of serious rebellions had been outmaneuvered, and there was peace of a sort in the Congo for a while.

REPUBLIC OF THE CONGO

TAN.

LAKE TANGANYIKA

ATLANTIC OCEAN

CONGO RIVER

● Carmona

● Luanda

10° S

A N G O L A

Benguela ●

● Nova Lisboa

Z A M B I A

S.W. AFRICA

20° E

BECHUANA-
~LAND

R H O D E S I A

100 STATUTE MILES

XXI

Angola: "The Forgotten War"

(1961)

AFTER THE four-hundred-year deceptive quietude of Portugal's African province of Angola was shattered by rebellion in 1961, a visitor asked a Portuguese administrator pleasantly, "Having been the first Europeans to come to Africa, I assume you intend to be the last to leave?" The Portuguese reply was steely: "You are mistaken, *senhor*. We do not intend to leave."

Other colonial powers—Britain, France, Belgium—were pulling out of

Africa, either peaceably or under fire, and new nations were starting off on wobbly feet all over the continent. Thirty-five of them were born in the decade between 1956 and 1966, some to sink into bankruptcy, some to be torn apart by tribal wars, some to show bright promise through their welter of problems—but none to request a return to the protection of colonial status.

To the Portuguese, however, Angola and their other overseas possessions are not colonies; they are provinces of Portugal itself, even more closely linked to the homeland than was Algeria to France. The British had brought a sense of Anglo-Saxon politics and law to her colonies; the French had brought French culture; the Belgians had concentrated on economic development. But the Portuguese had taken on the "sublime task"—in the words of her dictator, Dr. António Salazar—of the Christianization and assimilation of her African colonial peoples. And this she does not intend to shirk.

Portugal is the oldest of all colonial powers and her "spiritual conquest" of Africa began soon after her navigators first explored the thousand-mile stretch of West African shoreline that is now Angola's coast, ten years before Columbus discovered America. In 1490 a formal Portuguese embassy, including several missionaries, was dispatched to the kingdom of Kongo, where her navigators had reported the country to be incredibly prosperous. The king was soon converted to Christianity, and for two centuries thereafter the people of the Bakongo tribes, whose religion had been fetishism, accepted the crucifix as their fetish charm and every native was given a "Santu" or Christian name. Soon Portuguese interest drifted southward, and from the early seventeenth century she has held sovereignty over all of coastal Angola. In 1885, during the European "scramble for Africa," she fixed her interior boundaries in agreement with Germany, France and King Leopold's "Congo Free State." Today some fifty percent of all Angolans are at least nominally Christian.

As in Brazil, the Portuguese made no distinctions on the basis of color or race. Never in Angola have blacks and whites been separated as they have in other parts of Africa. There are many mixed marriages, and the mulatto offspring of even irregular unions are accepted without question. Visitors to Angola from other parts of Africa report in some wonder on seeing white waiters serving black customers in good restaurants, or white taxi drivers thanking black patrons for a tip. Black and white live side by side in the slums of the cities (though not so often in the best parts of town), and a few black Africans hold high positions in government, the law courts and the educational system.

This tolerance of color on which the Portuguese pride themselves is the visual proof of their ideal of *assimilado* in their relations with their colonial peoples. In Angola this assimilation consisted of raising the *indigena*, whom the Portuguese defined as "individuals of the black race ... who do not yet possess the enlightenment and the personal social habits ... of Portuguese citizens," to the status of *assimilados* by means of their giving up tribal affiliations, learning to speak Portuguese correctly, having a trade or profession which made them and their families self-sufficient, being of good conduct, and fulfilling their military obligations, all of which took schooling, money, time and a great many documents and applications. By 1950, after four hundred years of Portuguese occupation, some thirty thousand out of a population of more than four million, or .75 percent of Angolan Africans, were *assimilados*.

There were several reasons for this snail's-pace progress in assimilation. For many years Portugal sent few colonizers and paid little attention to the internal development of the country. Until the middle of the last century, the prosperity of this potentially rich province depended almost exclusively on the slave trade with Brazil. For a time Angola surpassed even the Guinea Coast as a source of "black ivory," as the euphemism was, for slave markets everywhere in the New World. It was only after slavery was officially abolished, in 1878, that Portuguese colonizers began to think of developing other resources.

Another reason was that the Africans themselves were not always eager to give up their tribal affiliations and the protection of their tribal laws for the stricter laws of the whites, nor were those willing to do this able to get the necessary education. In 1959 there were 1,639 elementary schools and 31 secondary schools available to both blacks and whites throughout the country. Illiteracy among the blacks was estimated at 97 percent. Among the whites it was 20 percent. But perhaps a more basic reason was that many an African preferred the timeless ways of his own culture to the Portuguese notion of the "dignity of labor."

The source of manpower had been curtailed not only by the massive export of slaves, but also by onslaughts of cannibal tribes from the interior in the earliest years, as well as large-scale emigration to a somewhat better life in neighboring territories during the later centuries, and the ever-present tropical diseases. Thus it was deemed necessary to mobilize, by whatever means, such available labor as there was to build up the country. Under a system of contract labor—barely more than a substitute for outright slavery—any African male between the ages of sixteen and sixty who could not prove he had done useful work for at least six months of the previous year could be forcibly recruited by a local official and shipped off to work on public projects or in agricultural, mining or construction jobs—to any company or landowner who needed labor anywhere in the province. The contract laborer's wages—which, when the officials were corrupt, he might not receive at all—were often no more than ten cents a day. The ideal behind contract labor was that by it the African could learn to become a productive member of his society. But, as with the ideal of assimilation, the practice was an ugly travesty of the purpose.

Both as to ideal and as to practice, assimilation—the open mixing of the races in an integrated Portuguese society—precludes any preparation for African self-rule. And although Prime Minister Salazar would like to keep Angola, as he has tried to keep his native Portugal, a peaceful, motionless, peasant society, the turbulent winds of change that swept through Africa in the 1950's seeped through even the blanket censorship, the police surveillance of suspected dissidents, and the tight border controls of Angola.

Not only Africans but liberal Portuguese spoke of the necessity for change. Captain Henrique Galvão, a colonial inspector, wrote a report in 1947 that was so critical of Portuguese administration and the practice of contract labor that he was jailed. When in 1958 General Humberto Delgado was allowed to campaign for president of Portugal against Salazar's candidate— though he was not allowed to win—white Angolans voted heavily for him. In 1960 a group of five whites, one mulatto and one black were given prison sentences for distributing pamphlets advocating Angolan independence from the control of Lisbon.

The purely African underground organizations agitating for independence were never anti-white, but anti-Portuguese-rule. Among their leaders, Holden Roberto, of the União das Populacões de Angola, or UPA, is a Protestant, trained in mission schools, who took his first name from a favorite missionary teacher. And both Agostinho Neto and Mario Pinto de Andrade, leaders of the Movimento Popular de Liberacão de Angola, the MPLA, are poets and highly educated men who are interested in a social revolution in Portugal as well as in Angola and have the sympathy of many whites as well as blacks. By 1960 these two organizations had their headquarters outside Angola and a rivalry for leadership had grown between them.

Coincidental with this awakening of self-interest among Angolans was a sudden influx of Portuguese into the province. There had never been many Portuguese settlers in Africa. At the turn of the century there were only some 9,000 in the entire 480,000-square-mile province of Angola, most Portuguese emigrants having preferred to settle in Brazil. But the growing press of overpopulation, underemployment and poverty in the homeland gave impetus to an increasing flow of Portugal's poor to Africa, and the government encouraged this migration. By 1940 there were 40,000 whites in Angola, and in 1960 there were 200,000. Although these newcomers were offered land and livestock in the countryside, many of them gravitated to the cities. And although the outward tolerance of color continued in the old easygoing way, the social and economic gulf that had in fact existed all along became more obvious as these new colonizers usurped the jobs of semi-skilled Africans and tightened the lid that kept them in the role of laborers.

The flow of Portuguese men and money into Angola—the visible sign of Lisbon's determination to keep tight hold of her colony while others were letting go of theirs—resulted in a new bustle of life, a new prosperity. But with prosperity, the peace that came of ignorance and servitude was threatened, as was the racial harmony that had long masked injustice and neglect.

In January 1961, Captain Galvão, the onetime colonial inspector, seized the Portuguese liner *Santa Maria* at sea and announced that he was heading for Angola. Even though he sailed instead to Brazil, his act of defiance against the government of Lisbon was enough to spark a minor uprising in Luanda, Angola's principal city. At dawn on February 4, bands of men, both black and white, organized by the MPLA, attacked the city's prisons, radio station and a military barracks, killing six white policemen and one black army corporal. Of the attackers, fourteen were killed, fifty-three wounded, and one hundred arrested. Next day a state funeral was held at the Luanda cemetery for the seven defenders who had died, and correspondent James Burke was there to photograph and report on it:

▶ Most of the more than 50,000 Portuguese whites of Luanda seemed to be out for the funeral of six white policemen and one black soldier killed in the previous day's attack on the Angolan capital's strong points. People lined the entire three-mile route to the cemetery, and the road was choked with cars and buses bringing other thousands. But of the 120,000 black residents of the city, only a scattered few appeared in the crowds. This seemed strange in view of the racial harmony and cooperation claimed by Portuguese officials in Angola. In this moment of crisis, only a negligible few Africans seemed to have ranged themselves alongside the whites.

At the gates of the high-walled cemetery a crowd waited tensely for the funeral cortege to arrive. Entire families, men, women and children, had come out on this cloudy late Sunday afternoon to pay their respects to the fallen heroes. The men were stern and quiet and some of the women were sobbing. Nothing like this had been seen in Luanda before.

Then the funeral cortege arrived, led by motorcycle police and limousines carrying the Governor General and the Provincial Military Commander. Seven flag-draped coffins were unloaded from military trucks and placed on individual hand carts at the cemetery gates. First in line was the coffin containing the body of the Negro soldier, and it was flanked by the Governor General and the Military Commander. The provincial leaders were obviously concentrating their respects on the black man. Yet, except for an honor guard of Negro soldiers and a Negro altar boy carrying a crucifix, the crowd around the coffin was mostly white.

As the procession moved slowly into the cemetery, the air of tension seemed to grow. In front of a small chapel at the center of the burial grounds there was hushed silence while the procession paused for a brief religious service. Then the lead coffin of the black soldier was wheeled off toward a line of freshly dug graves a hundred yards away.

Suddenly the emotionally charged quiet of the crowded cemetery was shattered by shrill screams from the direction of the gates. The cries spread nearer and were picked up by people around me. Then gunfire crackled. The crowd scattered outward as though blown on the shock waves of some explosion. Screaming women passed by, tugging their children. Men hurried families along with outspread arms. Women fainted, or simply sat on the ground in paralyzed terror.

As I ran in the direction of the firing, I noticed men running alongside me with sticks and stones in their hands. They were shouting, "*Mata todos! Mata todos!* Kill them all!" The rumor had flown that a force of blacks, presumably from the same rebel organization that had attacked the day before, had attempted to raid the cemetery and the police and troops at the gates had fired to scatter them. And now the white men in the cemetery, crazed with rage, erupted to hunt down the "raiders"—which meant, in the dimming twilight and the hysterical mood, any stray Africans in the vicinity.

The police tried to close the cemetery gates and keep the men inside. One officer slapped a berserk white man's face. But the mob broke through and raced across the fields, waving sticks and pistols and shouting hoarsely for a kill. The hunt centered around a nearby lumber mill and box factory where the retreating raiders were said to have disappeared. A terrified Negro woman and some youngsters were flushed from one of the buildings and allowed to pass through the first wave of the mob, though sticks and stones were thrown at them as they moved away.

Part of the mob around me closed in on the sawmill shed. Some pistol shots barked out, and when I reached the shed a black body was sprawled on the floor near a pile of logs. White men were crowding around the corpse, screaming at it, jabbing it with sticks and beating it with heavier pieces of wood picked up in the lumberyard. One man found a length of heavy chain and struck so hard at the body that he upset his balance, falling over backward on the floor.

Then the mob left him and ran on to a long warehouse building where another African had been cornered. As I approached, the trapped man crawled out through the roof tiles and stood up, silhouetted against the last light in the sky. The whites surrounding the building screamed for his death: *"Mata! Mata!"* and pistols cracked. The African disappeared over the rooftop, but I could not follow to see what happened to him. Two grim-faced Portuguese were holding me. Several others gathered around, sticks in their hands.

A white-uniformed police officer appeared and ordered the men to release me. As he led me away from them, some of the mob followed, and one man spat, *"Journalista estrangeiro!"* But the officer held up his hand and hissed for silence, and the men dropped away. He escorted me across the field to the cemetery road where my car was parked, and stayed with me until I was behind the wheel. Then he said in broken English, "You go. No stop car." I thanked him and drove off.

It was night now, and passing through the African city adjoining the cemetery area, my headlights picked up small groups of white men, sticks in hand, fanning out on a wider hunt for blacks.

The myth of racial harmony in Portuguese Africa had collapsed at the Luanda cemetery that afternoon. ►

Leaders of the underground organizations claimed that three thousand Africans were killed in reprisal for the February uprising, and in March the United Nations Security Council agreed to consider the subject of the recent events in Angola, but concluded that there was no immediate threat to international peace. Holden Roberto of the UPA had gone to New York to lobby at the United Nations and left instructions with his Léopoldville headquarters that, should the Security Council fail to debate the Angolan issue, UPA members in Angola were to start a campaign of sabotage, general disobedience and guerrilla attacks. When the council refused to schedule the debate, the word was passed. But what started as guerrilla forays by a few hundred rebels in more or less disciplined bands suddenly exploded in a horrifying wave of hatred and revenge. On the morning of March 15, thousands of Africans, most of them from the Bakongo tribe, ran screaming into the villages and plantations of the north, a few shooting primitive muzzle-loading guns, but most with only their curved *catana* bushknives or simply sticks and stones. Although they shrieked "*Mata brancos!* Kill the whites!" many Africans as well as Portuguese were slaughtered in the stampede. The tribesmen killed with obscene brutality, impaling women, castrating or disem-boweling men, dismembering children. Eight hundred whites alone were killed in that one day.

The Portuguese reacted quickly, although they had had no inkling of the coming attack. Only 850 of the 8,000-man Portuguese army stationed in Angola at the time were in the north, but the rest rushed to the area to bolster the Portuguese settlers, who were fighting back by shooting every African they saw—even their own servants who had stayed by them. In the retaliation of the next few days perhaps 10,000 Africans were slain, although the UPA claimed that the figure was nearer 130,000. Lisbon sent 20,000 additional troops to the area, not only to put down the rebels but to curb the settlers' vengeance.

The outburst lasted nearly five months, but by August it had subsided to the familiar pattern of isolated terrorist attacks and less discriminate army counterattacks. By air and motor patrol the army ranged the area, bombing and shooting up not only the rebels' hideouts but any village that might be thought to shelter them. More than 150,000 black Angolans fled across the border to the Congo, and perhaps as many more left their harassed villages and retreated into the inaccessible bush of the interior.

The savage outburst seemed to awaken the Lisbon government to the realization that their ideal of Christianization and assimilation had somehow failed. Having built their society in Angola upon slavery, they were now experiencing the long-pent violence of a slave revolt. In September 1961 the *assimilado* status was abolished and all Africans were offered full Portuguese citizenship. Reforms of all sorts were inaugurated in education, health care, the system of contract labor. The army's "psychosocial services" began teach-ing better farming methods, sanitation and child care over the radio, and earnest attempts were made to lure the thousands of refugees out of hiding in the backland bush to new village areas cleared and prepared for them.

But in the neighboring Congo a guerrilla camp had been set up to train Angolan fighters for independence. They were getting advice and arms from some of the most experienced insurrectionists in the world, primarily the Algerians. And of those frightened, hungry Angolan refugees in the bush, more were choosing exile in the Congo than were accepting the Portuguese invitation to resettle in the new villages.

In 1963 the leaders of UPA formed a Government of the Republic of Angola in Exile which was recognized by many African states, although the rival MPLA seemed to be getting the backing of both Russian and Chinese Communists. But neither organization was able to launch more than sporadic small attacks on isolated outposts, and over the years the smoldering rebellion in Angola lost the world's attention and became "the forgotten war."

Ironically for the rebel leaders, their efforts not only failed to weaken Lisbon's hold on her African province, but were the spur that jolted Portugal into a realization of her responsibilities there. With stubborn resistance to world opinion, the Salazar government speeded increased white immigration, economic development and announcements of great reforms. Just at the time when most European nations had put aside their colonial past with some relief, the Portuguese in Africa were beginning to take their colonial mission seriously.

THE VICTIMS

A SECTION OF PHOTOGRAPHS

Jewish refugee children from Poland are turned back from entering Palestine.

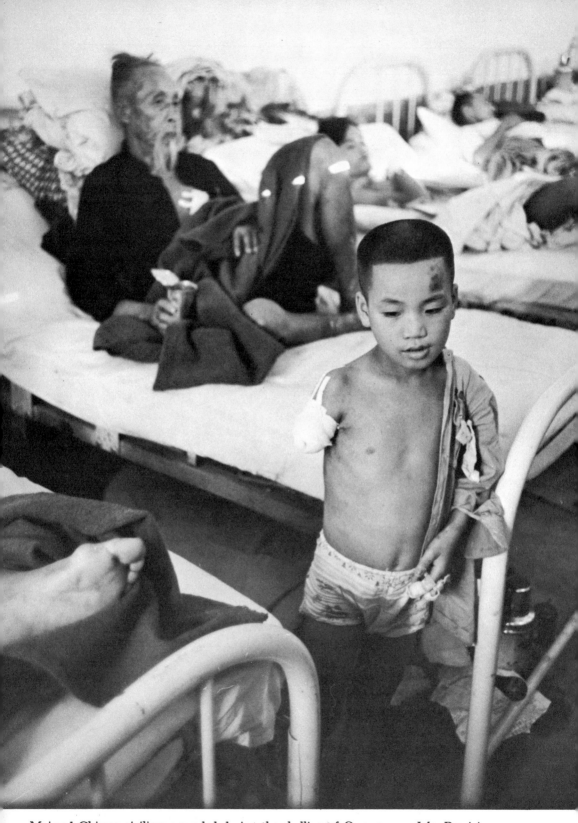

Maimed Chinese civilians wounded during the shelling of Quemoy. *John Dominis*

Dying American corporal, killed in the last night of fighting in Korea. *Michael Rougier*

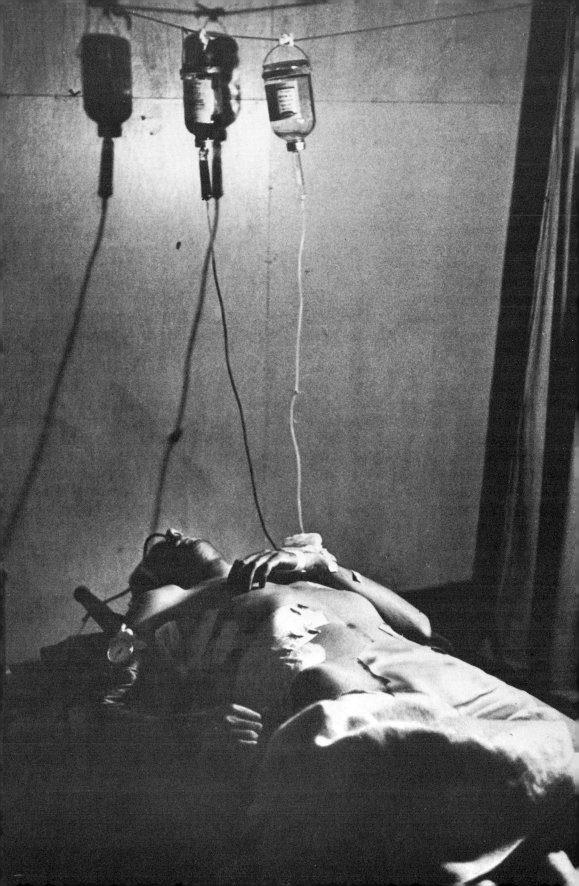

A refugee mother flees from the battle area in Korea.   *Carl Mydans*

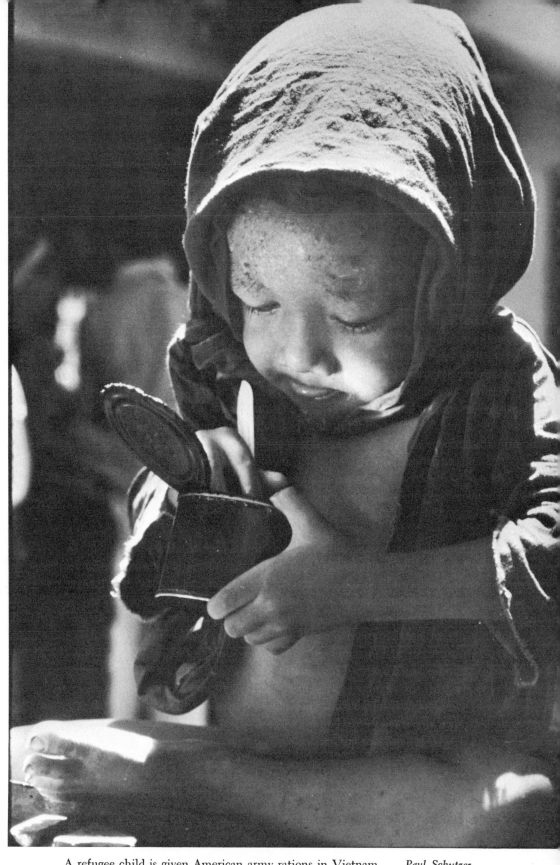

A refugee child is given American army rations in Vietnam.   *Paul Schutzer*

Refugee women and children rest on their way to a collection point in Vietnam.   *Paul Schutzer*

Homeless Koreans wade the Nakong River in their flight from the war zone.   *Carl Mydans*

Homeless Congolese take the road away from the enemy.   *Terence Spencer*

South Korean refugees carry their belongings along a mountain road.   *Carl Mydans*

North Korean prisoners, stripped to their underwear, are taken to a POW camp.   *Carl Mydans*

Chained by the neck, an Indonesian rebel is taken prisoner by the Dutch.   *John Thiessen, Jr.*

Eyes and mouth taped, a Viet Cong prisoner is held by the U.S. Marines.   *Paul Schutzer*

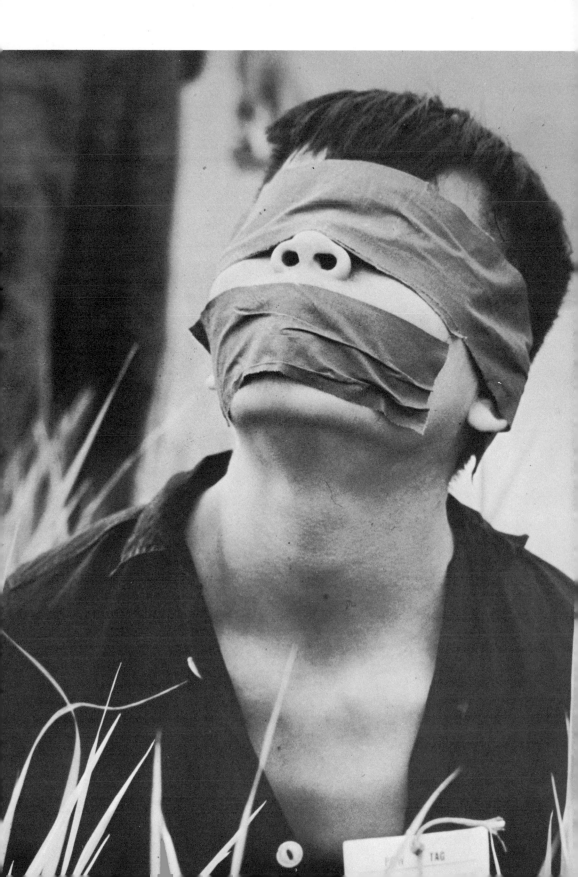

A Chinese civilian is beaten by Nationalist soldiers for showing disrespect to an officer. *Mark Kauffman*

American prisoners of war are marched through the streets of Seoul after their capture by North Koreans.

Wife, mother and grandmother weep for a young Communist killed in Korea.   *Margaret Bourke-White*

Captured mutinous soldiers of the South Korean army are taken to a prison compound.   *Carl Mydans*

Communist prisoners are jailed in Indonesia.   *Co Rentmeester*

Moslem refugees are abandoned by the road in India.   *Margaret Bourke-White*

A Chinese woman mourns her loss after the war passed through her village near Suchow.   *Carl Mydan*

Terrified Jewish children are carried from burning buildings in Old Jerusalem.   *International News photo*

Hungry Egyptians scramble for food from a looted supply depot in Port Said. / *Larry Burrows*

An impromptu People's Court in Communist China tries a fellow peasant for landlordism.

An FLN army firing squad in Algeria executes a fellow Moslem for collaboration with the French. *Dickey Chapelle*

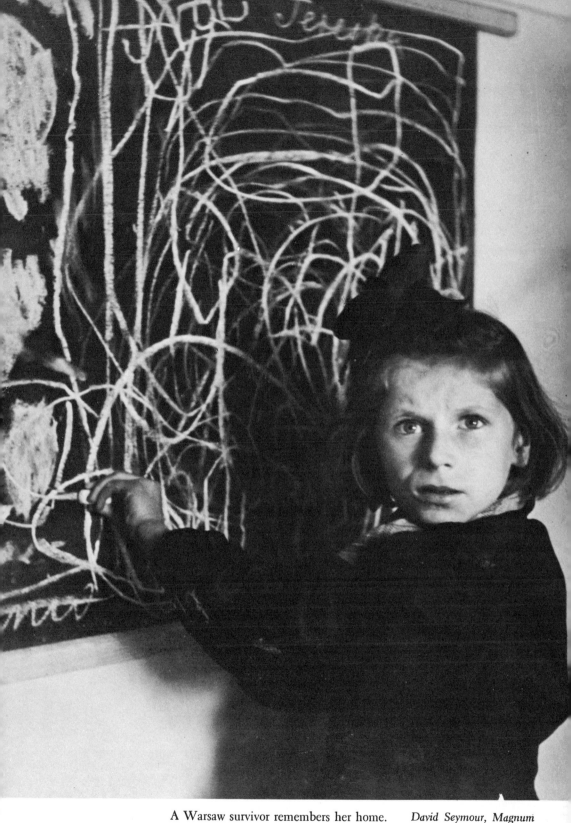

A Warsaw survivor remembers her home.   *David Seymour, Magnum*

A Viet Cong prisoner pleads for mercy.   *Larry Burrows*

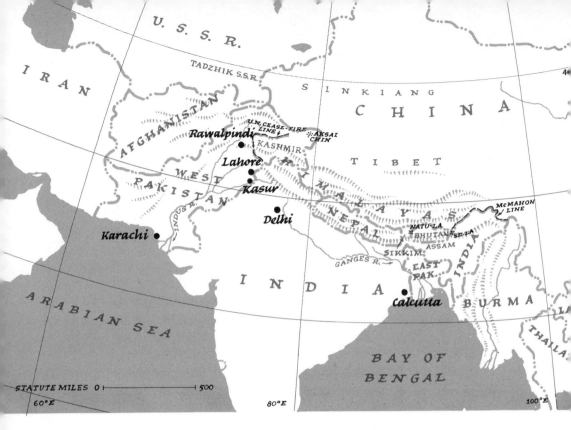

XXII

India: The Border Conflicts

(1962-1965)

INDIA'S NORTHERN BORDER stretches for 2,500 miles along the sky-high chain of the Himalayas and is hung with exotic names evoking the mysterious. And equally inscrutable seemed the activities of the Communist Chinese along that border from 1954 to 1965 when they invaded the territory of their neutralist friends the Indians, who had stood patron for them in the family of Asian nations.

At its western end the Ladakh area of Kashmir meets with the Chinese province of Sinkiang; in the east the North East Frontier Agency runs alongside Tibet. In between are strung the Himalayan buffer states of Nepal, Sikkim and Bhutan. So remote is the Kashmiri "desert of white stones"—the Aksai Chin of Ladakh, which juts between Sinkiang and western Tibet—that the Chinese had a labor force there for two years building a hundred-mile road across it before the Indian government became aware of this infringement on its territory. And in 1962, one week before 20,000 Chinese soldiers supported by artillery and heavy mortars poured into the North East Frontier Agency at Se-la, correspondent Charles Elliott visited the border there and later wrote:

▶ A week ago we stood at the top of the Se-la ridge and stared into fog, trying to see where the Chinese might be. Even when the fog blew away, there were too many mountains. The curved, heavy shapes blocked everything except the very tips of snowy Tibetan peaks many miles away. But although we couldn't see them, the Chinese in front of us were real, perfectly real. Today the news came that they had attacked Se-la and taken it, and the whole front, the biggest in the war, was blown wide open. Their columns must have traveled close to a hundred miles through gorges and over mountain ranges without being detected. ▶

The roots of the Chinese-Indian border dispute go back to the early years of this century. In 1911 the religious leaders of the Tibetan government took advantage of the tumultuous Chinese revolution to break away from the long tradition of Chinese suzerainty over their ancient country. And in 1913, when the Chinese Republic had been established, the British rulers of India called a conference of Indian, Chinese and Tibetan representatives to delineate the border in the unexplored Himalayan regions between Tibet and northeast India. They were aware that China, like the empires of the West, was subject to an inherent urge to expand, and that the new republic would look hungrily toward Tibet and perhaps beyond.

The conference was called by the British Foreign Secretary to India, Sir Henry McMahon, and the line the delegates drew—710 miles along the watershed of the Himalayan ranges from Bhutan to Burma—was known as the McMahon Line. In the spring of 1914 the conference recognized China's jurisdiction over Tibet with the understanding that it would not become a Chinese province, and all the delegates, including the Chinese, put their initials to the boundary line as drawn. But when the Chinese government heard what its representative had done, they recalled him, summarily dismissed him, and refused to recognize the McMahon Line, calling the agreement "illegal, null and void." Later their Communist successors added the epithet "imperialist."

When the Communists took over the government after World War II, China once more extended suzerainty over Tibet, establishing an autonomous Communist government there at the expense of the ancient religious oligarchy. Though India remained on very friendly terms with China, refusing to criticize the Communists' entry into Tibet, the move made the Indian government uneasy and it built fifty new checkpoints along the McMahon Line, which India considered the legal boundary, recognized by tradition if not by the Chinese government.

In 1954 these two still-friendly governments signed an amicable non-aggression pact concerning Tibet. But it was only three months afterward that the Chinese complained of Indian intrusions on their territory, producing old maps to show that land the Indians had always thought was theirs was really—they had maps to prove it—Chinese property.

In 1955 the Chinese began to build their Tibet-Sinkiang Highway across the Aksai Chin, and in 1957 included it on one of their ever-handy maps. The Indian government sent out a series of long-range patrols and one of them, at last, discovered the road, but it was empty of Chinese, so nothing was said. The Chinese build-up all along the Indian frontier and the occasional minor clashes of patrols could all be overlooked by the Indian government as understandable adjuncts to the Communists' reassertion of their overlordship of Tibet. There was ferment in that high and ancient country, and in 1959 a full-scale rebellion broke out, was ruthlessly suppressed, and the Dalai Lama with a horde of refugees escaped across the border into India. The smile of friendship between Peking and Delhi was growing strained. The Chinese accused the Indians of "trespassing and provocations" during the Tibetan rebellion, and Nehru accused the Chinese of "a deliberate program of aggression."

In August of that year a patrol of thirty-eight Assam riflemen were attacked by three hundred Chinese soldiers at Longju in the North East Frontier Agency, and in October a party of Indian border police probing the Aksai Chin far to the west suddenly saw a Chinese soldier waving at them from a ridge. While they sat on their ponies open-mouthed, machine guns and mortars opened up on them and nine were killed. Eight were captured and forced to sign confessions that they had violated Chinese territory. The tension in the diplomatic notes and all along the border line increased. The

Indians engaged in a series of "nibbling" operations against the Chinese road in the Aksai Chin, and the Chinese made excursions across the McMahon Line.

In October 1962, Nehru instructed the Indian army to "free our territory on the Northeast Frontier from Chinese intruders," but before they could start their operation, the Chinese struck. Twenty thousand well-armed mountain troops swept down from the Thag-la ridge and overwhelmed the five thousand Indians defending it. For three weeks the Chinese waited while the remnants of the Indian brigade regrouped and the Delhi government sent reinforcements. On November 7 the Indians re-formed to attack again, and again the Chinese overran them "like red ants," driving them eighty miles back down the valley. And at neighboring Se-la they launched a massive assault, capturing the Indian supply base, throwing the army headquarters at Tezpur into a panic, and advancing till the whole rich province of Assam lay spread before them. Then they stopped. On November 21, Radio Peking announced that China was ordering a cease-fire on all fronts and that, beginning December 1, their troops would be withdrawn.

Although their motives seemed inscrutable at the time, the Chinese chose, for reasons of their own, to stop the war while they were winning. But before negotiations could begin, the question had to be settled: Withdraw to where? The Chinese proposed that they pull back to some twelve miles behind the line of "actual control" in November 1959. This would still leave them in possession of considerable territory, including the Aksai Chin, which the Indians considered theirs. But at a conference of the Afro-Asian non-aligned nations held in Ceylon, the Chinese position was substantially upheld and the Indians agreed to it. The cease-fire was prolonged indefinitely and the Chinese did not break it—until 1965, when the temptation proved too great.

That year the smoldering Indo-Pakistan conflict over Kashmir flared into open warfare and the Indians were compelled to turn their attention from their northern border to that other cease-fire line, the one drawn by the United Nations across that contested province in 1949. For nearly two decades the relations between India and Pakistan had been characterized by mutual fears and resounding accusations, although in quiet practice these disaffected neighbors had solved many of the problems created by the agony of their partition. On the subject of Kashmir, however, their enmity was unrelenting.

In accordance with the agreement of 1949, India controlled two thirds of that onetime princely state to Pakistan's one third. But seventy-seven percent of the population of Kashmir is Moslem, and the Pakistan government, counting on this brotherhood to bring a favorable vote, repeatedly called for a Kashmiri self-determination plebiscite. The Pakistan army, meanwhile, was devoted almost exclusively to a defense against India, and India kept three quarters of its army posted along the Pakistan borders and in Kashmir—despite the pressure of the Chinese on the northern boundaries.

When in 1962 the Chinese stepped up that pressure to full-scale attack, the Indians were forced to take their eyes off Pakistan, transfer one third of their army to confront the Communists, and ask for help from the United States. As allied arms were rushed in to assist the Indians, the Pakistanis became increasingly uneasy as to the eventual use of those arms. Their press grew almost hysterically anti-American as well as anti-Indian, some going so far as to suggest that the Indian-Chinese border war was a mere hoax which Delhi had engineered in order to get more arms for use against Pakistan.

When the Chinese withdrew, the Kashmir quarrel became India's paramount concern once more. The United Nations tried to negotiate the argument, but both sides rejected outside help. In 1964 there were repeated skirmishes along the cease-fire line, and in August 1965 thousands of Pakistani "freedom fighters" filtered into Indian Kashmir to "help," as they said, "their Moslem Kashmir brothers seeking self-determination." The Indians responded by moving troops across the line to hit so-called "guerrilla bases" in Pakistan Kashmir, and Pakistan, thus countered, marched her soldiers deep into Indian Kashmir. With that the Indians opened a whole new front on September 6, sending a three-pronged drive directly into Pakistan across a previously undisputed border. What had been merely another set of skirmishes along the cease-fire line became a war. It lasted for seventeen days, until September 22, when both sides accepted a United Nations truce.

Although both governments made loud and warlike noises and the populace on each side was stirred to patriotic frenzy, the war at the front was conducted for the most part in a gentlemanly manner with a prudent reluctance to initiate the wholesale destruction characteristic of modern war. On September 10, correspondent William Rademaekers sent a report on both the prudent aspects of this seventeen-day war and on the effects that even the most gentlemanly conflicts have on the noncombatants of the area:

▶ On the southern front we watched the Pakistan infantry advancing, spread out in a jagged line, ancient Enfield rifles held chest high, netted World War II helmets bouncing with every step, the light brown khaki uniforms clashing with the bright green corn and rice against a backdrop of palm trees swaying in the breeze. It had all the unreal qualities of a movie set, and even the rumble of artillery fire and the swoosh of low-flying jets could not make it come alive.

There is a vast difference between the look of this war and the sound of its communiqués with their conflicting claims of major gains and victories on both sides. There is no way to explain what is happening here by comparing it with other wars of our century. Although each army is equipped with modern weapons of destruction, comparatively little damage is inflicted. Although each army has infantry that number in the hundreds of thousands, few of them are used. Although the terrain for the most part is open and inviting, little of it is exchanged.

Tempting targets such as bridges, powerhouses, roads, supply depots are largely untouched. It is a strangely shadowy and elusive war, political rather than military, where death and destruction are limited to the few vulnerable towns that can be raided without risk.

All along the main battle area the armies are squared off with a comfortable mile or mile and a half between them. This is good artillery and armor range and gives the air force on both sides room for maneuvering. Clashes, when they come, are usually armored battles supported by a few infantry, with gains measured in terms of yards rather than miles, and with units pulling back to re-form if by some fortuitous accident they break through enemy lines. You don't take or hold land with tactics like this, but you do defend well, and this is that kind of war. ►

But even in a gentlemanly war, people get hurt. Artillery and airplanes have their targets, and on their side the Indians found them in the Pakistan front-line towns of Sialkot and Kasur. And as when in a football game observers are dismayed to see a young man carried off the field, so in a war—especially a war like this—the normal man winces when he sees the devastation of a city. Of his experience in Kasur, Rademaekers wrote:

► Kasur lies in a pocket of Pakistan territory hard on the Indian border. Because of its nearness and vulnerability it was a favorite Indian target. The city is deserted now, its residents scattered in a fifty-mile radius across the countryside. Buzzards wheel overhead and settle with a flourish on the carcasses of water buffalo. Dogs stalk through the rubble, kicking up black clouds of flies in their effort to get at the putrid human flesh buried beneath the brick rubble. An old man sits atop the ruins of his house, shaking his head and wailing softly. A few policemen walk through the wreckage to prevent looting, but otherwise the town is a mixture of sickening smells and silence.

For Kasur the war began September 7, when Indian forces moved within two miles of the city and shelled it, beginning at six in the morning and continuing steadily until one in the afternoon. An early target was the American Protestant Mission school for girls, where shells tore into the walls and fell in the garden, spraying shrapnel and tearing up the red clay earth. Others exploded in a barnyard, sending chunks of flesh flying into the street, followed by a stampede of mortally wounded animals. A mosque collapsed in a spray of dust. Brick walls crumbled from the concussions. The people of Kasur fled from their city, taking only what they could carry.

Five days later, emboldened by a lull in the fighting and hungry to the point of desperation, they began drifting back into town. Then, on September 14, the Canberras came back, this time hitting the city with a brace of thousand-pound bombs, demolishing a two-block area in one part of town and destroying an entire complex on the outskirts.

Lying in a field with one's nose pressed firmly into Pakistani mud while four Indian jets wheel in an arc overhead, one is very much aware of this aspect of the war in which Kasur, a non-military target, has been shelled, bombed and strafed for more than a week while the military vehicles that pack the straight, open road between here and Lahore are largely untouched.

By first count, at least 120 civilians had been killed in Kasur and another 350 injured. But those who fled after the shelling and returned were forced to flee again. So the exact number of the dead they left behind is not yet known. There is no one in the town to dig the bodies out. ▶

It was this brief war and the involvement of the Indians in Kashmir that proved too great a temptation for the Chinese. Two years earlier they had signed a boundary agreement with Pakistan and they were eager to bring the alliance closer. At the same time, it would do no harm to embarrass the Indians, who had at last admitted their dependence on the West. In August, while the Pakistani "freedom fighters" were filtering into Kashmir, they found reason to send a warning note to India, demanding that it stop building defense posts on the Sikkim border a thousand miles to the east.

On September 7, the day after the Indian-Pakistan hostilities broke out in earnest, China offered to come to the assistance of Pakistan. In another ten days she had moved her troops into the Natu Pass, and on the 17th sent an ultimatum to the Indians that if the "military works" they had allegedly constructed on the Tibetan side of the border were not dismantled by the 23rd she would attack.

Again, as in 1962, a Chinese army lay somewhere hidden in the fog-bound mountain heights, a lure to correspondents eager to see this unpredictable, inscrutable enemy, these "red ants" who could come pouring down at will "like a human sea" over a Himalayan ridge. On September 22 correspondent Jerrold Schecter made a trip to the Natu Pass and described his findings there:

▶   At 14,500 feet the mountain flowers are purple underfoot. Yellow lichens and red moss brighten in the morning sun, and the heavy granite-block retaining wall of the road up to the Natu Pass curves in stony arcs to the Sikkim-Tibet border. Once a link in the golden caravan route through Lhasa to Samarkand, Natu-la, as the Tibetans call it, this week seemed aloof and foreboding as the morning wind and fog blew through it, for this week, on the pretext of Indian army border violations, the Chinese Communists threatened to cross the Sikkim-Tibet frontier into Indian territory.

The border here is formed by a natural barrier, a ridgeline watershed. Whichever way the rainfall flows down from the ridge determines the border. Heavy boulders, slate and granite outcroppings rise sharply from the heights, and below lies the Chumbi Valley, a dagger pointed between Bhutan and Sikkim. If thrust through the valley by Chinese Communist troops, the dagger could slash all the way to Siliguri and cut off the whole of West Bengal, Assam and the North East Frontier from the rest of India.

In a shrill note delivered to the Indian chargé d'affaires in Peking on September 17, the Chinese warned that India would face "grave consequences" unless "56 military works large and small" were torn down within three days and some "seized livestock" and allegedly kidnapped Chinese border inhabitants were returned. When the Indians proposed that a joint inspection team check on the disputed military works, the Chinese extended the deadline until midnight, Thursday, September 23.

All week they harassed the Indian positions near the pass, firing white parachute flares from their 82-mm. mortars and advancing against the Indian posts with bursts of rifle fire. In the early morning of the 21st, between two and three o'clock, there was a brief firefight, both sides

373

exchanging about a thousand rounds of small-arms fire. The Indians suffered no casualties, but the Chinese were seen dragging away at least two of their men from the foggy no-man's-land between the Indian positions and the ridgeline border.

On Wednesday morning there was tension all along the line. News of the India-Pakistan cease-fire had not reached the Natu Pass and the Chinese were still active on the ridge. Heavy white clouds lay on the mountaintops, only for minutes breaking to reveal glimpses of the gleaming Himalayan peaks, and in the night snow had begun to fall.

Along the mountain road from Sikkim's capital of Gangkok to Natu Pass the Indian forces are well dug in. Forty anti-aircraft guns stand in strategic spots near bridges, and security checks are constant. As you approach the front, you see, instead of the usual shaggy brown pack mules and glistening black yaks, khaki-clad Indian soldiers spread out along both sides of the pass, their American-made automatic weapons at the ready.

But at the border there are no "military works" as the Chinese claim. One look at the terrain makes it clear that all positions are dug in around the natural fortifications of granite blocks and sod. There are no concrete fortifications or pillboxes to be seen, nor any barbed wire. Obviously, the Chinese Communists are making a grandstand propaganda play on behalf of Pakistan this week, but even from high in the Himalayas the echo round the world has a hollow ring.

By mid-morning on the 22nd the fog had cleared through the pass; the colors of the vegetation and the rocks were intensified in the high altitude. Sunlight forced sharp clarity in the open spaces, while the huge rocks along the ridge line abounded in dark shadows. The curving road built of crushed granite looked starkly white and its manmade lines in sharp contrast to the jagged natural terrain. The scene seemed very peaceful.

"Look up there," said an Indian officer standing next to us. His face was shadowed by his heavy parka as he pointed across the road to the ridge line. "There on the left, on the top of that black slate. That's where they have their mortars."

I looked along the ridge that is the border of Tibet three hundred yards away, but even with field glasses only a black snout could be seen poking between green spikes of the wild rhubarb that grows on the mountain.

"Now look to the right and you'll see some Chinkos. That's where they've come over the top onto our side."

Again I could make out only the yellowish blur of a Chinese uniform. Smoke from a cooking fire rose beside him straight into the clear morning air. There were no signs of fortification. The only man-made stonework in the area was a memorial tablet on a flat table of land extending from the road. It marks the visit of Prime Minister Nehru and the Maharaja of Sikkim in September 1958. It is clearly on the Indian side of the frontier, but earlier in the week some Chinese soldiers in their yellowish wool overcoats had crossed the border and come down to it.

"Let's get a closer look," the officer said. He clambered down the ridge onto the road and I clambered after him. The pass seemed suddenly deserted. Only the clouds and the brightness of the morning were apparent. There were no sounds.

"If they open fire, get down," said the officer. "We'll take care of the rest."

A junior officer with an automatic weapon had accompanied us, and behind us a group of Indian *jawans* stood ready beside a granite fortification on the slope. Three more moved forward on our right to flank our party.

When we stood by the Nehru marker we could see the Chinese positions less than a hundred yards away. Following the officer's directions, I searched the shadows along the ridge. Suddenly a Chinese soldier popped up and then down again. In the distance we could see ten more, in yellow overcoats, marching in step. A group of three with cooking pots came walking casually along the ridge. With field glasses we could make out the red stars on their collars and peaked caps. They stopped to stare at us.

"The Chinkos were down here at the marker themselves yesterday," the officer said.

The three men with the cooking pots went on and disappeared behind the ridge. Others with automatic weapons took their place, then faded into prone positions behind the rocks. I looked around. The Indian *jawans* too had disappeared into the background of green grass and yellow moss. Nowhere was a soldier to be seen. Only the jutting outline of the ridge and the white clouds beyond.

"Better get back," the officer said with a smile. "You never can be certain what the Chinkos will do."

The breeze had started to quicken, blowing the fog through the quiet Natu Pass and across the top of the ridge. I felt it on my back as I climbed up the slope to our own lines. Overhead a Himalayan mountain hawk drifted in lazy circles, watching us. ▶

One thousand miles to the west, on that September day—one day before the Chinese ultimatum was to expire—the United Nations truce went into effect in Kashmir and the flare-up of that smoldering stalemate was quenched once again. The Chinese, having lost their opportunity, backed away from their ultimatum without a fight. The U.N. had succeeded in soothing the situation, and four months later the Russians managed to bring the leaders of India and Pakistan to talk peacefully together.

But the Kashmir fire was not out, it was merely banked. Many Indians still felt as Nehru did when he said that to sever Kashmir from India would be like slicing off a man's arm or leg. And Pakistan still argues for a plebiscite. The overwhelming sentiment of these Moslem people for their fellow Moslems in Kashmir was voiced by a cigaret vendor in Rawalpindi when he heard the bitter news that peace had come. "Kashmir is our right," he said. "If we did not take it today, we must take it tomorrow."

The Chinese likewise wait for tomorrow. They pulled their troops back from that confrontation in September 1965, and the Himalayan border quieted to little skirmishes when patrols, or merely wandering soldiers, strayed in those craggy ridges from one side of the disputed boundary to the other. Their actions might have seemed inscrutable to the casual observer in that their aggressive posture cost them the friendship of their neutralist neighbor to the south and set back the cause of Communism there. But from a purely Chinese point of view, they achieved a well-thought-out objective. Following their ancient military dictum, popularized by Mao Tse-tung, of "making a noise in the east while striking in the west," they acquired a year-round military passage from Sinkiang to Tibet in that most important and mysterious hinterland where China meets with Soviet Central Asia.

With all that noise at Natu-la, they continued to run their convoys over the "desert of white stones." And in the lofty passes of the east, while they resumed their silence behind the drifting fog, Chinese soldiers with their guns and cooking pots still wandered casually along the doubtful border.

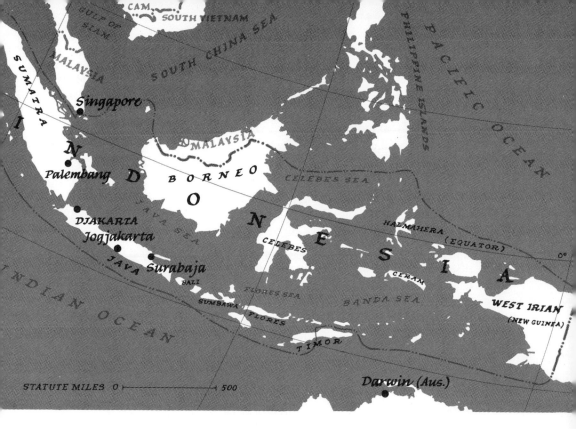

XXIII

Indonesia Runs Amok

(1965-1966)

IN THE eight months beginning in October 1965 a madness swept the
islands of Indonesia, leaving half a million dead. The roots of the madness took their nourishment from excessive nationalism, religious prejudice,
racism and the politics of the Cold War, but the dark force that carried it
along was something less understandable. It more resembled the blind drive
that lemmings follow in their rush to self-destruction than it did any willful

act of a society of men. The Norsemen created the word "berserk" to describe the violent passion that overcame them on the battlefield, making them howl and foam at the mouth and bite their shields. The Indonesians have another phrase. They call it "running amok."

About one hundred million people live on the rich and beautiful islands of Indonesia. Four centuries ago when the Dutch first came upon the land of these proto-Malayan people, they were astonished at the diversity of the archipelago: three thousand islands stretching along the Equator for three thousand miles like a string of jewels in a coral sea. And, like jewels, they represented wealth. The volcanic-fertile red-brown soil produces two rice crops a year, as well as copra, hemp, tobacco, sugar and teak. Many of the islands are scented by the spices they raise, once so rare and expensive that they were the lure which brought the early navigators in their galleons to exploit the East. Today some of the oil beneath the shallow Java Sea is of such high grade that it needs no refining for a diesel engine to run on it.

For 350 years these islands were a golden horn for the Dutch. Then in 1942 the Japanese overran them and held them until they lost the war in 1945. In the short vacuum between the end of the Japanese military occupation and the return of the Dutch colonialists, the Indonesian nationalists, led by the mystic revolutionary Sukarno, proclaimed the Republic of Indonesia and undertook self-rule. For four years they had to fight for this independence, but in 1949 the Dutch agreed to withdraw, and the new nation was on its own.

Yet Indonesia is hardly a nation at all. Rather it is a political entity of a very diverse people, divided by great distances, separated on their islands by open ocean, speaking seventy different languages and holding a variety of religious beliefs. And the government, controlled by untrained people in the early years, floundered in economic and political unrest. In 1959 Sukarno proclaimed himself the President-Premier with almost unrestricted powers to rule the country in a "guided democracy" under his dictatorship. In 1963 he was made "Lifelong President," but his rule only worsened the country's economic plight.

Wily, unpredictable and dazzling, Sukarno held a mystical sway over his people. Although ninty percent of all Indonesians are at least nominally Moslems and the rest are Hindus, Buddhists and Christians, primitive beliefs in spirits and sorcerers are very strong, and to many of his people Sukarno was an almost supernatural being, possessed of certain occult powers and beyond the touch of evil. In his heyday, palace servants sold his bathwater to peasants who believed that drinking it would give them some of his magical power.

And he in turn basked in this reputation, saying, "The Indonesian people will eat stones if I tell them to."

In his foreign policy Sukarno kept a precarious balance between the Western world and the Communists. To the Americans he sold himself as a truly democratic man, the bulwark against Communism in Indonesia. But in Moscow and Peking he posed as a fellow traveler, and to the Indonesians he said, "Don't be afraid of being leftists" and "We must dare to do a little gambling." In the same way, he stayed atop the shifting forces of the political power groups at home. These major power groups were two: the Indonesian Communist Party, called the PKI, and the high-ranking officers of the military forces.

The PKI was the oldest Communist Party in Southeast Asia and the third largest in the world. It claimed three million members, with 272 branches and cells on every Indonesian island of any size, as well as the control of worker and peasant organizations with another fourteen-million membership. In 1955 its leaders were the strongest influence on Sukarno's policies and they were gaining strength. But their mistakes were fatal: Sukarno himself, the charismatic leader, was above his people's criticism, he could do no wrong; but his policies of high-handed foreign dealings and his reckless spending on useless monuments, his government's corruption and inefficiency, had brought his wealthy country to the edge of bankruptcy and his peasants to starvation on their once-rich lands. In their eyes, it was the men around him who were responsible for this.

The enmity between the Communists and the Indonesian military leaders became increasingly bitter during 1965. By then both sides were waiting for the ailing, sixty-four-year-old Sukarno to die, knowing that with his death a showdown was inevitable in their grab for power. In September the Communist leaders were assured by three physicians from Peking that the President had not long to live and they decided that the time for the desperate grab was now.

In the pre-dawn stillness of October 1, truckloads of Communist soldiers, youths and women rumbled through the silent streets of Djakarta, Indonesia's capital. They were on their way to launch a coup d'état, capture or murder the army's topmost generals, and have Sukarno—who may or may not have been in on the plot—and the country to themselves. It was a bumbling and hastily mounted thrust, made hideous by the taste for cruelty that underlies the Indonesian's charming and artistic nature. The first of the generals they came upon, the Communists shot outright. But some were kidnapped and taken to a nearby training field known as the Crocodile Hole. Here young members of the Communist women's organization performed a diabolic rite, castrating live cats and cutting them to pieces, and then dancing naked, drugged with narcotics, before the captured generals. Afterward they mutilated the generals with small sharp knives and gouged out their eyes.

News of this obscene brutality spread quickly through the islands and the reaction was swift and ferocious. While Sukarno stood apart, denying any knowledge of the coup, the army tracked down leading Communists and arrested or shot them. And where there were too many Communists for the army to handle, they armed civilians so that they could make arrests, or simply turned the suspects over to anti-Communist mobs to be done away with. All of the bitterness and frustration that the people had suffered under their incompetent government was vented on those fellow citizens whom they called Communists—whether they were party members or simply ignorant farmers who had believed the Communist promises.

This was not the first time that the Communists had tried to launch a revolution in Indonesia. Twice before in the past forty years they had risen to take over. In 1926, when they tried to seize Djakarta and lead a revolt, the Dutch put them down. During World War II they grew in strength again, made a bid for power in 1948, and were smashed by the Indonesian army, hundreds of their leaders being arrested, executed or exiled. This time the military leaders were determined there would not be another rebirth. With their encouragement the Indonesian people took up their swordlike *parangs* and throwing-knives and entered the slaughter. On every island, in every town and village they simply ran amok, killing not only Communists but their families and friends, as well as Chinese moneylenders and men who were said to be atheists or whom they envied for their landholdings or who were simply, for one reason or another, out of popular favor—in all, perhaps one out of every two hundred citizens.

When it was over, calm returned. It was as though the scenes of horror existed only in a dream. No outsider witnessed them. No correspondent or photographer was present to report them. In an era of instant reportage of every minor incident in human affairs, news of this massive purge and national bloodbath came only fitfully to the outside world, like the flicker of distant lightning which accompanies a thunder too far to be heard. Only in the spring of 1966 were correspondents permitted to travel in Indonesia. Then the official figures were given them: 87,000 killed. But as they traveled, saw, and heard, they revised the figure upward to 100,000, 200,000, 500,000.

Correspondent Dan Coggin was one of those who made the first trip through the countryside after the slaughter. Scenes he reported of the aftermath indicate how such a figure could be arrived at:

▶ Tracing the course of this momentous upheaval, we began our tour on Java, heading east toward Jogjakarta. The real rural Indonesia begins to unfold its assets and its debits, first in hill country of ingeniously reticulated paddy fields, then in vast expanses of green and golden rice waving in the breeze interspersed with heavy rain forests and brooding brown volcanoes strung out in a majestic network across the island.

The volcanic soil is black and bounteous, water is so plentiful and irrigation so clever that in many areas the land provides two good crops a year. But the shirtless peasant bent over his rice seedlings under the searing sun is usually working the same acre his grandfather toiled over, with most of the old problems and a lot of new ones, including a government that insists he sell some of his rice to it at only a fraction of the free-market price so it can be supplied to shortage areas, civil servants and military personnel. His awakening political consciousness has brought more turmoil and turbulence than satisfaction, its most significant by-product being, of course, the wave of death which has just swept this silent and mysterious but outwardly peaceful land.

There was more to the killings than his awakening to politics, mostly by indoctrination. Part of the slaughter at least was the violent release of pent-up frustrations, economic and otherwise. He could listen to Sukarno's promises until he was blue in the face, but poverty was still there and social injustice was still there. When the peasant heard the anti-revolutionary clarion sounded against the Communists, here at last was something he could do himself and see results; he could pick up his *parang* and after the bloody business was over he could have a sense of accomplishment, bizarre and brutal though it be.

Nine miles east of Jogjakarta, the old Hindu-Buddhist temple town of Prambanan lies in the shadow of the conical, cloud-cloaked active volcano Mount Merapi. This was a Red stronghold estimated at sixty to seventy percent Communist. On October 27, with the arrival of a troop detachment in Prambanan, the "clean-up" began and continued until mid-April. More than 4,000 Communists were killed, about one out of every nine residents in this town of 35,000. Day and night, soldiers accompanied by mobs of civilians, many of them informers, scoured the dusty narrow streets and slum alleyways, dragging Reds and suspects out of their homes for arrest, investigation, interrogation and, usually, execution.

The Woro River a mile east of town was the receptacle of about 3,000 of Prambanan's dead. The hundred-foot-wide river flows only four months of the year, during the rainy season, and is now completely dry, as it has been since the executions there began. We walked for an hour alongside the gray, sandy riverbed flanked by rice and sugarcane fields, talking with three men from a nearby hamlet who helped with the grave-digging on soldiers' orders, witnessed daily executions between the first of November and the middle of April, and vowed heatedly that the river is haunted by ghosts of the victims who moan and scream at night.

Every afternoon, they said, two soldiers would come and set the male villagers to digging graves large enough for five or six corpses each. Just before sunset one or two green army trucks would turn off the highway at the river and bump down the dirt road beside it to the spot where the fresh graves were dug. There were eight to fifteen graves every day, and the number to die ranged from thirty to seventy. The Communists were prodded out of the trucks at gunpoint, mostly men but usually including three or four weeping women and boys of twelve or thirteen.

As the dozen-odd soldiers led the terrified prisoners down into the sandy riverbed beside their intended graves, the full realization that they would all be dead in ten minutes usually brought forth a pitiful, haunting chorus of wailing and weeping, moaning and pleading for mercy, though some in every group went stoically to their deaths. Then the prisoners, whose hands were bound behind them, were huddled together, here and there a married couple saying goodbye or a mother trying to comfort her young son. The soldiers quickly took five or six from the bunch at a time, prodded them over to one of the graves and made them kneel beside it. Then, with no ceremony, the soldiers shot each of them in the back of the head, shoving the corpse into the grave when it didn't fall in naturally. The grisly process was repeated in front of each grave until all were dead, and the soldiers climbed into the trucks and drove away, leaving the old men of the village shoveling sand into the graves in the twilight.

In the villages of Kutawinangun and Gendongan, which were almost one hundred percent Communist, it is virtually a life without men now. Only a handful remain in several hundred families. The widows work in the fields, old men tend the cattle, and older children look after the little ones. It has been this way since almost all the men were taken away by soldiers late in November.

In Kediri so many thousands of bodies were dumped in the Brantas River between October and March that the authorities in Djombong, a downstream town, complained formally of plague danger. Kediri's staggering toll: at least 25,000 in a city of 250,000.

In the town of Blitar, barefoot kids were playing in the yard of the large gray frame house where Sukarno was born. About 4,500 Communists were killed in Blitar. A local citizen, Kiai Haji Zahid, sat by his bungalow on the edge of the jungle across a swaying footbridge over a ravine. He scratched his several-day-old beard and gave Blitar what he considered the high distinction of being the first to start killing Communists and the last to stop. The Moslems of Blitar, as in many other areas, he told us, had joined in the killing because there weren't enough soldiers on hand to do it effectively alone. Also, he said, troops who came from far away didn't know who was a Communist and who wasn't. This was up to the local people like himself.

This lack of military supervision was one reason for the huge slaughter in the rural areas where most of the people live in small isolated villages with no soldiers around for miles. When the wave of killing started, there was no authority to stop it until it had run its course—a good three months after the military commanders called in vain for a halt. ▶

For millions all over the world caught in the humdrum of daily living, the word Bali has brought to the mind's eye visions of an idyllic tropical paradise of lush green forests, limpid mountain pools and crystal beaches, of nature in all its unspoiled glory and of happy islanders who work and play in childlike innocence. But the madness reached into paradise too. And the Balinese ran amok just like their brother Indonesians, and, like them, settled down without remorse when it was over.

Correspondent Don Moser toured the island and talked to those who had taken part in the massacre and felt its aftermath. He said in his dispatch from there:

▶ On Bali, this most beautiful of islands, the Balinese proved capable of the most exquisite cruelty. When they attacked the Communists, "it was like watching kids torture a cat," said one of the few Westerners who lived there during the killings. In Denpasar, students beat a classmate to death with stones. Around Negara, where Communists had dug graves for their intended victims, the reprisal took a toll of thousands of party members who wound up buried in the same holes that they had prepared.

In Klungkung, a village where beautiful objects are wrought from silver, a young Moslem matter-of-factly related his part in the anti-Communist campaign. One day his wife's uncle, an official in a Communist farmers' association, came to the boy's house in panic. The nationalists were burning his home, he cried. He was afraid for his life and wanted sanctuary. "No, I cannot receive you," the young man said. When the uncle begged, the young man sent a friend to complain to the local military commander that a Communist was trying to get into his house. The uncle was arrested and turned over to his niece's husband for execution. The young man discussed the matter with his wife. "You *must* do it," she insisted. "He is a Communist." And so that night the young man chopped off the head of his wife's uncle.

What kind of people are these who participated in such a slaughter? This question recurred to me constantly during my tour. Let us look at one who is a fair choice of many I have talked to as representative of the state of madness that has swept these islands. He is Hasan Hasri, a gentle-looking man of thirty who lives in a small, crude house in the village of Gelgel, where he helps to support his ten nieces and nephews. Hasan, a devout Moslem, was a farmer until the eruption of Gunnug Agung, Bali's great volcano, which destroyed his land. Then he became a laborer on the roads. Last December, though, when the army began bringing Communist prisoners down to Djumpai beach and distributing them to the villagers, Hasan felt the call of Allah. And so he took the sharp *parang* he had made from the leaf of an automobile spring and began to haunt the beach.

Every day the soldiers brought the Communists to the beach in trucks. They came at ten in the morning and three in the afternoon, and sometimes at night. There might be only a dozen prisoners, but often there were twenty-five or twenty-seven. Hasan was usually given two or three for himself. He led his Communists down to the beach where local farmers had dug the long pits, one and a half meters deep. Sometimes there were too many prisoners and the holes had to be lengthened at the last moment. The prisoners were seated on the edge of the pit, their thumbs tied securely behind their backs. Hasan shouted, *"Allah U Akbar, Allah U Akbar*—In the name of God." Then he began to chop. Hasan could usually sever the head in a single chop, he said. But sometimes at night he would miss in the dark and hit only a glancing blow into the head or neck. Then the prisoner screamed until Hasan finished him off.

Often he would chat with the men before killing them. He had nothing against them personally, he said. But they were Communists. Their names were on the party list. They were atheists, and Hasan was only carrying out the will of Allah. Once in a while the Communists begged for mercy before Hasan's auto-spring blade sliced down. But usually they were defiant and brave, and some yelled "*Hidup* PKI—Long live the Communist Party."

The first time he killed, Hasan was a little upset, he said. But after a while he settled down and then he acquired a thirst for the chopping. Eventually he quit his job as a laborer. "I had to chop every morning and every afternoon and sometimes I had to chop at night," he said. He did not worry about giving up his work on the road, for he knew that Allah would provide—and sure enough, his friends and neighbors donated food to Hasan and his family.

Why did the Indonesians destroy the Communists so mercilessly? Nothing can completely explain their ferocity, but they did have many grievances. In many rural areas the Communists had introduced a new land-reform program and administered it badly. The program was supposed to distribute land equitably, but the Communists not only appropriated lands belonging to highly respected members of the community but also attempted to take over lands belonging to the Moslem mosques. On highly religious Bali, where Hindu temples take a cut even on profits from cockfights, the Communists alienated villagers by telling them that their lavish and lovingly prepared offerings to the Hindu gods were nothing but a waste of good food.

The people were bitter, too, about the economic disaster that had overtaken the country—a disaster blamed on Sukarno's Communist advisers and administrators. By last fall *rupiah* notes were worth literally less than the paper they were printed on. Indonesian housewives had to carry suitcases of bills on routine shopping trips. Out in the countryside, peasants simply gave up trying to use the money and reverted to a trade-and-barter system. In lush Bali, where once a man could make enough in two days to live on for ten, he could not earn a day's living in a long day's work.

And everywhere people were irritated by Sukarno's lavish prestige projects, the enormously costly buildings and monuments that he was creating all over the country. "For these things," said one angry Indonesian, *"we* must eat stones." Yet it would be a mistake to think that all killings had genuine political motivation. Out in the countryside of Bali, people had no more conception of Communist ideology than they had of high finance.

The smiling young boys who bring flowers to tourists and guide them through the Balinese temple of Besakih bashed in the heads of three local Communists one night just outside the temple gates. When I asked their leader last week if he understood the difference between Communist aims and the aims of his own party, the Nationalist Party, he replied: "No, I just work here at the temple, I do not understand about politics." Did he hate the Communists? "No, I did not hate them," the boy said. Why *did* he kill them, then? "Some authorities just came by one day and said to get rid of them," the boy answered with a shy, pleasant smile. "And so we did." ▶

After the months of bloody violence came a period of calm. And the political victory of the military inaugurated many changes in the land. Before the attempted coup the nation was in bankruptcy; it was involved in a war of its own making with Malaysia; it had withdrawn from the United Nations; and it had lost the respect and confidence of a large part of the world with whom it had formerly traded and on whom it leaned for financial credit. The new government stripped Sukarno of his leadership. The war with Malaysia was ended. Indonesia again joined the United Nations and entered into trade with the Western world. Indonesian leaders spoke of sharing among their people the bountiful resources of the rich archipelago.

But the scales tip easily, and the enormity of the killings makes the road to peace unusually precipitous. In one of the villages that Dan Coggin visited, a *wayang*-play puppeteer and wealthy man, a Communist, was turned over to the mob and hacked to death after he had surrendered to the village headman for protection. His two eldest sons were away at college, but they have returned home to visit three times since then, and so far know the names of five of their father's murderers. They have a plan for vengeance, they fiercely whispered to Coggin. They will complete their education and then join the local paratroop unit so that as military men they may kill the five with less risk of reprisal.

In many instances the children of suspected Communists were slaughtered with their fathers in order to avoid just such revenge as this. But there are orphans enough in Indonesia to cast a shadow of future violence. And as yet the better life for the people that the military leaders speak of has not materialized.

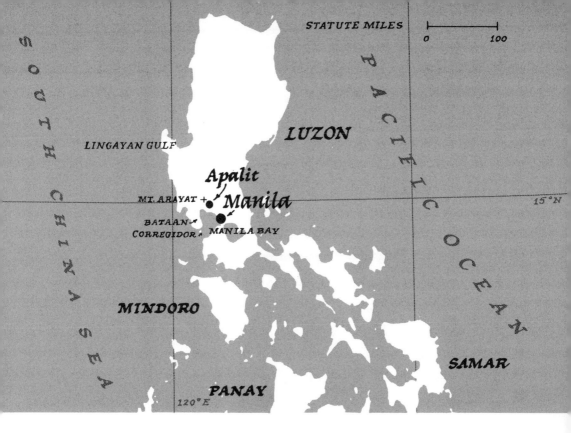

XXIV

Philippines: The Hukbalahap

(1966-   )

IN THE PHILIPPINES, whose government set an example of wise dealing with insurrection and put down a Communist-style rebellion in 1952, a new "war of liberation" was in the making in 1967. The causes underlying the unrest and the men who exploited them were much the same in the 1960's as those in the late 1940's, but the inspired leader who had successfully dealt with them was dead. And the desperate peasant farmers of Luzon island were once again the water, in the Maoist phrase, in which a

387

growing guerrilla movement swam.

The springs which fed that water lie deep in Philippine history. Although the Filipinos are of predominantly Malay stock and their archipelago of seven thousand islands stretches through the South China Sea from Formosa to Borneo, their land has always lain outside the mainstream of Asian development. The fleets and forts of the English, Dutch and Portuguese explorers made little contact with the people of the lands they occupied; but when the Spanish came to the Philippines in the sixteenth century, they went boldly into the countryside with both sword and cross, and the Christianity they planted took extensive root. The hybrid Asian-European culture that grew from it was different from any other in the Orient.

Similarly, the role that the United States played in the Philippines was unique among colonial nations in Southeast Asia. In 1898, at the end of the Spanish-American War, the islands had fallen to the United States as a territory won in conquest—somewhat to the dismay of the American people. With their own continent yet to be developed and their own fight for liberty still fresh in mind, they had no desire for a colony. But, given the *fait accompli*, it was considered imperative that the people be educated for democracy before they undertook self-rule. This mood was expressed by President McKinley when he said: "The truth is I didn't want the Philippines and when they came to us as a gift from the gods . . . there was nothing left for us to do but to take them all and educate the Filipinos."

It took the United States three years of fighting to subdue the rebellious Filipinos who had hoped for independence with the end of Spanish rule, but even while they fought, the Americans began this process of education. And for the next half-century, until final independence was granted in 1946, the U.S. government was almost exclusively preoccupied with the education and political development of her charges. The tragic consequence of this preoccupation was that the feudal structure which had resulted from three hundred years of Spanish influence on the original Malayan tribal society was left untouched. Even today the economy and the control of the land is in the hands of a few families. Almost 35 percent of all Filipinos are sharecroppers, many of whom are forced to pay up to 70 percent of their crops to landlords who may charge 100 percent or even 200 percent on loans to their tenants.

Long before independence a political structure had been built, with all the trappings of an executive office, a legislature and even political parties, but it did not work in the way the Americans took for granted it would work. With the goal of independence already promised free and clear, Filipino politicians devoted themselves not to the cause of nationalism, but more often to ingratiating themselves with those who held actual power: the landowners and the wealthy families who controlled the produce of the nation. This led to graft and corruption in the Philippine government from the very top right down to the provincial level.

Under the pressure of Japanese attack in 1941, the relationship between the United States and the Philippines was cemented by their mutual defeat. For a time the warmth between the two amounted almost to love, and the Filipinos fought for the return of the Americans virtually as much as for their own liberation from Japanese occupation. Among the guerrilla groups who were supplied by American air-drops and submarines late in the war was an organization which called itself *Hukbalahap*, a name derived from the initial syllables of the Tagalog words for "People's Army Against Japan," and further shortened to the nickname *Huks*. Some of the leaders of the Huks had been active in agrarian uprisings against the landlords before the war, and in the three years that they fought the Japanese they continued their war against the landowners. During that time they extended their control over much of Luzon, the Philippines' main island, assuming the functions of government, redistributing land, setting up cooperatives and operating drumhead courts of justice. Through ambushes and attacks on Japanese patrols and depots, they were able to arm thirty thousand men.

When the U.S. forces returned to Manila in 1945, independence was granted the Filipinos in a flow of emotional words, and the Hukbalahap, like the rest of their countrymen, rushed to welcome the liberating soldiers. But the American officers, finding too much of socialism, even communism, among the Huks, denied them recognition and declined to give them the back pay given to other resistance groups for their efforts against the Japanese. Manuel Roxas, the first President to be elected after the war, refused to seat the Huk leader Luis Taruc and some of his colleagues when they were elected to congress. The Huks retired to the hills and became an insurgent force.

The Philippines has a peculiarly appropriate climate for such an insurgent movement. In this predominantly Malay population of more than thirty million people with an overlay of Spanish and North American cultures, eighty percent are Catholics, seventy-two percent are literate, four percent own twenty-five percent of the wealth, and a fraction of one percent hold political power. The war had left great destruction, especially on Luzon. More than half the capital city of Manila had been laid waste. Hundreds of smaller cities and provincial barrios had been hit, and everywhere schools and factories were in ruins.

Even more important, three years of Japanese occupation had eroded the moral climate of the country. To survive under the Japanese, it had become necessary, even patriotic, to cheat, rob and kill. This immorality had been carried into the new government, where graft was taken for granted. Many people in the cities could not find work—schoolteachers and soldiers were seldom paid regularly—and farmers could no longer support themselves on the land. More and more drifted into the hills to join the Hukbalahap.

In April 1948, President Roxas died and his successor, Elpidio Quirino, granted amnesty to the Huks if they turned in their weapons. Luis Taruc himself led the move to accept the amnesty and personally negotiated the terms in Manila. But just at this time word reached the Philippines of the decision made by the newly re-created Cominform to carry armed warfare to Southeast Asia. Perhaps because of this, Taruc withdrew from the negotiations, returned to the hills and resumed hostilities. It was only then that he openly revealed that he was a Communist, and his insurgents—although they continued to be popularly known as the Huks—renamed themselves the "People's Liberation Army," or HMB.

By 1950—as in 1945—the Huks had control of large portions of Luzon. In some places they levied taxes and ran their own schools and newspapers. The regulars in their army now numbered some twenty thousand and they had the support of well over a million peasant farmers who supplied them with food and shelter and with intelligence against the Philippine constabulary forces with whom they were in sporadic but open warfare. Their Politburo drew up plans for the seizure of national power, and they seemed on the verge of such a takeover when a single man arose to change the course of events. He was Ramon Magsaysay, a congressman and ex-guerrilla who became Defense Minister in 1950, and later President.

Magsaysay understood that most of the rank and file of the insurgency were rebelling against poverty and injustice. He formed a policy of "All-Out Force and All-Out Friendship," which combined intensified military action against the hard core of the Huk regulars with programs to alleviate the sufferings of those who had turned to them in despair. "They want a house and land of their own," he said. "All right, they can stop fighting because I will give it to them." He opened new lands for the landless, created agrarian courts where peasants could find justice for the first time, and even persuaded the legislature to provide funds to buy virgin land, where he offered a plot of his own to any Huk who would surrender.

By 1954 Magsaysay had won his war. The Huks had dwindled to a few isolated stragglers, and their leader, Luis Taruc, emerged from the hills and presented himself for surrender. Seldom had there been such a clear victory over a concerted Communist attack. But the Magsaysay solution did not survive his death in an airplane crash in 1957. Land distribution, the key to his victory, was sabotaged by the congress, which, dominated by landlords, refused to allocate the needed funds. Relatively few of the hundreds of thousands of oppressed farmers on Luzon reached their promised homesteads, and all the old evils of corruption and abuse, which Magsaysay had fought to eradicate in his few years as president, returned, making the land fertile for Communist propaganda once again.

By 1967 central Luzon was once more the heart of a resurgence of armed unrest. Again the Huks were capitalizing on the erosion of law, the staggering incidence of corruption among officials, and the steadily widening gap between the rich and the poor. The new Huk "Supremo" was the aging and asthmatic Pedro Taruc, brother of Luis, who was still in jail, but the active leader of this second rebellion was Faustino Delmundo, known as Commander Sumulong. Their organization was small, dedicated and tightly disciplined. Their terrorist units roamed the countryside, meting out instant, violent reprisals to local mayors, government officials and police who defied their orders. Once again they set up their own courts of law. Their agents collected tribute and taxes. They enlisted military officers, city officials and congressmen in their cause. And, remembering their earlier mistakes, they no longer called for an immediate revolution, but turned instead toward a gradual subversion of the country's political system.

Once again a state of war existed between the Huk guerrillas and the Philippine Constabulary, with raids and ambushes and counterraids. In December 1966 correspondent Arthur Zich arrived just after the Constabulary had cornered a Huk commander and part of his squad and had shot it out with them. The Constabulary colonel, Rafael Ileto, gave Zich the following dramatic account of what had happened:

▶ It was a little after nine o'clock, Sunday evening, December 12, and Colonel Ileto was in his headquarters at Camp Olivas in the Constabulary's First Zone of Pampanga Province. He was waiting for information that might lead him to a Hukbalahap hideout. In the past few weeks the Huks had been on the move in the First Zone area, collecting taxes from the farmers, who had just finished their harvest, and—a new venture into the vacuum left by the central government—organizing the Huk equivalent of Barrio Councils. Four local policemen had defected to them, and a Constabulary trooper had been kidnapped. His body had just been found.

Colonel Ileto had ordered his roadblock checkpoints increased in the hope of forcing the Huks to lie low in one barrio long enough to fix their whereabouts and strike. Now the news that he was waiting for was brought. An informer was led in. "They are in the big, painted house between San Pablo and San Ecidio," he said. "They are all there, Oscar and the others." Oscar was the code alias for Ricardo Ignacio, a Huk company commander and the ninth-ranking man under Supremo Pedro Taruc. He was responsible for six towns which the Constabulary concede are under virtually complete Huk influence.

Oscar had been unknown a year earlier, but four months ago, when it became clear that this violent newcomer had been responsible for some twenty-five assassinations and kidnappings in the area, the government had set a five-thousand-peso price on his head. At that time, when the outspoken head of the local anti-Huk Mayors' League had been shot in an ambush, Oscar had boasted openly, "I am the man who killed Mayor Anastacio Gallardo." Now the informer brought news of his present hideout.

Three Constabulary teams and three Ranger teams from Camp Olivas, and a Twentieth Battalion Combat Team in armored personnel carriers from nearby Arayat converged on the big painted house the informer had pinpointed, and deployed around it. The house was dark and silent. The order to come out drew no response. Then, in the dark shadows behind the house, a man was seen slowly walking away. He carried a tin pail, and the troopers who saw him assumed he was a simple civilian out to get some oil for his lamps, as is common in the barrios. They held their fire. Out front a trooper had gone to the door and peered inside: a figure was climbing the staircase. The trooper shouted. From an upstairs window a Thompson sub-machine gun answered. A grenade thumped against the windshield of the command jeep—but failed to explode. The Constabulary opened up. The man with the pail broke into a run and plunged into a rice paddy in the dark. He had been the lookout. A thump on the pail was the warning he never gave.

Spotlights on the personnel carriers lit up the house, but it was silent again. Then a second-floor window was flung open. One man stood exposed in the spotlights, pleading to surrender. He cried out that he was one of seven Huks inside, but there were also thirteen civilians, including six children. The Constabulary promised to hold fire while the innocent came out. The man who was surrendering and a Huk "amazon," the wife of Commander Oscar, were among them. As they were filing out, the sound of creaking metal came from the back of the house. The spotlights swung. On the second floor was a doorway, covered with sheet metal, which led onto a flat tin roof. Even as the light hit it, the sheet metal came away and a man charged out, firing a Thompson. Trooper guns blazed back, the volley thudding into the man with such force that he was blown back into the house.

Two more men scampered out under fire, but the troops caught them. One man jerked upright, spun into the air and fell dead in a heap on the ground. The second man, hit in the hips and thighs, made a desperate dive and managed to crawl some twenty yards before he died. The last man out was Oscar. He appeared on the roof, and the bullets knocked him off it like a duck in a shooting gallery. He was as tough dying as he had been in life: both knees shot away, with more slugs in his belly and chest, he kept on wriggling when he hit the ground, and crawled almost to the edge of the rice paddy—some 150 yards from the house—before more bullets finally finished him. ►

One of the two Huks captured—the man who pleaded from the window to be allowed to surrender—was Potenciano de Leon, a gentle-voiced, soft-eyed family man, for years a policeman in the town of Apalit, but for the last nine months a member of Commander Oscar's killer squad. Now in prison, he had no hope of freedom, for he was marked for death outside the prison walls. Thus he talked willingly to correspondent Arthur Zich, who visited him soon after his surrender. How the Hukbalahap chooses a man, taints him by making him a known outlaw, and from then on uses him as a captive killer is revealed in Zich's interview:

► De Leon's story starts back in 1963, during the elections of that year. At the time he had been a permanent member of the Apalit police force for four years, but well before that, as a temporary policeman back in the late forties during the first rebellion, he had fought the Huks. "I was a wanted man by the Huks ever since," he says.

One fall night, as the elections approached, a Huk commander accompanied by Constabulary troopers entered Apalit and conducted a campaign meeting—out in front of De Leon's house, within which a terrified De Leon was hiding and listening. "When I saw the Constabulary among the Huks," he recalls, "I thought, here I am a policeman and wanted by the Huks. What chance do I have?"

Honorio Mercado became the new mayor. "I knew he was close to the Huks and I told my police chief what I thought, and I said, 'We'd better fight them now.' And he said to me, 'No, we will not fight the Huks. For if we do we will surely die.' "

One night Mayor Mercado invited De Leon to dinner. "When I came I found Mercado and Commander Oscar laughing and joking together, and when I sat down with them at the table, two Huks sat down one on each side of me with carbines pointing at me under the table. I ate very little. But after dinner the Mayor put his hand on my shoulder and said, 'There is no trouble now. We will let them go wherever they want in Apalit.'

"I was not wanted by them any more," De Leon said, and even after all these months he showed visible relief in the recollection. But now he knew he was committed to them.

"One day," De Leon recalls, "Domingo Yambao, a Huk Commander, came to me and told me that Commander Oscar had ordered us to liquidate someone. Oscar had said this fellow, Jose Garcia, was an enemy of the people. He was the head of a gang called 'The Seventh Fleet,' which had been terrorizing the farmers. We were to kill him to show the people that the HMB support the people who are oppressed."

On the night of March 19, De Leon and nine other men slipped into a barrio in Minalin. It was past midnight when they got to Garcia's house. De Leon was ordered to stand lookout, to make sure that he was spotted and could be recognized by any witnesses. Then they burst into Garcia's house and chopped him down with a Thompson sub-machine gun. But his common-law wife escaped, and when she did, De Leon noticed that she got a good look at him. "The barrio never moved during the shooting," De Leon recalls. "It was deathly still. Nobody would have come out even if Garcia had yelled for help. I pitied him. But I pitied myself more."

From that point on, De Leon was locked in, a man wanted by the law, floating from one barrio to another, moving every two or three days. Life among the Huks had begun.

In between skirmishes and missions, Oscar and his men carried on their job, which was agitation and propaganda and tax collections. "Nobody could say no to us," De Leon says, "because the Huks do not accept the answer no." And he began to learn that Huk life wasn't always bad. "The people were good to us. They took care of us—out of fear or whatever. Sometimes they would get up from their very own beds and give them to us. Families that could not afford it would kill a chicken for us for dinner. There was one family once. They slaughtered a chicken for our breakfast, another for our lunch, another for our dinner. And wherever we went they would wash and iron our clothes, run errands, buy us cigarettes, get us illegal unit patches for disguise Constabulary uniforms. And the women would act as our lookouts. One time in San Simon a woman carried a whole basketful of weapons right through an army detachment for us. They would gather information on the positions of government troops and tell us who the government agents were inside the barrios. And at the sound of alarm we would move out, or if it was too late to get out, they would hide us in their houses. The Constabulary cannot move inside the gate of a private house without the owner's permission or without a search warrant, and by the time they got the warrant we would be gone."

In early July, De Leon took part in the ambush and assassination of Candaba's Mayor Anastacio Gallardo. Sometime after that he began to sense that he had become suspect by the HMB. "I never took this off," he said, pulling from around his neck a Catholic medal, his mind going back to that terrifying period.

Finally, the December night came when the Constabulary staged the attack on the big painted house. "By then I knew that I was going to be liquidated," De Leon recalls. "I knew that I would be next. They thought I was informing. When the Constabulary turned their searchlights on us I realized my chance had come." ▶

De Leon told his Constabulary captors the details of eleven different assassination missions and named some forty men whom he knew to be members of Huk liquidation teams. But, far more ominous, he gave them a list of government officials who were deeply implicated in their relations with the insurgency. The situation in this central Luzon rice bowl, the heart of the Philippines, was dangerously similar to the situation there in 1950 when Magsaysay saved the government through his attack on the guerrilla fighters and his even more effective war on the graft and corruption and the cruel economic inequalities that were the basic reasons for the rebellion.

In 1967 the Constabulary were again attacking guerrilla hideouts, but as yet there was no Magsaysay in the Philippines to challenge the few ruling families who still held both the land and the power of government.

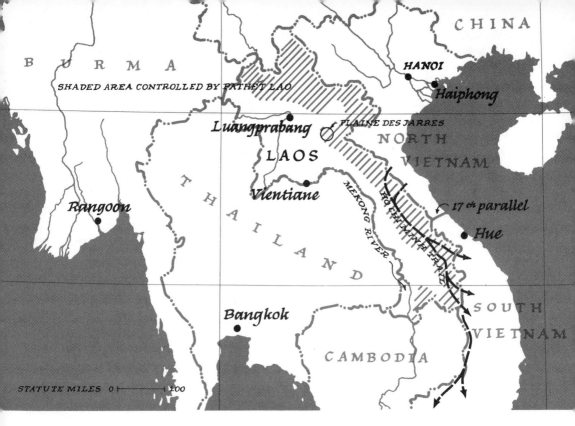

SHADED AREA CONTROLLED BY PATHET LAO

BURMA

CHINA

HANOI

Haiphong

Luangprabang

PLAINE DES JARRES

NORTH

LAOS

VIETNAM

Vientiane

Rangoon

THAILAND

MEKONG RIVER

17ᵗʰ parallel

Hue

Bangkok

CAMBODIA

SOUTH

VIETNAM

STATUTE MILES 0 ——— 100

XXV

Laos: The Beleaguered Neutral

(1954-   )

THERE ARE SOME LANDS that have been fought over until each time a
farmer plows his fields he turns up bones, and there are others where one
feels that war—no matter how pervasive it may be—is alien to the people of
that land. Laos, high in the mountains, beautiful and primitive, is one of the
latter. In 1954, when French Indo-China was divided into the separate
countries of Cambodia, Laos, North Vietnam and South Vietnam, Laos was

recognized as a sovereign state by both the Communist and non-Communist worlds and ever since has clung to a tenuous neutrality between her more populous and warring neighbors.

From time to time in history, Laotian princes ruled their own Kingdom of the Million Elephants and the White Parasol, but more often the area was under foreign influence. The Khmers of Cambodia, the Thai and the Annamese have ruled there, and in 1893 Laos became a French protectorate. Since 1959 the United States has become increasingly involved in a shadowy war waged in this strangely carefree but determinedly neutral land.

When the great post-war world conflict of the twentieth century burst into Laos, it was still a medieval state of feudal princes bickering for supremacy. And through the war these family rivalries continued, although the princes found it expedient to employ modern names such as "neutralist" and "anti-Communist." For with the North Vietnamese using Laotian territory as a sanctuary and an invasion route in their war with South Vietnam, this quiet country became a focal point where Communist and Western forces confronted each other.

That this confrontation was far less violent and less public than in neighboring Vietnam was due in some part to the Laotians' gentle passivity and insistence on neutrality. So while the Communists tried to obscure the fact that they were forcibly occupying much of Laotian territory, the United States was equally silent about providing massive economic and military aid in an attempt to bolster the Laotians into holding the line against Communist political erosion and military invasion which could outflank their position in South Vietnam and pose a threat to Thailand, Cambodia and Burma.

In 1962, at a conference in Geneva, fourteen nations signed an accord upholding the independence and neutrality of Laos. It was agreed that all foreign troops were to be withdrawn from Laotian territory, but North Vietnam disregarded the agreement and kept some troops—perhaps 25,000 as of 1967—guarding the Ho Chi Minh Trail, which filters through Laotian territory. The United States countered this in many ways, although it refrained from putting its own uniformed men in the field within Laotian boundaries.

At the time of the Geneva accord, a tripartite government was formed—a coalition of leftists, neutralists and rightists, headed by neutralist Prince Souvanna Phouma, with two other princes leading the leftist and rightist factions. The leftist was his half-brother Prince Souphanouvong, known as the Red Prince because of his alliance with North Vietnam. He withdrew from the coalition in 1963 and made his headquarters in the Communist-held north. He became the strongest political and military figure in Laos. Educated in Hanoi and Paris, he had joined the Viet Minh early in 1946, was trained by General Vo Nguyen Giap, and returned to Laos to fight the French. His forces, called the Pathet Lao, consisted in 1967 of some 30,000 skilled and dedicated Laotian troops filled out by North Vietnamese soldiers who were included in their ranks.

The third princely leader, Boun Oum, commanded the rightist faction and was supported by the United States, as was rightist strongman General Phoumi Nosavan, who replaced him. The royalist headquarters were in Vientiane, the administrative capital, and in 1967 Nosavan's anti-Communist forces consisted of some 60,000 troops of the Royal Laotian army which were intermittently allied with some 8,000 neutralist troops.

Premier Souvanna Phouma's position was remarkable among the leaders of countries involved in the complex of East-West conflicts. He received encouragement and support from both Moscow and Washington, holding a fine balance between Communist and non-Communist forces in his country. Both sides watched over Prince Souvanna's delicate position, careful not to violate too openly the agreements they established at Geneva lest they be drawn into direct confrontation. The Premier was aware of this and frequently threatened to retire to his property in France. "We want no help from the United States or any Western help," he declared moodily. "It would only mean more war for Laos. . . ." Still, he continued to accept the highest amount of American assistance in the world—$26 for every Laotian every year, or almost half the per-capita income—until surpassed by South Vietnam, which by 1966 was receiving $40 per capita.

Many of Laos' small, appealing, dark-skinned people would be astonished to be called Laotians, since they know themselves to be Meo, Yao, Youne or Khalom tribespeople who are hill men and quite different from the valley dwellers, who are a branch of the Thai peoples driven out of southern China by Kublai Khan seven centuries ago. Such rule outside their villages as they have known has been the rule of princes. And never having had any political control over their own lives, they view all happenings beyond their little communities as something that has nothing to do with them. They are not people who mix into world affairs; few of them read or write, and a recent American survey revealed that ninety percent of all Laotians believe that the world is flat and peopled mainly by themselves. The war that surges back and forth over their fragile houses and around their tiny patches of land belongs to another world, that of the princes or the foreigners. And it is wisest simply to bend before it, like the flexible bamboo, waiting only for it to pass before they spring back to their ancient way of life.

Even in Vientiane, the nation's capital, the war is taken somewhat in passing. Here live a hundred thousand of Laos' three million people, packed in with all the foreign missions, consulates and embassies which are established alongside each other, friend and foe. Here also are the headquarters of the International Control Commission made up of Polish, Indian and Canadian delegates—nominally the overseers of Laotian neutrality. And here a contingent of Pathet Lao troops is quartered a street or two away from a garrison of the Royal Laotian army. Usually these rival soldiers maintain a friendly peace, although once a battle broke out between them and they shot it out through the night. Only one man was killed, for Laotian soldiers are under Buddhist influence and are loath to kill any living thing. And not long after that, when during an eclipse "the frog was swallowing the moon," all the soldiers in Vientiane, left, right and center, joined forces to shoot at the frog and frighten him away.

The 1962 truce agreement was soon broken by sporadic military encounters, and on March 31, 1963, the Pathet Lao moved onto the Plaine des Jarres to bring formal battle to the neutralist forces there. The Plaine des Jarres has through the ages been the battleground for Laos. Whoever controlled that vast, grassy "Plain of Jars," named for scores of large stone burial urns dotting the area, has controlled the country.

General Kong Le was in command of the neutralist forces on the Plaine des Jarres. A small, dedicated man, he had risen from obscurity to become a national hero on the strength of single-minded views and independent leadership. An unknown captain in the neutralist forces in 1960, he led his battalion in a coup d'état against a right-wing government which he felt was subservient to the United States. Then, after being fêted and made much of in Peking, Hanoi and Moscow, he turned against the left-wing Pathet Lao, which he found to be a "lackey of Communism," and was now facing the Communist force on the battlefield.

In June that year, correspondent Pamela Sanders reached his battle station on the Plaine des Jarres and wrote about General Kong Le and the kind of war this neutralist general was fighting on that historic grassy battle plain:

▶ The Pathet Lao forces fighting for the Plaine des Jarres have been heavily reinforced and have now, in the third month of battle, pushed General Kong Le and his neutralist armies into a small corner of the northwestern edge of the plain. Here General Kong Le is clinging tenaciously, supported by American weapons and supplies, several thousand Meo guerrillas, and four battalions of the Royal Laotian army troops dispatched by his old arch-foe General Phoumi Nosavan, who is now also engaged in fighting the Pathet Lao.

Kong Le's logistical problem, already considerable due to lack of roads and an insufficient number of aircraft, is further increased by the daily deluge of the monsoon rains. Meanwhile, despite repeated attempts by the Meo guerrillas to cut the supply route to the Pathet Lao forces, northern truck convoys are getting through to supply the enemy.

The neutralist headquarters encampment, hurriedly constructed when General Kong Le's forces had to pull back last month, is a motley, makeshift conglomeration of tents and thatched huts, an ammunition dump and a repair depot where rows of Russian-made trucks lie useless for lack of spare parts. One kilometer to the west, in a valley nestled among the rolling lush green hills, stand four large olive-drab tents. The first belongs to the International Control Commission team, and the second to the six members of the French Military Mission, who are present for advising and training purposes when weather and battle conditions permit. The last two tents are the living quarters and field headquarters of General Kong Le.

One night this week the General sat in one of these tents with his neutralist chief of staff and the commander of the Royalist forces. The three men sat on stools around a small wooden table and in the wavering light somberly studied a map spread before them. A single hurricane lamp swayed on a rope overhead. Outside in the darkness the rain which had continued for eighteen solid hours still beat down incessantly, occasionally spraying the interior when the wind blew aside the tent flaps. Gullies of water snaking across the dirt floor had turned it into slippery mud. Their feet propped on the stool rungs, the three squinted at the positions marked on the map—the red for the Pathet Lao and Viet Minh, the blue for the neutralists and Royalists. Silently they began to rub the lines off and pencil new markings on the southern portion of the plain. Under attack for the past four days, two companies of neutralist troops, reinforced by Phoumi Nosavan's forces, had lost two key mountaintop positions and had retreated five kilometers to the west.

General Kong Le plucked fretfully at the vertical scar on his forehead and let out a sigh. "You see," he said, "the situation is very serious, very grave." Wearing a white T-shirt, a pair of levis and rubber shower shoes, the tiny, 5-foot-1½-inch, 115-pound General pointed his child-sized hand at the positions on the map and explained that with the loss of them, the Pathet Lao had moved toward absolute control of the main supply road; and, more important, they had now won the vital position they needed in order to assault the most strategic point on the Plaine des Jarres. Frowning again, Kong Le pointed at the lost positions and said: "We were there ourselves only yesterday. But what can we do? The Prime Minister Prince Souvanna has ordered me not to attack. He is always telling me I must not attack. I must not fight. It is very difficult."

Colonel Sabab, a neutralist paratroop officer, had entered the tent. He had the latest reports from the front lines. The news was bad. Thirteen neutralist soldiers were missing in one area and the Pathet Lao and Viet Minh were now heavily attacking another. He also reported that the roadblocks which the Meo guerrillas had established behind the enemy had been opened again and that a hundred-truck convoy carrying supplies had reached the Pathet Lao that afternoon.

Kong Le winced, shut his eyes and rubbed his forehead. "I feel dizzy," he said.

But Kong Le is a mercurial person and his moods are constantly shifting. Presently he lifted his head and, picking up a plastic globe of the world, smilingly said: "I will give it to Prince Souphanouvong and the Communists because this is what they want—the whole world." This brought small laughter from the other officers.

Kong Le went to his desk, pulled out several bottles of pills, took one of each, then lay back on his small wooden bunk. "My head hurts very much," he said. Kong Le suffers from frequent headaches and dizzy spells that seem to come on when the news is bad. He blames them on a blow he received when a rock fell on him on Corregidor Island while he was attending Philippine Ranger School there in 1957. He has lost a lot of weight and his face, once round, is now quite gaunt, obviously the result of fatigue and strain. After a while he began to talk again: "Some men do not know why they are fighting," he said. "But we know. We are fighting for peace. Everything depends on us. If we do not fight against the Communists, Laos will be lost and become a Communist state. And if we do not win here, all of Asia will be lost to them. It is true that we were with the Communists for two years, but what could we do? After the coup d'état in 1960 the Americans were against us. We needed help. At first the Communists were good to us. They gave us supplies and told us they were neutralists. A year ago I began to know the Pathet Lao were not fighting for Laos but for Communism. I knew then we would have to fight them. We do not want Laos to be controlled by anyone, not by the Communists or the Americans. My men and I fight for true neutrality and freedom."

The tent room again became quiet and General Kong Le picked up a copy of a book and began reading. It was Crane's *Red Badge of Courage*. He read curiously for a couple of pages and then, pointing to the title, asked if the book was about Communists. Disappointed when I said no, he put it down and presently asked one of the soldiers to sing a song. Listening to the plaintive tune, Kong Le said wistfully, "He is singing about a farmer who lived in Laos many hundreds of years ago. Someday, when Laos is free, I will go back to my village and be a farmer too. Laos is such a beautiful land. It is sad that we do not enjoy it."

Kong Le shares his tent room with three officers and four enlisted men. It has a spartan interior, although a guitar with broken strings stands propped against a locker and there are two or three pin-up pictures of American girls, and a transistor radio. Beneath General Kong Le's bed are five locked briefcases which I presumed contained important confidential documents. But once I was surprised to see him unlock one of them, take out a handkerchief and a pair of socks, and then carefully relock it. The lamp was put out around ten and only the candle was left flickering. The rain continued heavily and the wind snapped the tent flaps, and little rivulets ran through the mud on the floor.

It was still drizzling in the morning, but it was a lovely sight across the countryside. Cattle and water buffalo grazed quietly on glistening lime-green hills, and the smell of pine trees sweetened the air. Slowly a pale sun rose through the shower and a rainbow spread over the nearby purple mountains. Sounds of cowbells mingled with strains of *Les Sylphides* drifting out of the tent from Kong Le's radio. It was an idyllic pastoral setting.

But just two ridges away, in an equally pastoral setting, a curious scene was being enacted. Over the velvety landscape and through the soft summer rain rolled two Russian-made tanks and an armored car manned by neutralist soldiers. Before them stood a small conical mountain at the top of which was a Pathet Lao artillery emplacement. The tanks were going to try to knock out the emplacement and take the hill.

As the tanks chugged up the first rise, a herd of wild ponies scattered and galloped away before them. An armored car and one tank pulled over to the side and stopped while the second tank continued upward. Moments later a Pathet Lao gun flashed and a neutralist tank fired back. Both missed. Three rounds were exchanged while the tank slowly inched forward. It was obvious that the Pathet Lao could not depress their gun sufficiently to get the tank. Inexplicably, the tank suddenly halted. For ten minutes it did not move and there was dead silence. Then the first tank crept forward a few feet and the second followed a few feet, and again the Pathet Lao gun flashed. Both tanks answered and halted again. Why were they stopping? They were unquestionably out of Pathet Lao range and had therefore a clear field right to the top.

This painful crawling and stopping process continued for two agonizing, interminable hours. It was like watching a training film in which the reel is stopped every few frames and rerun in slow motion to point out mistakes. Then a few neutralist soldiers appeared and started climbing the hill. Slipping and sliding, they stumbled, fell, rolled backward, picked themselves up and stumbled forward once more.

Watching this lilliputian scene, one longed to pick up those little toy tanks and tin soldiers, wind them up, and push them to the top. What happened instead was that the tanks finally rumbled around the side of the hill and out of sight, the soldiers disappeared into a patch of trees, two of the ponies reappeared grazing quietly over that lovely mountainside, and none of us shall ever know what happened—if anything. ▶

That week, as correspondent Sanders was preparing to leave the Plaine des Jarres and General Kong Le was preparing still another pull-back from the pressures of the Pathet Lao attacks, the General showed her a ring he was wearing and said seriously, "It's magic, you know." Kong Le was noted for his magic. Widely popular with his troops and the Laotian people, he was believed invulnerable to bullets, and the cotton strings he wore tied around his wrists and the stone amulet he carried in a pouch at his waist to keep his thirty-two souls (one for each major part of his body) from fleeing protected him well, for he had never been wounded. Yet the spirit that guarded him must have lost its power, for he was driven off the Plaine des Jarres, and in 1966 he was removed from his command and sent into exile, far from the land he loves.

Meanwhile the war in Laos went on as before. The Pathet Lao took all of the Plaine des Jarres and continued to hold a thick belt of territory in the east and northeast and to run men and matériel over the Ho Chi Minh Trail. But within much of this Pathet Lao territory there were pockets of neutralist forces, and there were frequent skirmishes and some stiff engagements between government and Pathet Lao units.

From its inception, Laos was torn by violence, its villagers uprooted, their homes destroyed and their entire way of life thrown into disorder. Once a surplus food-raising area, the country was reduced to living on handouts.

With but three million inhabitants, it raised an army larger than that of Mexico and Canada combined. Once a land blessed with easy living, beauty and charm, it became a nation of refugees, four hundred thousand of its people wandering here and there, or languishing in makeshift camps. Driven from their homes by a violence which they did not understand and over which they had no control, they were tired and bewildered. Most of them were strangers, lost in their own country, for even the next valley was a foreign land to them. Now they were gathered in squalid temporary homes and shelters to live out the war. Almost all of them were farmers, and they had no land to farm and no work to do and had lost dignity and hope.

As they do in every land at war, the homeless in Laos have misery etched on their faces. The smile has gone out of them. And it is moving to talk to them, especially because few of them find anyone to blame—only their destiny.

Late in the war, correspondent Loren Fessler visited the Muong Cha refugee camp in a mountain valley south of the Plaine des Jarres. More than twenty thousand Laotians, most of them Meo tribespeople, were huddled in rows of grass-thatched bamboo huts or in long, tin-roofed sheds. Many of them had driven their cattle and goats and pigs on long-day marches through mountain trails. Some had straggled in from the fighting around the Plaine des Jarres. Fessler talked with Nao Same. She was thirty-five and had borne eight children, and now lay on a refugee camp cot eight months pregnant. Where was her husband? He was killed in the shelling of the village a month ago. Where were her children? She wasn't sure. Some were killed in the village shelling, some were hit during attacks on the trail. Others were lost along the way—she wasn't sure—somewhere. Only one son remained. She couldn't talk any more.

Nearby, Sao Yu lay on another bed. She was sixty. Her husband sat near her. He was seventy. Both had walked for two weeks. Now Sao Yu's feet were heavily bandaged. Their children were all married and gone, they said, so there was no one to help them when they had to flee from the shelling and the fighting. What had they lost? The husband replied: "Our pig and our horse and our cow." Sao Yu, weeping, broke in shrilly: "And our hen. The best layer we ever had. And our cow. We saved hard to buy her. She gave good milk and was with calf. Our two ponies, both so strong. Our ducks, they would have been good to eat and the male would have fathered many good ducks." The words turned into wailing.

The old man nodded silently. Then he said, "Now we have lost it all—all the quiet things."

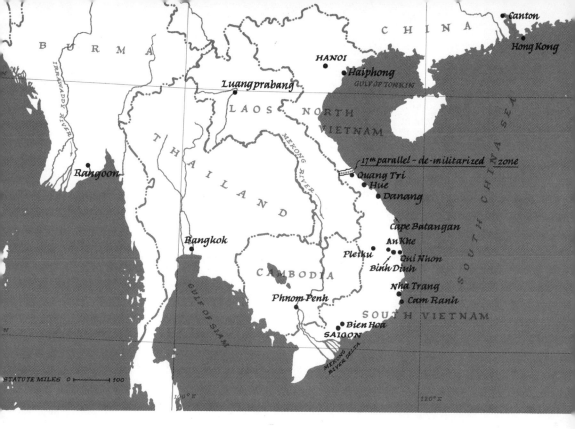

XXVI

Vietnam: The Continuing War

(1959-   )

W HEN THE North Vietnamese signed the Geneva agreements of 1954
ending the war against France and accepting a partition of Indo-
China, they did so under pressure from China and the Soviet Union, which
feared that a prolongation of the fighting might bring the United States into
the war. Time has shown these fears were justified, for Ho Chi Minh, having
won his dramatic victory over the French, treated the cease-fire accord as no

more than a pause in his effort to extend the Viet Minh control over all of the former French colony. And as resistance to him weakened, the United States was drawn in ever more deeply until, little more than a decade later, Americans were his chief enemies in the jungles and paddies of South Vietnam and in the air over the north.

The political situation at the end of the Indo-China war was that Ho, as president of the Communist Viet Minh government, became president in the northern "regroupment area," while Emperor Bao Dai, whom the French had persuaded to be their chief of state, appointed an uncompromising nationalist, Ngo Dinh Diem, to be his premier in the south. At the time of the Geneva cease-fire accord, it was agreed that elections for all of Vietnam were to be held in July 1956, and Ho, a national patriot, had vastly more appeal than the corpulent playboy Emperor, whom the Vietnamese considered a French puppet. It was a political necessity for Diem to rid himself of his chief of state, and this he did through a rigged referendum which neatly disposed of the Emperor and sent him off to his properties in France.

For two years after the division of the country there seemed a hopeful chance for peace. Thousands of Communists who had been fighting in the southern areas went north, and nearly a million refugees, mostly Roman Catholics, had been successfully resettled in the south. Under Diem the standard of living was rising, and American military advisers, who had replaced the French military training mission, were creating a South Vietnamese army to balance the Communist army of the north and the potentially dissident guerrilla fighters who had simply buried their weapons and remained in the south. As long as there was a chance for Ho to gain control of the country through elections, these fighters remained indistinguishable from the rest of the population. But there were fifteen million people in the tightly controlled north and less than twelve million in the south, and an election would almost surely have resulted in a northern victory; Diem therefore declared the Geneva agreement on this score "in contempt of Vietnamese national interests," and refused to hold the elections.

Feeling that he had been cheated of his elections as he felt he had been cheated by the Geneva accords themselves, Ho Chi Minh directed his guerrillas in the south to dig up their arms and called for violent political action to bring down the Diem regime. His people played on the interests of special groups: the politico-religious sects such as the Cao Dai; persecuted ethnic minorities; students; and particularly peasants who were unhappy with the government's unfulfilled promises of farm aid and land reforms. And his cadres once again began their terror raids. By 1958 it was clear that North

Vietnam was sending arms and men to the south to carry out subversion with the aim of overthrowing the Diem government. And in December 1960 the National Liberation Front was formed as a coalition of the Viet Minh with various nationalistic groups and religious sects under strong Communist leadership. In two years the military arm of the Liberation Front—known as the Viet Cong—had command of an estimated twenty-five thousand guerrillas. Using the tactics the Viet Minh had used against the French, they raided rubber estates, dominated rural areas by killing village officials, carried out reprisals against those who cooperated with the government, and slaughtered people on the city streets to demonstrate their power.

Premier Diem's increasingly repressive measures lost him the support of many groups in the south and he made no headway against the Communists. In 1963 the United States, convinced that Diem had lost so much public favor that he could not win against the Communists, publicly dissociated itself from his government, and late in that year Diem was murdered by his political associates. In the next nineteen months—until June 1965, when Air Force Commander Nguyen Cao Ky became Premier—South Vietnam had ten different governments, and with each change the Viet Cong benefited from the political turmoil. By now they were roving the countryside with impunity. General Vo Nguyen Giap, whose armies had destroyed the French, commanded the vast areas of the highlands and had virtually cut the nation in half. The South Vietnamese forces, bloodied and reeling, their reserves in tatters, were on the edge of defeat. Only a massive introduction of U.S. troops could prevent a Communist takeover.

The involvement of Americans in Vietnam was slow but inexorable and, like so many things in war that develop from action and counteraction, had its own chemistry. The early advisers who had taken over from the French were restricted to training and observation. Soon these advisers became assistants who flew planes but did not man the guns. Later they took over the guns but could fire them only when attacked; then they fired them to defend their bases. Now ground troops were sent out on patrol to keep the Viet Cong at a distance. And finally they engaged the enemy in the field.

In August 1964, after two American destroyers were attacked by North Vietnamese torpedo boats in the Gulf of Tonkin, the Congress of the United States, in what became known as the "Tonkin Resolution," empowered the President to "take all necessary measures to repel any armed attack against the forces of the United States and to prevent further aggression."

It was on the basis of this resolution that, in 1965, President Johnson made the most fateful decision of the war: to carry the conflict into North

Vietnam. Early in February the Viet Cong attacked a U.S. billet at Pleiku, killing eight Americans, and on February 7 the President ordered retaliatory air attacks against the north. A few months later the United States announced that it would come to the aid of South Vietnam with full military support, and by the end of the year a hundred thousand Americans were deployed in fighting positions. In late October and early November the first full-scale battle was fought between these troops and those of General Giap, and what had been a threatening but subdued conflict became a major international confrontation.

A number of conflicts overlaid each other in this war. In the first place it was a war resulting from the attempt of North Vietnam to dominate the south by political subversion and then by force of arms. In South Vietnam itself it was a civil war between the Viet Cong guerrillas of the National Liberation Front and the soldiers of the government army. And because Vietnam lies in a border region between the Western and Sino-Soviet worlds, it became a war of global confrontation. The roots of these wars were distinguishable, but the wars themselves blended into one: the struggle between North Vietnam with the backing of the Communist powers, and the United States—each supporting its chosen ally in the civil war—for the future of the people of South Vietnam and of their Asian neighbors.

The conduct of this war was further confused by the regional and religious conflicts within the country. Some regional antagonisms have their roots far back in the early tribal migrations; the religious differences stem from the introduction of various Buddhist sects and of Catholicism into the country in later years. And the war itself, like the Indo-Chinese war which preceded it, was fought over a fluid battlefield that covered virtually all areas of the country. The capture of territory in a particular engagement had little meaning; instead the measure of victory in a battle was the relative numbers of soldiers killed. Reports were made not of salient points won but of the ratio of the dead.

In 1965 the Viet Cong controlled about as much territory in South Vietnam as the Viet Minh did when the French were fighting there—perhaps two thirds of the country. Only limited areas were held securely by the government, and these were mostly around large cities, provincial capitals and major military installations. At night, as had been true under the French, a predominant part of the country still belonged to the guerrillas.

Shortly before the United States decided to throw the weight of American troops into the battle, Akihiko Okamura, a Japanese photographer who had been covering the war for many months, decided to go into Viet Cong country to report and photograph what was happening there. Taking his Japanese passport and a letter from his embassy saying that his government would appreciate any help given him and expressing hope that if anything happened to him his effects would be returned, he set off with a stick in the collar of his shirt on which fluttered a Japanese flag. There was a message on the flag in Vietnamese which was dramatically simple. It read: "I am Japanese correspondent. Mr. Okamura. Please do not kill me." This is his story.

▶ Early on an April morning I took the Route 13 bus north out of Saigon. There are plenty of buses out of Saigon these days, but most of the riders are women, since neither side usually fires at a busload of females. This weird war has been going on for almost twenty years, and most of the country is a broken and confusing no-man's-land in which ordinary citizens keep up the pitiful struggle of life while government troops and rebels haphazardly trade control of a bit of road, a village, a paddy field.

I began to see the tools of killing at the village of Ben Cat, twenty-seven miles from Saigon. There the government had much artillery dug in, American 105- and 155-mm. howitzers. Then, only about five hundred yards farther, we came upon five men with carbines, in the dark green uniforms worn by Saigon soldiers. Here was the Viet Cong, although I did not immediately understand it. They got on the bus. I tried to talk to them but they answered only in grunts. Two miles along, however, they halted the bus and politely invited me to join them. I did so. I still thought they were government soldiers, but as soon as we were down they announced that they were, in fact, rebels. I told them I wanted to go among the peasants.

"If you want to see how it is with the people, we will show you," one said. They stopped a passing truck. We climbed on, and within a hundred yards I had a scare. We were stopped by a U.S. personnel carrier full of government troops. My new VC companions were cool. It turned out the Saigon soldiers were only looking for food, and since our truck carried only grain, they waved us on. Soon the five VC jumped off and told me a village just ahead was filled with Saigon troops. They would by-pass the village afoot while I should go ahead and meet them on the other side of the town.

I was sitting in a roadside shop in the village sipping beer when a long government truck convoy guarded by both Vietnamese and U.S.

soldiers came through. While the convoy passed, the guards automatically sprayed the jungle crowding both sides of the road. As the convoy disappeared, fifty Viet Cong suddenly rolled out of the jungle on bicycles and followed the convoy to make sure it was leaving. I tell you, this war is crazy.

My five VC truck companions now showed up and took me in their protection again. I spent the next three kaleidoscopic days in villages about forty-five miles from Saigon. We slept in farmhouses and dormitories for rubber-plantation workers. In one village a Viet Cong political commissar appeared and befriended me. He was a colorful fellow—cowboy hat, police whistle hanging from his neck, an orange shirt, U.S. canteen belt and U.S. .45. He showed me how the Viet Cong—whenever the government troops were absent—patrolled Route 13 in a new jeep stolen from the government. They would stop every truck that came along, and if the cargo was something the VC wanted, they took it and loaded it on their own truck, which waited in the jungle. They also set up checkpoints and levied tribute from the traffic.

"If the stuff belongs to a businessman, we pay for it," Orange Shirt said. "They don't care who they sell to. But if it's government property, we confiscate it."

He let me watch while the VC hijacked nine government trucks. "They accuse us of getting supplies from Hanoi," he said. "But, you see, we can do quite well here at home." He sounded smug.

One morning I talked with a Viet Cong soldier on a bicycle, carrying a weapon and a child on the baggage rack. "I have a little shopping to do," he said. "I have only today with my family, then I must go back to Saigon to my work."

"What work do you do?"

"I am a government official," he said. "But when the rebels want me to do something, I take a few days off."

Most VC I met were friendly, but all the while I was aware that a war was going on. Constantly I heard the deep belly-throbbing grunts of artillery or bombs, and once the war got too close for comfort. I was in a roadside house playing with some children when suddenly small-arms fire crackled just outside. I jumped up to look out. An automatic weapon opened up on me and, with bullets coming through the walls, I jumped for the bomb-shelter tunnel. There is one dug into the dirt floor of every Vietnamese house. The children, being wiser than I, were already below. We pulled the cover shut and soon we heard somebody shout, "Who's down there?" The children's mother called back, "Only my family." But whoever it was in the house above us sprayed the shelter with a burst anyhow; it did no harm, for all these tunnels have angles dug in to deflect bullets.

When I went out again, I learned that the shooting had begun when government soldiers, riding in a bus with civilians, came into town and fired on the houses, just to keep everybody docile. The villagers told me that they often do that.

A day or so later Orange Shirt suggested that it was time for me to go on to a place really controlled by the VC and brought me an old, stooped lady of seventy-three—all her teeth black from chewing betel nut. He said, "Follow her." She scuttled off into a jungle path and I trailed. She shamed me. She would never let me rest. She kept going— jungle, plantation, paddy field, wading through streams, never talking, just turning her head to wave me on. She walked the legs off me. Whenever a government L-19 spotting plane came over, she dived into the brush. At dusk we came to a small plantation and she gave me over to the Viet Cong and, wordless, turned back again.

Four of the VC took me in charge. They were a different and more suspicious breed from those I had known earlier. We walked all night through the jungle and over paddy fields. Then, about three a.m., we came to a moonlit clearing and a log palisade with a barbed-wire gate. One of my companions clapped his hands sharply three times as a signal. We went through into denser jungle until we came to a series of three crude log bridges. A log cracked underfoot. I swayed and began to fall. One of my escorts caught my arm and snapped at me, "Be careful! There's a minefield under here!"

Across the bridge we were met by a new, husky Viet Cong wearing a U.S. .45. He said, "You will rest here two or three days. Please come with me." He led me to a rush-thatched hut with low, sweeping eaves, no walls, L-shaped. Five other VC were there. They had everything out of my knapsack, scattered on the floor. They whispered together. I was wet, tired, miserable. We had walked for nearly nine hours. They offered me one of two beds, about three feet high, mattressed with split bamboo. I spread my poncho liner and turned in. It was to be my bed for fifty-three days.

On the thirty-sixth day they still hadn't told me I was a prisoner—no one ever did—but I had a hint that something was going to happen. A strange VC officer came and asked me many questions about myself. On the forty-third day some soldiers came and began cleaning my prison hut, and shortly afterward a party of four came to see me. One of them was obviously the leader, and I decided to complain to him. "I am a prisoner here," I said.

"Have you been mistreated?" he asked.

"Robbed, starved and lied to," I shouted. I was getting angry.

One of the soldiers patted my shoulder. "Don't get so excited," he said. "This man is the second highest official in the National Liberation Front." If this was true, the man must be Huynh Tan Phat, the architect turned revolutionary politician and Viet Cong strategist. I asked if it was he, and he said yes. We talked that night and the next day. He assured me that the NLF would win. "If the Americans want to fight us on equal terms," he said, "they'll need at least four million men. They have been calling themselves 'advisers' to the Saigon forces. But soon there will be no Saigon forces and the Americans will be needing Vietnamese 'advisers.' When that begins, half of the Vietnamese 'advising' the Americans will be our own NLF agents."

He promised me that I would be released and we parted cordially, and at last, ten days later, two soldiers came to escort me away. It took them three full nights—mostly walking in circles, so that I estimated we walked seventy miles or more—to deliver me to a farmhouse near Route 13. I was still in jeopardy there, for I was now of neither side. But when the way was clear they sent me on with a group of refugee children on a bullock cart. At last I got on a bus. Then another bus. And at five o'clock on May 30, I staggered into my apartment in Saigon, just two months after I had left it for a visit to the Viet Cong. ▶

The Viet Cong permeated the countryside, but they never gave battle unless it was to their advantage, disengaging and slipping away before superior firepower—to seep back in when government troops withdrew. "The Americans are boxers fighting the wind," a Viet Cong officer said. The U.S. countered with a tactic known as "search and destroy." Even before it took over this operation, its guidance to the South Vietnamese army was to "find, fix, and fight the enemy." In October 1965 a government task force with American advisers was sent on such a mission in Binh Dinh province some three hundred miles north of Saigon.

Accompanying the task force was correspondent James Wilde, who described that experience as follows:

▶ It was dawn and the moon still played along the horizon. The hills were covered with mist. The village started to come to life. Roosters broke the night's silence. Buffaloes grunted to their feet. Somewhere a soldier softly strummed a guitar. Slowly the camp shook itself awake. Cooking fires were started and there was the click and snap of equipment being made ready. The operation was to begin at seven.

By the time the long column of Vietnamese marines started off down the road toward the encircling mountains, the sky was an implacable blue and the sun bored into every pore of the body. Sweat ran tickling down the back. It was harvest time. The peasants in black walked like an advance guard before the troops to their fields. They carried sickles, woven baskets and sacks, instead of automatic weapons, rifles and mortars. There was none of the usual singing and rejoicing that traditionally accompany the gathering up of the fruits of the earth.

Soldiers and peasants walked silently and almost side-by-side down the dazzling road. They were silent because they were in the presence of death. On either side lay the crisp black bodies of dead Viet Cong, with their white knee bones drawn up in supplication against the napalm which had roasted them there a week before. Their scorched helmets lay beside them like headstones. The sweet-nauseous, familiar smell of death hung heavily in the bright sunlight for nearly four miles. The dead would lie under the sky till they rotted into the earth because no peasant would bury them for fear of being accused of being a Viet Cong sympathizer. While the dead decayed in the sun, the peasants stuffed their noses with cloth and harvested their rice with gestures as old as time.

The Vietnamese marine task force of nearly fourteen hundred men, jaunty as Caesar's legions, moved up into the hills in two lines. By midday nearly every one of them was gasping. Their uniforms were drenched with sweat. Some fell by the wayside. Others collapsed where they stood. Still others vomited continually. It was then that the Viet Cong sprung their ridgeline ambush. Two Marines were killed instantly and five wounded. It was nearly impossible to tell where the firing was coming from in that thick, suffocating brush. Many men were exhausted beyond caring and could only hear the heat ringing in their ears.

But the task-force commander, Lieutenant Colonel Nguyen Thanh Yen, a bitter, brown, gnomish man of forty-two who had walked every step of the way with his men, snarled: "Get up, you bastards, it's only a few snipers. Get up and move after them." And then he pushed ahead, pulling his men up, shoving them forward till they located one of the

413

Viet Cong and killed him.

A veteran former French paratrooper of the Indo-China war with fifteen years of almost unbroken combat experience, Colonel Yen turned to his American adviser and said: "All our battles seem to be late in the afternoon at the end of a long marching day." Then he looked down the mountain at the villagers working peacefully in the fields and reflected: "It's probably their relatives, or sons, or husbands who are shooting at us up here. Well, maybe they will be happy now. Those airstrikes last week killed forty peasants down there as well as seven hundred Viet Cong."

That night, while Colonel Yen watched the moonlight creep up the Hoai Nhon ·valley, his guards nervously fingered their captured Chinese *Ka* sub-machine guns. There was every reason to be nervous and, indeed, bitter. Everything to the north was Communist. So was everything to the east and the southeast. And over the next line of mountains, in the Kim Son River valley, there were nearly two regiments of hard-hat Viet Congs and perhaps several regiments of North Vietnamese troops too.

What made it so hard to take was the fact that earlier this year this same task force had spent from February to June clearing this area at a heavy cost in blood and toil. "We killed the Cong here once," Colonel Yen said. "And we left a lot of our own blood up here too."   ▶

A few months after that, U.S. troops, entering the war in increasing numbers, were changing the character of the fighting, avoiding the long march and moving swiftly to the point of attack by helicopter. This new kind of "search and destroy" often carried them into areas close to enemy sanctuaries in neighboring Laos and Cambodia. In January 1966, correspondent Wilde accompanied an American unit which was helicopter-lifted into a region along the Cambodian border with orders to "catch the enemy and make him stand and fight" and, if he sidestepped across the border, to lure him to respond from his neutral refuge. It was an early exercise in the type of military action which was repeated with variations many times in this unusual war. What it amounted to, as one American said, was "going out and looking for someone to shoot at you." Wilde's account of this action points up its special character:

▶ The battle began early in the morning with salvo after salvo from the 8-inch guns shaking the ground. Jets screeched and whined, illuminating the skyline with startling bursts of napalm. Armed helicopters rattled overhead with salvos of rockets. Then dozens of slicks, troop-carrying helicopters, sneaked over at treetop level through the sunrise. They hovered like fireflies above the thick brush. It was impossible to land, so the troops tumbled fifteen feet to the ground. It was like dropping into a thick green sea. For several minutes each man was lost. But gradually the first sergeants growled things into order. The initial wave had landed—two kilometers from the Ton Le San River, which forms the Cambodian border.

Patrols moved out to secure the area. There was no contact with the Viet Cong, but two twelve-foot pythons were ripped apart by M–16 fire, and hundreds of small green snakes fled in every direction. Then in came the "Chinook" helicopters carrying fully armed platoons. As they hovered, the "Chinooks" disgorged aluminum ladders from their brown bellies some sixty feet above the ground and the troops swarmed down these swaying, shuddering arteries.

Hacking and slashing with machetes, the sweating columns inched through the undergrowth. Three hours later and only five hundred meters from the landing zone, the first patrol stumbled into a regimental-sized camp which stretched all the way to the Cambodian frontier. It had four hundred lean-tos, two hundred foxholes and a small hospital. Several other camps were discovered, all with well-defined trails leading to the river. There were several badly camouflaged sampans on the Cambodian side. Their contents were plain for everyone to see: ammunition boxes. At many river way-stations, fires were still warm and food was freshly laid out on tables. A group of twelve well-armed North Vietnamese soldiers in uniform crossed the river into Cambodia.

An American unit moved along the riverbank. It was a pretty spooky walk, for they were being used as bait. They advanced cautiously, glancing uneasily at Cambodia only fifty feet away. At one point they all stopped and watched their commanding officer flying his helicopter smack down the center of the river at water level. But even this tempting target drew no fire. The word came to pull back, and the airborne troops were lifted out. Then after a while the B–52's came over and blasted the area thoroughly. ▶

The inescapable paradox of the war was that the United States and its allies could not loosen their enemy's hold on South Vietnam without first winning the people. But it was next to impossible to bring the tremendous weight of a modern military power to bear on a rural country without killing and maiming civilians as well as the enemy guerrillas. This conflict of pur-

415

poses is dramatically revealed in the report of correspondent Michael Mok, who in November 1965 accompanied a U.S. Marine amphibious assault over the beaches at Cape Batangan, which fronts the South China Sea. Here is Mok's story:

▶   The Marines boil out of the landing craft and find themselves hip deep in water. Fire from the shore laces the surf. Crazy scramble to keep weapons and ammo from being inundated. Troops move out across the open beach feeling naked and exposed, but no one is hit. They form a skirmish line and head for the high ground, the squads leapfrogging each other, always covered by the squad to the rear. The Viet Cong fire slackens. They begin to pull back, leaving just enough snipers to slow the Marine advance.

Charlie Company, with whom we're traveling, is the first to reach the treeline, where there is a cluster of plaster-lath and thatch houses. They have been badly mauled by the pre-invasion strikes. A woman runs toward us, carrying a bleeding child in her arms. It is a little boy, wounded in the arm by machine-gun fire—evidently when the jets made their strafing runs. A medic takes the boy from his mother and runs with him to cover. He tries to bandage him, but the blood spurts so fast that the dressing is soaked immediately. For a couple of minutes the corpsman holds the child against his chest, staring impotently from the dying boy to the sky, where the banshee scream of jets can still be heard. Then he hands the child back to the mother, touches her awkwardly on the shoulder and hurries off to join his company.

Bravo Company has the mission of sweeping a complex of villages that lie beyond the paddies directly to their front. The most dangerous part of the job—the "downright hairy bit" as the Marines put it—is clearing out the labyrinthine tunnels and caves that honeycomb the villages. In the old days you merely chucked a grenade and went in shooting. To counter this, the Viet Cong makes a habit of dragging women and children into the holes with them. Now word has been passed that civilians should be spared at any cost. "If they fire on you from a cave, let them have it. But if no one shoots, hold your own fire and go down there with a flashlight and explore the damn thing. . . ."

A young lance corporal gets the first one, a narrow-mouthed tunnel opening off the trail. He strips off his helmet and flak jacket, wriggles head down into the hole. Seconds later, with only his feet sticking out, he screams and pops out backward, like a champagne cork. He had startled a sleeping cat, which ran across his face, clawing him. Nobody laughs.

416

Bravo starts to move through a stand of pine trees and the Marine on point spots five figures sitting on the ground, their backs to the tree trunks on the edge of a clearing. They appear so relaxed and unconcerned that he thinks they are Marines. "Are you people lost?" he hollers. "This is Bravo's sector. . . ." His answer is a burst of machine-gun fire. The Marines zero in on the group and two VC crumple. The other three melt into the forest. A trooper is sent forward to check the bodies. As he turns over the first one with his foot, the man, who has been shamming, pitches a grenade. The fragments wound the Marine in the leg, thigh and hand. His comrades move up and quickly dispatch the VC.

Beyond the piney woods lie the villages. A house-by-house search is made. The women sit silent, trying to stifle their fear. Then cave by cave, tunnel by tunnel, the Marines press their sweep. Suddenly from a tunnel mouth masked by a hedgerow arcs a grenade. The Marines scramble for cover. They pour automatic-rifle fire into the narrow aperture and draw a burst from beneath the hedgerow. A trooper squirms within a few feet of the hole and lobs in an explosive charge. The explosion makes the ground quiver like the hide of a cow dislodging a fly, and the tunnel collapses—not at the mouth, as we expected, but a full fifty yards away. The reek of cordite hangs in the air as the Marines plunge into the passage. They drag out sixty-six dead Viet Cong and six prisoners. They also lose a man of their own, a lieutenant who explored too long and suffocated from the foul air underground.

Investigation reveals that the cave is L-shaped and more than two hundred yards long. Then it is discovered that it had been used as a hospital. One of the wounded prisoners talked freely before he died. He said he was a medic and that all of the men killed in the tunnel were non-ambulatory wounded, too seriously hurt to be moved when the main body of the Viet Cong retreated before the assault today. The wounded man's story is substantiated when an intelligence officer reports to the colonel that they found about five hundred pounds of medical supplies in that L-shaped tunnel.

The colonel says something sharp and violent under his breath. Then aloud, but as if to himself: "Those boys of mine didn't have any choice after they were fired on, and if it happened again, they'd have to do it the same way. . . ." ▶

After the battle for Cape Batangan, Mok was told that he ought to go to a little village called Cam-ni, which the Marines had taken several weeks before. "The taking of real estate is just a beginning in this kind of war," he was told. "After that you've somehow got to win the hearts and minds of the people. Look up a Navy corpsman who's living with a squad of Marines in Cam-ni. But be careful. The Viet Cong still think they own the place. . . ." This is the story of Mok's experience in that little village:

▶ Cam-ni turns out to be a cluster of thatch-roofed shacks and a one-story cement schoolhouse with a shallow water well outside. In it we find our medical corpsman, Josiah Lucier, USN, originally out of Birmingham, Alabama, but for the last three years or so a resident of South Vietnam. He is a portly American Negro whose mischievous moon face calls to mind those Chinese idols whose bellies you are supposed to rub for good luck. He is twenty-nine years old and a career sailor who wears the sweaty utilities of the Marines, who call him "Doc."

Lucier says, "Well, I've got some calls to make out in the boondocks, so I'd better get my gear together." He ducks into the schoolhouse and soon reappears with his medical kit and a battered tin basin. (We learn later that wherever he sets that tin pan down automatically becomes a dispensary—be it a ruined temple, a cowshed or just a wide place in the trail.) I observe with some trepidation that Doc does not appear to be carrying a weapon. He grins and whips out a .45 automatic from one of his baggy side pockets. "I am a humanitarian and all that jazz," he says, "but I'm not completely out of my ever-lovin' mind. . . ."

We set out for Dong Song, a hamlet some five miles from the Cam-ni schoolhouse. As we walk Indian file down the paddy dikes and pick our way through the bamboo and bramble gates the farmers here use to fence off their property—watching out for boobytraps as we do this—Lucier tells us about his work. His main job is keeping the Marines in good repair. Then there is the job he does just because he wants to, which is holding sick call for all the villagers within walking distance. He tells us why he prefers to make house calls without an armed escort. "I figure it this way," he says. "Here these people are, minding their own business in their out-of-the-way *ville*, when all of a sudden along comes a bunch of strangers with guns sticking out all over them. They don't know it's friendly old John Wayne who wouldn't hurt a fly, so they're scared. Or if they're not frightened out of their minds, all those big guns and boots tromping around their yards is apt to give them the notion they're being occupied, which makes them feel small and put down. . . ."

Along the way we come to a little settlement which is no more than a dirt compound with rickety houses on four sides and a few scraggly

418

chickens and some equally scrawny children scratching around. It is his first sick call, and three kids appear from nowhere and rush the Doc. The fleetest of them seizes the washpan to fill it with fresh water, and Doc is in business. He gives a whoop to announce that he is there and old women in black pajamas come tearing out of their huts to flash their best bright-red betel-nut smiles. Josiah asks in Vietnamese, which he handles quite well, if anyone is sick. One of the crones goes into her hut and brings back a baby, which she hands to the Doc. Its head is entirely covered with an evil-looking scab. The Doc gently sponges the baby's head and after spreading the scab with some soothing unguent he applies a bandage, his fat fingers wonderfully deft and gentle. He hands the infant back to the mother and lectures her in Vietnamese on the topic of cleanliness and health. As he talks, the Doc lances boils, dresses cuts, cleans old wounds and dispenses medicines for dysentery. Presently the Doc gathers up his gear, tucks the tin washbasin under his arm and shambles off down the green-shadowed jungle track.

The walk back to the schoolhouse is tiresome and sweaty, and when darkness approaches, one of the Marines asks, "Are you sure you want to sleep here tonight?" The VC, whom the Marines call the Vincents, have been probing the place every night. We assure him that Cam-ni is just where we want to be. There is a huge full autumn moon and we sit around talking for a while. But after it sets, the crack of rifle fire jerks us up. Two or possibly three snipers are potting away at our positions, their slugs chipping hunks out of the schoolhouse wall. From the sound, the shots are apparently coming from a bamboo thicket at the edge of the village, maybe a hundred yards away. The sniper fire is suddenly drowned out by an explosion from the thicket. It is followed by a spine-freezing scream. A corporal sharing our quarters chuckles meanly: "They've been boobytrapping us ever since we got here. I thought I'd give them a taste of their own medicine. . . ."

An enemy grenade falls a few yards from the schoolhouse, making an angry orange flower in the dark and filling the air with powder stench and bone-tearing shards of hot metal. Then the Vincents cut loose with an automatic rifle. The fire seems to be coming from a tangle of undergrowth to the left, just beyond the ruins of a temple. "Listen," the corporal says. A .50-caliber machine gun drowns out the rattle of enemy fire. "That's the boss gun. I had them set it up in the temple just after dark. . . ." Above the hammer of the heavy gun rises a bestial shriek, perhaps that of a wounded animal. "That's one of our guys," the corporal

419

explains, "trying to draw fire."

All this builds up to an insane tattoo of shooting which goes on until dawn and then abruptly dies away. It is daylight at last. The Doc assembles the kit for his morning rounds. He is gray with exhaustion, for all his brown skin. "Nobody did much sleeping last night," I protest. "Why don't you pack it in for once and go over to the command post and see if the beer ration got there?"

"I guess not," says the Doc, managing to look sad and thirsty at the same time. He shambles off, dented washbasin flashing in the sun, every apprentice sniper's easiest score. Overweight and unsoldierly, but perhaps one of the Americans who are winning the war—such as it is. ▶

In the year after Mok wrote his report, the American involvement in Vietnam expanded step by step into a massive effort. The number of U.S. soldiers committed to the war grew from 100,000 to more than 400,000 and the first retaliatory bombings of North Vietnam were stepped up until the weight of explosives dropped on the targets there was nearly as much as that expended in all of World War II. The struggle for South Vietnam had become the third major war the United States had fought in a quarter of a century.

The weapons used were products of miraculous technology linked with seemingly endless money. But to frustrated Americans in the field it sometimes seemed like trying to swat a swarm of mosquitoes with an ax. And the primitive devices resorted to by the Viet Cong were surprisingly effective. The Americans had to take to steel-armored boots to shield against buried wooden spears, and although they were armed with the fastest-firing rifle ever made, some also supplied themselves with mail-order hatchets, which they found effective in close-in jungle fighting. Their incredible new hovering machine, the helicopter, had been known to fly home with an arrow, fired from a crossbow, in its belly. In some circumstances the elephant proved superior to any other means of transport. And massed labor forces stationed by vital roads could fill a bomb-cratered highway in less time than it took the multimillion-dollar super-bomber that blasted it to make the round trip from its base.

In January 1967, correspondent Robert Sherrod, experienced in the mass attacks and technological wonders of World War II, came with a fresh eye to observe this newly evolving kind of warfare that was taking place two decades later. The magnitude and the frustrations of this war were revealed in his report:

► Nothing I had read, no photograph I had seen prepared me for the immensity of the American effort in this war. The fantastic expense of Vietnam—$20 billion last year, $10 billion beyond the estimate—can only be comprehended in the viewing. Everything here is Texas-sized, from the new "Pentagon West" ($25 million), which will provide offices for most of the sixty-eight American generals stationed in Saigon, to a cantonment for sixty thousand troops under construction at Long Binh ($90 million). In World War II the engineers or Seabees would level a three-thousand-foot strip of topsoil, lay some pierced steel plank and report the airfield ready to receive planes. With jet planes it is different. Jets need dust-free, mud-free ten-thousand-foot strips of aluminum and concrete which cost five million dollars or more. We have built nine new jet fields between Danang and Saigon, and the total number of airfields in South Vietnam is now 282. Will these become the Stonehenges—or, more appropriately, the Angkor Wats—of Vietnam, the relics of a civilization which passed that way? Or will the Vietnamese dig up the concrete so that rice can be planted here again?

In less than two years the number of American troops based on Vietnamese soil has leaped from 25,000 to more than 400,000. To support them, 150 cargo vessels are always on the seas or at the docks—and new docks have had to be built to accommodate them. Saigon has three and nearby New Port will have four. To supply the big Marine Corps base at Danang they dredged channels and built three piers which, with a four-lane concrete bridge, will cost $120 million. The development of the great natural harbor at Cam Ranh Bay will come cheaper—only $110 million.

One evening I flew from the demilitarized zone down to Saigon, about three quarters of the length of this nine-hundred-mile stringbean of a country. Much of the coast was lit up by flares; artillery shells twinkled in forty or fifty different spots. No battles were being fought that night, but the Viet Cong, if present, presumably were being kept awake and the interdicting fire prevented them from traveling certain routes in case they intended going that way. This lavish use of firepower, whether effective or not, contributes to the cost of killing the enemy, which is currently calculated at $400,000 per soldier, including 75 bombs and 150 artillery shells for each corpse.

For every military operation that gets into the newspapers or on home television screens, a dozen or more never rate a mention because they turned out to be dry—or insignificant—runs. One morning I flew in an F-100F with a twenty-six-year-old Air Force pilot, Captain Dave Anderson, the first combat mission I had undertaken in a jet. Anderson, a stocky, phlegmatic young man, had already flown one mission a few hours earlier; he had also been shot down by enemy ground fire several weeks before, but since a helicopter had rescued him within seven minutes he shrugged it off.

Our mission was to fly from the airbase at Bien Hoa and help prepare a zone about thirty miles east of Saigon where a battalion of the 173rd Airborne Brigade could land. Our three-plane flight would drop bombs around the edges of the chosen zone in order to protect the helicopters as they hovered near the ground, bringing in the infantrymen. The ground crew armed our plane by slinging two 250-pound bombs and two napalm tanks under the wings. Our three planes hustled along the concrete and lifted smoothly into the air. To our left, beyond the snake-like Saigon River, lay Tan Son Nhut, its airfield cluttered with hundreds of planes and helicopters, its approaches choked with thousands of jeeps, cars, trucks, cyclos and bicycles. Like a thousand mirrors, the rice paddies shimmered in the noonday sun. Here and there a peasant in a conical hat and hitched-up black trousers worked his tiny, water-logged plot, possibly conscious that all of our jets, our napalm and bombs and soldiers and Marines were only part of an effort to persuade him over to our side.

Our flight sailed easily, almost silently, at 460 knots, between sky and paddy. Our target was as sharply outlined as a bull's-eye, a patch of light green in the dark green of the surrounding jungle. We knew from intelligence reports that three battalions of Viet Cong had been located within one to five miles of the landing zone. The Forward Air Controller was flying his little Bird Dog light plane far beneath us, just over the seventy-five-foot-high jungle, marking the targets with white phosphorus. On his instructions, our planes began their descent in single file. When our turn came, the Air Controller radioed to Anderson, "Put yours due east of the last one, in the heavy woods."

Half a mile from the designated area Anderson started our dive from 5,500 feet; the speedometer needle spun clockwise, up to 700 knots; the altimeter twirled the other direction. When we reached 2,600 feet, a dull klunk under the right wing told us that Anderson had released a bomb. In World War II we used to make one dive, drop our bombs and head for home. But I soon realized we were dropping our bombs one at a time, which meant that we would repeat our dive four times until we had laid all four of our eggs.

After all the planes had done their duty, the artillery—105's and 175's—opened up, firing from five and ten miles to the north. Then, 10,000 feet beneath us the helicopters (Hueys) swam into view, like so many minnows in a tank. The first ten choppers hovered over the landing area for about sixty seconds, until the 173rd's soldiers jumped out and started running toward the woods. Then ten more Hueys arrived, and ten more, until the full battalion had landed. Everything seemed to go off smoothly, so we headed back to Bien Hoa. The communiqué the next day gave one sentence to our landing and the newspapers didn't use a word of it.

It was two weeks before I had a chance to visit the 173rd Airborne to find out what had actually happened on the ground. I couldn't visit the scene of our operation, for by then the landing zone had lapsed back into Viet Cong control, but the battalion commander told me about it. "We didn't have any opposition. Only three snipers fired at us all day," he said. "We've been chasing that VC regiment for three or four weeks. These people aren't going to stand up and fight until they have an overwhelming advantage and I can't say I blame them." ▶

The problem of not only locating an enemy who habitually operated as part of the landscape but of forcing him to stand and fight to his own disadvantage was as old as the war in Vietnam. In the spring of 1967 the Americans tried a new technique to deal with this frustration: a combination of aggressive deep patrolling with sophisticated communications that made possible a more effective use of artillery as soon as the Viet Cong were located.

These new long-range reconnaissance patrols, or "Lurp Teams," often consisted of no more than four or six men—picked for their ingenuity and courage, rigorously trained—who were able to operate like the Viet Cong themselves, deep in the jungle. To see such men perform and report on the success of this new technique, correspondent Robin Mannock accompanied such a patrol in May 1967. "I am not a stranger to fear," he later wrote, "but I have never endured fear as intense or protracted as I experienced that night. I was so frightened I could hear myself sweat." This is his story of that patrol:

▶ As the lone helicopter dived for a tiny jungle clearing far out in Viet Cong country, Sergeant Clide Brown, a stocky, taciturn twenty-four-year-old Negro professional soldier, knelt behind the pilot's seat, scanning the treetops below. His five team-mates of this long-range reconnaissance patrol were sprawled on their backs on the chopper's

423

aluminum floor, pinned down by the more than fifty pounds of special equipment, explosives and ammunition each scout must carry in order to fight and survive in the jungle.

Four white faces had been stained mud-color and green with pancake camouflage makeup diluted with insect repellent. Brown and Specialist Henry Kiaha, a chocolate-hued twenty-two-year-old Hawaiian, had no need for this artificial blackface, but had smeared green on the highlights of their cheekbones. All the team wore mottled black-and-green "tiger suits" and, in place of the steel helmet, shapeless camouflaged cloth jungle hats with floppy brims. To ward off leeches the "Lurp Team" had sealed the gaps between their boots and trousers with green adhesive tape.

The lift ship circled and then dived for the jungle canopy. The men hoisted themselves to their knees and two troopers closest to the right-hand door swung their legs out into the air. Specialist David Carmon, twenty, going into combat after only six days in Vietnam, crossed himself. As the helicopter hovered six or eight feet above an overgrown strip of abandoned dirt roadway, the men jumped and raced for the undergrowth. The helicopter roared off into the failing late-afternoon light.

Wordlessly the team fell into patrol order with Pfc. John Jasinski, an eighteen-year-old on his second patrol, as pointman. Brown came next, then the team's radioman, draftee Pfc. Albert Ortiz, twenty-one, with nine missions behind him and less than two months to go in Vietnam. I was fourth, followed by Carmon and Kiaha, who was assistant team leader. His job was to watch behind as the team moved through the matted tangle of trees and "wait-a-minute" vines, creepers, bamboo and thorns. Jungle boots crunched desiccated leaves on the jungle floor as the men moved slowly, stopping every few yards to look and listen, harkening for the sound of other muffled footfalls above the shrill whine of crickets that echoed through the bush. Eighty-foot trees rose above the thicket and reduced visibility to less than ten yards.

After slithering little more than a furlong into the jungle, Jasinski spotted a fresh human footprint and signs of a trail. Next, he and Brown discovered the imprint of a sandal on a rotting log. Above the crickets' din, Kiaha thought he heard someone—or something—following the diminutive column. Each time the "Lurp Team" halted, the follower would stop a second later. Kiaha kept his suspicions to himself for fifteen minutes, then, with a feeling of growing certainty, he slipped forward and whispered to Brown.

The team leader made a sign with his arm and the men knelt on the jungle floor, each covering a sector with his automatic rifle. Brown and Kiaha crawled back to scout behind the team, but found nothing. After a few minutes the team resumed its march. Five hundred yards deeper into the team's patrol zone Brown called a halt for the night, and men used the brief minutes of tropical twilight to brush away dried leaves from the jungle floor and set up a tiny defense perimeter. Kiaha crept back and planted a Claymore mine, set to spew out seven hundred steel balls down the trail. For the first time it was possible to sip water from a canteen to replace some of the sweat that was pouring off the heavily laden scouts, soaking their fatigues. The team had been warned to conserve its water—there was none in the area to replenish canteens.

Brown unhitched his rucksack, lay back and listened. Birds and insects whirred in the jungle, which never fell entirely still. Then he heard a crackle—the sound of two fingers snapping. A minute or so later he heard the sound again. He estimated that the noise emanated from a spot less than thirty yards away. After a few moments there came the unmistakable metallic sound of a rifle bolt being drawn back. Brown got to his knees and motioned to his men in the gathering dark. "We're getting out of here," he whispered. "They're just behind us." Ortiz whispered for help into his radio, but there was no reply—dense jungle blotted out the signal.

Kiaha retrieved his Claymore and the team began its march northward on the prearranged escape route to the road. Darkness down in the undergrowth was total and a man five feet away was invisible. The team made its exit like a herd of elephants linked trunk to tail, each man gripping the coiled escape rope of the man in front. With one hand grasping a rifle and the other hanging for dear life to the rope, there was no way of warding off creepers and vines that caught a man by the throat. There was even less chance of moving with stealth. So Brown decided to mask his retreat with the sound of gunfire, waiting for a salvo of artillery fire to move a few yards, then stopping. "I figured the guns would confuse Charlie," Brown said afterward. "Besides, he can't move fast in the jungle, either. I thought we might be able to shake him off our tail."

Brown followed the escape route for about two hundred yards and then struck westward, hoping to find the landing zone—the only place within miles where a quick pickup was possible. The men following the team stuck doggedly to its heels. For more than two hours Brown counted each footfall to gauge his progress. "Every time my left foot had hit the ground sixty-seven times I calculated we had gone another hundred meters," he said afterward. Dripping with sweat and gasping with fatigue, the team finally reached the opening in the jungle where the road ran. A helicopter made its slow, imperious progress across the night sky, its red navigation lights flashing. Ortiz kept whispering: "Four seven—this is Poppa Two. Four seven—this is Poppa Two." After minutes of pained silence, a voice could be heard replying: "Four seven . . ." But the voice at the other end faded and fell silent before Brown could pass his message. He moved the team quietly across the clearing and set up behind some fallen logs. Each man lay on his back like the spoke of a wheel, with his head to the center of a small circle, his automatic rifle cradled and ready for instant use.

Now, to the sound of the night birds, yelping monkeys and the throaty voice of the gecko were added the eerie noises of two pieces of bamboo being knocked together softly. "That's Charlie," whispered Jasinski. "He does that to signal to the others." Bushes and grass rustled and the noise of clicking bamboo moved around the edges of the clearing. At one point, Brown estimates, the Viet Cong were less than fifty feet from the prostrate team. "He didn't know our exact location," Brown said later. "That's why he didn't come in to finish us off. If he'd made his move in the dark, he would have given away his own positions." Once or twice there was the sound of metal against wood as a rifle brushed against a tree. The team measured the slow passing of the night with each breath. Some tried to snatch some sleep. One man snored softly and had to be shaken awake, but I was so scared I did not close my eyes once. The clicking of bamboo continued and the bushes rustled. Helicopters and an occasional fixed-wing aircraft flew overhead. Ortiz whispered into his radio, but in vain.

Dawn and the moment of greatest danger seemed never to come. Clouds scudded across the sky and then Venus, the morning star, rose in the heavens. Pale yellow streaked the eastern sky. Brown alerted his men, but something made the Viet Cong stay their hand. The six men moved back into the undergrowth. Suddenly, less than two hundred yards inside the canopy, Brown spotted two men in black pajamas. He blasted off a burst of automatic fire and the men melted into the jungle. The team wheeled right and froze in its tracks. Brown signaled for withdrawal and each man fired into the bushes. A sniper hidden in a tree stitched a line of bullets among us. Kiaha lobbed a grenade into the bush as the team began a rapid withdrawal to the clearing.

426

As the team reached the open and set up a small defense perimeter in the tall grass, Ortiz spotted movement and cut loose with a withering burst. Kiaha stood up, ran forward and threw another grenade, and the members of the team flattened themselves to avoid its blast and flying shrapnel. Brown was busy on the radio, calling for a quick exit.

Ten minutes later Brown got the order: "Pop Smoke." He un-hitched a smoke grenade from his belt, and yellow smoke billowed across the landing zone. He ordered the team to split in two. Kiaha, Carmon and I were to go in the first chopper, Jasinski, Ortiz and Brown, the last man off the ground, in the second. Because speed was essential, the chopper pilots used two ships, each lifting three men. Gunships armed with rockets and machine guns began orbiting, and Brown instructed them to hose down the jungle about two hundred yards from the clearing to make sure they did not hit his team.

A lift ship swooped down and I saw its crewmen make anxious gestures as I sprinted for the door and threw myself across the floor. Carmon and Kiaha were aboard seconds later and the chopper lifted off with its lefthand machine gun chattering and the team men emptying their automatic rifles into the bush to make any Viet Cong keep his head down. Brown's chopper hit the landing zone immediately behind the first, and the team was soon in the air with the choppers skimming the trees, lifting us out of there. ▶

In the intense and continuous fighting it was easily forgotten that this was a limited war with the initial limited objective of stopping the Communists from forceably taking over the government of South Vietnam. Militarily, although this was a war of attrition where success was calculated by the numbers killed, by the end of 1967, after more than two years of full U.S. commitment, there were more Viet Cong and North Vietnamese soldiers under arms than at the outset. And politically the pacification of the countryside—the implanting of government influence in the war-ravaged villages—which had been attempted under nine different programs in a dozen years of French and American effort, was being given yet another try under a new name: Revolutionary Development.

John Mecklin, who had covered the wars in Vietnam for almost twenty years, wrote in 1967: "The pacification problem ranks as one of the most difficult goals the United States has ever set for itself. Yet its success is the only visible way for the U.S. to escape from Vietnam except in defeat." Keenly aware that this, which President Johnson called "the other war," was the war to be won, the Americans struggled with it from the very first. But every new formula for bringing lasting governmental order to the countryside was frustrated by the Viet Cong's counterattacks. It was at its crux a contest for the minds of the Vietnamese peasants, who make up eighty-five percent of the population. And, as a Vietnamese official pointed out, "They know that if they are caught by the government helping the Viet Cong they will be put in prison for a while. But if they are caught by the VC helping us, they will probably have their heads cut off."

A farmer, who with his family was being moved to a strategic hamlet for the second time, told an American pacification officer: "What we need most is security. I would even follow the Viet Cong if they brought security and gave me a chance to make a living. I'll follow anyone who will do that." But no one, in the midst of the ever escalating war, had found a formula for peaceful existence on a battlefield. And the second and more far-reaching U.S. objective in the war—that of preventing a Chinese takeover of Vietnam and perhaps the rest of Southeast Asia—was jeopardized by the very magnitude of the war itself. For if in crushing the Viet Cong they destroyed the land and the people among whom the Viet Cong moved, they would forfeit a historic obstacle to Chinese expansion. The Vietnamese, having been subjected to a thousand years of Chinese domination, continued to feel a deep-rooted opposition to encroachment from the north. But with their land in ruin, they might become easy prey for Chinese control of their country once again.

The dilemma brought by these contradictions was reflected in the confusion and dismay of the American populace. It was on the home front as much as at Dienbienphu that the French lost the Indo-China war, and Ho Chi Minh was well aware of this possibility in the war in South Vietnam. "Americans don't like long, inconclusive wars," he said. "And this is going to be a long, inconclusive war." And it was impossible for the American people to work up a war fever against their Viet Cong enemy, so small, so far away.

As never before, the civilians of an entire nation were drawn into the heart of war as television brought the battlefields into their living rooms. And perhaps it was the lack of hatred among the fighting men themselves that was reflected in this absence of vindictiveness against the enemy, as well as compassion for the noncombatants in the area. Among the men who fought, there was little feeling that they were crusading against evil in a "war to end wars" or to "make the world safe for democracy." Nor were they in search of glory. They fought because they accepted a responsibility and were sustained by the comradeship of the men who fought beside them.

In May 1967 a Columbia Broadcasting Company television team interviewed survivors of an American platoon which had been overrun in a skirmish in central Vietnam. All but eight of the platoon had been killed by the Viet Cong. Among the men interviewed was Pfc. Clifford Roundtree, who had escaped by feigning death among the corpses of his comrades for fifteen hours. Still shaken and exhausted, he tried to answer questions put to him, talking slowly, pausing for words and staring at the ground.

"Well," he said, "my one thought is that it isn't so much the—the laws or agreements or anything that's going to come out of it. It's—it has to be the will inside, in the hearts of both sides. We both want peace. . . . We've got enough problems, with disease and everything, to keep us real busy for a long time just helping each other without shooting each other."

The interviewer asked him if he didn't hate the enemy after his experience.

"No," Private Roundtree answered, "I can't say I hate anybody. I was doing my job and I guess they were doing theirs; that's what war is like. You'd be a fool to hate. You're only cheating yourself when you hate."

Many Americans agreed with Pfc. Roundtree, and yet they were committed to the fight, and this commitment bound them to spend increasing sums of money and increasing numbers of their men in an agony compounded of determination, guilt and doubt.

The paradox of this unwanted war was that while one side fought a holding action, waiting for the enemy to tire, the other side—the one with the military potential to destroy the enemy outright—was inhibited by the very nature of this potential from concentrating all its power on the goal of victory. Therefore it fought to obtain, not victory, but a negotiated peace. The question that tormented it was which road would best lead to peace.

XXVII

Arabs vs. Israel:

The Third Round

(1967-)

I N 1956 IT TOOK the Israelis seven days to defeat the Egyptians in the
Sinai Peninsula, and the world marveled at such a mighty blow. In 1967 it
took them four. In that time they also demolished the Jordanian army massed
on the west side of the Jordan River and in Jerusalem. And in another two
days they drove the Syrian army from the fortified ridges above Galilee, from
which it had been shelling Israeli farmers with impunity for years. In 1956 the

United Arab Republic lost two thousand men and fifty million dollars' worth of military equipment. But a far heavier loss to them was the killing blow to their pride and to their sense of mission as leaders of a united Arab world. Given eleven years, new soldiers could be found in an exploding population of thirty million. And the Russians not only replaced the arms the U.A.R. had lost, but made that loss seem puny in the flow of new equipment. In the decade following the Sinai debacle, they shipped more than a billion dollars' worth of planes and tanks and guns to the U.A.R., and another billion to the other "Arab socialist" states. Thus when the fighting started, on June 5, 1967, the Arabs were well-equiped, well-primed, with a total of some 450,000 men in arms ostensibly united under Egyptian command, for the avowed purpose of "driving the Israelis into the sea" and "wiping the shadow of Zionism from the earth." But where were the pride of leadership and the unity of Arab spirit?

It is as ridiculous to say that Arabs cannot fight as it was in the past to say that Jews were cowards. The courage of the Jews in 1948 and 1956 has been surpassed in the modern world only by the courage of the Jews in 1967. And in the past, men of Arab nations have been both feared for their bravery in battle and admired for their chivalry as victors. But in the mid-twentieth century the stock of courage and noble deeds among the Arab military leaders seemed to have been expended in bombast. The words were aggressive and full of confidence, but when the shooting started, Egyptian officers hardly seemed to know which way to run. Among the 11,500 prisoners taken by the Israelis were 9 Egyptian generals, 10 colonels and 300 other officers. Hundreds of undamaged tanks, armored vehicles and mobile guns were left standing in the desert when their crews fled. The vital fort of Sharm el Sheikh, which guards the Gulf of Aqaba, was deserted by its Egyptian defenders at the approach of Israeli torpedo boats and the mere threat of a paratroop attack. A Russian surface-to-air missile site guarding the Suez Canal—its radar van in a heavy concrete revetment, its missiles standing ready on their launching platforms—was simply abandoned. "Can you imagine," asked an Israeli officer, "can you imagine an army that would run and not try to destroy equipment of this kind?"

This retreat, astounding as it looked from a safe distance, did not take place without good cause. Even though the build-up for the conflict had been going on for many years and had risen to a pitch of quivering tension in the preceding two weeks, the Arabs were taken by surprise when the Israelis hit them with coordinated air attacks at eight o'clock Monday morning, destroying most of their aircraft on the ground. And the almost simultaneous

431

lightning attacks of four Israeli armored columns into Sinai and the Gaza Strip were enough to create panic even in a very stout heart.

The Egyptians had been pushed, perhaps, a little further than they meant to go. President Nasser, faced with the problems of an underfed and ever growing population and a near-bankrupt economy, with more than a billion dollars in outstanding debts and much of his state-owned industry closed down for lack of foreign exchange, badly needed to keep up his image as leader of a united Arab world. The obstacles to this were that the Arabs were anything but united and the struggle for leadership was bitter and beset by mistrust and betrayals. The only point on which Arab leaders were forced to agree was in their vocalized hatred of Israel. In actuality, rather than in words or dreams, the Arabs were hopelessly divided, not only between the Arab-socialist states of the left and the Arab traditionalists on the right—the one personified by Nasser and the other by King Feisal of Saudi Arabia, carrying on their war against each other in Yemen—but within each of these blocs. All through the winter of 1966–67 Syria had been challenging Egypt for the leadership of the Arab left—that is, for the reputation of active belligerency against Israel. It was Syria who encouraged the Palestinian terror groups to raid Israeli territory, supporting them not only on her own soil but on Jordan's. It was Syria who had been shelling Israeli farmers not only from within her own borders but from Lebanon. And when Israel retaliated with ever more aggressive strikes across her frontiers, it was Syria who alone called for "war now," taunting Egypt with hiding behind the United Nations units in Sinai.

If he wanted to keep his leadership, Nasser was forced to act. Thus in early May 1967, when Israel warned the Syrians that they were "very close to the area of danger," Egypt felt compelled to come to the defense of her ally, with whom she had signed a mutual-defense pact in November 1966. On May 16 they put their defense agreement into effect, and Egypt, for the first time since 1956, moved her forces into positions along the Sinai frontier.

This was the strip of border guarded by the United Nations Emergency Force, and in order to make room for his own troops, the Egyptian commander requested the U.N. commander to "withdraw [his] troops immediately," as his own forces were "ready for action" in the area. This startling request was forwarded to the United Nations Secretary-General, who asked for clarification from the Egyptian government and warned—perhaps in the hope of deterring a hasty decision—that if any U.N. troops were to be withdrawn from Egyptian soil, then all must be, not only from Sinai but from the Gaza Strip and the Sharm el Sheikh as well. After two days of pondering, the

Egyptians requested just that, and the international deterrent force was removed from between the antagonists.

On that day, May 18, as Egyptian troops poured into Sinai, Syria alerted her border forces; Iraq, Kuwait and Algeria promised to put their forces at the disposal of a United Arab Command; and Israel ordered a partial call-up of her men at arms. So far, although the crisis was building rapidly, the seeming rush toward war was not yet out of hand. On May 23, however, Nasser closed the Gulf of Aqaba to Israeli shipping, thereby cutting off her trade with the eastern half of the world. To Israel, this was an act of aggression, and in her cabinet the argument intensified between those who would continue to work for peace through a reliance on international powers, and those—personified by Moshe Dayan, hero of the 1956 campaign—who felt that Israel had no alternative but to fight for her life.

To judge by their public speeches, the closing of the gulf was taken as something very like an act of war by the Arabs, too. Although he reiterated that the Arabs would not be the first to attack, President Nasser, speaking of his troops' occupation of Sharm el Sheikh after the removal of the United Nations unit there, went on to say: "The Arab people wants to fight. We have been waiting for the right time when we will be completely ready. . . . This step makes it imperative that we be ready to undertake total war with Israel." That they were not "completely ready," even in Arab eyes, was due to the pitiable state of Arab unity. Even in this crisis, Nasser refused to convene the Arab League Defense Council because he was afraid to share his war plans with Jordan and Saudi Arabia, nor was the "Unified Arab Military Command" given any power. It was a command, in any case, that did not exist in more than words and was now completely by-passed, even forgotten. And Jordan, which has the longest border with Israel, was so far from being "unified" with Syria that they had broken diplomatic relations a few days earlier.

But now it was imperative that some sort of unity be achieved—that of immediate military objective at the very least—and tremendous pressure was put on Jordan's King Hussein until on May 30 he at last capitulated and flew to Cairo to conclude a mutual-defense pact with the U.A.R. On that occasion Nasser said: "The armies of Egypt, Jordan, Syria and Lebanon are stationed on the borders of Israel. . . . Behind them stand the armies of Iraq, Algeria, Kuwait, the Sudan, and the whole of the Arab nation. Today [the world] will know that the Arabs are ready for the fray. The hour of decision has arrived."

On the first of June the Israeli war party won their argument and General Dayan was named Minister of Defense. On June 4, President Nasser made yet another statement, perhaps for the consumption of the Cairo mobs that were thronging the streets crying "We want war!" but spoken to Israel: "We are facing you in the battle and we are burning with desire for it to start. . . ." At eight o'clock next morning the Israelis struck.

Hundreds of fighter-bombers rose from the fields around Tel Aviv and took off across the Mediterranean, flying low to avoid the defensive radar screens and sweeping in from the west to surprise Egyptian targets. With almost incredible accuracy they bombed and strafed the military airfields, including those in Sinai, and within three hours they had virtually destroyed the Egyptian air force, most of it on the ground. Other Israeli planes flew north to hit at Syrian airfields, and east to Jordan and Iraq.

At 8:15, as their planes were streaking toward their far-scattered targets, Israeli tanks and armored infantry, their engines roaring, treads spewing up the desert sand, plunged across the Egyptian border into Sinai and the Gaza Strip. The course of the battle was reminiscent of the 1956 campaign in the spirit and daring of the Israeli army, the speed of the attack, the tactics of seeking the enemy's strongest points and hitting, fighting, overrunning and moving on without pause. But this time the forces of both sides had been built up and the battles were larger, fiercer, the losses nearly ten times greater. And this time, unlike 1956, the Jordanians—true to the promise of their mutual-defense pact—opened a second front.

Before noon, machine-gunning and mortar firing started in the divided city of Jerusalem, and from the high point at Latrun, Jordanian batteries shelled Israeli positions even as far as Tel Aviv on the coast, so narrow is Israel's waist at this point. But the heart of the war with Jordan was Jerusalem itself. On Monday the Israelis began a pincer movement around the city, to take the hills to the south and north, and on Tuesday Jordanian resistance began to crumble. The pincers were closing and the Israelis turned to clear Jordanian soldiers from the encircled city. By Wednesday they were within the walls of the Old City and had pushed all the way to the west bank of the Jordan River. The Jordanians fought tenaciously—at the cost of six thousand dead and missing—but their air power had been destroyed in the opening hours of the war, and they were faced by even more tenacious and hard-hitting troops than their own. By ten o'clock Wednesday morning they were no longer a cohesive force, and Jordan accepted the United Nations plea for a cease-fire.

In Sinai the battle went almost as rapidly. By Tuesday the major Egyptian fortress of Abu Agweigila on the central Sinai front was overrun after twenty hours of fighting, and in the Gaza Strip the city of Gaza fell. By

434

Wednesday Israeli columns were converging on Mitla Pass, the key to the whole east bank of the Suez Canal, and in the south the fortress of Sharm el Sheikh—the presumed objective of the entire war—was abandoned by the Egyptians without a fight. It could be said that the war was finished sixty hours from the time it started, in contrast to the hundred hours that it took in 1956. But the battle of Mitla Pass went on for twenty-four hours, and the Syrian front was yet to flare into real fighting.

More than a thousand tanks were engaged in the battle for Mitla Pass, as well as armored units, artillery and aircraft. It was here that the U.A.R. fought the hardest and lost the most, for this was not only the access route to the Suez Canal, but the last path of retreat for its scattered forces cut off by the swirling Israeli advance. What was left of the battered Egyptian army was thrown into this last-ditch battle, and when it was over and the escape route plugged, the Israeli air force pounded the trapped Egyptian men and vehicles until the entire fourteen miles of the defile were scattered with blackened, twisted metal and charred corpses—the ruins of an army laid out in the white-hot desert sun. That night the U.A.R. accepted a cease-fire and the fighting stopped. Ten thousand Egyptians had been killed in the four-day war—a war they had said they wanted but, for all their sophisticated Russian equipment, they were not prepared to wage.

Only the Syrians remained in the battle, lobbing shells down from their fortified heights. On Friday noon the Israelis turned and charged them, driving their tanks up the steep ridge north of the Sea of Galilee, attacking the stone-and-concrete gun emplacements head-on, knocking them out and overrunning them, blasting through and around them, until by Friday night they were eight miles into this bristling defensive wall and the bulk of the Syrian force had fled. On Saturday the Israelis continued their drive until they held the key to this whole Syrian string of forts and were ready, at last, to accept the cease-fire called for by the United Nations.

It was a compact war, a brilliant show of military genius and fighting spirit on the part of the Israelis, a show of courage by the out-gunned and out-maneuvered Jordanians, a show of the tragic effects of disorganization and self-delusion among the other Arab states. It was a decisive war: in six days it changed the map of the Middle East—at least for the moment that the military victory seemed all-important.

But the conflict was not confined to a quarrel between Arabs and Israelis. It was a war with global overtones. The Russians, with more than two billion dollars' worth of military aid invested, were deeply involved in an attempt to win the Arab world for the Soviet sphere. The United States was committed to the existence of the state of Israel. And in the United Nations, meeting to carry on the war in words even while it was being fought in blood and flames, the delegates took sides, each in accordance with the self-interest of his own nation. The words seldom sought relation to reality, and they were used in various ways by various representatives of various cultures.

It might be said that the Russians use words in diplomacy as a fleet will use a smokescreen, billowing clouds of insubstantial but opaque material between themselves and their adversaries so as to hide their very real maneuverings. No more than the captain of such a fleet would they expect this floating smoke to be mistaken for their charted course. Americans, steeped in Western European culture, as are the Israelis, are more inclined to use words to convince. They lay them out as a pattern for their actions to follow. And when they lie, it is with the purpose to deceive on some selected point—a deviation from the pattern so as to catch the adversary out. But by and large they link their words to actions.

To the Arabs, words seem to have more substance, to take on a reality of their own. To them the word, once spoken, is the deed. If a thing is said, it is done. Thus can the President of the U.A.R., the "leader of the Arab world," say, "We are ready for the fray," and supply his troops with no more than one day's ration of food and water, and leave his war planes lined up wing to wing on his military fields. The word has been spoken: "We are ready. . . ." What need for more?

How confusing to an Arab, then, must be a Russian smokescreen. How terrifying for an encircled Israel to hear the words—which might be taken for intention rather than illusion—"We are facing you in the battle . . . burning for it to start." And how devastating for the Arab armies to be beaten, mauled and made fools of when the word was that they were ready, that they would win. Cairo took refuge from this humiliation in the lie that the United States and Britain were flying planes in Israel's defense. It was not Israel that beat them; it was the Big Powers of the Western world. But the Russians, carefully maneuvering through the disaster, believed no such tall tale. True to the rules worked out by them and the United States in the perilous years since each has had weapons capable of world destruction, they instigated calm and responsible conversations on the direct line to Washington, even while the smoke of verbiage was clouding the U.N. councils and the very real smoke of burning war matériel and men was darkening the desert sky. And when the shooting part of the war was over and the diplomatic war went on, the Premier of the Soviet Union and the President of the United States met to say quietly to each other that they wanted peace.

436

The word has been discredited before now, and in our present era it is being attacked not only for its unreliability but because it is out of date. Nevertheless, it still has power—to communicate, inform the mind and touch the heart. With it, reporters of crises in world affairs reveal, to all who can read, the heart of the matter: that is, the actions of human beings at certain focal points in human history.

Hundreds of correspondents rushed to the Middle East to report on the Arab-Israel war. Those who converged on Cairo found themselves cut off from seeing any action or hearing more than the patriotic slogans and martial music that issued from the radio. Nor were those in other Arab capitals able to see much more of what was going on. In Israel, however, those with skill and determination managed to reach the center of the war, to watch it from within, and to photograph and report on it.

Among these correspondents, three were killed. One was a photographer, Paul Schutzer, and with him was a reporter, Michael Mok. The two had worked together in other wars. They had a friendship; they were a team. Thus, correspondent Mok's description of an Israeli motorized assault over the border into the Gaza Strip the day the war broke out carries the impact of what war means to a man who is both observer and, in the sense of personal loss, participant:

▶ On Monday, as the war flared on three fronts, Paul and I were sitting in the shade of a little wood with the men from a battalion of mechanized infantry. Their mission was to board halftracks and, supported by tanks, spearhead an armored column striking across the Negev desert for the city of Gaza. Paul insisted that we ride in different halftracks. "If you ride with me, that cuts off one camera angle. No one wants pictures of your ugly face."

Schutzer, accompanied by a young lieutenant named Dov, the military liaison officer assigned to us, mounted the lead vehicle carrying the battalion commander. I was in the second tractor, commanded by a lieutenant they called Yacob. Scarcely had we squeezed in when the column began to roll. Schutzer gave the thumbs-up sign and shouted something I couldn't hear for the roaring of the engines. I got the message. It was "*L'ha-im!*" which means "To life!"

We jumped off from a fortified kibbutz called Nahal Oz and less than two hundred meters past the line of departure ran into heavy machine-gun and small-arms fire. Then mortar rounds came crumping in all around us. In our car, the bursting shells first wounded the machine-gunner, who sits in an elevated position up front. Blood welled down his face and made the stock of his weapon slippery, but he pressed it into his cheek and kept firing. The driver, taking evasive action, maneuvered the halftrack like a Dodge-em car at a carnival. The tracks threw up clouds of Negev dust that choked and blinded the troops who were blazing away with their Uzi sub-machine guns at dug-in Egyptian soldiers, now firing on us from all sides. Yacob, the vehicle commander, was bleeding from two wounds, one in the arm and another just below the left knee. He continued directing fire, however, shouting "*Oyev!*" (enemy) and then loosing a short burst to pinpoint the target.

We were within grenade range now. One of our troopers cast aside his Uzi and, face contorted, lobbed grenade after grenade at enemy soldiers trying to rush our halftrack. Some of the grenades burst so close I could hear their fragments whinging off the side of our vehicle. The driver, still maneuvering for our lives, suddenly jounced the car into reverse, landing us half in a cactus thicket. For a few instants the war forgot us and I stood up to have a look around. To our left front I could see one of our halftracks had sustained a direct hit and was blazing. The fire roared skyward with a fierce racking noise, and it was incredibly bright, brighter than the desert sun. "I hope Paul has a picture," I thought. And then, "Good Christ, what if he's inside . . ."

When it got dark, the crippled halftrack was still burning and we were busy securing a little airport that had signs both in English and Arabic saying "Welcome to Gaza." The boys used classic commando technique on the buildings: kick down the door, pitch in a grenade, rake the inside with a long burst, and then have a look around. After things quieted down—they were still mortaring our position, but not very accurately—I went from tractor to tractor looking for Paul. No one had seen him. No one knew where he was. Men who had chatted with us in the woods before the battle suddenly, it seemed, had forgotten how to speak English. They were the same ones who could speak it before, I knew, as I recognized their silhouettes by the light of the desert stars and the red lines of outgoing tracers overhead. "Maybe he went out with the first lot of wounded," someone said. So I headed back with the next bunch.

We loaded the casualties on a halftrack, with the walking wounded riding in the command car. We drove without lights, but incoming mortar rounds had ignited acres of cotton and rye, so we had no trouble finding our way. Two kilometers back, there was a large tour bus waiting for us. Its civilian driver had volunteered his vehicle to fetch out the wounded. It was hard getting the stretchers through the windows, and some of the badly wounded cried out, *"Adonai,"* which in Hebrew means "Lord." We had no morphine.

We went back through Nahal Oz, where it all started, pitch black now except for taped flashlights of the *kibbutzniks* who pointed us the way. Bouncing over potholes made the wounded scream. We finally got to the forward aid station. No Paul. But I found Dov, who had been riding with him.

"Is that you, Mike?" Dov asked. I was kneeling beside him.

"Yes," I said.

"Mike, I don't want to tell you this, but your friend is dead. Do you understand? Paul is out of it now. . . ."

I must have made some kind of noise because Dov reached up with a bulkily bandaged hand (the dressings used for burns are very awkward-looking) and patted me on the head. "Don't feel so bad," he said. "Please don't feel so bad." I rode back to Ashkelon hospital because somebody said Paul might have been taken directly in, by-passing the forward station. At the hospital I found another man who had been on Paul's halftrack. He was burned all over and couldn't see, but he recognized my voice. "Paul is dead," he said. "He was standing up taking pictures. They shot him through the head before the bazooka round hit us, before the halftrack caught fire. . . ."

Two nurses who were spraying him with some sort of soothing salve gestured for me to clear out, and I did. ▶

Even in modern war a correspondent can sometimes play the role of the romantic journalist of the past, wandering through the battlefield and from one side of no-man's-land to the other, notebook and sketchpad in hand. Such a man is George de Carvalho, sometimes called "the general" by other correspondents because he has seen so much of war, who covered the fight for Jerusalem in the old-fashioned manner—though he carried typewriter and camera—and sent reports of the action take-by-take as it progressed:

▶ When the war began Monday morning, I was driving up the Judean hills from Amman to Jerusalem in bright spring sunshine. At nine o'clock a news flash cut off the Beatles: "Fierce fighting between Israeli and Egyptian forces." The day before, King Hussein had told me he expected war "any day, any hour. The Arabs will fight united, with all their might for their lives, their land, their honor." This was the hour for the fight, but the Jordanian forces along the highway had not yet heard the news.

At 9:15 I drove into Old Jerusalem on the edge of no-man's-land and the Israeli border. The mellow old Biblical city was utterly quiet, with no sounds of war. But shopkeepers were rolling down their shutters and people were running about mindlessly. Green-clad Jordanian troops in their flat Tommy-type tin hats were dashing to their positions on the city wall. Shortly before noon, artillery fire started up, and all along the strip of gaunt shell-torn houses of no-man's-land, abandoned since the 1948 war, shells screeched in from both sides. The U.N. truce supervision team called a cease-fire at twelve o'clock and again at twelve-thirty, but you couldn't hear the difference.

I went over to the American consulate by the Mandelbaum Gate. Telephone lines and branches shredded by shrapnel littered the streets. The sheet-iron consulate gate was closed, but I wriggled over the wall just as Jordanian soldiers manning positions nearby began aiming at me. Later I dashed over to the YMCA building, normally a favorite hostel for pilgrim groups. A shell had blackened the entry and smashed the glass doors. Jordanian troops had turned the building into a strongpoint and they were getting hit hard. Inside lay a wounded soldier gushing blood. His corporal sent me packing with a kick and a slap in the face. A very hard slap. He cocked his rifle and shoved me out at gunpoint. So I drove over to the Mount of Olives. I asked a Jordanian major for permission to take pictures of nearby guns firing, but he refused. The Intercontinental Hotel, usually packed with tourists, was deserted. It was right in the target area. From the terrace I could see shells landing on Mount Zion and the U.N. headquarters.

From the Mount of Olives I went to the lower slopes of Mount Scopus, which is crowned by an encircled Israeli garrison of forty men and where Jordanian shells and machine-gun fire were hitting constantly. The garrison was firing back and seemed to be holding on. I left there and drove to Bethany. Jubilant Arabs told me that Jordanian troops had taken Jebel Mukabar, a smoke-shrouded ridge across the valley, "And tomorrow we will take Tel Aviv!" But Israeli jets were screaming over Bethany in wide circles, to dive down and strafe Jordanian armor massed in reverse positions back down the Judean hills near the Jordan valley and the Dead Sea. For ninety minutes as many as a dozen jets kept striking without any Arab air challenge. Ground fire flashed for miles around and hit one Israeli plane, which exploded in a bright red flash and puff of black smoke, and plummeted straight down. No parachute ejected. The others kept on hitting in steep, almost vertical dives, until dusk turned the hills of the Holy Land purple. Later I learned that the Jordanians were attempting to bring up seventy tanks and the Israeli jets claimed sixty of them.

I went back to the city, to the National Palace Hotel, on the edge of no-man's-land, where about thirty Arabs, mostly women and children, huddled in the basement listening to the Cairo radio. From the roof I could see Israeli searchlights from New Jerusalem beamed on the slopes of Mount Scopus, lighting up attacking Jordanian soldiers for the beleaguered garrison there. Red tracer bullets flashed through the sky and Israeli jets dropped flares over the hilltop and hammered at the surrounding Jordanians late into the night.

At first light, about four a.m. on Tuesday, the jets started hitting again, in and around Jerusalem but sparing the sacred Old City. The Israeli artillery, which had been concentrating on no-man's-land and around Mount Scopus, began firing a few hundred yards deeper into the city, and suddenly the Star of David was hoisted atop the Palestine Archaeological Museum well inside Jordanian territory. At nine a.m. Kol Israel began broadcasting to Arabs in the city: "Stay away from windows and rooftops or you might get shot." Minutes later, Israeli troops in brown-and-green camouflage uniforms began darting along the walls of Port Said Street, past this hotel. From the lobby window I sneaked some pictures. A blond Israeli soldier, crouched and tense, saw me and swung his gun around. I smiled and waved. He smiled and waved back, then ran onward, hugging the wall. Sniper fire sputtered intermittently, and still does.

A Jordanian soldier with his Lee-Enfield rifle and his old tin hat has just come into the hotel basement. He is trapped and lost, but still belligerent. Kids start crying and women wailing. The Arab oldsters persuade him to ditch his gun and leave. A patrol of Israeli soldiers, some with crinkly blond beards, come into the hotel and I assure them that there are no snipers here. They say, "Stay indoors." Jerusalem is fairly peaceful now, except for the crackling of some small-arms fire around the corner. ►

Correspondent de Carvalho took advantage of that lull to file his cable. Then he was back observing, taking pictures, writing the following description of the war as it looked late Tuesday afternoon and Wednesday:

► I went into the Israeli section of Jerusalem and at about five o'clock recrossed the Mandelbaum Gate toward the Old City. Israeli tanks and rocket launchers were lined up on Port Said Street and at five-fifteen they rumbled into action, wheeling around the walls and down into the Valley of Jehoshophat. As dusk fell, they opened up with direct cannon fire and terrific machine-gun bursts at the slopes of the hills rising to the east. There was little answering fire, and after nine o'clock the shooting dwindled.

At dawn on Wednesday, Israeli forces began hitting the last Jordanian positions overlooking Jerusalem. From my observation post less than a mile away, I watched the tank columns go forward and then a company of Israeli infantry advance in skirmish-line formation toward a piney wood where Jordanian machine guns were rattling. They took some casualties, but kept going, and dashed into the trees shooting. Inside the woods, Jordanian machine-gun fire spluttered less and less frequently, then stopped.

But snipers are still busy in the city. We have a grandstand view from our roof. Three red rifle-shot blips flash from a house window about two hundred yards to our left and another unseen but very noisy sniper keeps shooting from an unfinished building about a hundred yards to the right. A little while ago, firing broke out all around as Israeli troops went in to clean out the buildings. Soon they were herding some fifty Arabs, wearing civilian clothes and with hands held high, down the road toward the Mandelbaum Gate. But they didn't get that sniper in the building under construction. He keeps snapping bullets at passing Israelis below. He won't last long. ►

De Carvalho stayed in Jerusalem to watch the second-string Israeli reservists come in to take over the city that their troops had won. By now he had passed through the Mandelbaum Gate eight times, driven past Israeli troops at Gethsemane so often that the soldiers there were like old friends, had seen David Ben-Gurion at the Wailing Wall and gone to Bethlehem, and after a scary start had decided not to try to get back into Jordan through the scattered and belligerent retreating Jordanian troops. He went instead to Syria, to see the battle there. When it was over, he sent this report:

► At dawn on Saturday, when my Jerusalem taxi reached the frontal assault point after a horrendous night of fighting military traffic jams, the war was all but over. The taxi turned back and I thumbed and walked up the ridges past the battered, broken Syrian positions. An endless Israeli armored column of tanks, halftracks, and mud-daubed trucks—military, commandeered civilian, or captured Jordanian—crawled along the newly bulldozed road winding up the steep slopes right under the six-thousand-foot crest of Mount Hermon. Long lines of white tape laid by Israeli army engineers marked a safe track through the minefields and booby-traps.

In the trenches and fieldstone fortifications, gaping-eyed and open-mouthed corpses of Syrian soldiers sprawled grotesquely amid the garbage of war: spent brass cartridge cases, round loaves of Arabic bread, stained bandages and flamboyantly colored leaflets which show Syrian troops pushing Israelis at bayonet point into the Mediterranean.

This vast complex of military positions, devised by Soviet army engineers, looks almost impregnable. There are six rows of fortifications on these mountain ramparts dominating the valley and the Israeli *kibbutzim* far below. Almost at the crest stands an Israeli Sherman tank, its cannon aimed pointblank at a Syrian position only yards away. Inside, the tank is a shambles of smashed steel and shattered flesh. Alongside lies the only intact body, wrapped in a tent flap, an Israeli tank trooper with his padded helmet placed over his corpse. One Syrian bazooka man in a stone emplacement a hundred feet away had fired a Russian rocket which pierced the Sherman's armor. Amid the rubble of his blasted emplacement, the bazooka man is dead too, hit by another Israeli tank.

Now the Israeli army is well over the top, after fighting up impossible slopes against fantastic fortifications stronger than Hitler's Atlantic wall, as I can personally testify. Many of the units had come from the Jordan front. They had taken up their positions on the Jordan River when they got orders to move north and they just kept rolling for thirty-six hours, getting their detailed attack orders by radio enroute, until they hit the Syrian border. At the top of the last crest, in an abandoned Syrian village high above Galilee, I caught up with one of these outfits. The convoy had stopped entirely here, except for the lead unit—a potent force of Sherman tanks, halftracks and truck-borne infantrymen. They were going on ahead, so I loaded on a halftrack with a dozen dog-tired but grinning Israeli soldiers, all of them civilian reservists.

In tactical formation we passed the point where the Israeli attack had turned off to take the Syrian positions from behind. "From now on there are only Syrians ahead, but where are they? Running like hell," a

443

young lieutenant said. He added, however, that he thought the Syrians had fought well—much better than the Egyptians and almost as well as the Jordanians. The orders were to keep going until the cease-fire, so we rolled on, past abandoned Syrian artillery and strafed Syrian convoys, until just before dark the radio crackled the cease-fire order. In old Western wagon-circle style, the outfit parked for the night, ringed by tanks and machine guns, next to an abandoned Syrian camp. During the night two diehard Syrian snipers were shot and an incautious jeep ran over a mine.

At 4:30 a.m. the unit unrolled into tactical formation again, but the cease-fire stayed on. A top Israeli officer came in by helicopter and led the unit to defensive positions on ridges along the cease-fire line. He went like lightning, leaping from jeep to halftrack to tank, to escort company after company for miles along the Syrian front, setting up the positions. Toward noon, two U.N. representatives in official white vehicles showed up from Damascus and talked to our officer, who showed them the Israeli cease-fire lines both on a map and by pointing to nearby posts.

"You will stay in these positions?" a blue-bereted U.N. officer asked.

"Yes—unless the Syrians start any more trouble."

"And no harm will come to the Syrian general you captured?"

"Of course not. We are not Arabs."

The U.N. officers drove off toward the hills of Damascus, visible in the distance, and I turned back on the long road to Jerusalem. ▶

Though the pen is not always mightier than the sword, in the hand of a word-master it can wield great power. And in the tradition of masterful writers who turn themselves to reporting, Theodore H. White flew to Israel when the war started and saw the sweep of it—from Sharm el Sheikh to Syria—in the perspective of history. In the immediacy of what he saw and felt, he wrote the following story of the war:

▶   What happened on Monday, June 5, 1967, was more in the nature of a paroxysm than war—or rather, as if an awkward and ignorant hand had been toying with the fuse of a strange explosive of unknown power, and thus been blown to bits.

The shattered bits of the Egyptian army are now flung across the sands of the Sinai desert for two hundred miles. Under the blue and merciless skies of the desert, strewn across its sifting dunes, a museum of war's infinite agony is momentarily spread out. There, along the road one drives, held timelessly and silently in place, are fourteen Russian tanks, six to one side, eight to the other side of the road—as if on tactical demonstration, in perfect deployment, yet all black and silent. In the sun, an Egyptian soldier lies as if asleep, his poncho covering his head. The others lie nearby, grotesquely rigid, legs spread, toes pointing stiffly up, as in some antique Pharaonic frieze. Israeli scoop-shovels cover the bodies with sand, for the only thing that moves now in the desert is Israeli.

From the air, one sees along each road dead Egyptian tanks and more tanks, trucks and more trucks, tracks in the sand showing the agony of hopeless flight. By the airfields lie the burned-out MIGs. So do fragile helicopters, their rotor blades squashed, as if someone had stamped on spiders. Thus one comes to Mitla Pass—fourteen miles of destruction in the desert mountains, swatched either side with tipped-up trucks and burned-out tanks. The wriggling tracks show how they tried to thread the bottled pass, were stuck in sands and then were caught. Circlets of black show where fuel spilled and blazed.

One returns from the desert via Sharm el Sheikh, a spit of land where desert sand covers coral reef, pointing out into the beautiful green-blue waters of the Gulf of Aqaba. Here is where the blockade was closed. The reef stretched out into translucent waters with the tempting iridescence of coral. A beautiful· place to bathe, observes one of the Israeli soldiers stationed there. Too beautiful a place, one notes, to have triggered such a war.

The central front, with Jordan, also has its tormented showpiece— Jerusalem and the Wailing Wall, the last remaining outcropping of the temple destroyed by Titus in 70 A.D. As high as a man can reach by lip or touch, its stones have been polished smooth by centuries of kiss and stroke. Above men's reach grow the tufts of shrub which have found roots in the crevices of the gray and mellow stone. The Israeli army had placed at its foot a wooden ark of the scrolls of the Bible. Lest anyone mistake what it was, the crude Hebrew lettering of an army sign said, *"Beyt Knesseth"*—This is a temple.

I arrived in the north, the last of the three Israeli fronts, for the final day of the war. Down the slopes of Tiberias, Herod's city, came rumbling Israeli tanks enroute to battle. Beneath them lay the placid waters of the Sea of Galilee, and on the Syrian bluffs, above the waters where Peter fished, was the low haze of artillery smoke and the high, black, waving plumes of air strikes. We passed the memorial to Mary Magdalene, and

445

in the sky above it a helicopter ferried wounded from the battlefront across the lake. The helicopter drew one's gaze; slowly it flew low over the green grove of the Mount of the Beatitudes, where Christ had preached the Sermon on the Mount. The eye followed the helicopter across the barren hills strewn with black basalt boulders and purple thistles until it disappeared between the Horns of Hittim where, one August day eight hundred years ago, Saladin met the Crusaders in their heavy Frankish armor, routed them, and put them to the sword. This perspective was too large to grasp.

Only within sound of shellfire across in Syria did the perspective become real again: tanks and trucks lurching up the slopes; the dead beside the road under their tarpaulin covers; a platoon of Israeli mortar-men examining a Russian-built Syrian truck, tinkering with it, then dancing with glee as one of their number made it roar alive; a deserted Arab village, its honey-colored walls silent except for the echo of gunfire; and the call down the line of jammed armor and trucks, "Clear the road! Clear the road! Wounded coming back!"—and the ambulance delicately, slowly, seeking out the gentlest ruts in the rocks.

We came down from the front in late afternoon to wash and rest in Kibbutz Dan, northernmost of Israeli settlements. The kibbutz raises chickens, cows, apples, honey, and has a fishpond for breeding carp. Mobilization had taken fifty able-bodied men and women from the settlement's five hundred souls two weeks ago. Thus when the Syrians hit them on Tuesday morning at 7:30 only twenty-four middle-aged men were left to hold the trench line, with teen-agers to run the ammunition.

Baruch Fisher, a stocky, fiftyish apple specialist, was in command of the two 81-mm. mortars close by the chicken coops in the rear. When the Syrian company attacked, the four automatic rifles in the trench line pinned the enemy in the meadow under the grove; the trench command post called for mortar fire, and Baruch's two mortars, firing 150 rounds in twenty minutes, chopped them up. Some might see it as a miracle, for the answering Syrian shellfire dropped within the chicken coops, only fifteen yards from the mortar pits. A direct hit might have ended Kibbutz Dan's resistance. Baruch Fisher did not see it as a miracle. "For us," he said, "it was a very practical matter, not a matter of ideology. There was no place else for us to go—we stayed here or we died."

A final scene comes back—from a visit to Bethlehem a few days after its capture. In the dark cenotaph where, supposedly, Rachel lies buried, Israelis of every diverse strain had gathered—from the bearded

"Tremblers" in their long black caftans to the husky irreligious paratroopers from Tel Aviv and the kibbutzim. In the gloom, one of the Orthodox Tremblers, swaying back and forth, broke into the ancient Hebrew chant for the dead: "He who maketh peace in His heavens, He will make peace for us and all Israel, and say ye amen." Even the paratroopers bellowed, "Amen."

It was in this cruel and lovely land, two thousand years ago, that peace and mercy were first preached by a Jew of Nazareth as a universal doctrine. Every artifact and ruin, every ancient terrace hardened to stone, every fallen pillar and tumbled fortress from Acre to the marches of Sinai bespeaks the alternation between man's mercy and man's animal fear. It is Israel's turn now, for the first time in two millennia, to seek a balance. ▶

Israel and its Arab neighbors have been in a state of war since that nation's birth. Three times in two decades the heated words exploded into killing and destruction on a massive scale. Three times Israel destroyed the armies of those who threatened her. And still the tiny homeland of the Jews is surrounded by angry nations fumbling for the dignity of their past and hungry to avenge hurt pride. Three times war has seemed to Israel the answer, and she has shown a dazzling spirit when she has gone to war.

But when a questioner asked Moshe Dayan if he was not sometimes tempted to dispose of his enemies once and for all, that most successful warrior that the world has seen since World War II answered: "I don't think that in war there is any such thing as 'once and for all.' I don't think 'once and for all' can be applied to war."

XXVIII

What Is Peace?

I F "ONCE AND FOR ALL" is a phrase not applicable to war, can it hold true for peace? The history of the world does not hold out much promise. Certainly the state of peace—which has been described as "the absence of war"—goes back as far as history, and from as early a date men have attempted to define the rules of war, to limit it, or to eradicate it altogether. Long before the Christian era and outside its sphere, a set of laws to regulate the warrior caste of India was drawn: soldiers were not allowed to fight with men who had lost their armor or were fear-stricken, drunk or out of their minds. Women and children, fugitives, those who begged for mercy with clasped hands were safe from them, as were the farmer and his crops. Nor in the course of war were trees to be cut down or the land burned. The unwritten rules of war of ancient Greece, the codes of the Saracen warriors and of the Samurai in Japan all reflect this ideal of the chivalrous warrior, although they did nothing to prevent or limit war itself.

During the so-called Dark Age of European culture the Church did make attempts not only to restrict the knightly caste but also to put limits to warfare. The Peace of God forbade attacks on pilgrims, merchants, women, children, peasants and even cattle, as well as churchmen and church property. Churchyards, wayside crosses, even plows were set aside as sanctuaries for the hard-pressed. No man could make war on his enemy without due warning—one week's notice—of his intent. And the Truce of God prohibited all fighting between sundown of every Wednesday and dawn of the following Monday as well as in the seasons of Advent and Lent.

Similarly, the attempts to control war through a dictated peace date back to ancient times. There have been periods such as the two hundred years of the Pax Romana, when the Roman empire—stretching from the Rhine to Africa and from the wall of Hadrian eastward to Syria—enforced more peace and order than the world had known before. But this was the peace of the conqueror, maintained by an imperial army. And although many since—from the Hohenstaufen up to Hitler—have tried, in emulation of the Romans, to make peace by force and dominate the world, none has succeeded.

Attempts to prevent war through a balance of power have been successful within small groups of nations such as the Greek city-states of the Periclean period, the Italian states of the Renaissance, or in Europe during the "era of moderation" of the eighteenth century. But the balance has always proved too precarious to last. And the outlawing of war through moral sanctions, calling on man's best nature, has been successful only when an organized church—such as the universal Christian church of the Middle Ages—had instruments with which to enforce it: the threat of interdict or excommunication, forfeiture of property, or even physical punishment such as the loss of a hand. But even with these instruments the uncertain peace among the Christians was not long maintained.

The notion of world federation, too, has been a dream of rational men for centuries. Men like Pierre Dubois in the fourteenth century, Henry IV of France in the sixteenth, William Penn in the seventeenth outlined ideas for such alliances based on international understanding and enforced by an international police. In 1815 the idealistic czar of Russia, Alexander I, set forth the principles of a Holy Alliance in which the sovereigns of Europe were to cooperate in brotherhood to achieve peace, and the subsequent Quadruple Alliance actually sent soldiers to enforce that peace—but failed because their objective was to protect the status quo as much as to outlaw war.

With the birth of the twentieth century, when the potential of total war in the age of science struck men's minds, desperate conferences were held in an attempt to limit armaments, to set up sanctions against aggressors, even to curtail the claims of sovereignty when they infringed on international order. The last of these pre-war conferences was held at The Hague in 1907, and in 1914 the costliest war in history to that date began. Four years of unprecedented slaughter left forty million people dead. Out of the fear and horror of that war came the League of Nations.

According to its covenant, members of the League would not resort to war without submitting first to arbitration or to an international court of law. Means of enforcement were to be moral pressure and a universal boycott against the war-maker—but when Japan was confronted by the condemnation of her fellow League members after her conquest of Manchuria, she simply withdrew from the League. And when Italy invaded Ethiopia, some sanctions were imposed, but they did not much affect the course of that colonial war, and with Mussolini's victory the sanctions were lifted.

The League's attempt to limit armaments failed when it ran into the question of security. No nation would reduce its arms without a guarantee of national safety—and the members could not agree upon an effective guarantee. And despite the arms limitations put on the defeated nations of World War I, the build-up of arms continued. In the year following the hope-filled World Disarmament Conference of 1932, Hitler came to power and, rejecting any limitation on German armaments, resigned from the League.

Thus in 1939 the world again descended into unrestricted war, another struggle for world dominance by military power as in the days of Rome, a war fought not by a regulated warrior caste but by a universal conscription of the male population, a holocaust without the ethical restrictions of any powerful religion. The precarious balance of power had collapsed once more, and men's dream of an international federation had failed to serve them. It was a war without limitation as to arms, fought at a time when science had combined with savagery to produce unheard-of weapons.

Sixty million died in that war. And on their corpses, on the rubble and the radiated ruins of their cities, rose the United Nations. Normal men were frightened and disgusted, and once again they sought a way to peace.

Like its predecessors, the United Nations has been hampered in its efforts to keep peace by the overriding claims of sovereignty among its member nations. As one architect of American policy said in 1966, "The vital national interest must take precedence over abstract moral considerations," adding, perhaps in defense of this statement or in proof of it, "It always has." But peace in the twentieth century is not a "moral consideration." It is a necessity.

Years ago General Charles de Gaulle wrote, "Hope though we may, what reason have we for thinking that passion and self-interest, the root cause of armed conflict in men and nations, will cease to operate; that anyone will willingly surrender what he has, or not try to get what he wants? ... Is it really likely that the present balance of power will remain unchanged so long as the small want to become great, the strong to dominate the weak, the old to live on?"

Likely or not, hopeful men still seek a way to a more stable peace than that which we have now. They seek it in many ways, but those who are most concerned follow, for the most part, two main paths of thought: those of the pacifists and of the advocates of world government. The philosophical problem confronting the pacifists is that in their line of reasoning the concept of peace tends to be negative. When any cause, including that of peace itself, becomes a dominant ideal—that is, worth dying for—then pressure to achieve it mounts toward violence. And when one fights for peace, it ceases to be peace. Therefore, no man or group of men should believe in any cause— even that of peace—to the extent that they are unwilling to compromise or postpone it. Among the pacifists, only the advocates of positive non-violent action have been able to overcome this paradox.

The answer of the internationalists is that peace which tolerates war is no longer peace. They say that war will not be banished simply by wishful thinking and that, to be effective, peace must have a positive meaning. Peace between nations must rely on international justice. A peaceful world society, like any of its component communities, must provide itself with a police force—an international army—ready to use force to ensure peace. As Quincy Wright points out in A *Study of War*, such a concept of peace encroaches upon many established conceptions and interests, and the world public is not likely to favor it enough to achieve it unless it exists in more than symbols and myths.

The conception that it most encroaches upon is that of national sovereignty. And just as at one time powerful dukes and barons fought against surrendering their authority to a central kingdom, and individual states reluctantly gave up their rights to a federal government, so do modern nations balk at the thought of placing their future security in the hands of an international body. But, as Stanton Coblentz says in his *From Arrow to Atom Bomb*, "peace-making by its very nature is not a unilateral matter." It calls for the cooperation of all nations, "any one of which, like a mad carouser in an overladen canoe, could upset the balance and tip the rest overboard."

In nearly a quarter-century of existence the United Nations has attempted to keep the balance in that canoe, and it has succeeded better than any previous effort in man's history. It has arranged for cease-fire agreements in eight different conflicts and sent peace-keeping units to the continuing areas of tension in three. Twice it has mustered a multi-national army to act as a policing force under U.N. command. Although it might seem to progress only in little inching steps, hobbled by quarreling among its member nations as well as by the recalcitrance of the warring men it seeks to pacify, it has often acted with courage, and it has survived. Its business, after all, must be carried on by men among men, by the frustrated Swedish officer in a Cyprus village crying out, "For God's sake, why don't you stop shooting?" or by a platoon of Gurkhas under attack and desperately firing at Katangese insurgents.

It seems, indeed, an awkward progress toward universal, everlasting peace. But, as Walter Lippmann pointed out many years ago, "We must aim at the possible or we shall accomplish nothing at all. We must aim at a peace which is good enough to endure without serious interruption in the world as it is among men as they are for perhaps fifty years. . . ." The cease-fires that the United Nations has arranged have lasted less than the half-century Lippmann mentions, but with infinite patience, step by step, they can be prolonged and the warlike flare-ups along their lines can be minimized. Minute by minute, through such efforts, we may buy time.

War doesn't happen by itself. Men make war. But, once started, war seems to develop its own chemistry, operating beyond the control of men, as it did in the Middle East in 1967 when it snatched control from Nasser. Tolstoy found just such a takeover from Napoleon when his armies were smashed in Russia in 1812. "The fact shows perfectly clearly," Tolstoy wrote, "that Napoleon saw no danger in the advance on Moscow, and that Alexander and the Russian generals did not dream at the time of luring Napoleon on, but aimed at the very opposite. Napoleon was drawn on into Russia, not through plans—no one dreamed of the possibility of it—but simply through the complex play of intrigues and desires and motives of the actors in the war, who had no conception of what was to come and of what was the sole means of saving Russia. Everything came to pass by chance."

President Kennedy used to say that all recent wars, especially World Wars I and II, seemed to have resulted from grievous miscalculations by one or more of the belligerents. And unless there is a forum of some sort where nations can speak and attempt to understand one another, the chances of miscalculation are tremendous. As a diplomat who periodically visited Communist China said in a report to his government: "Watching China today is like looking through a window into a room full of brawling black cats on a dark night. Every so often a cat appears at a window. You don't know whether he is winning or losing. You don't even know for sure what's going on inside the room."

And an American official whose job it was to analyze what was happening inside the North Vietnamese power structure told of a despairing dream he had in which he found himself walking in a wood so dark he barely avoided falling into a pond which was distinguishable from the forest floor only in that it was slightly darker. He stood and stared at the pond and was fascinated when bubbles rose from the bottom and a little wave rolled across the dusky surface. Then one tiny fish leaped out of the water and splashed back in and disappeared. The pond became completely quiet. As he stood there staring, a friend walked up, slapped him on the shoulder, and asked, "What's going on in this pond?"

Yet, despite the threat of miscalculation and the power of chance, man's hope continues to lie in the considerable area of choice still left to him and in the reassuring thought that, as someone expressed it, "very nearly everything that has happened in history very nearly didn't happen."

In 1945 the bomb cut history in two. On one side lie the ages spent in the search for ultimate military power. On the other is the era in which we have arrived at that ultimate; the search must no longer be for better weapons but for new ways to exercise power and influence without them.

The fear of the nuclear potential has succeeded for more than twenty years in keeping the power nations from direct open warfare. And the shield of this fear has been enlarged by various international pacts to offer its protection to members closely allied to the nuclear nations. Outside these areas the United Nations has been able to operate. But there is a third battleground, one that has been the scene of growing violence in the last half of the twentieth century, for which the machinery of peace is not yet geared.

The trend of recent years has been toward proliferation and fragmentation. From 1945 to 1965 the population of the world increased from 2,230 million to 3,285 million. The number of independent nations almost doubled—from 71 to 125—and membership in the United Nations grew from 51 to 118. "Monolithic Communism" broke into factions, as did the solidarity of the capitalist nations. In reaction to the pressure to conform, the youth of the world flew to extremes of individuality; modern existential philosophy rejected the notion of a prior "essence" or cohesive idea of man and society; art was denying the necessity of a unifying form and turning to "happenings." So wars became fragmented. Even in such major international conflicts as the war in the Middle East, the "united Arab peoples" were in actuality a diverse collection of antagonistic governments, each acting on its own. The war in Vietnam was an interplay of several wars. And the majority of warlike actions throughout the world—though frequently exploited by an international Communist ideology—had more the aspect of a series of explosions.

The East-West tension, though it still existed, was superseded by the growing tension of despair among the poverty-stricken people of the world, a despair that bred violent challenges to the governments of more than eighty nations in the decade following 1958—most of them in the Southern Hemi-

453

sphere. More than half of the world's population lives in this underprivileged southern half of the world where most of the very poor nations are located. (The designation "very poor" has been given by the World Bank to those countries where the per-capita income is under $100 a year.) Very nearly every one of these lands where misery flourishes has suffered serious internal violence in the last decade. By contrast, in the rich nations of the world, where live about a quarter of the world's population holding seventy-five percent of the world's wealth, there has been only one internal upheaval of major proportions.

Thus, in stark black and white, the threats to peace in recent times have come not so much from the rich, white, powerful nations of the Northern Hemisphere as from the poor, dark, southern nations, many of them born in this decade, where post-war words like "liberation," "freedom," "self-determination" and "equality" have engendered just enough hope to make reality unbearable. As there have been periods of wars fought for religion, wars fought in the name of nationalism and more recently wars fought for "liberation" as against "freedom," the era now developing may well be known as a period of rebellious outbursts, popular upheavals and bloody rioting— localized sub-wars bred of despair and fought in the name of economic equality, a chance to live.

The line between war and peace has blurred, and the time is past when massive military force was the primary source of power in world affairs. As recently as thirty years ago Bertrand Russell wrote that economic power derived from military power which was capable of seizing the areas of natural resources which produce economic ascendancy. But General James M. Gavin, quoting him in 1966, noted that a fundamental change had taken place since then, and that modern technology can provide adequate resources for humans to live on this earth no less than it can provide the weapons system to destroy a major portion of the human race. Economic power and technological progress, rather than a reliance on armed force, are more appropriate weapons with which to wield influence and wage peace in this new age.

Peace is indeed the absence of war, but it is more than that. It is more than the temporary armed tranquillity of the status quo. Like good health, it is indefinable, appreciated most when it is lost. But as the object of men's hopes in every age, it implies a trust in brotherhood, a chance to live creatively, free from want and fear. To some it is the excitement of unlimited opportunity. To others, like the old Laotian refugee, it means the fulfillment of a simple longing for "all the quiet things."

454

The choice between peace and war is as basic to mankind as the choice between life and death. In the past few thousand years, man, one of many species, has pre-empted the earth; in the last hundred years he has proceeded from the internal-combustion engine to the hydrogen bomb to flights into space. Still, the roots of war are deep in his heart, lodged in fear, ambition, a thirst for vengeance, hate. Since every human being lives with these emotions day by day, the "absence" of them is difficult to conceive. But if true peace is a quality "which passeth all understanding," it is nevertheless the only alternative to death.

THE DEAD

A SECTION OF PHOTOGRAPHS

Lament for the dead is chanted by Greek women over the body of a civilian killed by mortar fire.

John Phillips

Korean women search for their own among the dead.   *Carl Mydans*

The bodies of Turkish Cypriots killed in the fighting are laid out in the mosque at Louronjina. *Brian Seed*

The bodies of Egyptian soldiers in the Port Said cemetery are identified by their women.   *Larry Burrows*

In an open-air morgue in Bogotá, civilian victims of the rioting rest in uncovered coffins. *Jean Speiser*

In a temporary grave in Korea, American soldiers are buried in army shrouds. *Carl Mydans*

In a military cemetery in Vietnam a family weeps.   *Robert Capa*

After the massacre at Suwon, Korea, the dead lie sprawled in the dust.   *Carl Mydans*

Index

Carl Mydans

Carl Mydans was born in Boston, the son of a musician, and grew up in Medford, Massachusetts. He attended Boston University's School of Journalism and worked as a newspaper reporter in Boston and New York. During this time his interest in photography sharpened, and in 1935 he joined the now famous photographic unit of the U.S. Farm Security Administration directed by Roy Stryker. When *Life* was born in 1936 he became one of its first photographers. He has remained on its staff ever since, covering world news and many of the wars fought in these thirty-two years, reporting with both camera and typewriter. He met his wife, Shelley Smith, at *Life*. Soon after they were married, World War II broke out and they were sent to Europe and later to Asia as *Life*'s first photo-reporter team. His first book, *More Than Meets the Eye*, reported some of his experiences during those war years. Mr. Mydans continues his dual role today as photographer-writer.

Shelley Mydans

Shelley Mydans was born at Stanford University, where her father was professor of journalism, and after attending college there she moved to New York, where she became a reporter for *Life*. There she met and married Carl Mydans. In Asia as a photo-reporter team, they were captured when the Japanese overran Manila and spent two years in prison camps. On their return to the U.S., Mrs. Mydans wrote her first book, *The Open City*, a novel about Americans interned by the Japanese. She then worked as a war correspondent in the Pacific, and after the war as a correspondent in Tokyo, where her husband was bureau chief for *Time* and *Life*. When the Mydans' second child was born, Mrs. Mydans retired, and during the time that she was raising a family she worked on the research and writing of *Thomas*, a novel about the life, murder and miracles of Thomas Becket. *The Violent Peace* is the first book Mr. and Mrs. Mydans have written together.

Carl Mydans

Carl Mydans was born in Boston, the son of a musician, and grew up in Medford, Massachusetts. He attended Boston University's School of Journalism and worked as a newspaper reporter in Boston and New York. During this time his interest in photography sharpened, and in 1935 he joined the now famous photographic unit of the U.S. Farm Security Administration directed by Roy Stryker. When *Life* was born in 1936 he became one of its first photographers. He has remained on its staff ever since, covering world news and many of the wars fought in these thirty-two years, reporting with both camera and typewriter. He met his wife, Shelley Smith, at *Life*. Soon after they were married, World War II broke out and they were sent to Europe and later to Asia as *Life*'s first photo-reporter team. His first book, *More Than Meets the Eye*, reported some of his experiences during those war years. Mr. Mydans continues his dual role today as photographer-writer.

Shelley Mydans

Shelley Mydans was born at Stanford University, where her father was professor of journalism, and after attending college there she moved to New York to work as a reporter for *Life*. There she met and married Carl Mydans. In Asia as a photo-reporter team, they were captured when the Japanese overran Manila and spent two years in prison camps. On their return to the U.S., Mrs. Mydans wrote her first book, *The Open City*, a novel about Americans interned by the Japanese. She then worked as a war correspondent in the Pacific, and after the war as a correspondent in Tokyo, where her husband was bureau chief for *Time* and *Life*. When the Mydans' second child was born, Mrs. Mydans retired, and during the time that she was raising a family she worked on the research and writing of *Thomas*, a novel about the life, murder and miracles of Thomas Becket. *The Violent Peace* is the first book Mr. and Mrs. Mydans have written together.